NEW YORK TIMES

ERNEST HEM

SECRET ADVENTUR

WRITER, SAILOR, SOLDIER, SPY

NICHOLAS REYNOLDS

P.S.
INSIGHTS,
INTERVIEWS
& MORE...

Praise for

Writer, Sailor, Soldier, Spy

"Reynolds looks among the shadows and finds a Hemingway not seen before." —*London Review of Books*

"[An] engrossing story of Hemingway's disillusionment with American politics, his sympathy with communism, and his attraction to adventure and subversion." —*Kirkus Reviews*

"Nicholas Reynolds has produced a thorough, well-researched, and highly readable account of Ernest Hemingway's engagement with espionage (American and Soviet), communism, and military adventurism. In particular, *Writer, Sailor, Soldier, Spy* is the first book to put Hemingway's dalliance with the Soviet NKVD in the broader context of Hemingway's life in a way that makes sense of this only recently revealed and unexpected aspect of Hemingway's adventurous life." —John Earl Haynes, coauthor of *Spies: The Rise and Fall of the KGB in America*

"Nicholas Reynolds's fascinating new research in *Writer, Sailor, Soldier, Spy* shows that [Hemingway] was in fact working for both the Russians and the Americans." —*New York Review of Books*

"The riveting, brand-new story of how America's greatest writer was shaped by his secret adventures as a spy for both U.S. intelligence and the Soviet NKVD: *Writer, Sailor, Soldier, Spy* is compelling, vivid, and essential reading for all Hemingway and espionage fans. Reynolds adds much critical insight to our understanding of Papa's jigsaw-puzzle character."

—William Doyle, author of *PT 109: An American Epic of War, Survival, and the Destiny of John F. Kennedy*

"Drawing on his intelligence background, Reynolds uncovers a trove of documents that point to American novelist Ernest Hemingway's recruitment in 1940 by the NKVD. . . . Reynolds ably researches Hemingway's World War II adventures, both in Cuba and Europe, including clandestine activities supporting America's war effort. . . . An intriguing study highlighting the tension between Hemingway's Soviet sympathies and his identity as a U.S. patriot. . . . Recommended for Hemingway enthusiasts and for readers interested in the history of Soviet espionage."

—*Library Journal*

"[A] thoroughly researched exploration of Hemingway's military adventurism."

—*Publishers Weekly*

"You'd think it might be hard to find new insights into one of the most famous lives in literature, but Nicholas Reynolds's new book does just that. *Writer, Sailor, Soldier, Spy* reveals a secret that a writer who stripped them from the lives of others concealed in his own—that he'd offered to be a spy for the Soviet intelligence and tried to spy for the U.S., too, during World War II. . . . I am fascinated."

—Scott Simon, NPR's *Weekend Edition Saturday*

"Fascinating."

—*Columbus Dispatch*

"Former CIA Museum historian Nicholas Reynolds pieced together a remarkable revelation: Nobel Prize–winning novelist Ernest Hemingway had served as a spy for a number of international agencies."

—*Sacramento Bee*

"A well-researched and written biography. . . . A tremendous accomplishment."

—Bookloons

"Captivating. . . . Reynolds reveals the covert side of Hemingway other biographers have not disclosed. . . . An important addition to the canon of one of America's foremost writers. Reynolds's unique biography reads like an espionage thriller. It is well illustrated, clearly written, and an engrossing read that adds more details to Hemingway's continually fascinating life." —*Missourian*

"The pace is breathtaking, and that's the effect Reynolds wants to achieve, because it is how Ernest Hemingway lived his life."
—*The Scotsman* (Scotland)

"Nicholas Reynolds ably weaves Vassiliev's revelation, unavailable to previous biographers, into the tangled fabric of Hemingway's event-filled life. Hemingway's readers . . . will find it fascinating."
—*The Times Literary Supplement* (London)

"Renowned American novelist Ernest Hemingway led a shocking secret life as a Soviet spy, according to claims in a new book. . . . The startling revelations are detailed in *Writer, Sailor, Soldier, Spy* by former CIA officer Nicholas Reynolds. . . . The book also offers an insight into the other complex set of relationships Hemingway enjoyed with American agencies." —*Daily Mail* (London)

"Nick Reynolds writes well. . . . His colorful, fast-paced narrative is supported by almost sixty pages of detailed, voluminous endnotes. *Writer, Sailor, Soldier, Spy* is not the usual stuff that is reviewed in JAMP, but no member will want to miss an opportunity to read this fascinating story." —*The Journal of America's Military Past*

"Adroitly written and evocative. . . . A controversial, but very important, part of Hemingway's life. Reynolds supports every assertion with detailed research, and he allows the exploration to speak for the Great American Author—55 years after his tragic death."
—*Idaho Statesman*

WRITER,
SAILOR,
SOLDIER,
SPY

WRITER, SAILOR, SOLDIER, SPY

Ernest Hemingway's Secret Adventures, 1935–1961

NICHOLAS REYNOLDS

wm
WILLIAM MORROW
An Imprint of HarperCollins*Publishers*

P.S.™ is a trademark of HarperCollins Publishers.

HarperCollins books may be purchased for educational, business, or sales promotional use. For information, please email the Special Markets Department at SPsales@harpercollins.com.

A hardcover edition of this book was published in 2017 by William Morrow, an imprint of HarperCollins Publishers.

FIRST WILLIAM MORROW PAPERBACK EDITION PUBLISHED 2018.

Designed by Leah Carlson-Stanisic

Library of Congress Cataloging-in-Publication Data has been applied for.

ISBN 978-0-06-244014-3

18 19 20 21 22 RS/LSC 10 9 8 7 6 5 4 3 2 1

I guess in our day fighting will be the cleanest way to live.

—Josephine Herbst to Ernest Hemingway,
March 16, 1938, in a letter about
the Spanish Civil War

CONTENTS

CAST OF CHARACTERS

Raymond O. Barton—U.S. Army general who commanded the 4th Infantry Division and facilitated Hemingway's work as a war correspondent in France in 1944.

Fulgencio Batista—right-wing dictator of Cuba overthrown by Fidel Castro on January 1, 1959.

Elizabeth Bentley—Vassar College graduate who joined the Communist Party in New York in 1935 and then became a Soviet spy. She was also the lover of Jacob Golos, who recruited Hemingway for the NKVD. After Golos died, she turned herself in to the FBI and testified against her former masters.

Alvah Bessie—American communist who fought for the Republic in Spain and wrote the well-received memoir *Men in Battle*. He became one of the "Hollywood Ten," a group of communist writers who went to jail for contempt of Congress in 1947.

Philip W. Bonsal—U.S. ambassador to Cuba in 1959 and 1960 who befriended Hemingway and tried to find middle ground between Castro's Cuba and Eisenhower's America.

Hayne D. Boyden—U.S. Marine Corps aviator who served as naval attaché at the American Embassy in Havana and supported Hemingway's antisubmarine war patrols in 1942 and 1943.

Spruille Braden—U.S. ambassador to Cuba from 1942 to 1945 who oversaw Hemingway's work with his subordinates Boyden and Joyce.

David K. E. Bruce—senior OSS officer who met Hemingway in 1944 in France. Together they played a role in the liberation of Paris. Bruce became a senior U.S. diplomat after the war.

Fidel Castro—Cuban revolutionary who overthrew Fulgencio Batista in 1959, establishing a left-wing dictatorship.

Roald Dahl—Royal Air Force officer (and future bestselling author) who befriended Martha Gellhorn and helped get Hemingway to Europe in 1944.

John Dos Passos—fellow novelist and Hemingway friend until their falling-out in Spain in 1937 over the murder of his friend José Robles by Republican or Soviet security organs.

Gustavo Durán—multitalented Spanish composer and soldier who rose to command a division in the army of the Spanish Republic; good friend of Hemingway until their falling-out in 1943; accused of being a communist spy by Senator Joseph R. McCarthy in the 1950s.

Chou En-lai—the charismatic longtime Chinese communist leader who met with Hemingway and Gellhorn in 1941.

Hanns Eisler—former German communist composer investigated by the House Un-American Activities Committee in 1947.

F. Scott Fitzgerald—fellow novelist and close Hemingway friend in the 1920s.

Francisco Franco—Spanish general and Nationalist leader who led the rebels against the Spanish Republic. When the rebels triumphed, he became the country's dictator, staying in power until his death in 1975.

Joseph Freeman—American communist writer, *New Masses* editor, and Hemingway acquaintance.

Martha Gellhorn—the writer's third wife, who accompanied him to Spain and China, lived with him in Cuba, and urged him to cover World War II in Europe.

Jacob Golos—ardent Bolshevik revolutionary who emigrated to the United States, eventually becoming an NKVD operative in New York; recruited Hemingway for "our work" in late 1940 or early 1941. He died on Thanksgiving Day in 1943.

Igor Gouzenko—Soviet code clerk who defected in Ottawa in 1945 and took with him a stack of secret documents about Soviet espionage in Canada and the United States.

Winston Guest—American socialite and sportsman who served under Hemingway in both the Crook Factory and on *Pilar*'s war cruise.

Gregory Hemingway—Hemingway's third, and youngest, son.

Hadley Richardson Hemingway—the writer's first wife, mother of John Hemingway.

John "Bumby" Hemingway—the writer's eldest son.

Leicester Hemingway—Ernest's younger brother, who sailed the Caribbean in 1940 looking for supply depots for German submarines.

Mary Welsh Hemingway—the writer's fourth, and last, wife, whom he met in London in 1944 and married in Cuba in 1946.

Patrick Hemingway—the writer's second son.

Pauline Pfeiffer Hemingway—the writer's second wife, a devout Roman Catholic and the mother of Gregory and Patrick Hemingway.

Valerie Danby-Smith Hemingway—the writer's last secretary, who, after his death, became the wife of Hemingway's third son, Gregory.

Josephine (Josie) Herbst—left-wing American novelist and Hemingway friend in Paris, Key West, and Spain.

José Luis Herrera (also known as Herrera Sotolongo)—Cuban communist and Spanish Civil War veteran who was Hemingway's personal physician and friend.

John Herrmann—Josie Herbst's husband, a novelist and undercover communist agent.

J. Edgar Hoover—longtime director of the Federal Bureau of Investigation.

Harry Hopkins—aide to President Franklin Roosevelt, director of the Federal Emergency Relief Administration (FERA), the New Deal agency that operated from 1933 to 1935.

A. E. Hotchner—American journalist and writer born in 1920 who went to Havana in 1948 to interview Hemingway, became his close companion, and, after the writer's suicide, authored five books and many articles about him.

Joris Ivens—Dutch communist filmmaker and Comintern operative who worked with Hemingway on a film about the Spanish Civil War.

Sir Anthony Jenkinson—a young British aristocrat who joined forces with Leicester Hemingway to explore the Caribbean early in World War II.

Robert P. Joyce—American diplomat stationed in Havana who befriended Hemingway and facilitated his intelligence work on land and at sea during 1942 and 1943.

Chiang Kai-shek—Nationalist leader of China during World War II who fought both the Japanese and the communists. He met with Hemingway and Gellhorn in 1941.

Ivan Kashkin—Soviet literary figure who played an important role in translating Hemingway's works into Russian and introducing them to Soviet readers.

Arthur Koestler—Hungarian-born journalist and writer who collaborated with Willi Münzenberg in Spain, then turned against communism and wrote the anti-Stalinist classic *Darkness at Noon.*

Charles T. "Buck" Lanham—U.S. Army officer who forged a bond with Hemingway on the battlefield in 1944 and became one of his closest friends. They corresponded regularly after the war.

Mary "Pete" Lanham—the wife of Charles T. Lanham.

John Howard Lawson—Hollywood screenwriter and dogmatic communist who refused to answer questions about party affiliation for the House Un-American Activities Committee in 1947.

R. G. Leddy—FBI special agent stationed at the American Embassy in Havana during World War II.

Archibald MacLeish—prominent American poet and writer who worked with Hemingway and Ivens on their film about the Spanish Civil War; appointed librarian of Congress by FDR.

S. L. A. Marshall—American military historian who was with Hemingway during the liberation of Paris in 1944.

André Marty—French communist who became a senior commissar in the International Brigades during the Spanish Civil War and achieved notoriety for ordering the arrest and execution of many soldiers suspected of disloyalty.

Herbert L. Matthews—*New York Times* journalist who befriended Hemingway in Spain and went on to cover Fidel Castro's rise to power in Cuba, writing a groundbreaking series of articles about Castro and his movement.

Joseph R. McCarthy—Republican senator from Wisconsin who conducted witch hunts for communists in Washington in the early 1950s.

Henry Morgenthau, Jr.—U.S. secretary of the Treasury, in touch with Hemingway around the time of his trip to China in 1941, interested in hearing his views on the situation in Asia.

Willi Münzenberg—German communist who brilliantly coordinated Comintern propaganda operations in Western Europe during the 1930s.

Joe North—American communist writer and editor who arranged for Hemingway articles to be published in Marxist journals. He may have introduced Hemingway to the NKVD recruiter Golos.

Alexander Orlov—NKVD *rezident,* or spy chief, in Spain from 1936 to 1938 who befriended Hemingway and enabled him to visit a guerrilla training camp before he himself fled to the United States to escape from other Stalinist henchmen.

Maxwell Perkins—Hemingway's longtime (and sometimes long-suffering) editor at Scribner's, Hemingway's publisher.

Gustav Regler—German communist who served as a commissar with the International Brigades in Spain, where he and Hemingway became friends. He subsequently turned against communism and Stalin, and went into exile in Mexico.

Alfred Rice—Hemingway lawyer and de facto literary agent from 1948 on.

José Robles—a Spanish academic who emigrated to the United States, became a professor at Johns Hopkins University, and then returned to Spain, where he served the Republic during the civil war. He was murdered under suspicious circumstances by Republican or Soviet security organs.

Andy Rooney—reporter for *Stars and Stripes* who encountered Hemingway on a battlefield in France in 1944.

John W. Thomason, Jr.—U.S. Marine Corps officer detailed to the Office of Naval Intelligence in Washington, DC, who supported and enabled Hemingway during his antisubmarine war patrols in Cuban waters in 1942 and 1943 and collaborated with him on an anthology about war.

Leon Trotsky—Bolshevik commander and Soviet leader who was Soviet dictator Joseph Stalin's main rival for power in the 1920s. Forced into exile in Mexico, Trotsky died at the hands of an NKVD assassin there in 1940.

Alexander Vassiliev—KGB officer turned journalist, researcher, and exile. In the early 1990s he signed a contract with the SVR (the post–Cold War Russian intelligence service) to read NKVD/KGB files and prepare summaries to share with Western historians, a project aimed at raising money for the KGB/SVR pension fund. One of the files that he read was that of Hemingway.

René Villarreal—Hemingway's housekeeper in Cuba who was known as the writer's "Cuban son."

Emmett Watson—Seattle-based journalist who interviewed Hemingway in 1960 and discovered the truth about his suicide in 1961.

Harry Dexter White—senior U.S. Treasury official who tasked Hemingway with collecting information about conditions in China in 1941. After the war, White was exposed as a Soviet spy.

Edmund Wilson—left-leaning American literary critic and writer.

Milton Wolff—American leftist who fought in the Spanish Civil War and continued to campaign for progressive causes throughout the 1940s and 1950s.

INTRODUCTION

In 2010 I was the historian for "The Best Museum You've Never Seen," the CIA Museum, which winds through the corridors of an Eisenhower-era building secluded on a secure campus in Northern Virginia. We were preparing to install a new exhibit on the Office of Strategic Services (OSS), America's first central intelligence agency, dating to 1942. I was tasked with finding out everything I could about this experimental organization, which included researching the company roster.

Hastily pulled together to fight the Axis, OSS was an odd creature—at once a collection of men and women from the upper crust of society on America's east coast, and a magnet for astonishingly talented and creative people from all walks of life, from Wall Street lawyers to Hollywood filmmakers to freebooters and soldiers of fortune, even the future chef Julia Child. In OSS they could almost literally design their own adventures. Few of them were attracted to the less tolerant cultures of the regular Army and Navy.

My head swimming in research, I made an offhand connection one day that would lead to uncharted waters. I remembered reading in the past that Ernest Hemingway and Colonel David K. E. Bruce of the OSS had "liberated" the bar of the Ritz in Paris from the Germans in August 1944. Now I wondered if there was more to the story. Hemingway would not have been out of place in OSS. He loved secrets, and the edge they gave him. He craved action, but was not cut out for conventional soldiering. He moved easily between social and economic classes—and across borders. I thought to myself that he had a lot in common with many of the men in the spy business whom I had met or read about. So had he been an OSS spy of some sort? What *was* the full story about Hemingway and intelligence in World War II?

I proceeded to check every source I could find. A reference at CIA pointed to a declassified OSS file, now in the National Archives at College Park, Maryland, outside Washington, DC.[1] No one at the archives could lay hands on the file, initially deepening the mystery and leading to many frustrating hours with finding aids in old-fashioned three-ring binders in a back room. There were even a few sources that were still indexed on 3x5 cards that no one else wanted to see. In the end a friendly Hemingway scholar shared a copy of the OSS file that he had unearthed in 1983. Along the way, I found other tantalizing traces of once-secret OSS, FBI, and State Department files.

After a few months of work, I started to see the outline of a Hemingway portrait that was very different from the others I had known. The writer had—almost obsessively I thought—tried his hand at various forms of spying and fighting on two continents from 1937 on, before and during World War II. The way stations were varied, often exotic: the battlefields of Spain, the backstreets of Havana, a junk on the North River in China. He seemed to gravitate to men and women who operated on their own in the shadows. At one point his third wife, Martha, secretly lobbied OSS to put him on the payroll. Deputy directors and branch heads considered her request, assessing his potential in frank handwritten notes on the margins of transmittal letters.

And then I learned something that surprised me: he had signed on with another intelligence service, one that did not fit the conventional narrative of his life. That service turned out to be the Soviet NKVD, the People's Commissariat for Internal Affairs, the predecessor of the better-known KGB that, despite its name, operated both at home and abroad during the Cold War.

I stumbled on the NKVD connection when checking to see if I had covered all the bases in my research. I looked in unusual places for any references to Hemingway and intelligence. On a fateful day

I pulled off the shelf a 2009 book cowritten by an estranged former KGB officer, Alexander Vassiliev.[2] The work featured a subchapter that incorporated verbatim excerpts from Ernest Hemingway's official Soviet file that Vassiliev had smuggled out of Russia. Vassiliev's evidence was solid. The records of Hemingway's relationship with the NKVD showed that a Soviet operative had recruited Hemingway "for our work on ideological grounds" around December 1940, at a time when Stalin ruled the Soviet Union with an iron hand and was aligned with Hitler under the Molotov-Ribbentrop Pact—to say nothing of the bloody purges that had started in 1934 and were continuing with no end in sight.

A lifelong Hemingway admirer, I felt like I had taken an elbow deep in the gut when I read he had signed on with the NKVD. How could this be? He had always had many friends on the left, but he had never subscribed to communism (or any other ideology). The characters he created embodied so many American values we still cherish: truth, bravery, independence, grace under pressure, standing up for the underdog. His voice was uniquely American—and revolutionary. He had changed the course of American literature in the 1920s. Weeks before he embarked on this relationship with the NKVD in late 1940, he had published one of the century's greatest political novels, *For Whom the Bell Tolls*. Why would such a man sign on with Stalin's henchmen? And why would he do it secretly, which would mean hiding the truth from his friends, families, and readers? His greatest work, after all, came from sharing, not hiding, his life experiences.

Now I was hooked. After finishing work on the OSS exhibit, I went in search of answers to the questions that troubled me. Was there some mistake—perhaps in translation or transcription? If not, how could this have happened? How did the recruitment fit into the bigger picture? And what did it mean for the Hemingway legacy?

The principals were dead—Hemingway's Soviet recruiter died in Greenwich Village on Thanksgiving Day in 1943 (like more than one of his capitalist enemies, he had a heart attack after a big meal);

Hemingway himself committed suicide in 1961. His closest confidants were almost all gone. I realized that, for the most part, I would be relying on printed sources like the Soviet record, never officially declassified, along with private papers and letters meant for only one set of eyes. I hoped I would find enough information in archives and libraries to understand what had happened.

And so I set out on a quest, day after quiet day, in reading rooms all over the country, from San Diego to Seattle, Washington to Boston. Early on I immersed myself in the Hemingway papers at the JFK Presidential Library. While I paged through his correspondence—he was almost as great a letter writer as a novel writer—I sat in a room that overlooked the cold waters of Boston Harbor but was decorated like his living room in tropical Cuba, complete with animal skins and, on a table next to the sofa, what looked like a real pitcher of daiquiris until you tried to pour it.

All my life, even before my career in the CIA, I have wanted to uncover the backstory. Research has always been seductive for me. It felt right for one visit to the archives to lead seamlessly to the next. One more obscure book about the Spanish Civil War, or World War II, or the Cold War was never enough. And so, over the next three years, I filled in the outlines of the new Hemingway portrait from my unusual sources, which now included such things as the private papers of an NKVD general in the *U.S.* National Archives, those of his FBI handler in another Washington archive, the records of a dispute with his lawyer that seemed at first glance to be about copyrights. A little-known cache of Hemingway letters, read under the dour gaze of John Foster Dulles at the Princeton University Library, was surprisingly revealing when put into context.

Ultimately I concluded that Hemingway's dalliance with the NKVD, and the political attitudes that explain it, made an important difference in his life and art, one that has been overlooked until now. It influenced many of the decisions he made during his last fifteen years: where he lived, what he wrote, and how he acted. This chain of events even played a role in his suicide in 1961. Much of the drama played out in his mind, where he magnified it out of proportion. The chapters of the Cold War—the Red Scare, the Cuban Revolution, and, two months before his death, the Bay of Pigs fiasco—made things worse for him. He did not understand politics and intrigue as well as he thought he did, and for long stretches of time he overestimated his ability to control himself and others, even to change history. In the end, he began to understand his limits, and came to the tragic conclusion that the only way to reassert control was to kill himself.

That is the story I tell in this book.

NICHOLAS REYNOLDS
Washington, DC

WRITER,
SAILOR,
SOLDIER,
SPY

CHAPTER 1

AWAKENING

When the Sea Turned the Land Inside Out

Hemingway was not there just to observe. On September 4, 1935, he piloted his new cabin cruiser Pilar *some seventy-five miles northeast from Key West to the Upper Keys to join in the recovery effort. Determined to do what he could to help the survivors of one of the most powerful hurricanes in American history, he had stocked* Pilar *with food, water, and the kind of supplies that made life outdoors a little more bearable. But there was hardly anyone to help. He had not witnessed a scene like this since serving on the front lines in Italy in World War I. On Labor Day the storm had torn through the narrow, low-lying islands and wreaked as much havoc as a days-long artillery barrage. Many of the biggest trees, Jamaican dogwood and mahogany, had been uprooted and lay on their sides. Only a handful of sturdy buildings were still standing, the rest now just piles of wood. Near the small post office at Islamorada, the train sent to evacuate relief workers had been blown off the rails, its cars scattered at crazy angles. Worst of all was finding the dead, their bodies bloated in the 80-degree heat of the late summer day. Many of them were floating in the water, which was still murky from the fifteen-foot storm surge. It was hard to miss the clump of dead men by a wooden dock, where they had lashed themselves to a piling to keep from being swept away. Two women were cradled in the branches of a mangrove tree that had survived the high water and the wind—had the victims tried to save themselves by climbing? Or did the waves toss them into their gruesome aerie? That did not make much difference now. The only way the great writer could help the dead was to write about them, to tell the world how it happened and who was to blame for the tragedy. He decided to bear witness in a way that would change his life.*

By 1935, the year of the great hurricane, Hemingway had climbed to the top of his profession. Born just before the turn of the century, this ambitious young man from Oak Park, Illinois, had started a revolution in literature while still in his twenties. His two bestsellers, *The Sun Also Rises* and *A Farewell to Arms,* reflected how much he had lived in his first three decades: wounded veteran by nineteen, then foreign correspondent for the *Toronto Daily Star* and member of the Paris branch of the "Lost Generation" of legendarily talented writers.

The Nobel Prize for Literature that Hemingway later received ably explains the appeal of his work: his writing "honestly and undauntedly" reproduced "the hard countenance of the age" with a trademark combination of simplicity and precision. When he wrote, he was the soul of brevity, telling compelling stories in spare prose that spoke to millions of readers. His central theme was personal courage: he displayed "a natural admiration for every individual who fights the good fight in a world . . . overshadowed by violence and death."[1]

Hemingway was so successful that he was now on his way to becoming a touchstone for every American writer, and a role model for not a few American individualists. They were reading Hemingway, quoting him, copying his behavior, and seeking his advice. While his voice was uniquely American, he was also recognized as one of the leading novelists in the world. He had only a handful of competitors. His fame had even spread to the Soviet Union, where literature was meant to serve politics. Increasingly, Soviet writers were not at liberty to tell the truth about the world as they saw it and instead had to cater to the government. That did not make much difference to the mostly apolitical Hemingway. But he did enjoy the fact that more and more Soviets were reading his works.

On August 19, 1935, at a time when American literary critics had made him feel underappreciated at home, Hemingway received a package from Moscow containing a copy of his selected stories translated into Russian. It was posted from a prominent young translator and literary figure named Ivan Kashkin, who had done more to promote Hemingway's work in the USSR than anyone else, at first among fellow writers and then with other readers, including a few members of the ruling elite.[2] Hemingway was happy to see the Russian editions and, "[h]ungry for compassion and empathy," eager to read an enclosed essay that Kashkin had written in praise of the American writer.[3] In the accompanying letter (to "Dear Sir, or Mr. Hemingway or maybe Dear Comrade"), Kashkin told Hemingway how much Soviet readers welcomed his work, almost uncritically: "[t]here is in our country no idle gaping at your brilliant and sensational achievements, no grin at your limitations."[4] Without delay Hemingway wrote to thank Kashkin and tell him what "a pleasure [it was] to have somebody know what you are writing about"—so unlike the usual critics in New York.[5] This was the first of many long, remarkably frank letters to the man he would long value as critic and translator.[6]

Hemingway wanted to make sure Kashkin understood that while he was happy to have Soviet readers, he was not going to become a communist, or even a communist sympathizer. The successful young writer would maintain his independence despite pressure to move to the left. He explained to Kashkin in a letter that his friends and critics had told him he would wind up friendless if he did not write like a Marxist. But he did not care. "A writer," he continued, "is like a Gypsy" who "owes no allegiance to any government" and "will never like the government he lives under." It was better for government to be small; big government was necessarily "unjust."[7]

No matter what he claimed, readers on the left began to find traces of class consciousness in Hemingway's writing when he wrote about the fecklessness of American politicians, or how the rich in America ignored the plight of the poor. Some critics pointed to his short story "One Trip Across," about a boatman forced by the failing economy to turn to crime; others, amazingly, cited a few remarks he made about conditions at home in America in his book *The Green Hills of Africa,* which was actually a travelogue about the rich man's sport of big game hunting.[8]

The story that Hemingway would write for *New Masses* would surprise more than one left-leaning American and focus Soviet attention on him. Edited by American leftists and communists, this Marxist literary review fell just short of being an official organ of the Communist Party of the United States (CPUSA). When *New Masses* first appeared in 1926, *Time* magazine characterized it as "a smoky vessel, ungainly but powerful, with daubs of red on her lunging bows and red marks here and there on her somewhat disorderly running gear."[9]

That disorder did not matter to a variety of writers who ranged from the world famous, like George Bernard Shaw and Maxim Gorky, to minor lights known only on the left, all of whom wanted their work published. Some of that work was political; much of it was not. Hemingway submitted articles on subjects as diverse as bullfighting and death in winter at a snowbound chalet in the Alps. He felt free to angrily denounce the editors after they published a scathing review of his novella *Torrents of Spring.* They only were revolutionaries, he wrote his old friend the poet Ezra Pound, because they hoped that a new order would see them as "men of talent."[10] The editors lashed back that Hemingway was too focused on the individual and did not understand the powerful economic forces determining the course of American history.

Those forces made themselves felt in 1929. That year the stock market crash led to a deep depression that challenged every assumption about the American dream. The engine of capitalism, Wall Street, had stalled, and could no longer move the economy.

Something like one-fourth of the workforce was unemployed. An estimated two million men took to the rails, hopping on to freight trains and roaming the country in search of work. Millions more went hungry. Once-prominent businessmen stood on street corners selling pencils or apples, and then lined up with the unemployed at soup kitchens. The nation's formerly prosperous farms did no better. The cities could not afford to buy as much meat and produce, and the Depression spread through the farmlands. A prolonged drought in the Great Plains made things worse; acre upon acre of farmland literally blew away, creating a vast dust bowl.

After 1929, *New Masses* moved still further to the left. The editors decided to descend "into the stormy arena where the day's battles were raging," and to send reporters "to the surging picket lines, . . . the worried farm sides, [and] the smoldering South."[11] The idea was to capture, firsthand, the many kinds of suffering caused by the country's near-perfect economic and environmental storm. The resulting stories would attract readers who were now willing to take a hard look at the shortcomings of capitalism.

From afar, the Soviet Union seemed to offer a solution. The Soviets talked about a future where no one would be unemployed or hungry. It was a beguiling vision of a just, classless society. Nazi Germany and Fascist Italy were, it seemed, made to order as counterweights to the Soviet Union. Hitler's speeches set the tone for Germany. Gesturing forcefully, with closed fists, he would build to an angry crescendo, blaming the Jews and the communists for the crisis that gripped Germany as badly as the rest of the world. His was another way out of the Depression: silence your enemies, mobilize for war, take what you need from your enemies. With this approach, Hitler and his fellow dictator Mussolini drove many American artists into the arms of the left, much further than they might otherwise have gone.[12]

Even before the Depression hit, Hemingway had moved to Key West with his second wife, Pauline Pfeiffer. It was a place where they could start a family and where the robust, handsome sportsman—six feet tall, solidly muscled, with a full head of dark hair and dark eyes that commanded attention—could still live a halfway rugged outdoor life, or at least dress as if he were living that way, barefoot, in a plain shirt, usually only half-buttoned, and shorts cinched up with a piece of rope.

The southernmost tip of the Lower 48, Key West is nearly the last of a chain of small islands that protrude into the Gulf of Mexico from Florida. In 1928, it was a poor man's tropical paradise, reachable from the mainland only by rail or boat. Many of the streets were not paved; many of the buildings had no plumbing or electricity. The closest thing to a grocery store was the small warehouse that sold necessities.

The beach was never far, the water always warm and clear. Even at a depth of fifteen feet the white sand at the bottom seemed close enough to touch. Fish of many kinds hovered above the sand, easy prey for locals. In deeper waters the fishing was even better. Fishermen sold or bartered the catch of the day to their neighbors, who rounded out their meals with rice and beans from a warehouse and fruit from their gardens. After dinner, anyone could sit on the town pier and watch the sun set over the ocean, then go to a rough-hewn bar first called the Blind Pig, then the Silver Slipper, and finally Sloppy Joe's. Whatever its name, it was a place of "shabby discomfort, good friends, gambling, fifteen-cent whiskey, and ten-cent . . . gin" where the concrete floor was always wet from melting ice.[13]

Hemingway first heard about Key West from fellow novelist John Dos Passos, an intellectual from Baltimore—tall, shy, balding, more thoughtful than passionate, not unlike a professor. Still, he loved the outdoors, if not in quite the same way as the great fisherman and hunter Hemingway. Dos Passos had come upon the place while hiking down the Keys in 1924 and told Hemingway about his find in a letter. Hemingway came to visit and he too was smitten, eventually settling in a solid, two-story limestone house on Whitehead Street. Built in 1851, it looked like the kind of place a riverboat captain would put up in New Orleans, with its high wraparound porch, ornate grillwork, and wooden storm shutters usually painted green.

By 1930, the island city was suffering from the Depression. By 1934, Key West was literally bankrupt, unable to collect enough taxes to pay its bills. The Florida branch of Franklin Delano Roosevelt's Federal Emergency Relief Administration (FERA) stepped in and took over.[14] Part of the island's charm was that the mainland was far away; now, preempting the local government, a national agency was stepping in to save the key from itself. Dos Passos did not think much of the results. Something he called "relief racketeering" was turning "a town of independent fishermen and bootleggers" into "a poor farm."[15] Hemingway agreed. Roosevelt's New Deal, the

As close as you can get to tropical paradise in the Lower 48: The Hemingway house on Whitehead Street in Key West. *NY World Telegram and Sun Collection, Library of Congress.*

president's way out of the Depression, was like "some sort of YMCA show" run by "starry-eyed bastards." From Hemingway's worldview, which placed a premium on rugged self-reliance, the New Deal was encouraging men to quit their jobs and go on relief.[16] It did not help that one part of the recovery plan was to transform Key West into a tourist destination, and to make the famous author's house on Whitehead Street one of the attractions. This would rob Hemingway and his family of their privacy. Even so, they would call the place home until 1940.

In the Keys, almost everyone lived close to nature, and for a man as acutely attuned to the weather as Hemingway, it was not difficult to sense when a storm was on the way. On the last night of August 1935, dark clouds and high winds came along with the falling barometer. After checking the newspaper to confirm his hunch, Hemingway leapt into action to prepare his home and especially his boat for the storm. His oak and mahogany cabin cruiser *Pilar* had been painstakingly built to his specifications, mostly for fishing but also for living well on the open water. She was this night moored close to the submarine pens at the Navy Yard, a few blocks away. It was there that Hemingway spent five hours doing this and that to give her the best possible chance in the heavy weather ahead.

In the end, the storm brushed past Key West without doing much damage, but it struck the Middle and Upper Keys with full force, much more than any other hurricane in recent memory. Hemingway waited until the storm was over before heading northeast to explore the damage and to see how he could help. It was there he found the devastation. The foliage looked like it had been stripped away by fire, and the land like it had been turned inside out by the sea.[17] That was what he saw *before* he reached one of the seaside camps for the World War I veterans who were working on a New Deal construction project. Here the devastation was far worse. The primitive wooden cabins, little more than boards nailed to two-by-fours, with canvas

Hemingway and Dos Passos, friends in fair weather, on a fishing boat out of Key West. *Ernest Hemingway Photo Collection, JFK Library.*

for roofs, had simply disappeared. Bodies were strewn about like so much flotsam and jetsam after a shipwreck at sea. Hemingway had not seen so many dead men in one place since 1918. He liked to say that, by going to war, he had grown accustomed to death. It was something that the soldier simply had to accept. But this was *not* war, and it was *not* acceptable.

When the sea turned the land inside out: the devastation that Hemingway saw when he sailed *Pilar* north to the Matecumbe Keys in September 1935. *Ernest Hemingway Photo Collection, JFK Library.*

In a long letter to his editor, Maxwell Perkins of Charles Scribner's Sons, Hemingway could not contain his raw feelings about the experience.[18] He shared more gruesome details about half-naked bodies decomposing in the sun than the proper New Yorker, the kind of man who went deep-sea fishing in a coat and tie, could have found comfortable. Hemingway concluded that the veterans had been "practically murdered." He blamed the president and the FERA administrator, former social worker Harry Hopkins, now Roosevelt's confidant. They had "sent those poor bonus march guys down here to get rid of them" and had finally "got rid of them all right."[19] (This was true only in the sense that the Roosevelt administration had offered the unemployed veterans, who had staged protests in Washington, a chance to work in the Keys.) For Hemingway the story was yet another example of what was wrong with big government and the New Deal.

Joe North, one of the communist editors at *New Masses* who would come in and out of Hemingway's life at odd intervals, cabled Hemingway to ask for a story on the disaster. North was looking for copy that would cast the New Deal in a bad light. The communist wisdom of the day was that the Roosevelt administration was not much different from the Hoover administration, with one exception: the new president disguised his capitalist policies behind an ever-ready smile.[20]

While giving the author enough leeway to write what he saw, North thought Hemingway might just produce the kind of article he wanted. This was in line with the Communist Party's general disposition to make use of big names when it could, regardless of their orientation. Party membership was not required, only a willingness to write.[21] Even though *New Masses* had continued to criticize his bourgeois outlook, often bitterly, Hemingway agreed to write for North.[22] After all, he had already written part of the story in his letter to Perkins, and he welcomed another outlet for his intense feelings. Besides, no one else had asked him.[23] To protect his reputation, Hemingway made certain his friends and correspondents knew he was not changing his mind about the *New Masses*' editorial line.[24]

The review put Hemingway's story, headlined "Who Murdered the Vets?," on the cover of its September 17, 1935, issue and introduced it as an attack on the Roosevelt administration's policy of "unemployment, starvation, and death" for the veterans.[25] It was an unusual story for *New Masses*. It started out well enough, making class distinctions between the rich and the veterans. Hemingway wrote that wealthy fishermen like Presidents Hoover and Roosevelt knew it was not wise to frequent the Keys during the summer. Especially around Labor Day, the weather could be treacherous and posed a danger to property. The veterans, however, were not property. They were, Hemingway continued, simply "unsuccessful human beings" who did not have the luxury of choice. They had been sent to the Keys to do "coolie labor" during the hurricane season.

Then Hemingway shifted gears and spent the rest of the first page on how he had cared for his material belongings, in particular his custom-made cabin cruiser, telling the reader all the many things he had had to do to keep her safe from the storm. This passage, a good primer for the well-to-do boat owner facing a hurricane, somehow got by the editors. Shifting gears again, Hemingway next launched into a series of accusatory questions interlaced with gruesome details about the disaster. He wanted to know: Who sent the veterans to the Keys? Who left them there during the hurricane months? Who failed to arrange for their evacuation, the "only possible protection"? He ended by asking what the punishment for manslaughter was.[26]

"Who Murdered the Vets?" found readers far beyond the relatively limited circulation of *New Masses*. For one, *Time* magazine featured Hemingway's article in its own coverage of the disaster, focusing first on the fact that the Florida state attorney, George Worley, had come to the conclusion that "no one was responsible for the failure to evacuate the veterans . . . before [the] . . . hurricane killed 458." Hemingway was the counterpoint to Worley. Without implying he was now a leftist revolutionary, *Time* quoted Hemingway's pointed closing questions, asking how the veterans were left to die.[27] Going further, the newspaper *Daily Worker,* which styled itself "Central Organ Communist Party U.S.A.," reprinted every word of the original article, putting Hemingway's name in the headline *and* the byline, then adding the tagline "Novelist Finds Bloated Bodies of Men Left to Die on Keys."[28] Kashkin himself translated the article into Russian for his literary gazette, making it available to Hemingway's growing Soviet base.[29]

The article also attracted attention in one other quarter in Moscow. The clerks in the clipping service for Soviet spies focused on the article, most likely committing it to a file that could be mined for future operations and adding it to an index to make information about Hemingway retrievable.[30] The idea would have been to keep track of him and other foreigners who sympathized with the working class, and might one day be useful in some way. This was passive collection, something akin to a preliminary market study that compiled lists of good sales prospects, ones who might one day buy the Soviet line. It was probably the first time that anyone in the NKVD, or People's Commissariat for Internal Affairs, took any interest in Hemingway.

By this time the NKVD was one of the world's most experienced and accomplished secret services. Eventually morphing into the better-known KGB (or Committee for State Security) after a series of name changes, the NKVD* stood on a solid foundation of Russian and Bolshevik traditions. Imperial Russia had had its secret police, the Okhrana. In order to survive as a revolutionary movement in opposition to the Okhrana, the Bolsheviks created a secret, disciplined, and conspiratorial party. After coming to power in 1917, the Bolshevik government abolished the Okhrana but continued and enhanced its business model, creating a far more powerful organization to protect and spread the revolution. At home it was an instrument of control. By the 1930s, the secret organs of the state touched almost every aspect of life and work in the Soviet Union—and not in a gentle way. Abroad it was (despite its name) the primary means for recruiting spies, collecting intelligence, and eliminating opposition to the young regime.

The arm of the NKVD that was interested in Hemingway was its foreign service, mostly under the First Chief Directorate, which had resident offices, known as *rezidenturas,* in many Western countries. In the United States, the *rezidenturas* were in New York, San Francisco, and Washington. Apart from keeping an eye on the CPUSA, their mission was to steal American technology and to understand, perhaps to influence, American foreign policy, an increasingly important goal after Hitler seized power in Germany in 1933. To

* I will use the abbreviation "NKVD" throughout this book rather than reflect that organization's many—and confusing—name changes.

that end, the NKVD looked at a broad range of Americans with access to the information it wanted. Targets in 1934 included men like David A. Salmon, chief of the State Department's Division of Communications and Records; and Laurence Duggan, a young man with the right education—Phillips Exeter and Harvard—and excellent connections, also at State.[31]

Early on in the process, the Soviets collected information about individuals who might one day be willing to help the cause.[32] Leads might come from Moscow Center, or from the local party faithful, known as "fellow countrymen" (presumably because they were the next-best thing to Soviet citizens). In the United States the *rezidenturas* worked closely with the CPUSA and relied on periodicals like *Daily Worker* and *New Masses,* believing them to be accurate reflections of political reality.

When NKVD officers read the Hemingway article, they focused on the way he had "chastised" the establishment. The article exposed "what the poor and downtrodden people of the state [of Florida] had had to endure, not as a consequence of the hurricane but at the hands of the Government."[33] Soviet spies believed the American public would accept political statements by Hemingway "at face value . . . because . . . [he was] a well-known and respected author."[34] Their attitude was not unlike that of *New Masses:* whether or not they were under Soviet control, public figures like Hemingway were worth courting. They had many potentially useful contacts, and they themselves might one day become conduits for the Soviet point of view.

Hemingway was now on the NKVD radar. At this point, it is unlikely that there was a plan to recruit him, but rather a disposition to take advantage of any opportunities that might present themselves. If that happened, the NKVD—or its surrogates—would craft a suitable approach, sending the appropriate man or woman to sound Hemingway out and find out how far he was willing to go.

CHAPTER 2

THE WRITER AND THE COMMISSAR

Going to War in Spain

The time was the spring of 1937, the place Spain. A photo shows that the once-elegant black sedan, something like a 1934 four-door Dodge, has been riddled with bullets, probably from a passing enemy fighter plane. It is now a wreck, front tire flat, windshield shattered, one headlight dangling from its socket. The car's engine is exposed, its hood lying useless a few feet away. The open door suggests that the passengers got out fast. Two of those passengers, Hemingway and a Dutch communist named Joris Ivens, stand between the camera and the wreck, miraculously unscathed.

For most of his life, Hemingway liked to live on the edge and take risks. But the expression on his face suggests that, at least this time, the brush with death was close enough for him. His mouth is closed, his hands are safe in the pockets of a long tan trench coat that is partly buttoned, its collar turned up against the cold on the overcast day. There is a small black beret tight on his skull. Though his eyes seem half-shut, the writer is looking in the general direction of the camera. But Ivens, standing next to the writer, has his eyes wide open, and he is looking directly into the lens. Like Hemingway, he wears a black beret and a winter coat, but it is open and his left hand rests casually in the front pocket of his trousers. There is just the hint of a smile on his face, an almost satisfied look, as if the world was going his way despite the attack.[1]

Still alive after an air attack in the spring of 1937: the writer and his would-be political commissar, the Dutch communist Joris Ivens. *Fernhout Photo, Nederlands Fotomuseum.*

Hemingway went to Spain in 1937 to report on the civil war that had broken out in the summer of 1936. The basic political calculus was straightforward, at least at first: a cabal of reactionary generals, among them Francisco Franco, led a so-called Nationalist rebellion against the legally constituted Republican government. It was a working democracy. But for the likes of Franco, the Republic had two things seriously wrong with it: it could not govern effectively, and many of its supporters were pushing the country much too far to the left. The fault line was soon as deep as any in the first half of the twentieth century, with the great landowners, the military, and the Catholic Church aligned against a bewildering array of groups to the left of center—socialists, communists, trade unionists, and anarchists—each with its own agenda.

The war became more complex when three foreign powers intervened. While the Western democracies stood on the sidelines, Hitler and Italy's Mussolini aligned themselves with Franco, providing arms, advisors, and soldiers. Stalin decided to side with the Republic in order to improve his standing with the European left and divert attention from the murderous purges that he had ordered at home. So, in the fall of 1936, the Soviets started sending the same kind of help as Hitler and Mussolini, except that they sent less equipment, fewer troops, and more advisors and secret policemen. Among them was a man who called himself Alexander Orlov.[2]

The model for the minor character Varloff in *For Whom the Bell Tolls,* Orlov had impeccable Bolshevik credentials. His life had been one of unremitting revolutionary struggle. During the Russian Civil War he was part of the brutal fight against White guerrillas who wanted to overthrow the new regime. In the 1920s, he became one of the early members of the organization that was to become the NKVD and later the KGB. A natural linguist educated in the law, he was as comfortable operating in Western Europe as in the Soviet Union, which set him apart from many of his colleagues who would never shake the provincial look and sound of Russian officials. Surviving photographs show a compact man with short, dark hair and a closely trimmed, almost Hitlerian mustache. There is no hint of emotion in his eyes. He seldom smiled.

In the 1930s, Orlov was remarkably productive in Western Europe. Among other accomplishments, he helped to develop Soviet networks, including the superspies known as the Cambridge Five: Kim Philby and other members of the British upper class who would use their impeccable credentials to penetrate the highest levels of His Majesty's Government.[3] There was also a stint in the United States, and work on a senior coordination staff at the Kremlin, where Stalin, the ultimate Soviet personnel officer, had gotten to know him.

The NKVD sent Orlov to Spain in August 1936 with a clear agenda. High on the list was intelligence and paramilitary support for the Republic, to include the training and employment of antifascist guerrillas. He helped to grow the Soviet presence in Spain, as well as the influence of the Spanish Communist Party.

Over time, more and more parts of the government came under Soviet control. Simultaneously, the NKVD embarked on the ruthless suppression of local "Trotskyites" (those linked with Stalin's archrival, the exiled Soviet revolutionary leader Leon Trotsky). The NKVD in Spain went on to persecute anyone, of whatever nationality, who seemed to be unreliable, or might become unreliable in the future. The target could also be a Spanish political group, like the anarchists or a party on the hard left, each with its own, non-Stalinist vision of the future.

Those who came under suspicion faced some combination of arrest, interrogation, torture, and execution, often at one of the *rezidentura*'s own facilities. The English sculptor Jason Gurney, a left-leaning idealist when he went to Spain to fight for the Republic, soon observed what "everyone knew": there was almost always an NKVD "prison and interrogation center somewhere in the neighborhood." At "the slightest hint of subversion or 'Trotskyism'—which might include almost anything—a man was likely to disappear and never be seen again."[4] At least one of these centers in Spain was complete with its own, very convenient crematorium.[5] The NKVD might lure a Trotskyite in for an appointment, then interrogate, kill, and cremate him, leaving no trace whatsoever.

To the extent that such paranoid practices had goals, the short-term goal was to strengthen the Republic by imposing unity among its supporters; the long-term goal was for Spain to become a Soviet puppet state.[6]

Orlov told his unlikely literary executor, a retired FBI agent named Edward P. Gazur, that the NKVD had engineered Hemingway's travel to Spain to become one of the voices of the Republic. "Through the efforts of the Republican Government, which was secretly motivated to do so by the Soviets, the North American Newspaper Alliance [NANA] in New York signed a contract with Hemingway. . . ."[7] Orlov's claim is hard to substantiate and even if true is only part of the story. The chain of events that led Hemingway to Spain had a number of separate links: his long-standing love for Spain; the call of another war; a news service willing to pay the amazing sum of a dollar per word; a chance to make a film for the Republic; and, not least, overcoming the U.S. State Department's reluctance to issue a passport for his travel to Spain. Before he could sail from New York, he had to go to Washington to meet with Ruth Shipley, the powerful bureaucrat who controlled the passport office, produce his contract with NANA, and assure her that he "had no intention of participating in the . . . conflict."[8]

The writer Josephine Herbst, a friend since Hemingway's Paris days who resurfaced in Key West and Spain, had a better understanding than Orlov. She intuited that Hemingway, like many others, "was undergoing some kind of transformation" and went to Spain as part of that process.[9] She also knew he wanted to be *the* war writer of his generation; war gave answers that could not be found elsewhere, even in the waters of Key West when the tarpon struck. "What was the deepest reality *there* was in extreme form *here*."[10]

Herbst was right to focus on process. Hemingway did not change overnight. He started with a general disposition to support the Republic and oppose fascism.[11] In December 1936, he wrote to his editor Perkins that Franco was "a son of [a] bitch of the first magnitude."[12] In another letter a few weeks later the tone was ambivalent. Neither side was right, and he was not about to throw his support to either. But he did care about human beings and their suffering, which meant that he sympathized with the people who worked the land.[13] He added that he did not think much of the Soviet regime, which was supporting the Republic: "[T]hat's a dirty outfit in Russia now but I don't like any governments."

A few days later, to his wife Pauline's family (who were Catholics and for that reason more likely to be sympathetic to Franco and the Nationalists), he admitted that the "Reds may be as bad as they say" but added that it was their country, not that of the absentee landlords, let alone the Italians and the Germans.[14] He also asserted he wanted to go to Spain to watch "the dress rehearsal for the inevitable European war" so that he could write "anti-war war correspondence" to keep the United States out of that war.

Then there was Martha Gellhorn, Hemingway's eye-catching new mistress, almost ten years younger than the great writer. She had walked into Sloppy Joe's in Key West in December 1936 and changed his life. Fit, blond, and energetic, she had a thirst for adventure married to a passion for writing and left-wing causes. She and Hemingway agreed to meet in Spain, where they would both cover the war, she for *Collier's* and he for NANA. The war sealed their relationship; they almost literally bonded under fire. In 1940 she would become his third wife. Of his four wives, she would be the one who came the closest to being an equal. During this war, she developed into a journalist and novelist with her own point of view. Often he was approving, but at other times he was resentful of her career ambitions. Still, he did pay attention to her focus on the suffering of ordinary people in the 1930s. Her presence in Hemingway's life in Spain made it easier for him to open up to the left.

Also guiding his leftward turn were fellow artists and writers, many of them longtime friends like John Dos Passos, the novelist who introduced him to Key West; and Archibald MacLeish, the future librarian of Congress who was already a famous poet. MacLeish and Dos Passos were, Hemingway wrote, the only two literary friends he could trust.[15] MacLeish was at this stage somewhat pessimistic about the future of capitalism, and Dos Passos was dedicated to social equality. Like Hemingway, MacLeish and Dos Passos had many communist friends and acquaintances. But all three had often disagreed with those communists, sometimes bitterly, and it would be more accurate to call them left-leaning and antifascist than "fellow travelers," let alone fully pledged communists.[16] With MacLeish and Dos Passos, Hemingway became one of the founding members of Contemporary Historians Inc., a group formed to make films about the Spanish Republic. Their goal was

Hemingway and Gellhorn in Spain, where they forged their relationship covering the civil war. Gellhorn looks cheerfully at the camera, while Hemingway has his back to it. A flask lies within arm's reach. *Ernest Hemingway Photo Collection, JFK Library.*

to generate favorable publicity about its struggle for survival and, above all, to move the U.S. government off its policy of neutrality.

The Historians would produce *Spain in Flames,* which Hemingway worked on even before he left New York; and *The Spanish Earth,* which he would help to film on location and then narrate in his own voice. *Spain in Flames* comes across today as a heavy-handed combination of history and propaganda. One flier screamed that the film showed "thousands massacred by Fascists with Hitler-Mussolini help," "women and children lying dead in the streets of Madrid." The same flier quoted Hemingway as saying that no man, no matter what his political belief or religious faith, could fail to be moved by the film.[17] *The Spanish Earth* would be more nuanced and artistic but still tell a compelling story. Its director, the cosmopolitan Joris Ivens, was by far the most politically committed among the Historians. Going well beyond his colleagues' intermittent support for left-wing causes, he was a dedicated communist for all of his adult life, through the collapse of the Soviet Empire in 1989. In the 1930s he was under the discipline of the Communist International, or Comintern.[18]

Nominally a revolutionary association of communist parties, the Comintern was separate from the NKVD. But like the NKVD it was an extension of Stalin's apparatus, under his overall control. Among the leading figures in the Comintern was the German Willi Münzenberg, a tireless, unkempt, creative, charismatic man. Once described as "the five most interesting men in Europe" because he was so versatile and energetic,[19] Münzenberg first met Lenin *before* the Bolshevik Revolution. In the 1920s it was Lenin himself who asked Münzenberg to create a mechanism outside Russia for agitation and propaganda—soon abbreviated "agitprop"—to generate good press for the revolution. Münzenberg was an excellent choice, and before long he was running a dazzling European empire for agitprop, sometimes called the Münzenberg Trust.[20]

First came the printed word: Münzenberg launched journals or newspapers to counter capitalist and fascist periodicals. Then there were plays, conferences, and cultural events of many kinds—"in breathless succession . . . a dozen or more International Congresses, Rallies and Committees."[21] Films were produced at home in the Soviet Union and abroad. The Comintern openly claimed some of the products as its own but also operated through a plethora of front groups. Collaborators might be witting or unwitting. The unspoken motto for much of the time was "everything for the party, but nothing in the name of the party." A professional filmmaker for the Dutch Communist Party, Ivens was just the kind of man Münzenberg wanted on his team.[22] The loyalty, energy, and creativity were there, and so was the discretion. Ivens knew that films that did not look and sound like propaganda were all the more compelling.

Ivens did not have to hide his affiliation from the Historians, who were aware of his background and comfortable with it. MacLeish was sure Ivens was the kind of "communist who [would] never let communism get in the way of his work."[23] MacLeish was perhaps too generous.

It seems the persuasive Ivens soon stepped into the role of "Ernest's Political Commissar," the man who would direct the writer's political education.[24] No one is likely ever to know whether the Comintern directed Ivens to work with Hemingway. There is no trace of a formal tasking in the voluminous surviving files of the Comintern. A computerized search of their 50 million or so digitized pages (they were revolutionaries with a passion for record keeping) for any reference to Hemingway will produce no results.[25] But Ivens may have been tasked in some informal, "see what you can do" way, like Münzenberg's charge to the then-communist newspaperman and writer Arthur Koestler to see what he could find out from the enemy's point of view. With no training, and less aptitude for spying, Koestler proceeded to Franco's headquarters on a mission that led to his arrest and almost cost him his life.[26] Equally likely, Ivens may just have decided to do what seemed right to him, and set out to make good use of the great author.

Hemingway and Koestler were not the only writers whom the Comintern enlisted for the duration of the Spanish war. Another target was Barbara Wertheim, better known later in life as the historian Barbara Tuchman, who would write the bestseller *The Guns of August*, which attracted the attention of President John F. Kennedy.[27] A New York socialite and Radcliffe graduate, Wertheim made her way to Spain in 1937 as a reporter for the *Nation*. After a time in Valencia and Madrid, she headed for Paris, where she encountered one of Münzenberg's principal deputies, the worldly, charming, and highly manipulative Otto Katz, who tried to recruit her for the Comintern. No communist, she refused the pitch. Katz's fallback position was to ask her to come up with an idea for a book that would support the cause by exploring historical parallels. This she did, writing her first book about Britain and Spain in the nineteenth century, "designed," as she put it, "to show how it had always been a cardinal principle of British policy to keep Spain . . .

free of control by the dominant power on the continent (currently Hitler)."[28] Intriguingly, a copy of Wertheim's little-known book on Spain found its way into Hemingway's personal library in Key West, where it was still on the shelves in 2015.[29]

Like Katz, Ivens would adapt his approach to fit the target. Born a year earlier than Hemingway, the Dutchman knew better than to start by urging Hemingway to sign up as an agent of the Comintern. Ivens would gradually introduce Hemingway to the flock, but he would not force him into the fold. Decades later in a remarkably frank interview with the Massachusetts Institute of Technology historian William B. Watson, Ivens remembered, "I had a plan for Hemingway, and I think I used the right tactics. For this kind of man. [*sic*] I knew how far he could go, and that he was not a traitor."[30]

Ivens put Hemingway to work, personally and directly, on the front lines of filmmaking, and made sure to expose him to the Comintern's antifascist line. Unlike a disciplined communist, Hemingway did not come with much by way of political consciousness, only his half-formed attitudes, like helping the underdog, fighting fascism, or keeping America out of another European war. Ivens would change that once Hemingway arrived in Europe in March 1937. "I was very politically involved," he told Watson; "he wasn't. . . . For myself I set the task to make Hemingway understand the anti-fascist cause," the way the Comintern understood it, no more and no less.[31]

Ivens started by forming a strong personal bond. He could build on the foundation of their work. For his part, Hemingway put his heart into the filmmaking. He made himself useful, arranging transportation, carrying equipment, and sharing his food and drink (typically whiskey and raw onions). Perhaps to test himself—he had not been in combat for almost twenty years—he seemed to relish going out onto the battlefield with the crew. Working on the front lines, and sometimes in the no-man's-land in between, the men took risks that only the combat veteran Hemingway fully understood. One day a bullet slammed into a wall next to Ivens's head, and Hemingway had the team move to a less exposed post. When it turned out that the cameraman had forgotten his camera, Hemingway crawled back on his hands and knees to look for it—while enemy sharpshooters marked his path with near misses, bullets that hit close by. Being able to walk away from such near-death experiences brought the men ever closer. In Ivens's words: "[I]f you are on the front line with a man . . . you come to know who he is. . . . The first two weeks in Spain we spent getting to know one another. . . . At the front these preliminaries go very quickly."[32]

Ivens introduced Hemingway to the "right" people: communist fighters. For this purpose, the International Brigades, created and run by the Comintern to fight for the Republic, were made to order. They were filled with tough, colorful, and educated men (as well as a few women) from various countries, including the United States, the kind of people who appealed to Hemingway. Some of them, like Milton Wolff, of the Brigades' best-known American component, the Abraham Lincoln Battalion, would become lifelong friends. They were not just scribblers or dreamers, but men risking their lives for their beliefs—they were *authentic*. Most were under communist discipline, willing to do whatever the party or the Comintern ordered them to do. Ivens did not have to lecture Hemingway about politics; he simply needed to take him to the front, especially where the Brigades were fighting, and let him absorb what those around him were doing and saying.

After a few weeks, Ivens decided Hemingway was ready for the next step: meeting the people behind the fighters. These were communist commanders, Soviet officials, and Soviet newspapermen. The best place to find them was only a few miles from the front, at the Gaylord in Madrid, which the Soviets had turned into an annex for their embassy in Spain. Set on the corner of two fair-size streets, the small, discreet hotel was easy to miss. With a few futuristic straight lines etched into its gray façade, it looked more like an apartment house than a luxury hotel with marbled corridors leading to well-appointed rooms. Only the sentries with fixed bayonets standing by the carport suggested there was anything unusual about the place.

The Soviets and their cronies lived, ate, and drank in grand style at the Gaylord while their soldiers fought and died in trenches a few miles away. It was one of the few establishments in the capital that had an excellent supply of food and alcohol, especially vodka and caviar. On an early visit, Hemingway apparently brought the two precious bottles of whiskey that wound up on a communal table already groaning under the weight of a huge ham (did he want to make sure that he would be accepted?).[33]

Part of the appeal for Hemingway was the Gaylord's exclusivity; only a handful of journalists were able to get in and mingle with the men who were deciding the course of the war. Ivens introduced the writer to Mikhail Koltsov, the chief correspondent for the Soviet daily *Pravda,* and the other communist leaders. Years later Ivens would remember how "that gave him [Hemingway] an edge, which for him was very important."[34]

Soon the bond between the two men was strong enough for Ivens to set tasks for Hemingway. Even more than seventy years later, from his letters to Hemingway, Ivens emerges as the kind of film director (or political commissar) who has trouble letting go; he is directive to the point of being tiresome. He told Hemingway whom to see, where to go, what to film, sometimes even what to say. One letter, from April 26, 1937, features a numbered to-do list, with entries about supervising the filming in a Spanish village; ordering transportation; sending an update no later than May 3; and keeping Dos Passos in line.[35] A short while later Ivens asked for Hemingway's help in finalizing a synopsis of *Spanish Earth.*[36]

Hemingway did not, by any stretch, do everything Ivens wanted him to. The relationship was more about influence than direction. But Ivens ran the agenda for Hemingway's first trip to Spain, leaving him little time for other pursuits, even courting Gellhorn. One of the camp followers, the British poet Stephen Spender, put it this way: Hemingway was "being pursued by this tough, aggressive lady." She was "always looking for him," but usually he had gone to the front with Ivens.[37]

It was no accident that Ivens expressed concern about Dos Passos. The professor was preparing to leave the fold. An underlying reason may have been the complicated rivalry between the two novelists; the immediate cause, however, was the murder of Dos Passos's friend José Robles. Originally from "a family of monarchical and generally reactionary sympathies,"[38] Robles's political journey took him to the left, but not to an extreme. In the 1920s, he emigrated to the United States and landed a job teaching Spanish literature at Johns Hopkins in Baltimore. When the civil war broke out, he happened to be in Madrid. He stayed and offered his services to the Republic. Since he knew some Russian, he became an interpreter for Spanish and Soviet officials when they discussed state secrets at the Ministry of War.

In the fall of 1936, Republican or Soviet secret police arrested Robles. Even today, the details are murky. Most likely his captors kept him in one of the small prisons the NKVD had established throughout Republican Spain, and interrogated him relentlessly. He was never tried or formally charged. Eventually it became inconvenient to keep him alive, and, early in 1937, his captors simply executed him and disposed of his body.[39]

As soon as he got to Spain in the spring of 1937, Dos Passos set to work uncovering the truth about his friend's fate. He rejected the theory that Robles had been a fascist spy as "the fabrication of romantic American Communist sympathizers," a dig at Hemingway and his communist friends. For Dos Passos, Robles's "case was pushed to the point of execution because Russian secret agents felt that Robles knew too much about the relations between the Spanish war ministry and the Kremlin and was not, from their very special point of view, politically reliable."[40] It was a story worth telling to

Americans at home because it offered "a glimpse into the bloody tangle of ruined lives" in Spain, an offset to "the hurray for our side" mentality, one that might help to "free our minds . . . from . . . black is black and white is white . . . partisanship."[41]

In this way, Dos Passos and Hemingway were moving in opposite directions between 1937 and 1940. As part of his transformation, Hemingway was becoming entranced with communist fighters and artists, and increasingly dedicating himself to saving the Republic from fascism. As Josie Herbst put it, Hemingway "seemed to be naïvely embracing on the simpler levels the current ideologies," while Dos Passos, with a better understanding of politics, was urgently questioning them.[42]

Ivens wanted to prevent fallout from the Robles affair, especially outside Spain. He did not want Dos Passos to say any more about his "friend-translator-fascist" when he returned home.[43] In his April 26, 1937, letter to Hemingway, Ivens expressed the hope "that Dos will see what a man and comrade has to do in this difficult and serious wartime"—that is, to consider the greater good, rather than the fate of one individual, a theme Hemingway himself soon echoed.[44] Without explicitly directing Hemingway to do anything, Ivens ended his train of thought suggestively: "You agree?"

Hemingway did agree. He worried Dos Passos could make it difficult for the film crew—his questions could "get everybody into trouble."[45] Now Hemingway assigned himself the task of ensuring that Dos Passos would not undermine their work after leaving Spain. Their conflict came to a head in Paris on May 11, 1937, just as Dos Passos and his wife were about to catch a train to the port of Le Havre, where they would board a steamer and continue the trip across the Atlantic.[46]

The Gare St.-Lazare was one of the largest and oldest stations in Paris. From the outside the elegant nineteenth-century façade made it look like a museum—it would not have been out of place next to the Louvre—but on the inside it was all function, a series of angular steel and glass roofs over the platforms and tracks. The sun had come out from behind the clouds around noon, and some light penetrated down to the platforms for the passengers who were looking for the 1:15 boat train. Having arrived late, Dos Passos and his wife, Katy, were struggling to load their many bags. Almost at the last minute, before the conductors called "En voiture" and banged the doors shut, Hemingway burst from the crowd of relatives and well-wishers. But he had not come as a well-wisher. He was scowling, and there was no cheerful small talk. Hemingway needed answers to important questions. Now. What exactly was Dos Passos going to say about Robles? Or for that matter about the war in general? Ever thoughtful and balanced, Dos Passos answered that he was going to tell his story to the American public: What was the point of fighting a war for civil liberties if you destroyed such rights along the way? Hemingway retorted: "Civil liberties, shit. Are you with us or are you against us?" Dos Passos shrugged like a professor making a point in class: he would write what he had to write. Lifting a clenched fist to Dos Passos's face, Hemingway said, "You do that, and you will be finished, destroyed. The reviewers in New York will absolutely crucify you."[47]

Katy Dos Passos (who was Hemingway's longtime close friend in her own right) could not believe what she was hearing. She told Hemingway she had "never heard anything so despicably opportunistic in all my life." Hemingway had no response, and when the train was finally ready to pull out of the station, he walked away without looking back.[48]

Ivens and Hemingway proceeded to edit Dos Passos out of their professional lives. It was as if Dos Passos had never been part of Contemporary Historians, which Ivens would later reconstitute as History Today Inc. to exclude the unbeliever. (The new organization would have, as Ivens put it, "no Dos Passos or so."[49]) In early 1938, Hemingway would return to the subject in a very angry cable sent from the French ocean liner *Ile de France,* followed by an only slightly less angry letter posted on dry land a few days later. The cable accused Dos Passos (who often had trouble making ends meet) of ratting "for money while better guys than you [are] still fighting"—that is, selling stories that exposed the Republic's faults.[50]

The letter started with an apology, but then deteriorated.[51] One of the milder sentences was still the kind of accusation that would end a friendship: for him to claim that, in this war, the communists were imposing their will on the people was "viciously pitiful."

For years to come, Hemingway would retell versions of the story, all of them unflattering to Dos Passos. He would claim Robles had been executed as a spy after a fair trial, or simply that "the boys" had shot the "worthless translator."[52] In 1954, Hemingway would cast himself as the one who had "had the heart to tell Dos" the truth about Robles, and that Dos Passos had "turned on me like I had shot him myself."[53]

Hemingway's attacks on Dos Passos reflected what he later called "the technical strain" of the great war against fascism that started in 1936, continued for a decade, and changed his life; he would use that strain to explain why he had turned on some of his old friends.[54] But he never disavowed what he said and wrote about Dos Passos or Spain in the spring of 1937.

A civil war within the civil war broke out in May in Barcelona, a city where the far left was realizing its vision of the future. At first the anarchists and the unorthodox Marxists in the POUM—the Partido Obrero de Unificación Marxista, or Workers' Party of Marxist Unification, appeared to have the upper hand. Elegant restaurants had become cafeterias for the people—the dining room at the Ritz was now People's Cafeteria No. 1. Factories were being run from the shop floor; priests were nowhere to be seen, their churches shuttered or put to other uses. One monastery had been turned into a tuberculosis sanatorium for children.[55] All of this ran counter to orthodox communist and Soviet policy: the revolution should wait until the war was over. Until that day, everyone should obey the central government.

The long-simmering conflict flared out of control, first at the telephone exchange, then in the streets, with both sides quickly erecting barricades of cobblestones and overturned vehicles. The fighting was confusing and heavy at times—on a quiet day it was "silent save for machine-gun and rifle fire."[56] While the Soviets intrigued in the background, exerting pressure whenever they could, the communists took advantage of the crisis and managed to replace the prime minister of the Republic. The new government moved against the POUM in Barcelona. Its headquarters was closed and turned into a prison, its units at the front disbanded, and its central committee arrested en masse.

In June, the party leader, Andrés Nin, paid with his life for his onetime support for Trotsky and outspoken criticism of Stalin, that "poisoned dictator."[57] The NKVD took Nin to one of its secret prisons, torturing him to confess that he was a fascist spy. Displaying amazing powers of resistance, he refused to confess, thereby saving the lives of his friends and comrades. The Soviets or their proxies then murdered him and dumped his body in the countryside. The NKVD *rezident* himself, Orlov, was on site at least part of the time; the case was that important to the Soviets.[58] To explain the affair, communist newspapers published lurid (and false) accusations of Nin's collaboration with the fascists. They eventually put out the story that he had been rescued by the fascists, and had found safety in Franco's or Hitler's hands.

Hemingway is unlikely to have known the truth about Nin's fate, or of Orlov's participation, but he heard the rumors. He mentioned Nin in his 1938 letter to Dos Passos, and later retold the NKVD's cynical version of Nin's death in *For Whom the Bell Tolls*. The character Karkov, modeled on the Soviet correspondent Koltsov, makes light of the whole affair. The POUM was a crackpot heresy; Nin had been in custody but escaped from "our hands." No one knows whether Hemingway naïvely accepted the cover story, or knowingly glossed over the truth in order to protect the Republic.[59]

During the troubles in Barcelona, Ivens and Hemingway were in the United States. From Spain, Hemingway had gone first to New

York and then to Key West, where he gathered up his wife and sons, and proceeded to Bimini in the Bahamas, his home base during the summer of that year. In early June, Ivens came south to discuss the film and a speech Hemingway was about to give.[60]

On June 4, the two friends flew to New York to attend the Second American Writers' Conference, sponsored by the League of American Writers. Touting the congress as a gathering of "men of letters of various political affiliations," the communist newspaper *Daily Worker* advertised the upcoming speech by Hemingway, "this most 'non-political' of writers . . . fresh from the bleeding battlefields of Spain."[61] But it was the CPUSA that set the program, casting its members in the leading roles, among them the dreary Stalinist Earl Browder, general secretary of the party; Hemingway's friend Donald Ogden Stewart, a Hollywood film producer who had become one of the faithful; and Ivens himself, who was still finishing his edits to *The Spanish Earth*.

The venue was Carnegie Hall, on West Fifty-Seventh Street in Manhattan. Built in 1891, it already looked old-fashioned, an ornate opera house with tiers of gilded boxes looking down on the orchestra pit and the stage. Tonight it was filled to capacity with 3,500 communists and their friends. Billows of cigarette smoke combined with the heat and humidity to make the air almost unbreathable. But the crowd paid close attention to the speakers. Ivens was third up, and showed clips from the film "made on the same front where I think every honest writer ought to be."[62]

Never comfortable speaking in public—one story has him going from bar to bar in midtown Manhattan to gather his courage[63]—Hemingway continued where Ivens left off. Constrained by jacket and tie, sweating profusely in the heat, the writer from Oak Park spoke in his flat, almost nasal midwestern voice, and had trouble reading his typescript. "[W]hen it didn't read right," Hemingway seemed to get mad at his text, "repeating the sentences with exceptional vehemence."[64]

The seven-minute speech was an attack on fascism that gave the benefit of the doubt to communism. Hemingway told the audience that the writer's problem was "how to write truly."[65] He went on to say that there was "only one form of government that cannot produce good writers, and that system is fascism"; a "writer who will not lie cannot live and work under fascism." He said nothing about what it was like to be a writer in the Soviet Union, where writers were forced to lie to survive. The members of the audience liked the speech as it was. This was for many the event they had been waiting for, and they were not disappointed. Whistling and stamping their feet, they rewarded Hemingway with waves of applause.[66] A few days later Max Perkins enthused that his observations about writing were "everlastingly true."[67] *New Masses* printed the text in its entirety on June 22.[68]

After Carnegie Hall, the Contemporary Historians faced a crisis. At one point, probably in late June, Ivens claimed he had to have $2,500 to finish the film. Hemingway decided to help Ivens, the man whom, he said, he trusted absolutely. He observed that various people, including MacLeish, said they could do nothing. But he was willing to make another financial sacrifice for the cause, and proceeded to borrow $2,500 at 6 percent, putting a dent in his finances but ending the immediate crisis.[69]

By the beginning of July the film had taken final form. Ivens drafted, and Hemingway edited, a script that reduced the war to a simple formula:[70]

> *We gained the right to cultivate our land by democratic elections. Now the military cliques and absentee landlords attack to take our land from us again. But we fight for the right to irrigate and cultivate this Spanish Earth which the nobles kept idle for their own amusement.*

Narrated by Hemingway, the film opens by portraying life in a Republican village, where the inhabitants are shown working collectively to make a better life for themselves. The film then shifts to footage of men fighting to defend that way of life, with scenes from the front and war-torn Madrid. Gellhorn would always remember the shelling scenes with women choking from the smoke and wiping their eyes, while men with "grave waiting faces" walked slowly toward the enemy they were about to attack.[71]

On July 8, Hemingway, Gellhorn, and Ivens showed *The Spanish Earth* to President and Mrs. Roosevelt. Gellhorn had reached out to her friend Eleanor and persuaded her to invite the filmmakers to the White House. At first, Hemingway did not think much of his host; when they met, the president was "all Harvard charming and sexless and womanly."[72] It was a hot day; he took them into a dining room that was not air-conditioned; the dinner was unremarkable: watery soup, rubber squab, wilted lettuce. But, after dinner, both Roosevelts watched the film intently. The president sat next to Ivens, and almost literally bent his ear when it was over. Perhaps, he started out, Hemingway and Ivens "should put more propaganda in the film."[73]

Hemingway and Ivens had planned to plead for a suspension of the arms embargo that stemmed from American neutrality. But Roosevelt talked so much that they could not make the pitch. The best Hemingway could do was to tell Harry Hopkins, Roosevelt's confidant, whom he now claimed to admire, that the Republic needed weapons to win. Neither the film itself nor this small initiative would lead to any changes in American policy, but it was a heady experience for the two artists to try to influence the president. Even years later, Ivens would remember the feeling: "We had tried, and we were quite proud that we had."[74]

The next day in her newspaper column, "My Day," Mrs. Roosevelt chatted with her readers about the three "very interesting people" who had come for dinner.[75] The Dutchman with curly hair and deep-set blue eyes was "a most artistic and fearless maker of films." She was struck by the way he had shown "the faces of the men and women . . . farmers, soldiers, orators or village housewives, all . . . interesting types whom you felt you would like to study."

For her part, Gellhorn wrote to Mrs. Roosevelt to thank her "endlessly" for arranging the visit, and asked, a little anxiously, "You did really like the film didn't you?" She hoped so: "Joris and Ernest were very happy about it . . . impressed that you and Mr. Roosevelt said to make it stronger—that's what it amounted to—by underlining the causes of the conflict."[76]

In mid-July, with Pauline instead of Gellhorn in tow, Ivens and Hemingway took their film to Hollywood, where they hoped to find friendly audiences able and willing to write large checks that the Historians would use to buy ambulances for the Republic.[77] Hemingway was lionized by the actors and producers only too happy to sit through a performance by the famous writer and his friend the director, especially for a left-wing cause. First there was a luncheon at MGM hosted by the Austrian beauty Luise Rainer, and then large affairs at the homes of two other stars, Fredric March and Robert Benchley. The performance at the Philharmonic Auditorium sold out.[78]

At the Philharmonic, Ivens spoke as if he were Hemingway; he almost "out-Hemingwayed Hemingway" with the remark that "I know that money is hard to make but dying is not easy either."[79] Not to be bested, Hemingway proceeded to make an articulate plea for help. After speaking about the cause—how the spread of fascism had to be stopped in Spain and how men he had loved had died for the cause, he made it even more personal:[80]

> *I don't know whether you have ever been wounded. . . . At the moment it happens, . . . it is not very painful. . . . But in about a half an hour when the shock has worn off the pain starts and . . . you will truly wish you were dead if the ambulance is slow in getting there.*

Scott Fitzgerald was in the audience at the Philharmonic and found the film to be "beyond praise," adding in a letter to Max

Perkins at Charles Scribner's & Sons (who published both Fitzgerald and Hemingway) that he had heard "something almost religious" in Hemingway's words.[81]

The grand tour of Hollywood turned out to be the high point for *The Spanish Earth.* Shown at venues like the 55th Street Playhouse in New York and the National Press Club in Washington, the film generated mixed reviews. Critics were ambivalent about the tension between cinematic art and political propaganda. Before long it faded into obscurity, becoming an interesting case study in the history of filmmaking.[82]

Then came Ivens's surprise announcement that he was through with Spain. He was going to focus on a new war, the one that was heating up in China. It was hard for Hemingway and Gellhorn to accept the sudden change, even though it was almost certainly on Comintern orders. They had gone through so much with the Dutchman, from the front lines to the White House. Now the team was breaking up, and one of its members was going to the other end of the earth. Gellhorn remembered thinking that Ivens and Hemingway were committed in different ways:[83]

> *In New York we were promoting* The Spanish Earth *as if the whole world depended on it. What always astounded me was that Joris did not return to Spain. Ernest and I went back there, he didn't. I believe he wasn't that emotionally involved after all.*

Hemingway worried, rightly, that the Comintern was starting to shift its focus from Spain, an unimaginable idea for him and Gellhorn in the summer of 1937.[84] The writer was still moving in the other direction, becoming ever more committed to the Republic, which in turn brought him closer to the Soviets—for him the Republic's best foreign friends. Even as Comintern stalwarts like Ivens redeployed, Hemingway deepened his friendships with the Soviet spies who remained in-country and were only too happy to respond to his overtures.

CHAPTER 3

RETURNING TO SPAIN

To Stay the Course

One of the hardest parts of the trip had been to persuade the garage owner to splash paint onto the near-perfect finish of the car to break up its outline. In the late summer of 1937, Hemingway wanted as much protection from enemy air attack as he could get for his trips to a Republican guerrilla camp in a remote corner of Spain, and homemade camouflage was better than nothing. After strapping an extra gas can or two to the bumper, he set out from Valencia on the smoother paved roads near the Mediterranean coast, then turned onto the smaller roads leading into the mountains of Teruel. Not designed for the army trucks and staff cars that now passed over them, the hill roads must have sprouted potholes and ruts. The car, probably another powerful Dodge said to have gears like a bulldozer, took about two hours to go some forty-five miles, climbing slowly but steadily around the hairpin turns.

Hemingway's destination, the small town of Alfambra, was pretty in an austere way, its barren hills framed by vegetation along the small river of the same name. He found the guerrilla commander he was looking for in a simple house that had been turned into a barracks, and quickly learned that Antoni Chrost, the plain-spoken Polish communist who was in charge, did not want visitors, especially not reporters. The name Hemingway meant nothing to him. Ernest produced a laissez-passer from the Army of the Center, covered with stamps that conveyed the power of the issuing authority. The pass charged every Republican commander with helping the bearer in his work, which, he liked to tell people like Chrost, was more like that of a writer than a reporter.

It was the pass that probably made the difference. Chrost eventually agreed to let the writer return three weeks later and go along on a sabotage mission—though he would assign a man to keep an eye on Hemingway just in case. The second time around, Hemingway was with the guerrillas for four days at their camp and in the field. They loaned him a revolver, and asked him to carry hand grenades and food on the fifteen-mile march to the objective.

Setting off at dusk, the thirty-man band slipped through fascist lines, traveled near (but not on) a road, and finally, under cover of darkness, crawled up to a set of railroad tracks on a small bridge over the Jiloca River. Before long they could hear a train in the distance, and see sparks from the locomotive lighting up the night sky. The train was moving slowly enough to give the dinamiteros *time to carefully prime their charges while Hemingway rummaged around in his pack for a camera. At Chrost's urgent request, he turned off the flash but was able to use the light from the explosion to photograph the attack: the bridge collapsing into the water just before the locomotive reached the riverbank, the cars coming off the rails, their iron wheels plowing up the earth before they came to rest, now useful only as scrap metal. The guerrillas did not wait for the enemy to react but started for home at once.*[1]

Hemingway returned to Spain three times after Joris Ivens went to China. The Dutch filmmaker would continue to write his American friend long, detailed letters, including a twenty-page note on January 28, 1938, urging him to stay the course.[2] Hemingway should continue to make the case for the Republic with his writing, just as he had in 1937; he should get his antifascist play, *The Fifth Column,* onstage and perhaps on film; he should stay in touch with people in the movement who could explain the events in Barcelona to him; if and when he was ready, if there was something he would "like to talk over with one of our leading people," he should not hesitate to "do it." Finally, he should come to China, the new frontier in the war against fascism.

Much of Ivens's advice fell on deaf ears. Hemingway would not go to China to work, let alone sign up with the Comintern. He would build on the foundation that Ivens had laid for him, making good use of his new Soviet and communist contacts. But he would support the Republic in his own way. He would be his own commissar. And he would be more than a propagandist for Ivens and his cause. Ivens did not seem to understand that Hemingway was also in Spain as a suitor, humanitarian, military advisor, and, above all, writer. As he had tried to explain to the guerrillas, the writer and the reporter were different. The reporter wanted facts for a story to file as soon as he could get it through the censor; the writer wanted to absorb the experience of wartime.

The man who came closest to replacing Ivens in Hemingway's life was the German communist Gustav Regler, one of the more interesting—and, ultimately, appealing—figures Hemingway would encounter in Spain.[3] He was movie-star handsome, as his cameo appearance in *The Spanish Earth* proved; he looked a little like a more cerebral Gary Cooper. Regler's combat record was a threshold qualification for friendship with Hemingway. In World War I, he had fought in the trenches for the kaiser. After the war, he became a dedicated communist, risking his life and livelihood for the party. This included working with Ivens on a propaganda film about Germany in 1934. The experience had left a bad taste in his mouth. Ivens was a little too slick, a little too manipulative for him. When he had encountered Ivens with Hemingway in Spain, he wondered if "the smiling Ivens" was going to make "another film of self-deception."[4]

In 1936 Regler was living in Moscow, where he started to understand, in a way Hemingway never would, what it was like to live under the dictatorship of the proletariat on a day-to-day basis. Often it ominously mirrored the ancien regime, or Nazi Germany. With a mixture of disbelief, disgust, and fear he took in one of the first of

Hemingway and the German communist Gustav Regler, the commissar with a heart who became a close friend. *Ernest Hemingway Photo Collection, JFK Library.*

Stalin's show trials: "I saw the prison-vans . . . pulled up behind the Bolshoi Theatre. They did not look very different from the vans used by the Tsarist police. . . . I [also] thought of [a prisoner] marching past me to his death in Munich."[5] Among the Soviet victims was one of his protectors, the great revolutionary Lev Kamenev, who was tried and executed in August. Regler wondered if he was next on the list, and was only too relieved when the Comintern approved his request to go to Spain. There he became a political commissar in the Twelfth International Brigade.

Unlike other commissars, some of whom took a much more heavy-handed approach, Regler saw his duty as maintaining the morale of the troops and working with the civilian population. In 1938 he would boast of saving priceless paintings from destruction and transporting women and children to safety from villages where battles were raging.[6] He was most likely sincere when he said that it was up to the commissars "to halt the cruelties . . . on both sides." It felt good to be waging the good fight again: for him the winds of "heroic Spain" were blowing away the "stink of Moscow."[7] He watched "the good Russia" come onto the scene, but worried that "the diabolical Russia" might not be far behind.

If Ivens tried to teach Hemingway about "the good Russia," and all she was doing to fight fascism, Regler did not hesitate to tell the American about "the diabolical Russia" and her ways. He told Hemingway a story that illustrated the difference. Members of a French battalion had, of their own accord, asked him to meet with them to discuss a problem. During a recent battle, two French soldiers had panicked, imagining enemy troops all around them and shouting for everyone to run. Regler had them arrested, then decided that they were suffering from combat fatigue. He sent them to a sanatorium and reported what he had done to the chief commissar of the Brigades, the French communist André Marty.

Marty had been a revolutionary since his days as a sailor in the French Navy. He was famous in communist circles for having organized a mutiny to keep his ship from firing on Bolsheviks after the October Revolution of 1917. When he appeared in Spain twenty years later, now as a senior official, the big man was running to fat, with a double chin and a receding hairline that he usually hid under an oversize beret. As if his black leather jacket and large pistol were not intimidating enough, he was more prone to shout than to speak, and to suspect almost everyone of treason.[8]

Regler's report in hand, Marty proclaimed he knew what to do, and took charge of the case. Then he ordered "a Russian execution squad" to shoot the two soldiers.[9] Regler remembered how Hemingway had exclaimed, "Swine!" and spat on the ground when he heard the story.[10] This gesture drew Regler close to Hemingway, and afterward he proved his friendship again and again, sharing confidences with the American:[11] "I told him the inside stories of operations and crises I had witnessed. I let him know about our losses and gave him advance information whenever I could, feeling certain that he really understood. . . ."

What even Regler does not mention in his memoirs is that he was the man who introduced Hemingway to another representative of the diabolical Russia, the NKVD chief of station Orlov. The meeting took place at the Gaylord, probably during the spring of 1937. Orlov was not introduced in his official capacity, but he assumed Hemingway knew who he was. (It was hardly a secret among the denizens of the Gaylord.) Not much happened at their first meeting. Drinking vodka and Spanish brandy, they spoke in English about their common interest in firearms, but not about politics. Gellhorn came along and charmed Orlov; they chatted about the Austrian food and music that both of them enjoyed.[12]

During the summer of 1937, Orlov followed the news about Hemingway's exploits in New York and Hollywood. In particular, he read in NKVD channels about the writers' conference at Carnegie Hall:[13]

> *[S]ources reported that Hemingway's speech was the high point of the convention. . . . [H]e had . . . torn into the Fascists and shredded them into small bits of unrecognizable bone meal. . . . [T]he fact that Hemingway had taken such a positive and firm political stance . . . in public took the [NKVD] by surprise.*

On the strength of Hemingway's performance in New York, Orlov decided that the NKVD would grant Hemingway carte blanche, good for any official help that he might need or want in Spain.[14] When Hemingway returned to Madrid in September 1937, he reappeared at the Gaylord and told Regler that he wanted to learn more about the Republican guerrillas, said to be performing great feats of derring-do in battle. With his ready access to the NKVD, Regler was able to tell Orlov in person what Hemingway wanted. Given his experience fighting White insurgents during the Russian Civil War, Orlov fancied himself something of an expert on guerrilla warfare, and liked the idea of showing off his program. Although he was going against the grain of the highly secretive NKVD, Orlov made an exception for Hemingway, who was both sympathetic to the cause *and* the most prominent journalist in Spain, one whom it made sense to court. And so Orlov arranged for Hemingway to visit Benimàmet, a secret guerrilla training camp in the NKVD domain.

Hemingway's tour guide at Benimàmet was Orlov's deputy, Leonid Eitingon, a barrel-chested NKVD officer who ran day-to-day guerrilla operations and impressed others as competent and direct. While photos of Orlov convey his intensity, those of Eitingon suggest toughness, charisma, and even some humor, which was remarkable since part of his job was to murder Stalin's enemies.[15] During the visit, Eitingon went to considerable lengths to impress Hemingway, taking him on a carefully orchestrated tour. The Soviets showed him every phase of the training in the camp, where whitewashed plaster structures set on a featureless plain gave it the kind of austere, no-nonsense look that appealed to the writer.

At midday, Orlov hosted a gourmet lunch served with fine French wines that he had been saving for a special occasion. He also poured a rare Polish vodka, Baczewski, a little something he asked an NKVD colleague in Vienna to ship to Spain for him on a regular basis. After lunch, Orlov and Hemingway went to one of the camp's rifle ranges to fire Soviet weapons. Considering the amount of lunchtime drinking, Orlov was surprised that Hemingway shot

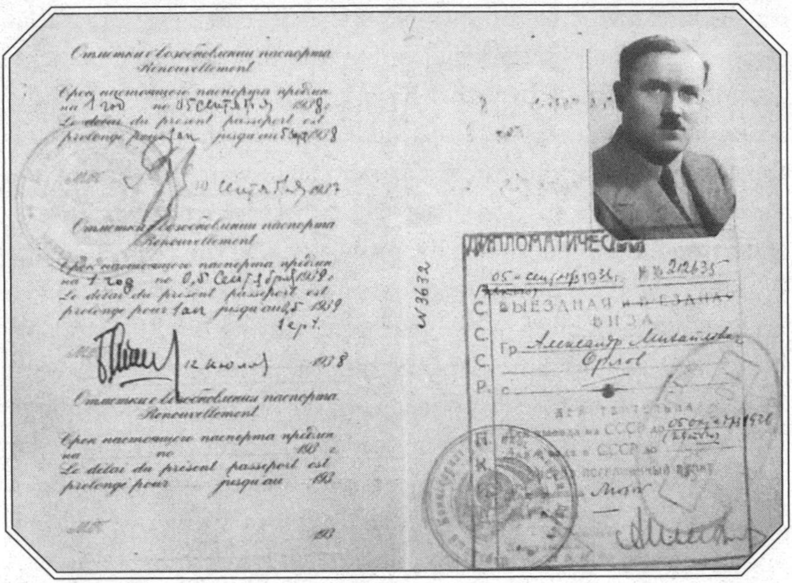

Alexander Orlov, the NKVD chief who ran the secret war in Spain for Stalin and made time to entertain Hemingway. *National Archives, College Park.*

very well by any standard. When the visit was drawing to a close, Orlov gave Hemingway one of his precious bottles of Baczewski to take back to his hotel. The Soviet thought Hemingway was "beside himself" when he expressed his gratitude for the hospitality that the NKVD had shown him.[16]

Orlov may have gone on to facilitate Hemingway's visit to Alfambra, the town where he spent the four days in the fall of 1937 with communist guerrillas. They in turn allowed him to witness the attack on the Nationalist train that would drive the plot of his novel *For Whom the Bell Tolls*. Some of the evidence is circumstantial: Benimàmet and Alfambra were about one hundred miles apart; Hemingway visited the two places at roughly the same time; Orlov would likely have exercised influence, if not control, over the Polish commando Antoni Chrost and his men, who may have trained at Benimàmet. Orlov himself hinted at a connection when he affirmed years later that "much of what Hemingway had written in the book" grew out of the visit to Benimàmet, adding how pleased he was to recognize himself in the character Varloff.[17]

Orlov met Hemingway again a few months later. The occasion was the official anniversary of the Bolshevik Revolution on November 7, 1938, which was also the second anniversary of the successful defense of Madrid. There were spirited celebrations across Republican Spain.[18] Over lunch at the Gaylord, Hemingway carried on at some length about the wonderful time that he had at Benimàmet and the most impressive bottle of vodka that he had taken home. After a few drinks, Hemingway started to speak freely. He "vehemently denounced Franco and the Nationalists" and had "nothing but praise" for the International Brigades and the Republicans. This turned out to be Orlov's last face-to-face meeting with Hemingway, but the astute intelligence officer had heard and read enough to draw some conclusions about the American writer. Orlov would remember Hemingway not as a man under Soviet control but as "a rugged individualist, great sportsman, but most of all a true believer in the Republican cause during the Spanish Civil War."[19]

Orlov, in fact, had reservations about true believers like Hemingway. When making decisions at work, Orlov was both cynical and realistic, less driven by ideology or belief. Years later he would imply that Hemingway, caught up in his own belief system, had not known when to quit: "the author, and people like him, were the prime motivators of the war in the sense that they swayed world opinion to the side of the Republicans . . . , which needlessly prolonged the war."[20]

If he had known about it, Hemingway would have been pleased by Orlov's opinion about his influence. He considered himself to be more influential than he actually was, believing that others lived by what he said and wrote about Spain. For one, the young communist writer Alvah Bessie was surprised to learn that Hemingway believed that it was his speech to the faithful in New York City on that hot day in June 1937 that had motivated Bessie to travel to Spain and join the Abraham Lincoln Battalion, the largely American unit raised by the Comintern to fight for the Republic.[21] In his memoir, *Men in Battle,* Bessie quoted Hemingway as saying that he knew "that speech influenced a lot of the boys to come over here."[22] This was, Bessie continued, "the kind of egomania the guy suffered from. . . . I had decided to go to Spain long before [I heard his speech]. I was trying to find a way out of my marriage."

On the battlefield, Hemingway continued to alternate between witnessing and participating in the fighting. He logged many miles with fellow American journalists Jay Allen of the *Chicago Tribune* and Herbert L. Matthews of the *New York Times,* and did not hesitate to set aside his notebook and pen when a Loyalist needed his help. In December 1937, after showing Allen how to protect his eardrums during an air raid by clamping a pencil in his jaws to hold his mouth open, Hemingway called on his colleague to help move an artillery piece stuck in the mud, and got angry when Allen refused, claiming that he was hired to write, not fight the war. Nor did Hemingway appreciate the lecture on the laws of war that followed, how reporters had no legal right to carry sidearms.[23]

Hemingway pitched in again one sunny day in the spring of 1938. With Joe North (of *New Masses* fame) and Matthews, Hemingway was driving along a mountain road in Spain behind a truckload of youths singing Republican songs and raising their fists in the Republican greeting. It was, he commented, a uniquely moving sight. In the next instant, the truck driver miscalculated a turn; the truck turned upside down; boys were strewn along the roadway. Hemingway leapt from their car and started giving first aid, while Matthews got out his notebook and started asking questions of the injured. North remembered hearing Hemingway shout at Matthews to get the hell out of the way before he, Hemingway, killed Matthews—and feeling that he, North, and Hemingway were kindred spirits.[24]

By the spring of 1938 more than one neutral observer was starting to give up on the Republic. The Nationalists were consolidating their hold on the northern half of the country, and attacking to the south in order to subdivide the remaining territory of the Republic. At the end of March, even Hemingway thought it prudent to prepare for the worst, and joined with two other journalists to ask the American embassies in France and Spain for help in planning for the repatriation of Americans who had been caught up in the war, especially the wounded.[25] Hemingway was again willing to shoulder more than his share of fund-raising and organizing. He made a point of stressing the need for secrecy since he did not want to give the impression that he had lost hope in the Republic, and was relieved when the military situation "incredibly" stabilized a few days later.[26]

When Hemingway and Matthews encountered Bessie on the battlefield in early April, Hemingway once again sounded like a Republican cheerleader. They met near the town of Tortosa, where the half-trained infantrymen of the Abraham Lincoln Battalion were helping to hold the line against a powerful fascist offensive. Bessie did not think much of Matthews, who seemed "bitter," "gloomy," and "ascetic" to him. On the other hand, the taller, heavier, red-faced Hemingway seemed like "one of the largest men you will ever see." He was "eager . . . like a big kid," asking question after question about the fighting. Hemingway refused to be discouraged. He praised the communists for their "example, unceasing agitation and unquestioned loyalty," which had helped to create a unified, antifascist army. He went on to conclude the war would enter a new phase, that the government's resistance would redouble because good people everywhere were getting madder and madder the more "women and children and old men" the fascists killed in cold blood.[27]

As long as there was any chance of victory, what Hemingway said and wrote about the war was generally upbeat and reflected well on the Republic. The point was to maintain the Popular Front against fascism. His articles for the North American wire service, to say nothing of what he wrote for the Soviet newspaper *Pravda*, read as much like propaganda as reporting.[28] He attacked the fascists, and especially their habit of bombarding civilian targets, which he equated to murder. He described the hardship, suffering, and valor of the Republic. He defended Loyalist troops against charges that they were committing atrocities, and he called on the democracies to repeal their policy of nonintervention.

Like so many others, Hemingway believed, with passion, that Spain was the place to stop fascism. If the democracies did not act, and the fascists triumphed, the former would deserve "whatever fate brings them."[29] He did not explore the Republic's shortcomings in any depth, and he did not want to report on the war from the Nationalist perspective. When asked to do so, he made only one, halfhearted attempt to enter Nationalist territory.[30] Hemingway even changed his mind about serving as an editor for the start-up *Ken* after the journal ran two anticommunist cartoons, because, he thought, "red-baiting" could undermine the Popular Front.[31]

Hemingway's 1937 play *The Fifth Column* concerns the business of catching spies.[32] It is the story of an American by the name of Philip Rawlings, who, like Hemingway, lives at the Hotel Florida in Madrid with a blond girlfriend, is a regular at the Chicote Bar, and has a cache of food that he shares with the less fortunate. But unlike Hemingway his main occupation is not that of writer. Rawlings describes himself as "a policeman," a specialist in "counter-espionage" who "signed up for the duration" of a series of "undeclared wars." Rawlings speaks such infelicitous lines as "my time is the Party's time," and "there's only one thing about orders. THEY ARE TO BE OBEYED." He has been in Spain for some twelve months, working for a hawk-nosed security officer named Antonio, a character who, most scholars agree, was modeled on a ruthless secret policeman named Pepe Quintanilla (who happened to be the brother of the artist Luis Quintanilla, whom Hemingway had befriended before the war). Rawlings is very good at catching spies—"members of a secret 'fifth column'"—by keeping his ears open as he makes his way around town, and by interrogating prisoners. He even leads a raid against an undercover artillery observation post manned by the fascists, capturing the men who are calling in artillery strikes against civilian targets in Madrid. The reader is left to conclude that the Republic needed men like Antonio and Rawlings to survive.

Where did Hemingway stand at this point? Looking back more than a decade later, he would admit that, during the war that started for him in Spain, he had become "so stinking righteous" that it gave him "the horrors to look back on."[33] For Hemingway the Spanish Civil War was not just an outlet for a writer who wanted to be a fighter, or just a source of material for his next dispatch or book. In words and actions, literally on and off the battlefield, Hemingway fought for the Republic and against fascism, both when it furthered his career and when it did not. He was willing to make personal and professional sacrifices.

More than once Hemingway came close to declaring that, in this war, the end justified the means. He had fallen in love with the antifascist, pro-Republican cause like so many other writers and intellectuals on the left. It was the one political equation that, in a decade of confusing crises, seemed to make absolute sense: freedom versus oppression, democracy versus dictatorship, progress versus reaction, the common man versus the oligarch, life over death. It was a cause that a thinking man could idealize. The great British poet W. H. Auden wrote for many in his immortal poem about Spain when he asked:[34]

What's your proposal? To build the just city? I will.
I agree. Or is it the suicide pact, the romantic
Death? Very well, I accept, for
I am your choice, your decision. Yes, I am Spain.

In his eulogy for Jim Lardner, a young American killed in one of the last battles that the Brigades fought, Hemingway came close to matching Auden's idealism and fatalism:[35]

> *[O]ur dead are a part of the earth of Spain now and the earth of Spain can never die. Each winter it will seem to die and each spring it will come alive again. . . . [N]o men ever entered earth more honorably than those who died in Spain. . . .*

The official reason for disbanding the International Brigades and sending the Republic's foreign volunteers home toward the end of 1938 was to placate the Non-Intervention Committee, set up by European governments to limit foreign intervention in the war. But their departure was also another sign that the prospects for victory were dwindling. The government hastily arranged a farewell parade in Barcelona in late October, when the foreign soldiers marched through friendly crowds, estimated at three hundred thousand. The crowds tossed so many flowers that the march turned into a shuffle through inches of petals, past large photographs of Republican leaders and Stalin. They listened to the words of "La Pasionaria," the over-the-top communist leader and orator Dolores Ibárruri, who told the Brigades that they could go proudly; they had done their duty; they were now history, legend. After the speeches, buglers blew "Taps" for the Internationals who had been killed in action, and, in the (sympathetic) words of one eyewitness, "all Barcelona bared its head and wept."[36]

The event shook the faith of the true believer in Hemingway when he learned about it in early November in Valencia, the Repub-

Barcelona, 1938: the day the Internationals marched out of the war.
Robert Capa Photo, ICP.

lican capital, in 1938. Unable to find a way to be optimistic about the future, he broke down. At their hotel during an air raid, Hemingway and Gellhorn encountered one of the Internationals, the Italian Randolfo Pacciardi, who had commanded the Garibaldi Brigade. Now he was on his way out of Spain and did not have a home that he could return to (Italy having fallen under fascist domination). He was, Gellhorn remembered, heartbroken, stateless, and penniless, but he did not complain about his fate.[37]

After seeing Pacciardi, Hemingway and Gellhorn continued on their way upstairs to their room. Soon she heard Ernest crying. He was leaning against the wall on the steps, and crying for Pacciardi, saying, "'They can't do it! They can't treat a brave man that way.'"[38] Hemingway was, Gellhorn wrote, crying for the way the government had dismissed the Brigades, with perfunctory thanks, letting men like Pacciardi go "without . . . money, or papers or any future."[39] The first and only time that Gellhorn heard Hemingway cry, it made her love him all the more.

Hemingway's own explanation for breaking down in Valencia was that "there is no man alive today who has not cried at a war if he was at it long enough. . . . [S]ometimes it is from a great injustice to another, sometimes it is at the disbanding of a corps or a unit that has endured and accomplished [much] . . . and will never be together again."[40]

Like Pacciardi, many Internationals went to uncertain fates when they left Spain. The British, Canadians, and Americans could go home but, tainted by their association with the many communists in their ranks, would face official suspicion for having fought for the Republic. The Soviets and their allies could return to the Soviet Union, but many would die in a new round of senseless Stalinist purges. The Germans and Italians could not go home, and looked, often in vain, for other countries to shelter them.

Hemingway left Spain for the last time at about the same time as the Internationals. He knew the Spanish war was all but over. And yet he was still far from ready to give up his personal fight for Republican values. Like his character Rawlings, he was fond of saying he had signed on for the duration, and pledged more than once to continue the fight against fascism for however long it took to defeat the enemy, even for fifty years of undeclared wars.[41]

CHAPTER 4

THE BELL TOLLS FOR THE REPUBLIC

Hemingway Bears Witness

By early February 1939, after Franco's troops had captured Barcelona, tens of thousands of Republican soldiers, camp followers, and sympathizers were taking to the roads that led out of the city to the north and east, away from the fascists literally drunk on victory. They were shooting anyone who resembled a Republican. The two-lane highways—really more like country roads with dirt shoulders—overflowed with refugees in cars and trucks, on foot and on the backs of donkeys. Farm women carried chickens and led goats; mothers led their children, all on their way to safe haven in France.[1]

A few of the trucks were loaded with fascist pilots, prisoners somehow still under the control of the Republican Air Force. The pilots and their enemies traded insults, swearing never to forgive and telling each other to go to hell. But mostly the Republican troops marched quietly and in good order. On a clear, sunny day just before they crossed into France, there was one last formation, then a small parade reviewed by a handful of officials, including the infamous André Marty. Next the soldiers added their rifles to the many piles of arms and other war paraphernalia that littered the rocky ground on the Spanish side of the border. Some of the Internationals who had stayed on to fight to the end closed ranks and sang as they marched into France. They felt a chill when French gendarmes ordered silence, shouting, "Singing prohibited!"[2]

From Key West, the writer read about the death throes of the Republic. His heart was still in Spain, but he finally accepted that the end was near. His attitude was like that of the first veteran to make it home only to hear that his comrades in arms are still fighting. He felt both angry and guilty. He was angry about the journalists who wrote about atrocities by the Reds or claimed that Franco's men were more humane (certainly a stretch, but one that more than one reputable journalist made). In a letter to his mother-in-law (Pauline Pfeiffer's mother, to whom he was still deeply attached despite his relationship with Martha Gellhorn) he wrote that the charges were simply not true.[3] He had seen "town after town bombed to the ground, the inhabitants killed, the columns of refugees on the roads bombed and machine-gunned again and again." It was the "sort of lying [that] kills things inside of you." He could not bear to think about his good friends who were still in the thick of things. It was better to be with them. He had slept "good and sound every night in Spain through the whole war," he added, and was always hungry but had never felt better. He concluded that "one's conscience is a strange thing and not controlled either by a sense of security, nor danger of death."[4] A day later he wrote Max Perkins that he had "bad dreams every night. . . . Really awful ones in the greatest detail."[5] It was strange because he had never had any bad dreams in Spain.

None of this changed his feelings about politics. He was still angry that the democracies had done so little for the Republic. Spain had "been betrayed and sold out a dozen different ways."[6] For him the British were still the main villains. He was still promoting his play, *The Fifth Column,* with its message that antifascist ends can justify harsh means. The producers in New York were in no hurry to stage the play, perhaps because "the war has gone bad," but Hemingway wanted it produced all the same. "Christ how I wish I'd written *that* as a novel," he told Perkins.[7] But busy with the war, he had not had the time.

A few weeks later, in March, the war was finally over. When they marched in to Madrid, the Nationalists behaved barbarically, as though they were following a script written by Republican propagandists. At first it was like a party. To celebrate, the conquering army ate and drank everything its soldiers could put their hands on. Priests, Nationalist policemen, and Royalists pulled out their telltale colors and uniforms and felt free to wear them openly again. Along with the celebration came thoroughgoing repression. Bonfires of "Marxist" books raged in the large cities. Just as in Barcelona, Republicans and Republican sympathizers were purged from the body politic. The least they could expect was to lose their jobs and businesses. Untold thousands were simply shot. No one will ever know exactly how many more—perhaps tens or hundreds of thousands—were herded into makeshift camps. Some languished in detention for months or years; many others were sentenced to long terms of forced labor, sometimes after drumhead courts-martial.[8]

On the road to France, Republican soldiers and refugees flee from Nationalist terror in 1939. *Robert Capa Photo, ICP.*

The Republicans who managed to flee from Spain did not always fare much better. Except for Mexico, none of the democracies welcomed the refugees. The democracy that was closest, France, was soon overwhelmed and grew more ambivalent as the numbers swelled past the two-hundred-thousand mark. Most Republican refugees in France found themselves in another set of camps, with bad food, poor sanitation, and little protection from the elements.

For Hemingway and Gellhorn, the democracies' stock could hardly have sunk any lower. The record on Spain was bad enough. But now there was also Czechoslovakia, betrayed at Munich in September 1938. To avoid war, British prime minister Neville Chamberlain and French prime minister Édouard Daladier had given in to Hitler's demands for the Sudetenland, the "rightfully" German territory inside Czechoslovakia. Hitler went on to absorb the rest of the country into his sphere of influence, completing the process in March 1939. Like Hemingway, Gellhorn blamed the French and especially the British for what was happening: "Chamberlain has given Europe to the dictators."[9]

For Hemingway now was the time to withdraw from the world and work. On March 23 he wrote to his Russian literary friend Ivan Kashkin: "The only thing about a war, once it has started, is to win it—and that is what we did not do. The hell with war for a while. . . . I am not killed so I have to work."[10] He went on to tell Kashkin he was now writing a novel; he had already put fifteen thousand words on paper. He let Kashkin see that his heart was still in Spain, criticizing those who had done nothing to defend the Republic and were now attacking those who had. "We" had "fought as well as possible, and without selfishness." Two days later he wrote to Max Perkins in a similar vein. After the way the French had treated the Republic, he felt no obligation to side with them against the Germans. It was, in any case, more important for him to write short stories and a novel about the war.[11]

Hemingway had already written five stories about the war, including "The Butterfly and the Tank," "The Denunciation," and "The Night before Battle."[12] All three describe wartime life in the Republic in unvarnished (and sometimes tedious) detail. The upbeat Hemingway whom Alvah Bessie had met on the battlefield was now the realistic Hemingway, willing to air the Republic's shortcomings and wish that its leaders had been more competent. "The Butterfly and the Tank" sets the tone, telling the story of the senseless death of a man whose practical joke in the bar called Chicote's (the real-life Hemingway haunt) leads to his death. Like a butterfly coming up against a tank, the man's prank clashes with the seriousness of the war. "The Denunciation" is a grim story about the need to denounce a fascist officer who has surfaced in Madrid at his favorite bar (not surprisingly, Chicote's). The problem is that he is now in Republican uniform and asking a lot of questions about the war effort. The story's two protagonists arrange for the secret police to come for the interloper, taking him away to be shot as a spy. In "The Night before Battle" an American communist soldier is sure he will die in a senseless attack the following day. He believes in the cause and understands the dangers that soldiers must face. But he questions the competence of the leaders who have ordered the attack.

While Hemingway was writing, the situation in Europe continued to deteriorate. The Continent was gearing up for war in the near future. The Western Allies engaged in talks with the Soviet Union, exploring possible military cooperation against Germany. But it was a halfhearted effort that led nowhere. On August 23, 1939, the Soviet and German foreign ministers announced that they had signed a nonaggression pact, promising not to attack each other for ten years. Hitler signed because he wanted a free hand in the west. For his part, Stalin wanted to be sure he would not have to fight Germany until he was ready. (He needed more time to prepare for war because he had murdered so many of his best officers.) Both dictators happily entered into a secret addendum that carved up the small countries of Eastern Europe, starting with Poland, which would soon have both a German and a Soviet zone. Two days later Britain concluded an Agreement of Mutual Assistance with Poland, formalizing earlier guarantees of Polish sovereignty.

The Nazi-Soviet Pact was the bombshell that shattered the remaining barrier on the road to war.[13] His eastern flank now secure, Hitler's forces could focus on the French and the British in the west. The alliance between communist Russia and Nazi Germany also rearranged the political spectrum on the left. It was the end of the Popular Front, that shaky (and often mythical) alliance of liberals, socialists, and communists against fascism; and of the Comintern, which had spent the 1930s promoting antifascist thinking of the Popular Front variety. For many Comintern leaders who would die in the seemingly inevitable purge, the pact was a death sentence. Internationals who had fought for the Republic under the Comintern banner were recalled to Moscow, arrested, and murdered because they were now too cosmopolitan, tainted by having lived in Western Europe. The brilliant Willi Münzenberg, who had served the cause so well, was now on his own. He would be found dead under a tree in France in 1940, probably killed by the NKVD. For left-wing Jews the party was no longer a comfortable political home base from which to fight Hitler and anti-Semitism. If they stayed in the party, they would now find themselves on the same side as their mortal enemy Hitler, a man who made no secret of his intent to eradicate them.

The party line had always been dogmatic, as if there were only one ideologically correct way to view the world. There was never much room for nuance or for individual interpretations. But most members had been able to focus on one or two basics, like fighting fascism, that resonated with them. Now, all of a sudden, the party stood that core doctrine on its head and required the faithful to defend the change. The reversal made liars out of honest men and women.

This was too much for the 25 percent of the Communist Party of the USA who abandoned the movement, never to return. Some of them were literary figures like Granville Hicks, who had been one of the editors at *New Masses*. He was more than willing, in his low-key, intellectual way, to explain why he was leaving the fold. Astounded by the party's dictatorial pronouncements, he found them "completely devoid of clarity and logic. . . . If the Party leaders could not defend the Soviet Union intelligently, they would defend it stupidly."[14]

Another significant defector was Hemingway's friend, the humane commissar Regler. At first he could not believe that Stalin had made a separate peace with Hitler. Wasn't it just another irresponsible, impossible rumor? Only after he saw the newspapers was he convinced that it was true. Like Hicks, Regler could not stomach the kind of doublethink the party was now calling for. He shook his head at what he was hearing from a communist doctor, a brave man and strong healer, who claimed that the pact had prevented "the outbreak of real war," and that it was "for the benefit of the proletariat."[15]

What did Hemingway think of the Nazi-Soviet Pact? There are a few hints in Regler's books. Regler and Hemingway's relationship had continued after the Spanish war. They kept in touch through letters, and Hemingway did what he could to help Regler in 1939 and 1940, sending money while the latter was a refugee in France after the collapse of the Republic. Later Hemingway agitated for Regler's release from senseless internment as an enemy alien at the start of World War II.[16] "We were," Regler would write in his memoirs, "without money and without friends, except for Hemingway, who stood like a rock."[17] Eventually the French released Regler, and he made his way first to the United States and then to Mexico, where he and his wife eked out a living as painters and writers, turning out works that were interesting but did not sell very well. His books would include two novels about the Spanish Civil War, one of which was transparently autobiographical.

Published in 1940, *The Great Crusade* is the story of a communist with a conscience who comes to reject Stalinism. The hero fights on two fronts: against the fascists on the battlefield, and against the Stalinists who undermine the cause. The book is long and often difficult to follow, but it is written from the heart. A passage from one of the chapters suggests how painful the process of disillusionment was for the faithful. The revolutionary intellectual Nikolai Bukharin, forced to confess to imaginary crimes during the purges in the 1930s, questions the meaning of his life, completely devoted to a revolution that has gone terribly wrong. Searching for answers, he finds nothing but "an absolutely black void."[18]

Perhaps without reading every page of the book, or thinking overlong about its implications, Hemingway interrupted work on his own novel about Spain to write the preface to a book about "the golden age of the International Brigades." He was full of praise for Regler and the Twelfth International Brigade, which Regler had served and which Hemingway visited often. That was where his heart had been during the war, Hemingway wrote. The men of the brigade were wonderfully brave, and nearly always happy, because the period when they thought the Republic would win the war was "the happiest period" of their lives.[19]

Hemingway went on to write that he was bitter about "a single, idiotic, stupidly conceived and insanely executed" attack in the hills above the Jarama River that had decimated the brigade. He approved of the fate of the man who planned and ordered the attack, and was "afterward shot when he returned to Russia." Hemingway did not use the commander's name, but it was almost certainly the communist soldier János Gálicz, described as a Hungarian who hated newspapermen and "should have been shot at the time." Once again Hemingway was giving the Soviets credit that they did not deserve. It is unlikely that the NKVD shot Gálicz for incompetence. Rather, he was almost certainly shot simply because he had served in Spain, which made him suspect in Stalin's paranoid worldview.[20]

In the preface to *The Great Crusade,* Hemingway also addressed the Nazi-Soviet Pact. His approach could not have been more different from Regler's. The German faulted Stalin first for giving up on the Spanish Republic and then for sacrificing communist ideals by making a tactical deal with Hitler. Hemingway, on the other hand, was willing to give Stalin the benefit of the doubt: "The Soviet Union was not bound by any pact with Hitler when the International Brigades fought in Spain. It was only after they [the Soviets] lost any faith in the democracies that the [Nazi-Soviet] Alliance was born."[21] Hemingway's support for the pact leaps off the page at the reader and seems out of context. But it *was* typical of his thinking at the time. He was saluting Stalin for supporting the Republic and the Internationals from 1936 to 1938, and arguing that, after Munich, the Soviet dictator could not be blamed for doing what he needed to do to protect himself.[22]

Regler seemed to understand how his friend thought, describing Hemingway as basically "unpolitical." Ernest had a better grasp of the law of the jungle than of politics. He was more like a hunter than a politician; he thought "in terms of black and white," of life or death.[23] He did not see that "modern dictators had no respect even for the law of the pack."[24] In a similar vein, Regler commented to one of the more sympathetic Soviets in Spain that Hemingway did not stand for Western democracy but for experiencing life in all its fullness in places like the hills of Africa or the waters off Key West.[25]

The months that followed were a confusing time. In September Germany invaded Poland. France and Britain declared war on Germany but could do little for Poland; Hitler easily conquered his hapless neighbor and cleared the way for Stalin to take his share of eastern Poland under the terms of their pact. What happened next was incredible for many devout communists. In November Stalin invaded his small, democratic neighbor, Finland. It was an old-fashioned, great-power landgrab, the sort of thing that a czar or a kaiser might have done. The Finns resisted in a David versus Goliath struggle that lasted until March 1940. Meanwhile Britain and France faced off against Germany along the heavily fortified border of France and Germany. This was the so-called Phony War during the winter of 1939–40, when nothing much happened.

The Phony War ended in May 1940, when the German army attacked through the heavily wooded and supposedly impassable Ardennes Forest in Belgium. Long columns of tanks and motorized infantry outflanked the border fortifications and rolled up the Allied lines with little difficulty. In six short weeks Hitler had conquered France and driven Britain from the Continent. The country that Hemingway blamed most for not supporting the Spanish Republic now stood virtually alone against the Axis, supported only by her dominions overseas. The new prime minister, Winston Churchill, was determined to fight, but Britain's prospects were grim. Many Americans doubted that she would be able to win against Hitler or that she deserved America's support. Gellhorn was not alone in thinking that the "English seem to be paying at last for Spain and Czecho [*sic*], Poland and Finland."[26]

During the first months of World War II, Hemingway remained deeply absorbed in his book about the Spanish war, occasionally surfacing to write letters or tend to Gellhorn. She commented in a letter that he was "like an animal" with his manuscript, keeping it close to him or hiding it in a drawer under other papers. He never willingly showed it to anyone, and would not talk about it.[27] When Gellhorn went off to Finland to cover the Soviet invasion, Hemingway focused only on her pluck in going to this war and, unlike more than one disillusioned communist, said nothing about the way the Soviets had attacked their neighbor.[28] When he turned his gaze to the Western Front, it was to denounce the British again. In May 1940, for example, he reminded Max Perkins how degenerate they were. In Spain "they gave us the worst bitching anyone did [while] we fought both Hitler and Mussolini for them for nothing and could have kept them tied up there indefinitely if they had only given any aid at all." He predicted that they would engage in something he called "Coitus Britannicus"—that is, they would withdraw from the field of battle and leave their allies in the lurch.[29]

The catastrophe in Europe spurred Hemingway's sometime friend Archibald MacLeish to speak out against American neutrality. In a series of talks and articles in the spring of 1940, the recently appointed librarian of Congress lamented the fact that so many young Americans were cynical about war to the point of pacifism. This he blamed on antiwar books like Hemingway's World War I classic, *A Farewell to Arms*. Hemingway shot back angrily that MacLeish had gotten it wrong. The Germans knew how to fight, and the Allies didn't, but it was not on account of antiwar books. MacLeish must have "a very bad conscience" while he, Hemingway, did not, "having fought fascism in every way" he knew how.[30] He suggested that MacLeish read *The Fifth Column* (his play about the counterspy who is not afraid to get his hands dirty) and take another look at *The Spanish Earth* (the film they had produced together). He included a barb about the front lines in Spain, where he had been

Hemingway reworking a draft of his great novel *For Whom the Bell Tolls. Robert Capa Photo, ICP.*

and MacLeish had not. Three weeks later Hemingway went on to complain about MacLeish to Max Perkins, writing that "there is so much panic and hysteria and shit going around now I don't feel like writing any flag-waving stuff."[31]

MacLeish had picked the wrong target. Hemingway's great novel of the Spanish war, *For Whom the Bell Tolls,* turned out to be all about engagement in the struggle at hand. It was very different from *A Farewell to Arms,* published in 1929. The earlier book is a love story about disengagement from the world. The soldier Frederic Henry has left the war behind, forced by an unlucky chain of events to desert. He is headed for neutral Switzerland with his lover, Catherine Barkley. The world shrinks to a tiny sphere around Henry and Barkley, who is carrying their child. The baby is stillborn, and Barkley dies of complications soon thereafter. By contrast, the very title of the Spanish book tells the reader to look for the connection between the story and the outside world; the phrase "for whom the bell tolls" is part of a John Donne poem that begins with the line "No man is an *Iland,* intire of it selfe."

Based on Hemingway's experience with the communist saboteurs, the new novel tells the story of four days in the life of a guerrilla band operating behind fascist lines. Their mission is to blow up a bridge to impede fascist movement when the great offensive starts. Far from deserting, the American guerrilla fighter Robert Jordan is ready to give his life for the cause. Jordan has a restless mind and cannot keep himself from thinking about how his life is caught up with politics and the war. He knows why and how the war is being fought and, like Hemingway, believes the Republic needs communist discipline to win against the fascists.

For Jordan, communist discipline was not perfect; it was just the best there was at the time. Jordan admitted to himself that some communist leaders were murderously incompetent and that their actions undermined the cause as surely as if they had been fascist spies. Foremost among them was the Frenchman André Marty, the chief commissar of the Internationals, whom Regler had told

Hemingway about. Certain enough about the picture he was painting, Hemingway did not bother to disguise Marty's identity in the novel.[32]

It was a given for Jordan that the fascists committed atrocities, such as the gang rape of his lover, Maria. Jordan also knew that the Republican record was far from unblemished. He hears of an atrocity not unlike an event that occurred in a place called Ronda during the war.[33] In the novel, after capturing the town, the Republicans decide which of its prominent citizens (who are either actual or suspected Nationalist sympathizers) will be forced to run a gauntlet of men wielding hooks, flails, and sickles. All of the Nationalists die with more or less dignity, not as fascist demons but as individuals. "I try," Hemingway told Kashkin, "to show all the different sides of [the war] . . . , taking it slowly and honestly and examining it from many ways."[34]

Hemingway's even-handedness met with approval from many critics. Edmund Wilson celebrated the demise of "the Hotel Florida Stalinist" that was Hemingway in 1937 and the return of "Hemingway the artist. . . . It is like having an old friend back."[35] But the same balance cost him friends on the left. When he read *For Whom the Bell Tolls* in late 1940, Julio Alvarez del Vayo, the onetime foreign minister of the Spanish Republic, spoke for many when he wrote that his fellow exiles were "indignant" about Hemingway's book, which, for them, had not captured the true "us or them" nature of the war.[36] For American communists like Alvah Bessie, who had felt a kinship to Hemingway after meeting him on the battlefield, it was a betrayal, a cruel misrepresentation of a noble cause. With a tinge of regret, Bessie wrote for *New Masses* that Hemingway could have written a great book about the people's war, but that instead he fell into the trap of individualism, writing "a *Cosmopolitan* love story" against the backdrop of the war.[37]

Bessie was angry that Hemingway had depicted the commissar Marty as "a fool, a madman, and . . . a murderer."[38] The attack on Marty would give comfort to "our universal enemy." Bessie conceded that Hemingway may not have intended to libel the Spanish people or the Soviet Union. But the way he told the story had that effect. "Hemingway praises the individual heroism of individual Communists, . . . [but] impugns and slanders their leadership, their motives, and their attitudes."[39] Other critics like Milton Wolff, the Lincoln Battalion commander and Hemingway friend, complained that the book overlooked, or minimized, atrocities committed by the Nationalists that, he stressed, were a matter of policy. The Nationalists killed people systematically; the Reds did not.[40] (Or at least not to the same extent. This was true if you overlooked the NKVD's campaign against Trotskyites and other left deviationists.) Joris Ivens eventually joined in the criticism, but not the outrage. He would offer the mild judgment that by writing the novel Hemingway had "returned to his old [apolitical] point of view."[41]

Ivens was wrong. The war *had* changed Hemingway. He had become passionately pro-Republican and antifascist. He was still that way. The only thing that had changed in 1939 was that he no longer had to censor himself in order to protect the Republic. He could now tell the whole truth as he saw it, something that some former Republicans like Regler were encouraging him to do.[42] During the war, Regler had shared party secrets with Hemingway, but the writer did not use the material because the party was actively fighting for the Republic and the Republic still had a chance.[43] Only after the war did he feel free to attack those who had undermined the cause. The communists had wasted time on things that did not matter: what was wrong with the Abraham Lincoln Battalion, and by extension the other Internationals, was "too much ideology and not enough training, discipline, or materiel."[44] Too often they were uselessly sacrificed by incompetent commanders.

Regler concluded that countless readers learned things from Hemingway's fiction that they refused to learn in real life. With the hunter's hatred of the poacher, the writer had depicted "the spy-disease, that Russian syphilis, in all its shameful, murderously stupid workings."[45] Regler the humane commissar knew there was more than one way to impose revolutionary discipline. Like the hunter in his metaphor, he was not against killing. But he was against killing without a license, when it was against the law. Regler was reasonably sure that Hemingway felt the same way as he did. Less than two years later, the German would change his mind and question Hemingway's judgment.

CHAPTER 5

THE SECRET FILE

The NKVD Plays Its Hand

The temperatures in New York were in the eighties on the eleventh day of a heat wave in July 1940. In Hemingway's suite at the Barclay Hotel, located a block from Grand Central Terminal in midtown Manhattan, the window in the living room was open and an electric fan on the coffee table was stirring up the hot, humid air. Ice cubes melted in a bucket. Bottles of White Rock beer perched on windowsills and tabletops, while a fifth of scotch occupied a central position on the floor, within easy reach of any beer drinker who needed a shot of something stronger. The writer received visitors in an unbuttoned pajama top, his ample chest hair on display. Friends and acquaintances, speaking English, French, and Spanish, drifted in and out. One was a lawyer; another was a civil war veteran with an enviable record in battle. The telephone rang every few minutes, interrupting talk about the fates of other Republican soldiers: detained in France, recalled to Moscow and shot, suffering in a Nazi concentration camp.

A *Times* reporter named Bob Van Gelder captured the mix of concern, energy, and above all triumph for his readers. Despite the distractions, he could not miss how cheerfulness kept breaking into his interview with Hemingway. With a shock of thick, dark hair falling away from his forehead, the novelist "looked elephant-big, enormously healthy." He could barely contain himself, leaning forward as he talked and edging his chair toward his listeners. He *was glowing with satisfaction because he had just delivered his war novel to Scribner's.*

After seventeen months of solid work, he knew instinctively that For Whom the Bell Tolls *was a masterpiece. But, with the bad news from Europe, he could not rest on his laurels. The world had exploded into war. Franco's ally was on the march; Hitler had captured Paris on June 14 and now dominated the European continent. That meant, as Hemingway told Van Gelder, the "fight in Spain will have to be fought again."*[1] *As ever, he did not plan to miss the action.*

By the summer of 1940, Hemingway was already thinking of new ways to harness his energy to the cause he had embraced. In July, when he was staying at the Barclay in New York, Ernest told Max Perkins in a letter that he would continue to fight the enemy but only on his own terms.[2] One way of challenging fascism was of course to write and document the struggle, just as he had done in his wartime works, *The Fifth Column* and *The Spanish Earth.* His new novel, *For Whom the Bell Tolls,* also sounded the call to battle. Writing was not the only way to fight, of course, and he was open to exploring other options. He was even willing to downplay his public persona for the duration. As he would later put it in a letter to his son Jack, whatever he decided to do in this war he would do "quietly and without loud announcement."[3]

The search for the right kind of war work was already under way in October 1940 even as Hemingway's personal life was reordering itself. The divorce from his second wife, Pauline, was nearing its final stages as he and Gellhorn planned their new life together. The ever-restless bride-to-be was looking for work as a correspondent overseas, hoping to travel to Asia soon after the wedding. The possibility of such a trip first shows up in one of Hemingway's letters on October 21, a week after *For Whom the Bell Tolls* appeared on the shelves of Scribner's Bookstore at 597 Fifth Avenue.[4] Ten days later the plans were off, only to be on again shortly after the wedding in

Cheyenne, Wyoming, on November 21.[5] From Cheyenne the newlyweds drove to New York, where they honeymooned in comfort at the well-appointed Barclay.

While in town, Gellhorn firmed up her assignment for *Collier's* magazine to report on how the Chinese were faring against the Japanese invaders in a stop-start war far away that had been going on for so long—the first skirmish dated to 1931—many in the West had forgotten about it. Somewhat grudgingly, Hemingway agreed to come along, and arranged with his friend Ralph Ingersoll to do some reporting for his new left-of-center tabloid, *PM*.

It seems Hemingway also agreed to "look into" a thing or two for the U.S. secretary of the Treasury, Henry Morgenthau, Jr., a powerful figure in the Roosevelt administration who liked the idea of tasking the colorful world traveler.[6] Months later, during a meeting of his inner circle on January 27, 1941, Morgenthau would ask breezily, "How's Ernest?" A man named Harry D. White would answer, telling the secretary that Hemingway was all right and that "he will be glad to look at anything [for us]."[7] White was the second most powerful man at Treasury. He had apparently approached Hemingway on Morgenthau's behalf, stayed in touch, and arranged for him to meet personally with the secretary. As Hemingway himself would explain in a July 1941 letter to Morgenthau, White had asked him to study "the communist-Kuomintang difficulties and try to find any information that could be of use to you."[8]

White was checking on the creditworthiness of a borrower. The department had been providing economic support to China and was about to enroll that country in the Lend-Lease Program, which was a way to buy arms on favorable terms so long as the arms were used to fight fascism. He and Morgenthau wanted Hemingway to go on a fact-finding mission, a common practice at the time that was sometimes a precursor to spying. A senior government official might ask a prominent citizen or politician to travel overseas, immerse himself in the local scene, and report his impressions. This is what William J. Donovan, a leading New York lawyer and Republican internationalist, did for the secretary of the Navy and the president in 1940 when he traveled to Britain to report on her staying power in the fight against Germany.[9] Donovan toured extensively, met with the political and military elite, and returned with a detailed report that helped lay the foundation for the Office of Strategic Services (OSS), the spy agency he would found in 1942. Morgenthau wanted something similar from Hemingway. For his part, Hemingway was flattered to be asked. This was the kind of recognition he craved. In his mind he was more than just a novelist or a journalist: he was a sophisticate who understood how the world worked, and could use his understanding to help shape events.[10]

The newlywed couple decided to spend Christmas at Finca Vigía, the home they had first rented, then purchased outside Havana. In the new year they would retrace their steps to New York before heading for the west coast. Hemingway would stay in town long enough for a remarkable set of meetings.[11]

A man named Jacob Golos urgently wanted to see Hemingway before he left for China. Golos was one of those true originals who surface from time to time in the history of espionage. He was born in 1890 in the Ukraine, at the time part of Czarist Russia, into a well-to-do Jewish family. His first arrest, at the age of eight, for distributing anti-Czarist propaganda, suggests that his family was, to put it mildly, left-leaning.[12] (More than a few Russian revolutionaries were Jewish, one reaction to the state-sanctioned anti-Semitism and the resulting pogroms that occurred with frightening regularity.)

The first arrest did nothing to dampen Golos's revolutionary ardor; he continued to distribute, and later to print, Bolshevik propaganda. After his second arrest he claimed to have survived a mass execution by falling to the ground and pretending to be dead. His third arrest was in 1907 at the age of seventeen. Now a seasoned Bolshevik, this time he was banished to Siberia. Within two years he had escaped by heading *east,* making it to China on foot and then to the United States via Japan. He pursued the same line of work in the United States as in Russia—that of revolutionary. First in Detroit and then in New York, he integrated himself into exile communities, mixing with expatriate plotters who never much cared for America and spent their time thinking obsessively about politics in the old country.

By 1915 Golos had become an American citizen. In 1917, the revolution finally came to pass; the Bolsheviks seized power in Russia. Golos stayed in the United States and became one of the first members of the CPUSA, which put him on the road to becoming one of its leaders as it grew. The party had various names and branches over time, but there was one constant: it was always Moscow's instrument in the United States and an arm of Soviet intelligence. Party members could become spies in their own right, or they could play a supporting role. Before long, Golos developed into a facilitator par excellence, the kind of man who could serve as a bridge between Soviet intelligence and American society in a way that was good for the Soviets but not for America.

No matter how long he lived in America, Golos looked and sounded like a Russian revolutionary. He was stocky and short, only five feet two inches; he had blue eyes, thick lips, and a receding hairline. In pictures the remaining hair, said to have been red, looks bushy and dense, creating a halo effect. He never lost his accent. His clothes were shabby, his shoes usually scuffed. This revolutionary cared little for creature comforts. His personal possessions were weighted in favor of party paraphernalia and pamphlets. But he was self-confident enough to substitute his own judgment for that of his NKVD masters from time to time. (From the Moscow perspective it looked like he was hoarding information and sources. In the spy business this was akin to the sin of falling in love with your agents, and often signaled that the handler cared as much for them as for the mission.) His operational judgment was not perfect, but more than good enough for an amateur. Since childhood, he had been a member of one of the most conspiratorial political parties in history, and he had an instinctive feel for intrigue. His people skills were well developed, and he had a way with the ladies. (One of his paramours went so far as to call him the "cutest man in Russia" while he was on a kind of sabbatical in the Soviet Union in the 1920s.[13]) Holding American citizenship and knowing his way around New York were enormous added benefits.

More than anything else, Golos was a true believer. Throughout his life he held a candle for the ultimate victory of communism, which he believed would usher in a workers' paradise. Though he could be highly manipulative, the sincerity of his revolutionary ardor shone through and made him more effective when it came to recruiting and working with spies. He was someone who could bring foreigners into the fold and motivate them to steal secrets

Jacob Golos, the old Bolshevik who recruited Hemingway for the NKVD. *National Archives, Washington.*

for him. While it is hard to compare Golos to other communists whom Hemingway had met, his independence and authenticity made him something like Regler—that is, someone the writer could like and trust.

In 1932 Golos became the head of World Tourists Inc., a prototype for the communist front in the United States. It appeared to be a travel agency, promoting its main destination, the USSR, but its main purpose was to serve as a support mechanism for Soviet spying. First the NKVD wanted Golos to procure genuine American passports for its agents, which he did by recruiting a U.S. passport clerk with a gambling problem that the NKVD could use as leverage. As time passed, Golos took on more operational work, recruiting and running spies. He even became responsible for vetting all new American spies whom he did not recruit himself.[14]

Toward the end of the decade, a unique constellation of events, set in motion by Stalin, made Golos almost irreplaceable. The dictator's purges had affected the American stations as much as those in Europe; experienced English-speaking NKVD officers were called back to Moscow on the flimsiest of pretexts. In Stalin's paranoid worldview, the very cosmopolitanism that made them effective also made them suspect, and the NKVD liquidated many of its best men, including officers from New York. At the same time, the Soviet appetite for secret political, economic, and technical information about the United States continued to grow. There was more work to do but fewer people to do it. Golos was one of those people.

He eventually found himself with three demanding jobs: the head of World Tourists, a senior CPUSA officer, and a pillar of the NKVD station in New York. Some days he met with station officers as many as three or four times a day. (This was an amazingly high number for a secret or even a discreet relationship; KGB doctrine in the Cold War dictated three or four meetings *a year* with sensitive agents.) In 1940 and 1941 he was said to have been grooming between ten and twenty Americans for secret relationships. He may not have been a professional intelligence officer, one who had been handpicked from party cadre, then trained and evaluated at the institute outside Moscow, but he knew more about America than most NKVD careerists, and was more productive than they were.

This was a time when the CPUSA membership was becoming increasingly American; the party would no longer have to depend so heavily on émigrés. There was opportunity in that trend. Native-born American party members or fellow travelers had the potential to infiltrate government and industry that émigrés did not. And as the number of such spies grew exponentially, so did the need for Americans who could serve as go-betweens (also known as "cut-outs" in spy jargon) between NKVD officers and American spies. For example, an American-born woman with a college degree would attract far less attention when meeting a senior American government official than someone like Golos, who seemed so Russian.

One of those Americans was Elizabeth Bentley, a colorless Vassar graduate who would come out as "the Red Spy Queen" after the war. What Bentley saw of the Depression troubled her social conscience, and she became a member of the CPUSA. Attending meetings and enjoying the company of other comrades took some of the edge off her loneliness. Golos spotted her potential, and gradually recruited her for "special work." He turned her into the perfect cutout.[15]

Journalists could play an equally important role. A prominent reporter with good contacts could also serve as a go-between *and* gather information himself or spot potential recruits. His potential would be even greater if it was well known that he was *not* a communist. The ability to travel outside the United States added value. Hemingway fit the bill on all accounts. For the NKVD he was as much an accomplished and sympathetic journalist as a novelist. A recruiter could draw on the information in his file in Moscow, which documented his 1935 attack on the American establishment in *New Masses* and his antifascist/pro-Soviet reporting from Spain, not to mention his over-the-top antifascist speech at Carnegie Hall in June 1937.[16]

The details are still locked away in Moscow, but the NKVD's decision to approach Hemingway was almost certainly made between October and December 1940. Alexander Vassiliev, a former KGB officer who read about Hemingway in KGB files in the early 1990s, has speculated that Golos read *For Whom the Bell Tolls* when it was first published. Unlike the doctrinaire leftists who attacked the book, Golos apparently looked beyond Hemingway's portrayal of the Republic's faults and saw his spy potential.[17] Perhaps Golos understood that, by reaffirming his independence, the writer had become an even more attractive target. Then there was his admiration for the communist irregulars who waged guerrilla warfare. The NKVD may even have been aware of his defense of the Nazi-Soviet Pact in Regler's book; in its fall 1940 review of the book, the Moscow-based Cadre Department of the Comintern noted that Hemingway had written the preface.[18] He was still a passionate antifascist and, for that reason, pro-Soviet. He was even willing to overlook Stalin's sins and to criticize American foreign policy. In so many ways, then, Hemingway had what the Soviets wanted.

No one in the West knows who introduced Golos and Hemingway, but they had a number of mutual acquaintances. Joe North, the New York–based communist with the friendly smile, spotted other potential recruits for Golos.[19] North's path had already crossed with Hemingway's more than once: when he persuaded Hemingway to write the *New Masses* piece in 1935 and when they shared moments of high drama in Spain. After the civil war, Hemingway wrote a passionate foreword to North's celebration of the American antifascists who had fought in the Abraham Lincoln Battalion.[20] They had last seen each other in the summer of 1940, when North had covered a conference on Spanish refugees in Cuba. The reunion had been an unexpected pleasure for both men. Hemingway had invited North to join him at the bar La Florida in Old Havana where the writer was a regular. The two veterans had made themselves comfortable under the slow-turning ceiling fans and talked for hours.[21]

Or the intermediary might have been an American communist like the mostly unsuccessful novelist John Herrmann, a longtime

Joe North, *New Masses* editor who ran Hemingway's stories and may have introduced him to Jacob Golos. *Abraham Lincoln Collection, Tamiment Library.*

Hemingway friend who worked underground for the CPUSA for years.[22] (Between 1926 and 1940, he was also the husband of Josephine Herbst, a good if not close friend.) According to one account, Herrmann was the man who, with one of his introductions, helped to set the stage for at least one very successful recruitment, that of the perfectly placed State Department official Alger Hiss.[23] A final possibility is Hemingway's good friend Joris Ivens, the filmmaker who was in New York off and on from 1939 to 1941 and had more than once encouraged Hemingway to meet fellow communists. One of his attempts was a cryptic two-line telegram that reads like an attempt to arrange a discreet meeting: "Tried to get you on phone but you went to the country . . . they say [they] wanted to have the other drinks with you today."[24]

If the intermediary remains a mystery, we know Gólos met Hemingway at some point in late 1940, probably during his honeymoon in New York. It is fact that they met, and that Golos's purpose was to recruit Hemingway for the NKVD. However, we must rely on conjecture, based on Golos's history and Soviet practices, to fill in the details of their meetings.

Both Golos and the intermediary knew that a personal introduction was a more promising way to start a secret relationship than a cold call. The intermediary may have picked Hemingway up at the Barclay and driven him to the kind of out-of-the way eatery on the Lower East Side that Golos had chosen for other meetings—like the small, quiet restaurant on Second Avenue where he had met with Bentley. The décor and the menu would have been unremarkable. There was probably a back room, or at least a quiet corner where they could talk. The working-class clientele would have been unlikely to recognize the great writer.

The intermediary would probably have left them alone to get to know each other, another prerequisite for a secret relationship. Hemingway would have ordered something to drink. After a bit of small talk, perhaps about the new novel, each man would have presented his credentials, perhaps exaggerating his accomplishments. The American might have talked about Spain, claiming he had been a fighter, not just a writer, and the Russian might have hinted at the important special work that he had been undertaking in the United States. Golos would have played on the theme of antifascism and talked about the Soviet Union as the ultimate bulwark against that ideology. He almost certainly would have flattered Hemingway about the important role the writer could play if he worked against fascism with the Soviets. Guessing what the burly American with the healthy ego might like to hear would not have been difficult for someone as experienced in intelligence work as Golos.

At roughly the same time, either before or after their first meeting, Golos would have interested the NKVD's New York station in the possibility of recruiting another prominent journalist for spy work. Given Hemingway's stature and Golos's experience, it is unlikely that this was a spur-of-the-moment, "it seems like a good idea" kind of recruitment. That might have happened in a Comintern operation, but it was far less likely in an NKVD operation against a high-profile target. The Comintern had its secrets but existed primarily to create and spread propaganda; the NKVD, by contrast, was a professional spy service. Men like Ivens produced films; men like Golos recruited and ran spies. He answered to a headquarters in Moscow that hated surprises and usually insisted on exercising as much control as possible.

If the Soviet spymasters were running true to form, it is likely that the case generated a number of cables between New York and Moscow *before* Golos made the recruitment pitch to Hemingway. The cables would have described the initial contacts with Hemingway as well as the station's thoughts on his potential as a spy. The Center would likely have summarized the information in the files about Hemingway, perhaps including Orlov's reflections on meeting Hemingway in Spain. At some point Moscow would have given its approval for New York to proceed with the recruitment attempt. Its preference would almost certainly have been for Golos not to pitch Hemingway early on, but rather after they had gotten to know each other better. Something like this happened; there was a process: first the writer agreed to help the NKVD and then the two made arrangements to stay in touch.

The records that have survived and are available to researchers make it clear that Golos was reporting to Moscow on his efforts to engage Hemingway as a spy. One of the landmarks among those records is a summary of Hemingway's file in the secret archives unearthed by Vassiliev.[25] Based on documents in the writer's file, which would have included cables from New York, the summary was written for internal consumption and never intended to be read outside a Soviet vault. This fact lends it a high degree of authenticity.

Dating from 1948, the summary states that "before he left for China, [Hemingway] was recruited for our work on ideological grounds by [Golos]." In the language of intelligence, this meant Hemingway had accepted a proposal to enter into a secret relationship with the Soviets. Golos may have explicitly referred to the NKVD, or he may simply have talked about Soviet "special services," a shorthand that would not have been a mystery to Hemingway. The reference to "ideological grounds" meant he agreed with the Soviet agenda (or at least part of it) and was not accepting the pitch because he wanted money or any other kind of compensation. It also virtually rules out blackmail or coercion; no one would have had to coerce an ideological recruit, especially one as prominent as Hemingway.

The transcripts from the secret file are silent about what specific tasks, if any, Golos laid out for Hemingway. Golos may have been content to recruit Hemingway solely on the strength of his potential as a journalist spy, that is, someone who could use his extensive network of contacts for the NKVD's ends.[26] This would not have been unusual for the Soviets, who commonly used a probationary period to test a new recruit and find out what he was best suited for. For his part, Hemingway may have thought that he knew what the Soviets wanted. Witness his brushes with their spies in Spain, his account of guerrilla warfare in *For Whom the Bell Tolls,* and his excursion into the world of the counterspy in *The Fifth Column*. Perhaps the NKVD wanted him to act like the hero in that play, who was a member of the secret police and reported on the persons of interest whom he met in bars—except now it would be on a much larger scale and would include the information he could gather from the rich and powerful in the course of his work.

There was one task that Golos, like any good recruiter, could not overlook. That was to make arrangements for clandestine meetings with someone else. He was already suffering from the effects of overwork and ill health and could not travel very far from home. So how would the NKVD get in touch with its new recruit in China (or anywhere else)? How would Hemingway know whom to trust? In a report to Moscow, Golos voiced his opinion that the NKVD must attempt to meet with Hemingway in China or, if he traveled via the Soviet Union, in the motherland. Golos wrote that he had prepared Hemingway to meet "our people" outside the United States. The writer had given the Russian a few "stamps," presumably something unique like Cuban postage stamps, and learned that he should only trust someone who produced them. Golos closed with a confident prediction: "I am sure he will cooperate with us and . . . do everything he can."[27]

Bearing a 1941 date stamp, this message from Golos is remarkable for a number of reasons. The wording reinforces the conclusion that Hemingway and Golos had established a relationship *before* Hemingway finalized his itinerary (which changed more than once); Golos's report makes sense only if they had an ongoing relationship, the basis for the comment that Hemingway would cooperate with the Soviets.[28] That Golos refers to Hemingway by his true name rather than by a code name shows that the secret relationship was young; the NKVD would not get around to issuing him a code name until later in 1941, when he would become known as "Argo." (The NKVD typically used code names for recruited spies. The names often fit the spy: the college-educated Bentley was "Clever Girl," a congressman on the take "Crook." Someone in the NKVD had a literary background and, more than likely, a feel for Hemingway's seafaring life. In Greek mythology *Argo* was the name of the ship that Jason and the Argonauts sailed in search of adventure.) Meeting the new recruit in the Soviet Union or China made good sense; this would be an opportunity for both sides to get to know each other without having to worry about being spotted by the FBI, which had been keeping an eye on Golos since 1939.

One of the next steps the NKVD took was to add *For Whom the Bell Tolls* to its holdings, sending a copy from New York to Moscow by pouch on January 8, 1941.[29] When he read Hemingway's file,

Vassiliev concluded that Stalin's henchmen at the Lubyanka, their headquarters in an old insurance building in downtown Moscow—with offices upstairs and prison cells in the basement—acquired the book for the purposes of rounding out the file of the newly recruited Hemingway.[30] The novel was, after all, a useful guide to Hemingway's thinking about antifascism.

At first glance, the story of Hemingway's recruitment appears to rest on a tenuous foundation. The records are fragmentary. There are obvious gaps between the surviving cables and memos, and the way they are dated is confusing. The originals themselves are not available, only handwritten copies and notes. Copies of all of the documents in the NKVD file, like the facsimiles that the FBI released in the 1980s, would make the case that much sounder.[31]

The FBI release allows the reader to piece together virtually everything the Bureau thought it knew about Hemingway. The story emerges from a series of messages, memoranda, and marginal comments, all written for internal consumption, most for a very specific purpose—to record an incident, update an earlier report, or request approval for an operation. It is not like writing a story with a beginning and an end that makes sense to the general reader. But it is the stuff of intelligence work. In this way, the "complete" FBI file and the "incomplete" NKVD file are similar. Each is a collection of fragments, some of them wrong or only partially right. But the fragments create a pattern, and the imperfections add to the ring of authenticity.

The same is true of the circumstances under which the story came to light. It is too fantastic to have been invented or to have been a conspiracy of some sort.[32] The collapse of the Soviet Union in 1991 was the very cataclysm its secret service had been created to prevent. The NKVD and its successor the KGB were the shield and the sword of the revolution, which in turn would care for those who served it. Once the Soviet Union was gone, KGB veterans felt like the employees of a company that suddenly went out of business without fully funding the pension system. They were on their own, facing economic and political chaos, not to mention a public that was now free to criticize them. What could anyone do about this? What did they have that they could use? Spy agencies usually exist to steal new secrets, but maybe they could also sell old secrets and use the money for a retirement fund.

Crown Publishing Group, a subsidiary of Random House (now Penguin Random House), saw an opportunity and came up with a proposition for the SVR (Sluzhba Vneshney Razvedki), the agency that took over the KGB's functions in the new Russia. In return for a substantial contribution to the agency's pension fund, the SVR would supply Crown's authors with historic information about KGB operations. Not only would such stories make for interesting reading, but, at the same time, they might improve the KGB's image by showing how well it had served the state. The SVR's senior management enthusiastically endorsed the arrangement, over the objections of many KGB traditionalists.

Each book would have at least one Russian researcher, handpicked by the SVR. That researcher would comb through the original KGB files and make handwritten notes, then use his notes to summarize his findings. An SVR review board would vet the resulting narrative before sharing it with a Western historian. The plan was not to share the raw notes, only to use them to prepare the summary. No one would identify any sources if their identities had not yet come to light. The result would be a book about the glory days of Soviet espionage but not a tell-all.[33]

First to appear was a biography of Alexander Orlov, the NKVD chief of station in Spain from 1936 to 1938, the man who had met Hemingway in 1937 at the Gaylord Hotel, where the Soviet secret policeman often went to relax in luxury.[34] The Orlov book was published in 1993 and looked like a good model for future volumes. Portraying Orlov in all his complexity, it did not sidestep controversy or paper over murderous truths about his career. To satisfy the skeptics, there were pages of facsimile documents of the original files.

Among the other planned titles in the series was to be a book on Soviet espionage in the United States during the 1930s and 1940s. The SVR picked Alexander Vassiliev to be the Russian researcher for that book. A journalist who had served as a KGB officer, he would be able to understand and summarize the files in a way no outsider ever could. He started work on the project in 1993, sifting through mountains of files about Americans who had spied for the Soviet Union—and finding there were many more than anyone had imagined. He was allowed only to take handwritten notes, in Russian, on what he was reading. Oftentimes he prepared verbatim transcripts of the documents, copying them word for word. When he was fairly well along in the work, he prepared the narrative summary for the official approval that would clear the way for a Western historian to start work.

Then the ground shifted in 1995 and 1996. Crown had to cancel the book project because it ran short of money. Hard-liners once again took control of the SVR. They believed in the sanctity of official secrets and had no time for any liberal notions of openness. One of those hard-liners told Vassiliev that they "were going to deal with him" after they had replaced the new management.[35] Vassiliev took this as a threat and fled to the West. He later arranged for his research notes to be smuggled out to him, including his original handwritten notes with his copies of parts of Hemingway's file.

The fact that none of this raw material was ever supposed to be released enhances its credibility. Hemingway scholars can now read transcripts of original Soviet documents about the writer, some of them written while the operation was unfolding. The perfect source would be the NKVD's entire original Hemingway file. But until the SVR opens its archives in the distant future, Western researchers can rely on Vassiliev, a competent witness who was able to do that work on our behalf.[36]

Is there only one side to the story of Hemingway's becoming a spy? The historian can lean on the incomplete but authentic Soviet account, but did Hemingway himself ever say anything explicit about the matter? Probably not. Ten years later in letters to his best friend he would write that he had done "odd jobs" for the Soviets in Spain and, after the civil war, stayed in touch with "Russkis" who had shared secrets with him—though he would not elaborate.[37] Otherwise there is no evidence he ever spoke to a third party about Golos and the NKVD, not even to Gellhorn, who shared many of his political views but was very much the junior partner in their marriage.[38] His relationship with the Soviet spy service was a serious undertaking, not something to discuss with friends over drinks or to write about, as he had done during the Spanish Civil War and would do again after some of his other, less secret World War II adventures. He understood the need for secrecy, one of the foundations of good spycraft. Hemingway thought that spying was one more of his many life skills, and he was not wrong.

When, in early 1941, Hemingway offered up the stamps to Golos, he was playing an active role in a secret transaction with a Soviet spy. (The stamps were the signal that the man or woman who produced them could be trusted, much like the irregular halves of a Jell-O box that other Soviet spies used—the person who produced the matching half was the fellow spy you were looking for.) Such material passwords are not necessary for normal, everyday transactions, only for secret business. If there is nothing secret about a relationship, the author or the newcomer could carry a simple letter of introduction, like the kind Ivens wrote for Hemingway during the Spanish Civil War. But if the relationship is secret, the material password works much better. By itself it tells no tales. Its true purpose is known only to the initiated.

Hemingway had not changed much between November 1938, when Orlov listened to him expound on the Spanish Civil War, and January 1941, when he dealt with Golos. The commitment to the struggle against fascism was still so strong that it surprised longtime communists, perhaps because they had not seen the real thing for so many years. Hemingway was an ideological recruit—Golos was right about that. But he was not like the "true believers" in communism. He did not believe in Marxism or Leninism; he was "just" joining the antifascist team that got results. Or at least that is the way he thought of the NKVD. He knew how it had trained guerrillas, destroyed railways behind fascist lines, and tried to bring discipline to the Spanish Republic.

Although he was different from many ideological recruits, Hemingway did share more than one trait with other spies. The recruitment process often started with an event that upset the emotional status quo, and changed the way the future spy looked at the world. For Hemingway it was the hurricane in the Florida Keys in 1935, which led him to attack more angrily than ever before the American establishment for its apparent lack of concern for the World War I vets who had died by the hundreds. Then, in the Spanish Civil War, he committed himself with whole heart to the Republic and developed a fascination with intelligence work. He was now taking the next step. He agreed to become a spy because having a secret life, not to mention the thrill from the risks that came along with it, met a need for him. For many spies there is some kind of frustration that drives that need. In Hemingway's case he had done everything he could in the fight against fascism, but he had failed to get the democracies, especially his own country, to listen to him. He would now resort to other, secret means, not unlike the spouse who starts an affair because his marriage is not working well enough for him (as Hemingway did more than once in his life).

Another trait he shared with other spies was an assumption that everyday rules did not apply to him. Hemingway had been living by his own code for decades. In literature it had to do with his revolutionary writing style. Breaking ground with his great political novel in 1940, he had just done it again. He was exultant, confident, and ready for a new adventure. In a letter to MacLeish's wife, Ada, he described how it felt "almost too good" to write as well as he could, and then to have his work sell. He wished he had had as much money "in the old days when there was a world to move in." Still, he mused, traveling thousands of miles to China would give "a man some lee-way."[39]

Hemingway was looking for that leeway in politics and war. He loved things military and being around soldiers, but he did not want to join any man's army. His preference was for loose affiliation with other irregulars, especially guerrillas, which made him feel like he was a part of the action but left him free to come and go as he pleased. He was not a communist, or even a fellow traveler, but he was willing to produce films for the Comintern and then to join with the NKVD in the fight against fascism, his overriding political passion.

If Hemingway had written about his meetings with Golos, he might have admitted that he liked the seasoned revolutionary and was attracted to his proposal. Hemingway agreed to a second meeting, then a third, and so forth. Finally, by January 1941, the American novelist agreed to work with Moscow. Like many spies, Hemingway would not have used the word "recruitment." While he knew he was entering into a secret relationship with the Soviet spy service, he likely viewed that relationship more as a partnership than as the first step on the road to taking direction from Moscow.[40] But "recruitment" *is* the word that the Soviets used. They believed that, when Hemingway agreed to Golos's proposal, it was the beginning of a secret relationship they intended to shape and control. The idea was for the agent to do what Moscow told him to do. In return he would receive something from the NKVD. That could take the form of money, freedom from blackmail, safety for his family. In Hemingway's case there is no evidence of anything beyond a general commitment to fight fascism and keep the relationship secret. But that was enough.

Hemingway would not have thought that he was betraying his country. He did not have much good to say about the New Deal, and he was still angry that Roosevelt had not supported the

Spanish Republic. He could barely contain his frustration that the United States was not doing more to fight Hitler. But he did not plan to betray his country. One day in 1940, after reading his daily mail, which often included unwanted letters from fans and critics, he answered a note that asked how a loyal American could buy a home in a foreign country and settle there. It was, he wrote in a telegram, "an unqualified obscenity" to ask if he planned to become a citizen of any country but the United States. He had many American Revolutionary forebears, but "none of them was named Benedict Arnold."[41]

Would the Department of Justice have agreed? Was this treason? Did Hemingway break any laws by agreeing to work with the NKVD? The American espionage laws of the day were not particularly robust and would not have applied. Hemingway was not a government official, and he did not have any official secrets to betray. Nor was he giving aid and comfort to the enemy in wartime. The United States was not at war, and the Soviet Union was not an enemy. After Pearl Harbor the two countries would even join forces for the duration of the war. At worst, Hemingway might have run afoul of the 1938 Foreign Agents Registration Act (FARA), which required public disclosure by anyone acting as "a political or quasi-political agent" for a foreign power.[42] This would certainly include affiliation with a foreign spy service; there would be prosecutions against Soviet spies (including Golos) under FARA.

Still, Hemingway's relationship with the NKVD was secret for good reason. Even before the war, American officials were suspicious of the far left. The FBI was keeping an eye on the CPUSA, and Spanish Civil War veterans faced discrimination. He himself had generated the applications that went into the Hemingway dossier at the State Department that included his assurances that he would not get involved in the Spanish conflict.[43] He did not want that (or any other) dossier to grow and interfere with his work. Then there was his reputation for independence. More than once he railed about the need for writers not to become indebted to governments or political parties. As he himself had put it, writers who espoused a political cause, worked for it, or believed in it would still die like any writer; their corpses would just stink more.[44] Hemingway may have imagined that he was joining forces with the NKVD to fight the common enemy, but he never wanted to read a newspaper headline that screamed: "Hemingway Unmasked as Red Spy." This was a secret he planned to keep for the rest of his life.

CHAPTER 6

TO SPY OR NOT TO SPY

China and the Strain of War

One day in April 1941, Martha Gellhorn went by herself to the market in Chungking, China. She relished its liveliness, a contrast to the drab part of town where the Hemingways were staying. There was a symphony of sensations in its narrow alleys—the smell of "food and spice, the aroma of flowers, roasting chestnuts, incense, the sweetness of opium," mixed with the "singsong" chants of peddlers offering everything from timber to cotton to cat's bells, knives, and ear cleaners.[1] *She did not expect to encounter the tall European woman "wearing a man's felt hat and a flowered cotton dress over trousers" who sidled up to her and asked if she and Hemingway wanted to meet Chou En-lai.*[2] *Gellhorn was instructed to return to the market the next day with her husband, but only after wandering around until they were sure that no one was following them. When she asked Hemingway about the name that had meant nothing to her, he told her that Chou was an acquaintance of their good friend from the Spanish Civil War, the Dutch communist filmmaker Joris Ivens. They would go meet him. For Gellhorn, "There followed a scene straight from James Bond but long preceding James Bond."*[3]

The woman in the man's hat led the couple deeper into the market than Gellhorn had gone the day before—the route was like a maze—before blindfolding them and putting them in a rickshaw. When the blindfolds were removed after the ride, they found themselves in a small, whitewashed room. There was a table and three chairs. Seated at the table was the communist leader who would become the premier of China from 1949 to 1976, dressed in a plain open-necked white shirt, black trousers, and sandals.

Hemingway and Gellhorn's trip to China in 1941 might have been a second honeymoon. Instead she would call it the "super horror journey."[4] Hemingway still had mixed feelings about going with her to the Far East so soon after their wedding. She would label him her "Unwilling Companion," or "U.C.," in her mostly good-natured and entertaining memoir, *Travels with Myself and Another.*

Even apart from Hemingway's attitude, it was a long, difficult trip, much harder than the often unpleasant and sometimes risky business of figuring out how to get into wartime Spain from supposedly neutral France. Although the United States was not yet at war, much of the rest of the world was, and it had not been easy to find and book passage, even for someone as famous as Ernest Hemingway. They eventually had to settle for a thirty-eight-year-old steamship called the *Matsonia.*

Accustomed to more comfortable crossings on the Atlantic, the couple was surprised to discover how rough the Pacific could be from San Francisco to Honolulu. In early February 1941, when they arrived in Hawaii to an enthusiastic welcome, Hemingway was not in a good mood. He angrily exclaimed that he did not like to have flowers draped around his neck and would "spit back" into the mouth of the next person who said "Aloha!" to him.[5] His mood did not improve when he and Gellhorn toured the naval base at Pearl Harbor. There, in the sheltered, tropical bay they saw American ships and airplanes all lined up in rows. Hemingway told Gellhorn that the United States was using a system that had been popular but disastrous during World War I: "Get everything and everyone packed in one place and [risk getting] . . . the whole lot wiped out."[6] He knew that the way to keep losses to a minimum, to protect them from the kind of air attack that the Japanese were already planning, was to spread your hardware and your people out. A few weeks later, in May, he would imply bitterly that U.S. forces had been asleep since the mid-1930s while he and Gellhorn had been doing their best to fight fascism.[7]

The journey continued. From Hawaii the famous couple made their way across the Pacific to China by Boeing Clipper on Pan American World Airways. It was a five-day trip, with stops at the tiny islands of Midway and Wake in the middle of the ocean, then on to Guam and Manila, before the final leg to Hong Kong.[8] This was the heyday of intercontinental air travel. The great seaplanes were like flying lounges: comfortable, well appointed, and well served. When the clippers touched down to refuel and take on fresh provisions, passengers were able to swim in idyllic lagoons or simply to bathe, dine, and sleep in even more comfortable surroundings. Hemingway was a man who did not mind hardship, especially in the service of a cause he believed in, but he also handily tolerated luxury.

On February 22, Hemingway and Gellhorn finally arrived in China. It would have been hard to find a better setting for intrigue. For years the Chinese had been fighting the Japanese, who had joined Nazi Germany and Fascist Italy to form the Berlin-Rome-Tokyo Axis. It was a brutal war that seemed unlikely ever to end. What the Japanese wanted was relatively simple—mostly raw materials and territory—and they did not care what they had to do to get it, which usually meant killing large numbers of Chinese, both civilian and military, sometimes randomly and sometimes with purpose. Here was an aggressor whose crimes were on a scale that Franco could never have imagined. If, as Hemingway liked to write, the Nationalists were killers during the Spanish Civil War, the Japanese were mass murderers in China. Even so, the outside threat brought only a semblance of unity to the Chinese side. Beneath the surface there was intense conflict between the old regime and communist revolutionaries.

The old regime was embodied by the warlord Chiang Kai-shek,

who was head of the Kuomintang, or Chinese National People's Party. Chiang was in nominal command of the government and army. Under Mao Tse-tung and his deputy Chou En-lai, the communists had their own, much smaller (and more disciplined) army. The two sides spent nearly as much time warily facing off against each other as fighting the Japanese. The Soviet Union, the Germans, and the Americans had all, at various times, provided support to Chiang and his military. At one point Hemingway and Gellhorn came across a display at a Chinese training academy that told the story graphically; on the wall, in a row, one after another, were portraits of Roosevelt and Chamberlain alongside the likes of Hitler, Mussolini, and Stalin.[9] To complicate matters even further, there were colonies in and around China governed by European countries that still believed in their power to control events in the Far East.

One of those colonies was Britain's Hong Kong, the gateway to China for Hemingway and Gellhorn. In early 1941 it was a kind of never-never land. In her travelogue Gellhorn recorded that it was far from the modern city of skyscrapers on the bay that it would become after the war. At its heart was the mountainous island of Victoria. A surprisingly wild district known as "the Peak" overlooked the working city of Hong Kong. The colony's rulers lived in comfortable homes on the hill; the higher their status, the higher their perch. Life down by the water could not have been more different. People there lived in shacks that seemed to have been nailed together yesterday from scraps of tin and wood. The streets around them were noisy and colorful, jammed with people, rickshaws, and bicycles.[10]

Although the mother country had been at war for well over a year, and Japanese forces surrounded the colony, time seemed to be standing still in Hong Kong. Hemingway later reported for Ralph Ingersoll's tabloid, *PM*, that the city's restaurants were among the best in the world and that there were still peacetime entertainments like horse racing, cricket, rugby, and association football.[11] Hemingway did his part to add to those diversions, introducing his own signature Bloody Mary mix to the colony and entertaining fellow writers with "tales of far-off places," such as the time he beat up a relative of the Norwegian fascist leader Vidkun Quisling in a bar in Idaho.[12] On another evening he and a Marine officer demonstrated "dagger and sword tricks," showing how easy it was to cut off a man's head without breaking a sweat.[13]

As negative as ever about the British, Hemingway pointed to the air of unreality when he wrote that "danger had hung over the place so long that it had become absolutely commonplace."[14] The city was "very gay," with "morale high" and "morals low" on account of the beautiful Chinese girls who had flocked to Hong Kong to spend time with the Chinese millionaires, five hundred of them by Hemingway's count, who were now living in the colony. The great writer seemed happy to report that the official British position was that there was no prostitution to regulate.

Hemingway had still more to say about the British. With relish, he recounted an anecdote about a Chinese general who wanted to know what the British really thought of the Chinese army.[15] The American writer mimicked a British officer who had told him, "We don't think very much of the Chinese, you know. . . . Johnny [Chinaman is] all right and a very good fellow. . . . But he's absolutely hopeless on the offensive, you know. We have absolutely no confidence in him ever taking the offensive." The Chinese officer countered with a riddle: Why do British staff officers wear a monocle? The answer was so that they would not see more than they can understand. Hemingway concluded the British in Hong Kong would die "trapped like rats" when the Japanese attacked the colony.[16] In this he would prove as prescient as in his assessment of U.S. naval forces in Hawaii; before the end of the year the Japanese would seize Hong Kong—they attacked eight hours after they struck Pearl Harbor.

It did not matter to him that Britain was the only great power then at war with Nazi Germany. She continued to wage her lonely life-and-death struggle for the survival of democracy in Europe. The other great antifascist power, the Soviet Union, was still at peace with Germany under the provisions of the Nazi-Soviet Pact of August 1939. Then, in April 1941, Stalin signed a second nonaggression pact, this time with Germany's ally Japan.

For many, including the Chinese communist leadership, it was a stunning betrayal. The American journalist Theodore White, who happened to be in China at the time, wrote in his journal that the "Russo-Jap Pact" was "like a clap of thunder."[17] When he passed the electrifying news to Hemingway and Gellhorn, White was taken aback by their cool, matter-of-fact response. A few months later Hemingway explained his attitude in another article for *PM*. He applied the same test to the second nonaggression pact that he had applied in Spain—that is, he did not look at what the politicians *said;* he looked at what they were *doing*. The Soviet Union had been providing aid to the Chinese government in its fight against the Japanese. Was that aid continuing to flow? Were the Soviet advisors still in China and still working? The answer to both questions was yes. "Soviet Russia has given China more aid than any other country has supplied" and was continuing to do so.[18] That being the case, who could fault Stalin for guaranteeing his own borders against attack from the east?

Hemingway did not address the argument that the pact freed up troops on both sides for other objectives. For the Japanese their mission was the war in China. In other words, Stalin had made it easier for the Japanese to fight in China. The irony is that everything else Hemingway said and wrote during his trip to China in 1941 was aimed at strengthening the Chinese hand against the Japanese, just as in Spain he had wanted to do whatever he could to help in the fight against the fascists.

Although Hemingway may have started out as Gellhorn's Unwilling Companion on the voyage to the Orient, they traded roles as the trip unfolded. Fastidious almost to a fault, Gellhorn was increasingly put off by the unsanitary conditions and general disorder they encountered in China. Hemingway was very nearly the other way

Hemingway and Gellhorn with Madame Chiang Kai-shek in Chungking, 1941. *Ernest Hemingway Photo Collection, JFK Library.*

around. He felt no need to wash every day or to keep his living space clean and tidy. When things did not go according to plan, the adventurer in him kicked in and he seemed to enjoy himself even more. That the adventure included meetings with Chinese leaders made it all the more enjoyable. Hemingway was usually happy to encounter political leaders who treated him like an equal.

For more than a week the couple stayed in Chungking, for her the "grey, shapeless, muddy" wartime capital.[19] There they met Chiang Kai-shek and the communist leader Chou, as well as a number of Chiang's generals and officials. The Generalissimo, as the supreme Nationalist warlord styled himself, and Madame Chiang (for Gellhorn "still a beauty and a famous vamp") invited the couple to an exclusive lunch in their private quarters, which put Gellhorn in mind of a modest, clean house in Grand Rapids, Michigan.[20] Thin and bald—the American general Joseph Stillwell nicknamed him "Peanut" after the shape of his head—Chiang was dressed in a plain gray uniform. Without his false teeth he looked "embalmed." Fluent in English, Madame Chiang translated her husband's rant against the communists, finding a number of ways to tell their visitors that Mao's forces were not making any significant contribution to the war effort. On the contrary, the sixty divisions that the Nationalists kept in reserve in case of a Japanese offensive also served "to watch the Communists."

Chiang observed that the communists were doing an excellent job of telling their story to American reporters; they made it seem as if their troops held the key to victory. At one point, while Madame Chiang was trying to charm Hemingway, Gellhorn questioned why the government did not take care of the lepers who survived by begging on the streets. To this the Chinese first lady countered that her countrymen were more humane than Westerners; they refused to lock lepers away from society. Besides, she went on, China already had a great culture when Gellhorn's ancestors were still "living in trees and painting themselves blue."[21] Gellhorn concluded that "these two stony rulers could care nothing for the miserable hordes of their people."[22]

Gellhorn contrasted the Chiangs with their rival, Chou. Thirty years later Gellhorn could not remember the substance of the conversation with the communist leader in the whitewashed room where they had met him. But she did recall the supremely positive impression Chou left on them: "For the first and only time we were at home with a Chinese. . . . We thought Chou a winner, the one really good man we'd met in China. . . . If he was a sample of Chinese Communists, then the future was theirs."[23] A few weeks after the meeting, Hemingway would describe Chou as "a man of enormous charm and great intelligence [who] does a fine job of selling the Communist standpoint."[24]

The European woman who arranged the meeting turned out to be one Anna Wong, a German who had married a Chinese communist. Her approach to Gellhorn raises some intriguing questions. Was this the hand of Joris Ivens reaching out from afar? Or was this perhaps the kind of secret contact that the NKVD spy Golos had hoped to arrange for Hemingway in China? The answer to both questions is a qualified *no*. Ivens was long gone from China and at that point back in the United States, looking for work. If he brokered the contact, chances are that it would have been only in the very loose sense of suggesting to Hemingway or Wong that they should meet if they were ever in the same place at the same time. If Golos had played a role in arranging the meeting, that fact would likely have been reflected in Hemingway's NKVD file. But there is no record of a secret meeting in China. On the contrary, the NKVD functionary who reviewed the file in 1948 noted that "contact was not reestablished with 'Argo' [Hemingway's code name] in China."[25] Even though Hemingway and Golos had gone to more than a little

The Chinese leader who did impress: Chou En-lai, ca. 1938. *Robert Capa Photo, ICP.*

bit of trouble to lay the groundwork for a secret meeting in China by agreeing on a password, it went unused in that country.

The more likely backstory of the meeting with Chou is that he was aware of Hemingway's presence in Chungking, a town where it was hard to keep a secret, and decided to exploit it. At the time Anna Wong was working as a kind of press officer for the communists, which would make it natural for her to arrange for Hemingway and Gellhorn to hear the communist point of view now that they had heard the Nationalist point of view.[26] The meeting was private so that Chou could speak without any interference from Chiang's functionaries, making it more like a background briefing than anything clandestine. Gellhorn did not have it exactly right when she described James Bond–style intrigue.

Hemingway used what he learned from the Chiangs and from Chou the way a journalist or a government emissary would employ such information: to write articles and prepare reports. What he did reflected the practices of the day, as well as the policies that he supported. His reporting for *PM* was generally upbeat, like his reporting during the Spanish Civil War. In an interview he explained that Chiang's army was important because it was keeping the Japanese occupied while the United States prepared to defend its outposts in the Pacific.[27] He praised the communist forces for the "marvelous fighting" they had done. He did not dwell on the tensions between the communists and the Nationalists because he did not want to say or do anything that would undermine the all-important cause, which remained fighting fascism.[28] For that reason he also kept his negative comments about British and American prospects in the Pacific to himself and a few friends or acquaintances.

The intriguing, unanswered question is this: What happened to the secret meeting that was supposed to take place during Hemingway's lengthy sojourn in the Orient? Why did Golos go to such lengths to make arrangements for a meeting that apparently never took place?

One possible explanation is that it was simply too difficult to arrange a meeting in the midst of wartime disorder. Hemingway and Gellhorn did not themselves know where they would be from hour to hour, or day to day; transportation and communication were erratic in the extreme. Gellhorn's travelogue is a tale of missed and haphazard connections, along with hair-raising plane or boat rides that almost end in disaster. This explanation, that it was too difficult for Hemingway and the NKVD to meet, loses some of its force in light of the meeting between the Hemingways and Chou En-lai. If Chou's people could find Hemingway and hold a discreet meeting, could NKVD operatives in China have done the same? Hemingway himself had a friendly encounter with a contingent of Soviet military advisors in Nationalist territory. They are unlikely to have deployed without some sort of NKVD supervision. The commissar on duty that day would have reported the presence of the irrepressible foreigner who had forced the congenitally secretive Russians to pay attention to him, when he put himself in their path and greeted one of the officers he happened to know with a casual, "How are you doing, *Tovarich*?"[29]

There are two other possible explanations. The first is that, like many spies, Hemingway may have had second thoughts after signing up with a foreign power, even one that he still admired. A psychiatrist who has studied spies describes it as "the morning-after stage," one that often sets in a few months later.[30] It is like buyer's remorse: you negotiate and close an important deal, then you wonder if you bought the right thing at the correct price. Maybe you want a little—or a lot—of distance from the salesman.

In late 1940 it had been relatively easy for Hemingway to convince himself that working with the NKVD was the proper thing to do. His anger at the democracies, mostly over Spain, and the way he sympathized with the Soviets took care of his doubts. And the success of *For Whom the Bell Tolls* empowered him. But becoming a spy was still an enormous step out of the American mainstream. It was a step that few Americans would understand or forgive. Hemingway enjoyed being an insider. Being in a secret relationship, dealing in secrets, the truest of "the true gen" that he liked so much, conferred a sense of superiority.[31] But it came at a price. He could not share who or what he knew. This was the enormous burden that he probably began to feel in 1941.

During the Spanish Civil War Hemingway had learned just how small—and unpopular—the far left was in America. He knew that many of his friends whose only crime had been fighting fascism in Spain had not been welcomed home. Even wounded veterans were often shunned. Time and again, after 1939 Hemingway showed that he was willing to stand up for them, just as he had supported the stalwart Gustav Regler when he had nowhere to go after the end of the Spanish war. But that did not necessarily make the writer comfortable outside the pale, where spies subsisted.

Another explanation is that Hemingway's near-manic level of activity was wearing him out. During the previous four years he had immersed himself in a series of life events that would have exhausted most mortals: infidelity, divorce, and remarriage; committing himself heart and soul to a lost cause in Spain; cutting his ties to Key West and moving to Cuba; writing a 470-page masterwork of world literature; and traveling to another war in an unknown part of the world. Agreeing to spy for the Soviet Union, an extremely stressful proposition for most Americans recruited by the NKVD, was only one entry on the list. It all contributed to what he himself later called "the technical strain of war [against fascism] from 1936 to 1946" in a letter to his literary friend Archibald MacLeish.[32] In a follow-on letter to MacLeish's wife, Ada, he added that the strain had made him "insufferable" for "decades."[33]

What Hemingway said and did when leaving China is consistent with buyer's remorse and exhaustion. The newlyweds decided to travel home separately. She had more work to do for *Collier's* and proceeded first to Singapore, still a British colony, and a few days later to Batavia (later known as Jakarta), then under Dutch control, to round out her reporting. Almost immediately the Unwilling Companion started missing his mate, to whom he would write a bittersweet series of letters on his way home. Without her, the pleasures of traveling in Asia were beginning to wear thin. A letter from his editor, Max Perkins, with news of the deaths of the writers Sherwood Anderson and Virginia Woolf, did not help his mood. He noted edgily that writers were "certainly dying like flies."[34] He had little in common with Woolf, but he would miss Anderson, just as he was feeling the loss of the writers who had died in 1939 and 1940, especially his onetime close friend F. Scott Fitzgerald.[35] After he started to fly east by stages from Hong Kong, he grew ever more surly, drinking bad Chinese liquor by himself during the long flights over water and snarling at his many admirers during layovers. A fellow journalist remembered him as "curt and belligerent," especially to anyone who asked him what he had been doing in China.[36]

From May 6 to 12, the impatient traveler stopped in the Philippines, then a dependency of the United States. It was the country's farthest—and most exposed—military and naval base in the Pacific, one that would be overrun by the Japanese in less than a year. While in Manila, Hemingway met with the local G-2, the designation for American military intelligence. He appears to have shared his impressions of the war in China, most likely including some reflections on Japanese intentions and capabilities. As he put it in a letter to Gellhorn a few days later, he performed "several G-2 errands" in Manila, spending time with officers who "seemed very grateful for the stuff" he gave them.[37] But he quickly added that there were limits to what he was prepared to do for the government. In the next line he continued, "You and I must *not* get fucked up with this present *goofy* war set up." Eventually they would have to pitch in and help win the impending war. But for the time being they owed it to themselves and their "childies [*sic*] and mother and the Holy ghost" to focus on their "trades of writing."[38]

What was on Hemingway's mind when he wrote this strange

letter? He still had mixed feelings about the American (and British) government, a holdover from the Spanish Civil War. It would take him a long time to get over his anger at the democracies for neglecting the Republic and not doing more to fight fascism early on. But perhaps a bit of his world-weary attitude now also applied to the Soviets. A few months earlier, after completing his bestseller *For Whom the Bell Tolls* and marrying a vibrant young woman, he had been ready for more adventure. On that upswing he had accepted the pitch from the NKVD and declared himself ready to travel to yet another war on an unfamiliar continent. But as his energy began to wane toward the end of the trip, he sounded ready to withdraw from the world again, at least for a while, as he had when he returned from Spain.

In mid-June, the untimely death of his fishing companion Joe Russell, the owner of the Key West bar Sloppy Joe's, took a further toll on him. (Even in his formal letter to Morgenthau, Hemingway described Russell as "one of my best friends" and said that he had canceled a trip to New York and Washington on account of Russell's death.[39]) It was once again time to rest and recuperate and to focus on writing before the next adventure: the coming war between America and the Axis, which he believed was not far off. Anyone who wanted to make serious demands on Hemingway's time and energy would simply have to wait. This included any Soviet intelligence officers who wanted to coax some production from the new recruit with such good potential.

In the meantime Hemingway was still happy to expound on his views and respond to one-of-a-kind calls from powerful political figures. By June 1941 he found himself in New York, where he sat for the interview with Ralph Ingersoll that was published in his daily *PM*. It was a classic Hemingway tour-de-force: some tall tales, interesting facts, one or two good insights, and many sweeping generalizations.[40] From New York he proceeded to Washington, where he met at least briefly with Treasury secretary Morgenthau, whom he was still eager to please.[41] The details of the meeting are lost, but it is a fair bet that he made predictions about the future and offered free advice.[42]

A few weeks later Hemingway wrote a long letter to the secretary.[43] The writer elaborated on a topic he had not covered in detail during their last meeting—namely, the friction in China between the Nationalists and the communists, something that was hard to exaggerate. He judged that there existed a serious risk of civil war. Hemingway was respectful but not shy about recommending a policy: making "it perfectly clear at all times that we will not finance civil war in any way."[44] That is, the United States should withhold aid if Chiang turned his guns on the communists.

Strictly speaking, Hemingway was not spying in China. There were no secret meetings. No one gave up, stole, or bought any state secrets. But he and Gellhorn had been granted private audiences, and confidences had been shared. Both the communists and the Nationalists used him to deliver their messages to the American public and the American government, while the secretary of the Treasury got a personal briefing from an experienced traveler fresh from China. It was not too different from going to the Gaylord in Madrid in 1937 and 1938. Once again Hemingway found it gratifying to be an insider dealing with senior officials.

The meeting with Morgenthau was especially gratifying. The difference between Chiang or Chou and Morgenthau was that the secretary wanted to hear what Hemingway had to say, not the other way around. Part of Hemingway's motivation for dealing with the NKVD was that Washington had not listened to him during the Spanish Civil War. Now that was changing. Talking to politicians may not have been quite as exciting as spying, but for someone who was tired of international intrigue it was not a bad substitute. Perhaps this is why Hemingway does not appear to have done much to follow up on his meeting with Golos; he now had other things to do that suited him just as well.

The man who had brokered the relationship with Morgenthau and given Hemingway something to do other than spy for the

Soviets was himself "the most highly placed" Soviet spy in the American government.[45] A longtime communist sympathizer, Morgenthau's right-hand man Harry Dexter White was secretly passing privileged information to Soviet intelligence. He knew exactly what he was doing and what the risks were. From the Soviet point of view, the problem with White was that he was not good at taking direction. Not unlike Hemingway, he was a man who believed that he could and should run his own foreign policy. He decided what to share with the Soviets and how to meet with them.

There is no evidence that the Soviets directed him to contact Hemingway or that White passed Hemingway's information along to the Soviets. Nor is it likely that either suspected the other of having a special relationship with the NKVD. It is hard to imagine that these two secretive men would have taken the enormous risk of sharing their secrets. When White asked Hemingway to report on China, he was almost certainly acting on behalf of the Treasury, not Moscow.

A further irony is that the mission in China segued into a relationship with another intelligence service that would come to mean much more to Hemingway than his relationship with the Soviets. The story begins with an eccentric soldier of fortune named Charles Sweeny, said to have been an officer in the French Foreign Legion. He and Hemingway had been friends since the 1920s. The writer always had time for Sweeny, especially when there was a war on and he was promoting some sort of wild scheme with his trademark passion. Sweeny attracted friends who, like himself, did not fit any particular mold, which made it natural for him to take Hemingway to meet another American original, the U.S. Marine lieutenant colonel John W. Thomason, Jr.

Impeccable in his formfitting uniform, with his short dark brown hair parted in the middle, this proud Texan was a veteran of World War I, a hero of the grim fighting in the trenches in 1918. He was a heavy drinker, even by the liver-challenging Marine standards of the day, as well as an accomplished sketch artist and short-story writer. (His sea stories, especially those collected in his first book, *Fix Bayonets,* were on the road to becoming cult pieces for generations of Marines.) Hemingway and Thomason were already aware of each other's existence. Among other connections, they shared the same editor, the redoubtable Max Perkins.[46]

In the summer of 1941 Thomason was in the Washington Office of Naval Intelligence at "Main Navy," a plain concrete office building that had been put up as a temporary headquarters in 1918.[47] It was part of the sprawling complex of rectangular "tempos" that had taken over the mall between the Lincoln and Washington Memorials. Since they would have entered Main Navy through the portal on Constitution Avenue, Hemingway and Gellhorn probably did not notice the building's only redeeming feature—its location alongside the Reflecting Pool, which Lincoln looked out on. Instead it was the bureaucracy that left an impression on Gellhorn; she remembered later that she and Hemingway had been "convoked . . . to answer questions about China" and "went surlily" to tell "desk Intelligence Officers that the Communists would take over China, after this war."[48]

She was right about everything but the surliness. The tone of the meeting was upbeat. Impressed with her analysis, Thomason commented to Perkins, with just a hint of condescension, that "she appears to be something of a person herself"—that is, not just an appendage to "the very sensible and decent" Hemingway.[49] Above all, Thomason was happy to finally meet the legendary author and hoped to see a lot more of him. He would get his wish. In the months to come, the world war would spread to the Americas, and the two warrior-writers, Thomason and Hemingway, would look for ways to fight the Nazis in the Caribbean together.

CHAPTER 7

THE CROOK FACTORY

A Secret War on Land

In 1942 Special Agent R. G. Leddy of the FBI was assigned to the American Embassy in Cuba, on the elegant Paseo del Prado, which ran from the harbor to the capitol and separated the old town of Havana from the new. The Prado featured a raised promenade shaded by laurel trees and graced with marble benches in between the two lanes of traffic. The embassy was located in a columnated mansion-turned-chancery built by former president José Miguel Gomez for his family sometime after the turn of the century.

All we know about Leddy's life and work is that he represented the Bureau in Cuba, and that Hemingway detested him for that reason. One afternoon that spring at a jai alai match—the game akin to squash, but played with a hard ball that careens around the court at dangerous speeds—Hemingway introduced him to a Cuban friend as a member of the American Gestapo. Hemingway later said that he was joking, but Leddy did not believe him. The writer soon showed his true colors again, when the Havana police picked up a tall—six-foot-five—young American sportsman named Winston Guest, who was working for Hemingway, took him to the central police station, and roughed him up. When they released him, Guest drove out to the Finca to report to Hemingway.

Guest's story enraged the writer. He saw the hand of the FBI behind the arrest, imagining that the Bureau was working against him, Hemingway, through its liaison officer with the Cuban police.

Even though it was now well after midnight, Hemingway loaded Guest, still dressed for dinner in black tie and tuxedo, into his car for the ten mile drive to a modest studio apartment near the Havana waterfront. It was the home of an American diplomat named Robert Joyce who was doing his best to coordinate the work of the FBI with that of amateur spies like Hemingway. When he opened the door, Joyce saw that the normally easygoing Guest was on the verge of tears, and that Hemingway was "in a towering rage." It would not be easy to placate him.

Playing the honest broker, Joyce summoned Leddy and told him to pass the word to the Cubans to leave Guest alone. While Hemingway glared at him, Leddy "listened grimly," then "silently departed." Joyce's intervention defused the immediate crisis but made no difference in the long run. Hemingway's attitude toward the FBI would only worsen over time, with unforeseeable consequences for him.[1]

Hemingway was in love with the island country that was only ninety miles from Key West, but already foreign and exotic, with its own tropical, Hispanic lilt and louche ways. It was the exceptional marlin run in 1932 that had first pulled Hemingway to "the great, deep blue river," his name for the Gulf Stream off Cuba.[2] That year a two-week expedition had stretched into two months. It was the beginning of the longest love affair of his life.

The Gulf Stream very nearly abutted Cuba's capital city, Havana, running some two hundred yards from El Morro, the massive sixteenth-century Spanish fortress that guarded the entrance to the harbor. The lighthouse keeper at the fortress could glimpse the Stream when he looked out to sea. Looking the other away, across an inlet, he could see the old city, with its church spires and pink, yellow, and blue townhouses that started at the water. Said to be the third highest in the world, the dome of the capitol was impossible to miss. To some this clone of the American Capitol in Washington, DC, looked out of place, which perhaps made it a fitting reminder

that the powerful neighbor to the north liked to reserve the right to interfere in Cuban politics.

After 1932, Hemingway was repeatedly drawn back to Cuba, usually on fishing trips. By the end of the decade, he had made the island his home. It was around the time of his meetings with the NKVD recruiter Golos in 1940 that he bought Finca Vigía—literally, "Lookout Farm," after its position on a hill a few miles outside Havana, the ocean just barely visible in the distance. On the Finca, thirteen acres of banana trees, tropical shrubs, and casual gardens surrounded a ramshackle but inviting one-story stucco villa built by a Catalan architect in 1886 and usually painted some shade of white. An ancient ceiba tree spread its branches in welcome near the front door to Hemingway and his wives and their cats and dogs and especially their books. Most rooms would soon turn into branches of the main library in Hemingway's study. Stacks of books sprouted on almost every available surface; by 1961 there would be something like 7,500 books in the house.

The American writer liked the choices and the freedom that this island offered the well-to-do expatriate. Life in Cuba was more colorful and exciting than life at home. The rules were different—that is, when there were any rules at all. Of course there was the superb fishing, but, as Hemingway told his readers back on the mainland, there was also the shooting club, where you shot at live pigeons instead of clay discs; cockfighting, already illegal in many American states; and Cuban baseball, where the old uncle at bat could tap his young nephew to run the bases for him when he hit the ball. The uncle and the nephew were among Hemingway's accepting neighbors in San Francisco de Paula, the village down the street from the Finca, and they made for another draw. Last, but hardly least, Hemingway enjoyed the cool and quiet early mornings in Cuba, as conducive to writing as any other time and place he knew. He liked to get up at dawn and work by himself, at first in his workroom in the heart of town at the Ambos Mundos, the somewhat formal, European-looking hotel that he favored when he first came to Havana; and after 1940 in one of the breezy, sunlit rooms at the Finca. When he wrote, a cat or a dog almost invariably padded into the room and stretched out at his feet on the cool yellow tiles.

Cuban society also suited the native of the rule-bound suburbs of Chicago. It was much less formal than American society. As he noted happily, a man only had to put on shoes when he went into town, and even most special occasions only called for a clean white shirt and long pants. The first time the American ambassador to Cuba invited Hemingway to dine at his residence, Spruille Braden found out that the expatriate writer did not have any "dinner clothes," and had to borrow jacket and dress shirt from friends.[3] (The jacket fit, but not the shirt, and Hemingway had to cinch the black tie up to close the collar.)

Braden called the Cuban form of government "gangsterismo."[4] Like many former colonies, Cuba had a small, corrupt ruling class that lived in privilege and comfort well apart from the lower classes that it took for granted or abused with indifferent cruelty. Even though he always said that he opposed the right-wing Cuban dictatorships, Hemingway could move with ease in both high and low circles. He was able to enjoy his memberships in clubs for the elite, and to connect with men who worked with their hands. This was especially true if they had a skill that he valued, usually something to do with fishing, boating, or shooting.

Cuba was where Hemingway found himself after China, settling back into the pleasant rhythm of island life. He seemed to be keeping his options open, telling a friend in August 1941 that he should not try to plan on doing anything together with Hemingway, because there was "a very good chance" that he would travel to China again or even to Russia in the near future.[5] This was a reflection of his—and Gellhorn's—restlessness during the summer of 1941. The burning question for them both was—still—what part they would take in the new world war. Gellhorn continued to feel an urge to ride to the sound of the guns, where she could write stories about great events. Hemingway still wanted to engage, but adopted more of a wait-and-see attitude.

The Soviet Union was now engulfed by war. Hitler had spent the first part of 1941 priming his war machine to invade. This was a massive undertaking that was nearly impossible to disguise, but Stalin willfully ignored the many warnings that came his way. One of those reports came from the great Soviet spy Richard Sorge, a German communist accredited as a foreign correspondent in Tokyo. Pretending to be a good Nazi, he worked his way into the confidences of the German Embassy in Tokyo and repeatedly risked his life to send secret messages to Moscow by shortwave radio.[6] Another warning was from the British prime minister, Winston Churchill, who was more than a little frustrated when Stalin did not react. Churchill later described how the Soviet leadership "supinely awaited . . . the fearful onslaught that impended upon Russia. We had hitherto rated them as selfish calculators. In this period they were proved simpletons as well. . . . So far as strategy, policy, foresight, competence are arbiters, Stalin and his commissars showed themselves at this moment the most completely outwitted bunglers of the Second World War."[7]

The German army and air force tore into the Soviet Union on June 22, 1941. About 145 divisions attacked along a front that stretched one thousand miles from north to south. From one moment to the next, the Soviet borderlands—part swamp, part featureless plain—went from subsisting as primitive backwaters, remarkable mostly for not being remarkable, to serving as the first line of defense, where hundreds of thousands of soldiers clashed in epic battles.

Its leadership gutted by Stalin's purges, the Red Army was not ready to fight, and the Germans won battle after battle in the first few months of the campaign, advancing relentlessly to the east (and for a while reducing Stalin to something like a catatonic state—even he had to admit to himself how badly he had miscalculated). In the third and fourth quarters of 1941, more than 2,993,000 Red Army soldiers were killed or went missing in action, to say nothing of the staggering numbers of prisoners captured by the Germans, some 400,000 in the first few weeks of the war alone.[8]

Late in the year the Soviets counterattacked with fresh troops from the Far East, stabilizing the front just west of Moscow and setting the stage for three and a half more years of savage warfare. The Eastern Front was, unquestionably, the most manpower- and matériel-intensive theater in the war. Its scale dwarfed most other battlegrounds of this, the greatest armed conflict in world history. Statistics tell the story clearly: between 80 and 90 percent of the German casualties in World War II would occur on this front. This meant that something like four *million* German soldiers would die in the East, along with an estimated eleven *million* Soviet soldiers.[9]

Now, more than ever, it made sense to think of the Soviet Union as *the* premier antifascist power. The Soviets seemed to be the only ones doing any real fighting, and they deserved the world's support. The *New Masses* editor Joseph Freeman (who had met Hemingway in the 1920s, helped to introduce his writing to the Soviets, and written a memoir, called *American Testament,* that was on Hemingway's bookshelf in Key West) thought the same way. The inevitable had finally happened. The two diametrically opposed systems were now fighting, and the outcome would be decisive:[10]

> *The Nazi system must be exterminated completely before the world can make any further progress, and the USSR has hurled into the breach the greatest single force capable of dealing that system a mortal blow. America ought to give the Red Army all the help it needs so that it may give us all the help we need.*

When, in the summer of 1941, Hemingway mentioned the possibility of traveling to Russia or returning to China, he may have been thinking of another stint of war reporting from the front lines. That is what the context and his most recent history suggest. Why not just continue the stream of reporting that he—and Gellhorn—had begun in China?

There was another possibility. He may have remembered that the Soviets still wanted him to travel overseas on spy business. A few months later, in November 1941, a message from Moscow Center directed the NKVD's New York station to "look for an opportunity for him [Hemingway] to travel abroad to countries of interest to us," presumably to interact with the elite and collect information as he had in China.[11] Underlying this message was the assumption by NKVD headquarters that its station in New York was in touch with Hemingway, or at least had a secret means of getting in touch with him. No one can tell from this tantalizing fragment whether New York acted on the message. But the Soviets did reach out to Hemingway in another way.

Sometime after the German invasion, Hemingway received a telegram from the Soviet foreign minister, Vyacheslav Molotov, one of the architects of the infamous prewar Nazi-Soviet Pact, cordially inviting him to visit the Soviet Union. Molotov said that a large sum in rubles would be at his disposal, representing royalties from the sale of his books.[12] Since the ruble was not traded in the West—it could not be exported or exchanged for dollars—the Soviets could not simply send Hemingway a check, but they could invite him to spend the money in their country.

It is hard to take this proposal at face value. This was not a good time to sample the delights of the Soviet Union. The western half of the country was a charred battleground. No Soviet official could forget for a minute that armies of German tanks were advancing on Moscow and, in the north, on Leningrad, the cultural capital. Did the cynical hard-liner Molotov, or a subordinate permitted to act for him, actually take time off from the struggle for survival to worry about paying royalties to a foreigner? Or was this invitation a pretext for getting Hemingway to Moscow, where the NKVD could spend time with him, getting to know him and turning him into a productive spy? The Soviets desperately needed friends and material support. Perhaps they could induce Hemingway to intercede in some way with the influential Americans he routinely met. At the very least, he was likely to write a favorable article or two about the Soviet army, which he said he admired so much.[13] It would not have been the first time that the nearly all-powerful NKVD had requested, or directed, the Foreign Ministry to act on its behalf. Seeing the Germans at the gates of the capital might have completed the conversion of the half-committed antifascist spy—just as the defense of Madrid had pushed him to the left four years earlier.

Hemingway never did travel to the Soviet Union. Early on the morning of Sunday, December 7, 1941, Japanese navy planes struck the American naval base at Pearl Harbor, on the Hawaiian island of Oahu, wreaking havoc on Battleship Row and killing some two thousand American servicemen. The day after the attack, while smoke was still rising over the wreckage, President Roosevelt spoke to Congress, committing December 7 to history as the day that would "live in infamy" and asking the joint session to declare war on Japan. Then, in a somewhat unexpected chain reaction, Germany declared war on the United States. America was now at war on three continents, from one side of the globe to the other.

Hemingway heard about Pearl Harbor over the radio when he was driving south across the Texas state line on his way back to Cuba from an idyllic autumn in Sun Valley, Idaho, spent hunting with Gellhorn and his sons. Once again he felt grimly vindicated. The predictions he had made when he visited Pearl in early 1941—that American ships and planes were vulnerable because they were clustered together—had come true. Four days later, from one of the first motor hotels in Texas, the Park Mo-Tel at 3617 Broadway in San Antonio, he wrote Max Perkins that "the myth of our matchless navy has been exploded."[14]

Hemingway's short-term remedy for the disaster was straightforward: the secretary of the Navy should have been relieved within two hours and "those responsible at Oahu . . . shot."[15] (Since the American way was different from the Soviet way, Admiral Husband

E. Kimmel and General Walter C. Short, the two officers who had been in command at Pearl on December 7, would not lose their lives. But they would die another kind of death, as a never-ending series of official investigations questioned their competence and their honor.)

At 5:45 the next morning, Hemingway was at it again, writing his publisher, Charles Scribner, that through "laziness, criminal carelessness, and blind arrogance we are fucked in this war as of the first day and we are going to have Christ's own bitter time to win it if, when, and ever."[16] He did not use the same terms for the wartime Soviet leadership, whose record in the early months of their war arguably was far worse than that of their American counterparts.

On the contrary, his positive opinion of the Soviets was still on display in March 1942, when he and Gellhorn went to Mexico City to attend a few bullfights and visit friends.[17] At the time, Mexico was second only to Spain in its devotion to bullfighting. Many Mexican cities featured a bullring downtown, and organized festivals around fights, like the one in Pamplona that Hemingway had made famous in his early masterpiece, *The Sun Also Rises.* Mexico was also still one of the few countries to welcome political refugees from the left. The best known refugee was Leon Trotsky, Stalin's archenemy, who spent the last years of his life on a quiet, tree-lined street in the part of Mexico City called Coyoacán, not far from the bright blue home of his sometime lover, the famous Mexican artist Frida Kahlo.

Trotsky's house was much less welcoming. It was more like a small fortress, with high walls, iron shutters, and armed guards in a watchtower overlooking the street. Trotsky was trying to protect himself from the long reach of the NKVD. Local party members harassed the great revolutionary, and not just with placards and insults. In May 1940 the NKVD dispatched a carload of Mexican communists, including the well-known artist David Siqueiros, to fire machine guns at the doors and windows while driving by. They missed Trotsky but hit his grandson and abducted one of his bodyguards, whom they later murdered. A few months later, in August, an NKVD assassin posing as a friend killed Trotsky with one blow to the back of the head from an ice ax, the kind that mountain climbers carry.

Hemingway's close friend from the Spanish Civil War lived in a humbler part of town to the south called Ajusco. The former commissar Gustav Regler had fallen on hard times. By now he had openly left the fold. "The Communist Party issued a secret order—'Regler is no longer with us, therefore he is against us.'"[18] This led to vicious cartoons in a Mexican newspaper depicting him as a Nazi and a Trotskyite, a ridiculous combination but still serious business if it incited local communists to do harm. Unknown youths started watching Regler's house. When he came to visit, the writer acknowledged the threat but did not seem to grasp what it represented. "He saw nothing but the physical danger," the German wrote in his memoirs, "and gave me money for a revolver."[19]

Hemingway urged his friend to look past the attacks in the press. Probably after a bullfight, Hemingway, Regler, and Regler's wife, Marie Louise, went for drinks at the Tampico Club. It was a restaurant that attracted the well-to-do and the artistic alike, in Mexico City's *centro historico* among elegant Spanish colonial buildings. The drinks loosened Hemingway's political inhibitions, just as they had when he drank vodka with Orlov in Spain and enthused about the Republican cause. Once outside the club, Hemingway could not restrain himself. He had something important to say to Regler. He "clapped his hand" on Regler's shoulder and "thrust [him] against the marble facade" of the restaurant.[20]

"Why did you leave them [the communists]?" Hemingway wanted to know. Marie Louise tried to intervene, but Hemingway would not take his hands off his friend, who was still weak after being wounded in Spain and then interned by the French in primitive camps. Hemingway "was in an alarming state of emotional confusion. 'Why did you believe [in] them in Spain? There has to be an organization and they have one. Go back to them!'" Hemingway finally let go of Regler, but he was not finished. Calmer but with no

A thinner and more pensive Gustav Regler at work in his home office in Mexico, ca. 1944. *Copyright © Annemay Regler-Repplinger.*

less urgency, he told Regler that the democracies were all but helpless against the Nazis. "The US is finished, just like France. . . . The Russians are the only ones who are doing any fighting."[21]

Neither Regler nor Hemingway ever forgot their encounter in Mexico. In a remarkable letter that he drafted in February 1947 in his own distinctive hand, Hemingway lamented that his good and very brave friend had left the Communist Party at the time of the Nazi-Soviet Pact.[22] Communism for Regler had been "like religion to a . . . *croyant* [a believer]," Hemingway wrote. In Mexico in 1942 Regler had been "as miserable as an unfrocked priest." He and his friends spoke as if the NKVD torture cells had played the central role in the Spanish Civil War. It came down to that for Regler. He focused only on the atrocities, apparently unable to remember why he had fought for the Republic. Hemingway admitted he knew "about the people *we* [emphasis added] shot in Spain, many times wrongly," but that was only the "smallest part of what went on." While he acknowledged the shooting of innocents, he focused on what he saw as the greater good, the struggle against fascism, driven by the Soviet Union in 1942 as in 1936.

Pearl Harbor changed the complexion of life in America. Early on, the attack spawned a wave of nativism. Many perfectly honest and patriotic citizens who happened to have ties to Japan or Germany came under suspicion—or worse. In the states on the Pacific Coast, tens of thousands of Japanese Americans were interned for the duration of the war, ostensibly to prevent them from committing acts of sabotage or espionage. Along the way they lost their homes and businesses.

Cuba joined the United States in the war against the Axis, and the situation on the island was not much different from that on the mainland. Here, too, the hunt was on for subversive enemy aliens. With their Spanish Civil War experience, Hemingway and Gellhorn were confident that they understood the threat. As Gellhorn would write to her editor at *Collier's,* Charles Colebaugh, a few months later, there were "770 Germans . . . and 30,000 Spaniards . . . [in] the [local] Spanish Fascist secret society."[23] They could organize a Fifth Column, a secret corps of activists, to undermine the government. It was important not to overestimate the threat, but it was something to keep in mind. Among others, the U.S. ambassador was "constantly and intensely concerned with local Nazi activities."[24]

Gellhorn knew that otherwise reasonable American officials were listening to all manner of far-fetched stories and that they were reporting these accounts to Washington. Many, if not most, of the reports were just gossip or rumor. As early as September 1939 the embassy in Havana, for instance, found "increasing confirmation of the pro-Hitler sentiment among perhaps the majority of local Spanish merchants . . . [who] are, however, guarded in betraying their real feelings," which must have left readers in Washington wondering how anyone could know what those "real feelings" were.[25]

Another pointless report, this one generated by an FBI confidential informant, sent to Washington and circulated at the highest levels of the FBI and the State Department, contained information on an unnamed older Italian gentleman with buck teeth who worked on the ship *Recca* and visited a youth named Hoppe, bringing him hawthorns and other fresh fruits.[26] There was nothing to explain what made any of this suspicious or worth reporting.

Along the way, Embassy Havana took note of Hemingway, the militant antifascist who knew his way around town—and seemed to understand the mysterious art of intelligence. The naval attaché, a Marine colonel named Hayne D. Boyden, reported to Washington that Hemingway was not afraid to confront fascists whenever and wherever he found them. There was, for example, the case of a man named Michael Pfeiffer, "one of the most disagreeable and loud-mouthed supporters of the Hitler regime [who] . . . sounds off at every opportunity . . . [and] would have engaged in a fist fight with Ernest Hemingway over the qualifications of the *Führer* [Adolf Hitler] if he had not feared a beating."[27]

Another man at the embassy who was cultivating the writer was the Yale-educated diplomat Robert P. Joyce. In his official photo Joyce looks like an intelligent, perhaps intellectual, member of the eastern establishment. He is stylishly dressed in a dark blue pinstriped suit and stares at the camera with a hint of arrogance. In the accompanying photo, his wife, Jane, seems cool, elegant, and handsome. She looks like the perfect complement to this young man on his way up.

The relationship between Hemingway and Joyce did not start well. When they first met in the late spring of 1941, Joyce perceived in Hemingway "a mild but polite hostility and a complete lack of interest in any future meetings. This attitude, I soon learned, was his habitual stance of dislike and suspicion in all his dealings with civilian government officials and authority in general. [But] . . . Ernest soon found out I was a poorly disciplined, inefficient, and unenthusiastic bureaucrat."[28]

The American diplomat Robert Joyce, perhaps Hemingway's best friend at the American Embassy in Havana, ca. 1941. *National Archives, College Park.*

Joyce was actually a man with considerable bureaucratic skills, just one who was not hobbled by convention. His approach to life made it possible for the two men to become friends. Joyce became a regular at the Finca, where he and Jane were often the only guests at dinner on Sunday afternoons, and would linger over drinks deep into the tropical night with Hemingway and Gellhorn. Joyce was comfortable with them even though he shared "none of Ernest's outdoor enthusiasms such as . . . the shooting of animals or people in wartime."[29] Hemingway toned down some of his more extreme views, enabling the two men to join in hating what Joyce called

"Hitlerism, Marxist-Leninist totalitarian communism, . . . [and] petty bourgeois conformity."[30]

It was probably in early 1942 that the writer first told Joyce that he, Hemingway, could do his part for the war effort by setting up a counterintelligence bureau in Havana. The members of the bureau could keep an eye on actual and potential Axis sympathizers, those Germans and Spaniards whom Gellhorn had written about. Hemingway explained how he had learned the necessary skills in Madrid in 1937 when he had worked with Republican counterintelligence. (His play *The Fifth Column* had hinted at his ability to uncover fascist spies in Spain.) He said he would even be willing to use his own money to fund a similar endeavor in Cuba.[31]

This idea was quite different from spying for the Soviets. Hemingway had not ended his relationship with them, but at least for the time being wanted to devote his time to a different kind of intelligence operation, one that he would initiate and control himself. Taking charge was something that he wanted throughout his life as spy.

Hemingway's idea was worth discussing with Joyce's boss, the other Yale man at the embassy, Spruille Braden. Ambassador Braden had the kind of physical presence that Hemingway understood; he was a powerfully built man who had been a champion swimmer and boxer in his youth. He was still agile, and his energetic, graceful tango "belied his 260 pounds."[32] In the summer of 1942 the ambassador agreed to meet at La Florida, a sign of his flexibility. Hemingway's downtown haunt—*Floridita* or "Little Florida" to regulars—was too casual for most diplomats. The stucco on the outside was usually pale pink; the interior featured black and white tiles and a long, mahogany-colored bar in front of a large mirror framed by wooden columns. Patrons wandered in and out through the eleven doors that were open to the street, which made it easy for Hemingway to invite anyone who made him angry to step outside for a fistfight. Later on the waiters would take to wearing slightly comical red jackets.

Braden and Hemingway quickly found common ground, even if Braden was careful to keep some distance between them. (When Hemingway later asked the ambassador to box with him, the older man declined after feeling the writer's arms and finding them "as large as the average man's legs and hard as rock."[33]) But Braden liked the idea of setting up an amateur counterintelligence bureau so much that he later claimed it as his own.

Braden had what he called "one of my better brainwaves" when he realized that Hemingway was "friendly with all kinds of people" in Havana and that the embassy could exploit his circle of friends.[34] In August 1942 the ambassador told the members of his staff about his plans for enlisting Hemingway's services.[35] Keeping track of enemy aliens actually fell under the purview of the FBI, which stationed a few special agents at the embassy, but the legal attaché's office would be shorthanded for a few months. In the meantime, there was Hemingway. When Braden summoned the writer to the embassy, the ambassador declared that "these Spaniards have got to be watched," now and later, and asked Hemingway to take up the slack. The novelist-cum-spymaster readily agreed and got to work on what he came to call "the Crook Factory," his variation on "Crime Section," the more bureaucratic term that the embassy used for the operation.

As head of the Crook Factory, Hemingway reported to Joyce, for whom Braden had created the unusual position of the embassy's chief of intelligence. This meant that the unfortunate diplomat was caught up in all sorts of turf battles, between the Army and Navy as well as Hemingway and the FBI.[36] Coordination was something that no one in the United States government was good at; every department and agency was notoriously independent, best at protecting and serving its own interests.

Braden was right about Hemingway's ability to mobilize what the ambassador remembered as "a bizarre combination of . . . bartenders; . . . wharf rats; . . . down-at-heel pelota players and former bullfighters; . . . Basque priests; assorted exiled counts and dukes; several [Spanish] Loyalists."[37] In all there were between twenty and twenty-five members of the Crook Factory, a few working as full-time informants and the rest on a part-time basis. Starting in September 1942 with a budget of about five hundred dollars a month, they went about their work in unusual ways.[38]

Joyce liked to tell a story about a "rich playboy" whom Hemingway code-named R-42 and sent on a mission to Mariel, thirty miles from Havana. Hemingway told Joyce he had "instructed R-42 to put up at the local bordello which is the best place to stay at Mariel. It's clean and serves well-cooked food. The Madam is a retired Havana whore; she is a friend of mine and a good woman. [To pass the time when off duty] I gave him to read . . . [Ernest] Renan's *Life of Jesus*."[39] When Joyce asked how the agent had liked the nineteenth-century French bestseller that portrayed Jesus more as a man than a god, Hemingway replied: "Bob, R-42 was so fascinated with the book that when he was half[way] through he turned to the last chapter . . . to find out how it all came out."[40]

Simply to focus on the bizarre combination of characters in the Crook Factory, or to write off R-42—almost certainly Hemingway's loyal and accomplished assistant Winston Guest—as a rich playboy, is to sell them short. True, Hemingway had an odd assortment of friends that he put to work. True, the Factory was not a professional counterintelligence service that built cases in a systematic way through surveillance or infiltration. There were no guidelines for targeting. It was not clear what the agents were looking for; they would somehow know it when they saw it: perhaps a foreign businessman standing at the long curved bar in the Floridita asking too many questions about the ships in port, or a socialite in black tie at a late-night dinner party telling Winston Guest how the Axis would win the war. When they had something to report, the agents would make their way out to the Finca, settle in among the bookcases and overstuffed chairs in Hemingway's fifty-foot-long living room, and drink while they talked in a haphazard mixture of Spanish and English. The bottles never seemed to run out and the "staff meetings" would last well into the early morning hours.

Hemingway's leadership style may have been unconventional but it was effective. He inspired loyalty and enthusiasm in his workforce. Despite the alcohol, Hemingway made his agents focus on detail and debriefed them thoroughly. After the meetings, he might stay up for the rest of the night, painstakingly writing and editing reports, before driving the twelve miles from the Finca to the embassy after daybreak. Forgoing the front door under the official seal that faced the Paseo del Prado, he would enter by a discreet side door and deliver his take to Joyce, who was impressed by Hemingway's diligence. After the war, he would remember that the author had "produced a great mass of reports."[41]

Not surprisingly, the Bureau did not think much of the Factory's work; Leddy informed Washington that its products were worthless.[42] But the most important customer at the embassy—the ambassador himself—found them at least as useful as the other reports that were crossing his desk. He cabled Washington in November 1942 that Hemingway was "developing information on Spanish activities . . . [that was] accurate, carefully checked, and rechecked, and is proving of very real value."[43] In other words, while the Factory did not uncover any fascist spies, or enable the ambassador to shift the balance of power in Cuba, it did cover a subject that he cared about.

That Joyce and Braden generally sided with Hemingway did nothing to improve his standing with the FBI. When Joyce had announced that the embassy planned to enlist Hemingway's services, Leddy had "pointed out to Mr. Joyce . . . that some consideration should be given to the question of the relationship between Mr. Hemingway and the Bureau representatives."[44] Leddy remembered that Hemingway had signed an open letter denouncing the FBI in 1940 for arresting activists in Detroit who had supported the Spanish Republic, which was a violation of the Neutrality Act. For that reason, Hemingway was "accused of being of Communist sympathy, although we are advised that he has denied and [continues to] . . . vigorously deny any Communist affiliation or sympathy."[45] Then there was the way Hemingway had introduced Leddy at the jai alai match in Havana. It was Joyce who tried to reassure Leddy that Hemingway was not against the FBI: the writer was always signing one petition or another without focusing on its content and had been joking when he compared the FBI to the Gestapo.[46]

This was not true, and Joyce knew it. Joyce and Hemingway were shaping the message to fit the audience and the job at hand. In reality, as Joyce wrote later, "Ernest [typically] reacted with violent hostility to the F.B.I. and all its works and personnel."[47] For one thing, he apparently believed that because many FBI agents happened to be Roman Catholics, they were Franco sympathizers. He liked to refer to the FBI as "Franco's Bastard Irish" and "Franco's Iron Cavalry." Hemingway felt that, in Joyce's words, the FBI understood "nothing about the subtleties of sophisticated intelligence in wartime." To him they were "simple-minded, flat-footed cops" without overseas experience. He considered them to be amateurs while he, with his experience from the Spanish Civil War, was the professional.[48]

Hemingway was wrong when he accused the Bureau of lacking sophistication. Declassified FBI records show a nuanced reaction to his encroachment on its turf. While at least one agent believed the FBI should confront the amateur Hemingway and unmask him as a "phony," J. Edgar Hoover himself stepped in to ensure that the Bureau would tread carefully. On the one hand, the director instructed his representative in Havana "to discuss diplomatically with Ambassador Braden the disadvantages" of allowing someone like Hemingway, who was not a government official, into the fold.[49] On the other hand, Hoover did not want to press the case, because Hemingway had the ambassador's ear as well as ties to the White House. (The president himself told Hoover about Hemingway's initiative for the United States to help Europeans interned in Cuba, most of them victims of fascism, while Hemingway made it clear to a special agent in Havana that "the FBI had better get along with him because he carried a lot of weight in Washington."[50]) None of this changed the director's attitude to employing the writer. For Hoover, Hemingway was "the last man . . . to be used in any such capacity. His judgment [was] not of the best" and his record of heavy drinking made his aptitude for intelligence work all the more "questionable."[51]

Hemingway's interest in intelligence was enduring but some of his adventures in spying were short-lived. One enthusiasm could yield to the next after a few weeks or months. The Crook Factory was one example of this. Before long the author was ready to move on. Joyce surmised that this was because Hemingway had come to doubt that the Factory was the best use of his time. But since the amateur spy did not want to turn his back on his creation, he looked for a way for it to continue under new leadership.[52]

Whatever his motivation, Hemingway told Joyce that he wanted to turn the operation over to a Spaniard named Gustavo Durán, who had been "active with him [Hemingway] in intelligence work on the Republican side during the Spanish Civil War."[53] Durán was yet another one of the remarkable men who came in and out of the author's life. Along with angular good looks, he possessed an amazing array of talents. In Hemingway's words, Durán was "a military and intelligence genius of the type like Napoleon that comes along once in a hundred years."[54] He started out as a composer and art impresario with left-wing sympathies. In 1936 Durán committed himself wholeheartedly to the Spanish Republic. Although he had virtually no military training, just an instinctive talent for combat, he rose to the level of division commander and was also briefly head of the Military Intelligence Service, the SIM, which worked largely under the direction of Alexander Orlov, the NKVD chieftain who had befriended Hemingway in 1937. After the war Durán made his way to the United Kingdom, where he married an American socialite named Bontë Crompton.[55] About this time Hemingway wrote Durán into *For Whom the Bell Tolls,* where he appears as "a damned good general," the friend Robert Jordan longed to see at the Gaylord in Madrid after blowing up the bridge.

When Hemingway asked, Joyce arranged for Durán to get American citizenship so that he could come to Cuba and run the Crook Factory.[56] By the fall of 1942 Durán was in Cuba, spending most of his time at the Finca on the day-to-day affairs of the Factory. It did not take him long to conclude that its reports were "trivial and without significance."[57] To make matters worse, he found Hemingway's precautions—like the revolver under the shirts in the chest of drawers—childish and unnecessary.[58] By the end of the year he had shifted his focus to the embassy, where he turned himself into a kind of cultural attaché and speechwriter for the ambassador.

It enraged Hemingway that Durán thought there was something more important for him to do than run the Crook Factory. And so Hemingway once again appeared at Joyce's door late one night to vent his frustrations. "Bob, I want to report to you that Gustavo is a bastard and that I have fired him as head of the Crook Factory."[59] That was the end of a great friendship, and of an unusual and only somewhat productive spy operation that had occupied Hemingway's time and energy for a few months in 1942 and 1943. He was already devoting more energy to a spy adventure of a different kind, one that would also leave little time for the Soviets.

CHAPTER 8

PILAR AND THE WAR AT SEA

A Secret Agent of My Government

At 11:30 A.M. on December 9, 1942, while anchored for lunch inside the Colorado Reef near the city of Bahía Honda off the northwest coast of Cuba, Hemingway looked out across the water from his perch on the flying bridge of his cabin cruiser, Pilar. *On this calm, clear day he did not have to strain to see the large plume of smoke that a ship was trailing across the sky. She appeared to be steaming toward him. By noon she was still a few miles away, but looking through his 10-power binoculars, he could now make out the four red and gold Spanish flags painted on the starboard side of her white hull and identify her as the ocean liner* Marqués de Comilla.

Then, at 12:10, he noticed another ship, "a gray painted vessel," about six to eight miles away, that made his pulse quicken.[1] *She looked like a Coast Guard cutter with something long and low like an oil tank in tow, but she had no funnel. By 12:15 he decided to put to sea to investigate, proceeding north-northwest at the moderate speed of seven knots, right for a boat that wanted to look like she was fishing, not speeding to a fight.*

When the distance closed to about three miles, the gray vessel turned broadside to Pilar, *presenting the silhouette of a conning tower on a long, low deck. "Moving majestically on the dead-calm sea,"*[2] *she was so large that she looked like an aircraft carrier to Hemingway's friend Winston Guest, now serving as first mate on* Pilar's *war cruise. The writer-sailor's reply, one that he would weave into his stories after the war, was: "No, Wolfie, unfortunately she is a submarine and pass the word for everyone to be ready to close."*[3]

This was the moment that captain and crew had trained and hoped for each time he took his cabin cruiser past the breakwater into the Stream. He continued to steer toward the probable U-boat, closing the distance between them "dry-mouthed but happy," eager to attack.[4] *The crew broke out submachine guns and hand grenades, readying these weapons out of sight of the target. Hemingway wanted to hide his violent intentions; the Germans would only see* Pilar *trying hard to catch fish until it was too late. A strike from a large barracuda reinforced the impression that she was just a fishing boat.*[5]

Slow minutes passed. At 1:25 P.M. the submarine changed course and sped up. Pilar *attempted to pursue but her target was now moving too fast. Within fifteen minutes the submarine slipped from sight, and* Pilar *floated alone on the ocean. The event was a disappointment for Hemingway the warrior, ready to die for his country; he and his crew would, he wrote later, have all gone to "Valhalla" for eternity, "happy as goats."*[6]

Pilar was at the heart of Hemingway's wartime adventure at sea. He called her a ship, but at thirty-eight feet she was a mere boat. She had a black hull and rode low in the water, hard to see even during the day. Her angular lines gave her a bit of an Art Deco look. For the writer Paul Hendrickson, who devoted a book to her, there was "something ghostly" about *Pilar*.[7] When Hemingway cast her as a spy ship in 1942 and 1943, it was a good fit.

Hemingway had liked the mahogany and fir design that he found in the catalog of Wheeler Shipyard, which sat on the banks of the East River in Brooklyn, New York. He ordered changes to the basic model, making it a little less comfortable as a cabin cruiser but more functional as a fishing boat, with such things as a small trolling engine, auxiliary fuel tanks, and copper-lined fish boxes. The result, Hemingway wrote to a friend, was a boat that was "a marvel for fishing."[8] She could take most any sea, and turn in her own length to chase a fish. Able to troll half the day on less than twenty gallons, she could speed up to sixteen knots in seconds. Though functional, she was still comfortable enough for extended trips, with five good-size bunks and roomy decks.

Pilar had played an important role in Hemingway's life from the day he brought her home to Key West. Before the great hurricane of 1935, he had spent as much time storm proofing the boat as his house on Whitehead Street, and it was on *Pilar* that he had made his way northeast after the storm passed. Off Upper and Lower Matecumbe Keys he had eased her through the debris and used her as a floating aid station. The experience had been grist for the inflammatory article that he wrote for *New Masses* that caught the attention of spymasters in Moscow.[9]

The pleasure boat that went to war: Hemingway's *Pilar* under way. *Ernest Hemingway Photo Collection, JFK Library.*

At the end of the decade, Hemingway had taken *Pilar* across the straits from Florida to Cuba. In Cuban waters, boat and master made themselves at home in the Stream, where for days on end he, family, and friends could troll for the great fish—marlin, tuna, and swordfish—that lived in its midnight blue depths. Hemingway loved few things more than being out on the water in *Pilar.*

Working at the Crook Factory had far less allure. The Factory was Hemingway's first foray into a wartime occupation after Pearl Harbor. While unusual, it was not the strangest thing that happened in the early days of the war. Hemingway met a need that the embassy perceived, and was able to operate largely on his own terms. But the work was not as exciting—or productive—as he might once have hoped. Even before the Factory hit full production, Hemingway picked up a thread that stretched back to the week he and Gellhorn had spent in Washington in June 1941 after their return from China.

It was then that the couple had met Lieutenant Colonel John W. Thomason, Jr., in the old Navy office building on the mall in Washington. The World War I hero was a man with many of the same friends and interests as Hemingway: war, literature, and art, to say nothing of strong drink. Hemingway and Thomason had bonded quickly. For Hemingway, the marine was a man worth listening to, someone who had one "of the most intelligent minds I have ever talked to."[10] They were soon exploring ways of working together. In the spring of 1942, they started collaborating on the anthology *Men at War: The Best War Stories of All Time,* published in the second half of that year.[11]

Hemingway's introduction to *Men at War,* written in Cuba in the summer of that year, was unabashedly patriotic. By collaborating on the book, which he dedicated to his sons, he was contributing to the expanded war against fascism. He would give young Americans a taste of what lay ahead for them. "This book," he began grimly, "will not tell you how to die."[12] But it would tell the stories of many men who had fought and died over time. "So when you have read it you will know there are no worse things to be gone through than men have been through before." With characteristic praise for Soviet and Chinese communist fighters, he singled out as one of the finest stories in this book that "you must not miss" an over-the-top piece by the American communist (and Soviet spy) Agnes Smedley.[13] The old China hand who had met Hemingway in Hong Kong wrote in glowing terms about the long-suffering fighters in Mao and Chou's Eighth Route Army, some of them mere boys, all of them ready to make any sacrifice for the cause.

For the introduction, Hemingway softened his usual criticism of American leaders. Pearl Harbor had happened because they had "forgotten" how the Axis had struck without warning against the Soviet Union.[14] But, he continued, it was not his intention to fix blame for the disaster, only to caution against underestimating our enemies, and to remind his readers what we were fighting for. So different from his blazing criticism of the democracies in the 1930s for not doing more to fight fascism, his description of American war aims could have been written by the White House press secretary. The country would fight for its constitutional rights and privileges, "and woe [be] to anyone who has any plans for taking those rights and privileges away from us."[15]

Hemingway now proposed to fight his war at sea on *Pilar*. He was ready to become what he would call "a secret agent of my government."[16] To be exact, he wanted to be a seagoing agent for Thomason and Naval Intelligence, the only American sailing in Cuban waters on secret orders. It was an imaginative way to combine his love for *Pilar* and the sea in an adventure that could have come from the pages of the magazine *Outdoor Life* (and would appear in his posthumous novel, *Islands in the Stream*). He would be contributing to the war effort without leaving the home waters that he loved, but doing work that would be more muscular and risky than classical espionage for the Soviets or counterespionage for the American Embassy in Havana. Above all, he would literally be captain of his own ship.

The basic idea of this more independent service was for Hemingway and his crew (many of them from the Crook Factory) to patrol the north coast of Cuba in *Pilar* in search of German submarines, the formidable fighting machines that were sinking Allied ships in many parts of the Atlantic.[17] Ideally Hemingway would key off a U.S. Navy signal that reported a possible sighting. *Pilar* would then proceed to search for the intruder and, when spotted, report his presence.[18] The next part of the plan was for *Pilar* to sink the U-boat—despite its far greater size (up to 250 feet), weight (up to 1000 tons), and armament, especially its 10.5 cm deck gun, able to blow a small boat out of the water with a single shot.

What the Germans would see was a fishing boat going about its business. The hope was that the enemy would come alongside to buy (or seize) fresh fish and water. But the crew of *Pilar* would be ready to attack with bazookas, machine guns, and hand grenades. There would even be a satchel charge, "a huge explosive device, shaped like a coffin, with handles on each end."[19] Hemingway would use Basque jai alai players, expert at placing a fast-moving ball where it needed to go, to lob the grenades down the open hatches of the (hopefully) still unsuspecting U-boat. If even one grenade exploded in a confined space, the result would be devastating. If it could be manhandled into place on the submarine's deck, the infernal machine would finish the job.

Hemingway himself later admitted that the whole operation was so fantastic, "just so improbable," that no one would ever believe that it had happened.[20] How then did it come about?

Americans started to worry about German submarines in home waters after the war in Europe started in September 1939. The Hemingways were prominent among them. In December 1939, Ernest told his brother Leicester about a young Englishman who "had a title, a bank account, and a naval intelligence assignment."[21] Tall, slim, stylish, and perhaps a little arrogant, Sir Anthony Jenkinson—Tony only to his friends—was a passably good writer with two adventure travel books to his credit by 1940.[22] (Only later would Hemingway call Tony a "non-fighter and vague prick," behind his back.[23]) Now Jenkinson was looking for "someone who liked sailing, could navigate, and wanted to do something adventurous"[24]—an invitation that sounded like many other wartime recruiting pitches for intelligence work and appealed to men like Ernest and Leicester. (The typical pitch could be summed up as, "We can't tell you exactly what you will be doing until after you agree to do it, but we guarantee that it will be exciting.") The concept was for them to sail around the western Caribbean and look for "possible and actual" German sub bases. Ernest helped to outfit the expedition.

Ernest could be very hard on the much younger Leicester (who was born in 1915)—scathing in his criticism, dictatorial with his advice—but this season he was "his most considerate self."[25] A picture of them in Havana Harbor shows the Hemingway brothers and Gellhorn drinking beer while they work on the twelve-ton wooden schooner that looks small and best suited for day trips close to land, not a long voyage across the Caribbean. Everyone is smiling. Leicester almost looks enough like Ernest to be his double but the body language makes it clear who is in charge. Leicester was in Ernest's debt, and he knew it—writing later that he could not thank Ernest "enough for the hundreds [of dollars] and the unbuyable [*sic*] help."[26]

Outfitting the schooner took somewhere between a few days and a few weeks, enough time for the brothers to have "many dinners together" and for the young sailors to help Ernest entertain his publisher, Charles Scribner.[27] Once they were ready to sail in early 1940, Leicester and Jenkinson plotted a course that would take the *Blue Stream* into barely charted waters. They entered quiet bays and estuaries, and landed on remote islands, places where the two young adventurers encountered smugglers, profiteers, and unusual people, some of them obviously European transplants.

Ernest corresponded with Leicester and Tony while they were sailing, offering bits of advice and encouragement.[28] Upon their return, they wrote in an article for *Reader's Digest* that they had "discovered Nazi agents, Nazi propaganda, [and] stocks of Diesel oil waiting for Nazi raiders."[29] The article concluded that they had witnessed "preparations for German naval action off the coast of Central America."[30]

The amateur spies offered their observations to Naval Intelligence, at least on the American side of the water. Their work was not well received. Rear Admiral T. J. Wilkinson wrote that, after careful study, the Office of Naval Intelligence (ONI) did not believe that Leicester was likely ever to collect any useful "naval, hydrographic, and subversive information."[31]

The admiral was partly right. Tony and Leicester's conclusions *were* far-fetched. The Germans never had an organized shore establishment in the Caribbean, as the young men had claimed. For most of the war, German subs were resupplied by other submarines, not by sympathizers onshore. But Admiral Wilkinson could have been more charitable. He made it sound as if Tony and Leicester were operating on the fringe. In fact, they—and Ernest—were in good company.

At least since 1940, Embassy Havana had shared their concerns. Early on, the mission had wanted to know about Leicester and Tony's quest. Hemingway reported to his mother in July 1940 from the Finca that "U.S. authorities here were very pleased with . . . [Leicester's] work."[32] Phantom submarines played a role in the spy scare that had led to the creation of the Crook Factory. Perhaps the Germans were putting spies ashore from submarines?

This was one of the things that Hemingway was exploring when he stationed agents like R-42 along the coast to watch for any signs of sub-to-shore activity.[33] Then there were the persistent rumors about colonies of Axis sympathizers along the coast who maintained secret supply depots for the German navy.[34]

The submarine threat itself was far from imaginary. In early 1942, there were not enough U.S. Navy or Coast Guard ships and planes to patrol the shipping lanes. After Pearl Harbor, the young, aggressive German skippers began to take full advantage of what they came to call "the happy time" along the east coast. It was so much more pleasant than, and often just as productive as, the war in the North Atlantic. They could position themselves in deeper water east of the coastal shipping lanes, and wait until a freighter came into view to fire a spread of torpedoes. Sometimes at night the targets were backlit by oceanside cities like Miami, where there was no blackout. It was as if the Germans were both spectators and actors in a deadly light show.

Farther south, the situation was not as dire, but there were both sightings and sinkings off the Cuban coast—eventually peaking around fifteen sinkings a month in the spring of 1942. Almost every day red-eyed survivors covered in fuel oil and molasses, the cargo many ships carried from Cuba, landed in Havana and found shelter at Hemingway's old haunt downtown, the Hotel Ambos Mundos. To respond to the crisis Embassy Havana came up with much the same approach as the U.S. Navy did for the east coast. The overstretched Navy had called on civilian sailors to patrol the Atlantic shoreline in their own boats, and keep an eye out for periscopes or submarines on the surface. They were to report any sightings, without attacking the enemy. This semiofficial initiative, which ran through the third quarter of 1943, came to be called "Hooligan's Navy," an "assorted collection of yachtsmen and Sunday sailors [who] would serve with distinction and verve, if not effectiveness."[35] A little more than a month into the war, the ambassador in Havana said he wanted something similar. In January 1942, he wrote Washington that "the submarine menace [was] . . . coming more close every day."[36] The solution he recommended was for the Navy to take over some cabin cruisers, outfit them with a weapon or two, and turn them over to the Cubans to run as patrol boats.

It is not clear exactly how and when Hemingway developed the specific idea of taking *Pilar* to war in this way. Leicester's adventure played a role. Hemingway was willing to grant that his brother did not do too bad a job on what he called "your snoop cruise." He still had a way to go, but he *was* learning how to spy (his exact words were that Tony and Leicester's work had grown "steadily less childish" over time).[37] But he revealed that he was "disappointed" they had not had "more violent contact with the enemy."[38] For Hemingway the perfect mission would be one that started with some kind of spying, and then ended in the destruction of the enemy.

This concept of operations started to take shape when John Thomason and Hemingway first met in Washington in June 1941. Hemingway told Thomason about Leicester's odyssey, and they discussed a possible follow-on mission, this time under the auspices of ONI. The upshot was that Ernest told Leicester to "get a hair-cut, . . . wash your face good" and then go talk to Thomason, offering to place the *Blue Stream* and her crew at his disposal.[39]

At some point—almost predictably—the focus shifted from Leicester to Ernest. The Baron, as Ernest liked to call his younger brother, wound up taking a war job in Washington, DC, for two years and did not go back to sea. But Hemingway himself also had a boat that he could put at ONI's disposal, and Thomason and Hemingway moved to exploring her potential for doing the job.

Perhaps unaware of this background, Ambassador Braden would claim that the plan had been hatched in his office in Havana, much like that for the Crook Factory. In his memoirs, he has Hemingway virtually demanding a quid pro quo for those "patriotic services" as Factory head. According to Braden, Hemingway said, "Now I want to be paid for all the work I've done."[40] When Braden asked him how he wanted to be repaid, Hemingway went on describe how *Pilar* would find and sink U-boats, and summed it all up with a martial flourish: "I can really have myself a party provided you will get me a bazooka to punch holes in the side of the submarine, machine guns to mow down the people on the deck, and hand grenades to lob down the conning tower."[41]

The ambassador knew that what Hemingway wanted "was against all regulations."[42] But since he had done "such an outstanding job" at the Crook Factory, Braden was willing to "scrap . . . the regulations" and underwrite the new initiative. Hemingway appreciated the support, and as long as the operation lasted, felt that he was "working for the Ambassador."[43] High-level support from the right people still mattered to him.

In the late spring or early summer of 1942, the Embassy took the next step, summoning John Thomason to Havana for consultations.[44] The marine showed up at the chancery on the Prado wearing his uniform, complete with the colorful ribbons that recalled his exploits in combat on the Western Front in World War I. Twirling his eyeglasses on a black silk ribbon and draining at least two tumblers of some kind of drink, he and the ambassador listened while the writer outlined his amazing plan. Invoking history, Hemingway explained how in both world wars surface combatants had disguised themselves as merchantmen or sailboats to entice an unsuspecting enemy to approach, and then opened fire when he was in range. Thomason granted that the idea was not impossible, "only crazy," likely to end with Ernest crawling "out the small end of the Cornucopia."[45] One round from the U-boat's deck gun, and *Pilar* would cease to exist—along with her skipper. But, Thomason allowed, it would be a boost to Allied morale if Hemingway somehow pulled it off.

This would be a secret American undertaking, run by the embassy without the knowledge of the Cuban government.[46] Hemingway would work through the naval attaché at the embassy, the Marine colonel named Hayne D. Boyden. With the improbable nickname of "Cucu" or "Cuckoo," Boyden appears to have been a seasoned, devil-may-care pilot, who had flown flimsy planes in every kind of weather during Marine operations in Haiti and Nicaragua. Better suited for flying than running an office, Boyden's temperament put Hemingway in the position of being the one who focused on the details. At one point, he would comment to the coordinator of intelligence at the embassy, his friend Bob Joyce, that his dealings with the colonel were getting a little too "sketchy" for his comfort, and ask Joyce to generate a plan, something in writing on who was supposed to do what.[47]

Thomason and Boyden eventually arranged for Hemingway to receive munitions and radio gear, both to transmit reports and to locate the enemy, along with a Marine warrant officer named Donald B. Saxon, described as "a lovely uninhibited character" whose pastimes were hard drinking and bar fights.[48] Saxon would help train the crew, then sail on board *Pilar* and work the equipment. There was even a flimsy cover story that Hemingway was doing research for the American Museum of Natural History. Boyden prepared a "get out of jail free" card on official letterhead that Hemingway could carry with him. It was written in a charming mix of English and Spanish that asked the reader to believe that Hemingway was making experiments with official radio gear while "engaged in specimen fishing for the American Museum of Natural History."[49]

Hemingway knew that the success of the undercover operation depended on, in his words, "surprise and a well-trained crew."[50] He would do everything in his power to keep *Pilar*'s secret (especially from the enemy) and to prepare his men for combat. Deciding what risks to take and fighting the ship would be up to him, which was exactly the way he wanted to operate. Even so, there was only so much anyone could do to improve *Pilar*'s chances. As Hemingway remembered a few years later, Thomason's final instructions summed up the bidding: "Get in there, boy, and God bless and God pity you. All I can guaranty [*sic*] is that we won't hang you and neither will the British. But, Ernest, you are certainly going to have to improvise."[51]

Pilar's war cruises began in the summer of 1942, at first on something like a trial basis with local training exercises. Then as Hemingway became more confident and received more equipment, he ranged farther afield. Hemingway remembered operating out of Havana, off the northwest coast of Cuba, and from Cayo Confites, a barren spit of sand at the eastern end of the Old Bahama Channel where his crew set up a makeshift camp.[52] In September 1943, he invited a person who happened to be a confidential FBI informant to lunch at the Finca, and told his guest that the "usual procedure" was to patrol for twelve hours, pretending to fish, and tie up at a nearby dock for the night.[53] Many of the cruises that Hemingway commanded lasted for days, at least two ran for close to three months. For long stretches the crew members had only each other for company. They endured every kind of weather. Perhaps seeking to capture some of the hardship, Hemingway decided to name the operation after one of his many cats, the less-than-fortunate-sounding Friendless.

Martha Gellhorn had mixed feelings about Operation Friendless. At one point, she praised Hemingway for his discipline and patience, for doing his duty in his "floating sardine box."[54] But at other times she said that the operation was just a way for *Pilar*'s skipper to get scarce wartime fuel for his boat so that he could fish and drink with his friends.[55] More than once he did give that impression—for example, when he brought his underage sons along on a "war" cruise, something that he did not mention in

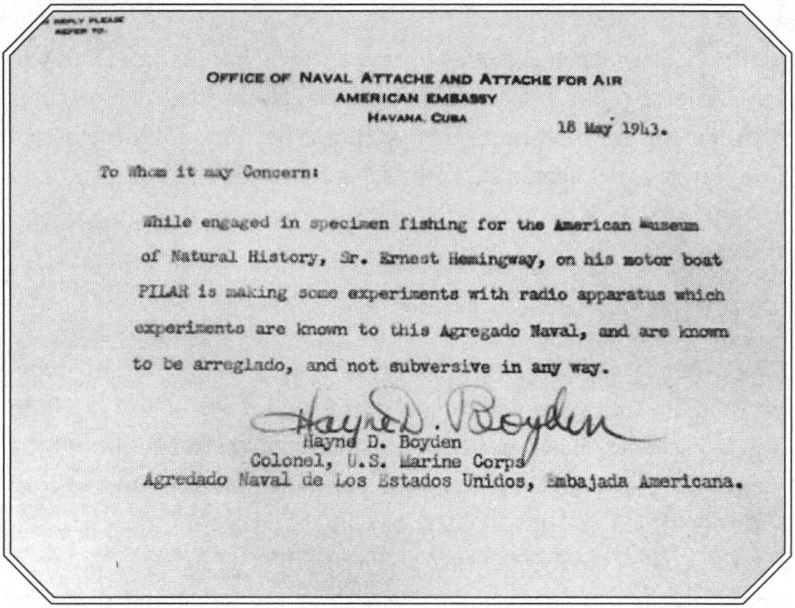

OFFICE OF NAVAL ATTACHE AND ATTACHE FOR AIR
AMERICAN EMBASSY
HAVANA, CUBA

18 May 1943.

To Whom it may Concern:

While engaged in specimen fishing for the American Museum of Natural History, Sr. Ernest Hemingway, on his motor boat PILAR is making some experiments with radio apparatus which experiments are known to this Agregado Naval, and are known to be arreglado, and not subversive in any way.

Haynd D. Boyden
Colonel, U.S. Marine Corps
Agredado Naval de Los Estados Unidos, Embajada Americana.

Neither English nor Spanish: the cover letter that the naval attaché wrote for Operation Friendless, *Pilar*'s war cruise. *Ernest Hemingway Collection, JFK Library.*

1948 when a friend was writing the history of the operation.[56] But on the whole he took the work seriously and put his heart into the mission. It was a matter of wartime luck that *Pilar* did not encounter any U-boats at close range. There were not a few Navy and Coast Guard captains who also did their duty, patrolling diligently and never actively engaging the enemy. But that was still honorable service.

Much of what we know about Operation Friendless comes from Hemingway himself—what he later told family and friends and what can be gleaned from the ship's log that he kept. It is written on an old calendar of medical history that had somehow found its way onto *Pilar*. Fragmentary entries are interspersed with the scores of long card games at sea. The entries read like something written on the fly, but they also appear to be valuable contemporary observations, made within minutes or hours of the events they describe. The entry for December 9, 1942, records in great detail the probable U-boat sighting that Hemingway had been hoping for—and his frustration when the gray vessel sailed away before *Pilar* could get close enough to attack.

Hemingway is not the only source for the incident. When he radioed Havana to report his sighting on December 9, the U.S. Navy took it seriously enough to retransmit it to the fleet and pay him and his crew a small compliment:[57]

> HAVANA REPORTS SUBMARINE BELIEVED TO BE GERMAN 740 TON TYPE IN SIGHT FROM 1210 Q TO 1340 Q 22-58 N 83-26 W X INFORMANTS TWO RELIABLE AMERICANS ACCOMPANIED BY FOUR CUBANS

Ambassador Braden was even more complimentary. He believed that Hemingway had made a real contribution to the war effort. After *Pilar*'s last war cruise in the summer of 1943, when it was clear that the U-boat threat in Caribbean waters was receding, he wrote Hemingway to thank him—effusively—for his service on land and sea. The ambassador praised the sailor-spy for taking "personal risks" despite the "ever-present danger":[58]

> *This work . . . was conducted with skill, judgment, and perseverance, against long odds and during protracted periods of physical hardship. I know too that it was conducted at no small personal financial sacrifice to yourself. . . . It must suffice for the present that I send you this tribute to your patriotism and your achievement, together with the assurances of my personal admiration and enduring friendship.*

Hemingway responded almost immediately, writing to the ambassador on his personal stationery, off-white, with the words "Finca Vigia, San Francisco de Paula, Cuba" printed in a simple but elegant red font at the top of the page. For him the language was flowery. He acknowledged that serving one's country was "a simple obligation which . . . deserves no praise." But serving under Braden had also been a "privilege" that had brought the writer "a great happiness."[59]

Hemingway treasured Braden's letter, and carried it with him for quite some time. It was not just that he felt the obligation to serve his country in wartime. Operation Friendless fulfilled the parts of the Hemingway code that called for skill, courage, and perseverance on his own terms. Though he had been in command, he had not worn military rank. As he wrote his friend Archibald MacLeish in May 1943, he had been working "very quietly and as well as possible with neither . . . the good old fish-eating predator nor the stars of the sky on . . . [my] collar"—and he had never been happier.[60]

The ambassador's letter was still in Hemingway's pocket in 1944 when he encountered Leicester in London. They met at one of the city's best hotels, the Dorchester, a few steps from Hyde Park and almost literally around the corner from the American Embassy on Grosvenor Square. Nearly as soon as they had started on their first glass of scotch in the dimly lit, wood-paneled bar, Ernest told his younger brother that he had a secret to share so long as Leicester promised "not to tell anyone. . . . *Anyone*, you understand."[61] Ernest then reached into an inner pocket and brought out Braden's letter, now in a dog-eared envelope. Reading the letter, Leicester immediately grasped how good Ernest felt about the work that he had performed in Cuba.[62]

Where did this leave the NKVD, the spy service with a long memory? Someone in the NKVD, most likely in Moscow Center, remembered in 1943 how the writer had agreed to become a spy some three years earlier, but had never realized his potential. While Operation Friendless was winding down, an NKVD "worker"—presumably a Soviet intelligence officer—met Hemingway in Cuba to take his operational pulse.[63]

Again the record is fragmentary. Most likely there was a message from Moscow to the man on the ground in Havana, asking about Hemingway. That man, or "worker," would have determined the best way to make contact with the author, and, since they were not trading atomic secrets, may have opted for a direct approach. Perhaps the Soviet decided "to hide in the open" and simply call Hemingway at the Finca, like so many other friends and admirers who hoped for a few minutes of his time, and then invited him to meet at a local restaurant. Perhaps he showed Hemingway the material recognition signal—the stamps that Hemingway had handed over in 1941 to make it possible for a new contact to prove that he really was from the NKVD. Once the "worker" had authenticated himself, the two most likely chatted, with the Soviet probing gently for information about Hemingway's activities. Hemingway may have talked about *Pilar*—it was his favorite topic in 1943—and about the war, perhaps heaping on praise for the great Soviet victory over the Nazis at Stalingrad early in the year. Even if he did not want to become an active spy for them, Hemingway was still full of admiration for the Soviets, and their record in the war against fascism going back at least to Spain in 1937.[64]

Though they probably never met, Hemingway and a man named Michael Straight had similar experiences with the NKVD. If they had met and compared notes, they would have realized that the Soviets knew how to deal with reluctant but well-placed American spies. Straight eventually wrote his memoirs, and described how the NKVD had applied gentle but persistent pressure.

Straight was a well-to-do American whose mother had married an Englishman after Straight's father died. He matriculated at Trinity College, Cambridge, in 1935 and by almost imperceptible degrees became a socialist, then a communist, and finally, in 1937, a spy for the NKVD. The stages included a visit to Soviet Russia and the death of his friend the communist poet John Cornford, who was killed fighting for the Republic in Spain. Straight claimed to have had second thoughts about spying soon after he left Cambridge, his episode of buyer's remorse. After he crossed the Atlantic, and used his many connections to find a job in the State Department in Washington, he hoped that he had left the NKVD behind him. In the spring of 1938, a Soviet who said his name was Michael Green dashed that hope when Straight picked up the phone one day to hear a heavily accented voice convey "greetings from your friends in Cambridge."[65] Green was waiting for Straight in a nearby restaurant, and started to talk after the waitress had taken their order and left them alone. The Soviet apologized for not producing their material recognition signal. It had taken him a while to find Straight, and the NKVD's part of a drawing, torn in half, had gone missing. (Straight would presumably have kept the matching half.)

The friendly, easygoing spy who spoke good English asked about Straight's work and suggested mildly that, if he saw any interesting documents, he should take them home to study. Straight said no one routed any notable documents to his desk. Green simply nodded; he did not press the point. After dinner, Green paid the tab, and promised to call again in about a month to see how Straight was doing. This was not what the young American wanted, but he could not bring himself to turn his back on his Cambridge friends, or to tell the low-key NKVD man who had not asked for much that he did not want to see him again. It was easier to postpone a confrontation. Besides, did anyone know if or how an agent could quit? In the end, Straight chose a middle course. Green's appearance may have been "a disaster" that Straight had wanted to avoid. Yet, as he wrote, they had "parted as friends."[66]

There are parallels between Straight's meeting with the man who called himself Green and Hemingway's first meeting with the NKVD in Cuba. In both cases the outcome was inconclusive. The Soviet worker and the American author did not come up with any concrete plans. But, like Straight and Green, they parted on good enough terms. The door stayed open for the Soviet to come back one more time to continue the process of building a relationship before Hemingway left for Europe in the spring of 1944. The NKVD file states that there was a second meeting and implies there would have been a third meeting in Cuba if Hemingway had stayed on the island.[67] Not ready to give up, the Soviets would find another time and place to call on the sympathetic if elusive writer. The NKVD still believed in his potential. There would be a need for prominent American spies for some time to come.

CHAPTER 9

ON TO PARIS

Brave as a Saladang

For a few days in August 1944, while American and French forces fought the Germans defending the approaches to Paris in the French countryside, Hemingway served as the unofficial chief of intelligence at Rambouillet, a small city or, depending on your point of view, a large clearing in the ancient forests around the capital. Reconnoitering the routes that the Allies might take to get to Paris, the writer turned war correspondent and his driver, Private Archie Pelkey, were by themselves in a jeep on a country road when they encountered a small band of French irregulars, all but two of them naked from the waist up.

The Frenchmen were radical communists, not too different from the guerrillas Hemingway had known in Spain, and quickly found common ground with the large American, even making him their leader. Together they traveled to Rambouillet, and, finding it on the friendly edge of the no-man's-land between the Allied and German armies, established themselves in a charming country hotel, taking eight of the thirty-some rooms in the Hôtel du Grand Veneur. There Hemingway created "a rather well-organized if tiny headquarters," complete with large maps tacked to the wall marking German positions and friendly patrol routes.[1]

Speaking English, French, and broken German, all salted with curses, the ostensible war correspondent took charge. In his shirtsleeves, he received "intelligence couriers, refugees from Paris, and deserters from the German army," methodically gathering infor-

mation and writing reports that he passed to Allied intelligence officers.[2] *To gather more information, he planned and ran patrols into the no-man's-land.*

More than once, he accompanied the patrols himself, risking his life when the Germans fought back. "Some of the patrols we made would scare you worse than Grimm's Fairy Tales," he would write his new mistress, Mary Welsh, a few days later.[3] *Hemingway was so busy that he did not have time to organize the gear that built up in his sleeping quarters: "Carbines stood in each corner, revolvers of every nationality were heaped carelessly on the bed. The bathtub was filled with hand grenades, . . . the [wash] basin with brandy bottles, while under the bed was a cache of army ration whiskey."*[4] *He was ready for whatever fate might throw his way.*

Following the summer of 1943, there was not enough war in Cuba. Hemingway had hoped to make himself useful without leaving the island. His wish had almost come true. He could hear and see German submarines in the waters around the island; he knew that at least one real German spy had made his way to Havana and sent secret messages back to Berlin. But despite their hard work, the writer and his comrades had had little to show for their efforts. Now the focus of effort was clearly shifting to the other side of the Atlantic.

U.S. general Dwight D. Eisenhower's forces invaded northwest Africa in late 1942 and advanced inland to link up with the long-suffering British Eighth Army. By the spring of 1943, the Allies had corralled some 225,000 Germans and Italians in a pocket along the Tunisian coast. German wags took to calling the place "Tunisgrad," evoking the recent German defeat at Stalingrad in Soviet Russia, where the war continued to rage at fever pitch. In May Colonel General Hans-Jürgen von Arnim had had enough, and surrendered the once-proud Afrika Korps and its attachments. It was now only a matter of time before the Western Allies would invade the mainland of Europe.

Martha Gellhorn had never stopped wanting to ride to the sound of the guns in Europe; she knew that the Caribbean was at best a sideshow. The war on the Continent was "increasingly unbearable to read about."[5] She found it nearly impossible to sit down, to think, to settle for the quiet life in Cuba. Instead she traveled around the Caribbean, but the material she gathered was mostly about invisible threats: the crew of a B-17 bomber dutifully patrolling the Caribbean, with nothing to report on most days; or a quiet port city in a European colony where Fifth Columnists might be at work. But the stories in North Africa and Europe would be about epic battles for the future of civilization. So, in September 1943, she left Hemingway and Cuba and, a month later, found her way across the Atlantic to become one of the few female war correspondents in the European Theater.

Though a milestone on the road that would eventually lead to her divorce from Hemingway, Gellhorn's decision to report from Europe was not the end itself. She wrote long, loving letters back to Cuba, filled with details about her life and work, and urged Hemingway to join her.[6] The tempo of operations was about to speed up; he needed to come as soon as he could. Hemingway resisted stubbornly, unwilling to abandon Operation Friendless and urging her instead to return to Cuba to keep him company. She was loath to give in to his entreaties—but also not ready to let him go.

Gellhorn went so far as to involve American spies in a bid to save her marriage. On her travels in Europe, Martha had encountered Bob Joyce, the renegade diplomat last met at the American Embassy in Havana. Now he was in Bari, Italy, in the Office of Strategic Services, or OSS, as the local base chief. Like many others, Joyce had joined America's first civilian spy service in search of excitement. He could not get away from the State Department and the Foreign Service fast enough; that life was too stuffy and hidebound for a free spirit like himself.[7] He knew that, under the charismatic leadership of the World War I hero William J. Donovan, OSS was filled with many of the best and brightest that America had to offer, and that the young agency was running a broad range of intelligence operations overseas, everything from ferreting out the enemy's secrets to conducting black propaganda, even infiltrating saboteurs behind enemy lines. Joyce thought that the change would be liberating. That made him just the kind of man that Gellhorn was looking for. He knew what Hemingway had done in Cuba and he could now offer an entrée into the OSS.

She laid the family issue out for him: she was hitting her stride as a reporter. But Hemingway wanted her to come home. She was prepared to obey "the orders of her lord and master," but desolate at the prospect of giving up her plans to cover "the big show," meaning the Allied invasion of France. She supposed that Hemingway was making plans to come to Europe in some capacity, but had run into transportation and perhaps passport difficulties.[8]

Joyce heard the plea for help and cabled OSS headquarters. He suggested that his boss, Whitney Shepardson, the sophisticated international businessman who was head of Secret Intelligence (SI), consider approaching Hemingway. The idea was to enlist him for SI, the part of OSS dedicated to classic espionage—that is, dealing with spies and stolen secrets.

OSS officers scratched their heads as this message made the rounds. Just what could Hemingway do for the fledgling spy service, wondered Lieutenant Commander Turner McWine, the chief intelligence officer in the Middle East. The author's prominence and temperament would make it hard for him to fit in.[9]

About a month later, Joyce addressed these concerns in a long letter to Shepardson. He listed Hemingway's attributes: he was an authority on Spain who knew more non-Franco Spaniards than "any other American"; he had already run intelligence operations in Cuba; and, from the Spanish Civil War, he had firsthand knowledge of guerrilla warfare and special operations. Joyce defended Hemingway against traditionalists like the head of military intelligence, Major General George V. Strong, a perennial thorn in the side of OSS who had apparently criticized Hemingway. Strong's criticism was more about the writer's lifestyle and sympathies for the Spanish Republic than of his abilities. What did it matter if Hemingway had been married three times? Joyce summed up that Hemingway was a man "of the highest integrity and loyalty," about as much of a communist or fellow traveler as the head of Chase National Bank. Joyce repeated his suggestion that Shepardson invite Hemingway to Washington to explore how he could be useful, perhaps in Spain or Italy.[10]

OSS Headquarters staffed the request carefully. Shepardson solicited the opinions of Deputy Directors Brigadier General John Magruder and G. Edward Buxton. Like his subordinates, Magruder expressed reservations about Hemingway's temperament and left-wing politics, not to mention Joyce himself, "an extremely intelligent and somewhat temperamental individual who would not be improved by association with . . . Hemingway."[11] For his part, Buxton wondered if Hemingway might have more potential for Morale Operations (MO), the OSS's black propaganda arm, than for SI.[12] The file duly made its way over to MO, whose leaders concluded a few days later that Hemingway was too much of an individualist even for the highly unconventional MO mission of trying to demoralize the enemy (by, for example, circulating counterfeit German stamps that featured a skeletal image of Hitler).[13] No one suggested that the forty-four-year-old Hemingway was suitable for a role in OSS's paramilitary branch, whose members operated behind enemy lines as guerrillas, exactly the sort of thing that Hemingway (and his fictional hero Robert Jordan) had done in Spain. That kind of war was for much younger men, wasn't it? In the end, Shepardson cabled back to Joyce in April that OSS had "[d]ecided in the negative about Hemingway. We may be wrong, but feel that although he undoubtedly has conspicuous ability for this type of work, he would be too much of an individualist to work under military supervision."[14]

How did the Gellhorn-Joyce initiative end? Did Joyce ever get back to Gellhorn to deliver the bad news? If Hemingway and Gellhorn talked about her approach to Joyce, how did Hemingway react?

It is impossible to know. Gellhorn and Joyce were out of touch in April, and wartime censorship would have made it difficult for him to give her the news in writing. By then Gellhorn had given in to Hemingway's entreaties and made her way back to Cuba for a brief reunion.

The fastidious Gellhorn returned home to a husband who was drinking even more and washing less than usual. He had grown a bushy salt-and-pepper beard, so disorderly that mice played in it. (At least that is what he claimed in a chatty letter to his first wife, Hadley.[15]) He had been sleeping on the floor amid stacks of unanswered letters after having a few drinks. This was all right with the crew of *Pilar,* and Hemingway's five dogs and eleven cats, all of whom made themselves comfortable in the disorder. The stage was now set for a private war. Hemingway talked about submarines in the Caribbean, Gellhorn looked to great battles to come in Europe, Hemingway defended Operation Friendless, Gellhorn attacked it. Some part of Hemingway had known for a while that Gellhorn was correct, but he did not want to admit it, certainly not to a woman who did not dutifully stand by her man and had gone instead on her own wartime adventures. That made her a bad wife who put her career before her marriage.[16]

Even after Hemingway raged at her, even waking her in the middle of the night to tell her how insane, irresponsible, and selfish she was, Gellhorn did not give up on looking for help from Allied intelligence.[17] Just as she had approached Bob Joyce and OSS in Italy, Gellhorn turned to another friend for help in getting Hemingway out of Cuba and into the war. This time she called on her friendship with Roald Dahl, another warrior-writer-spy. He was a British fighter pilot who could no longer fly because, after being wounded in a crash, he lost consciousness at altitude. His official title was Assistant Air Attaché at the British Embassy in Washington. Most attachés are spies in uniform, charged with collecting information about the host country. This was not enough for Dahl, who had another, unofficial portfolio from the organization known as British Security Co-ordination (BSC). Its job was to influence the American public and its leaders. BSC wanted to get them to support British war aims, work that involved a little bit of spying, the occasional press placement, and discreet pressure on the right person at the right time.[18]

Dahl had already begun his literary career by writing a combination of war stories and children's fantasies, one of which had even caught Walt Disney's attention. Impossibly tall at six feet six inches, with an exotic uniform and accent, to say nothing of his wartime record and literary credentials, Dahl was a prized commodity in Washington social circles. In October 1943, he had been invited to the White House for dinner and a showing of the film adaptation of *For Whom the Bell Tolls* in what he called the president's "private cinema." The hostess was Eleanor Roosevelt, who, Dahl wrote to his mother, "poured a lot of cocktails." One of his dinner partners was Gellhorn, "a good type" who "uses as much bad language as her husband does in his books."[19]

A few months later, in March 1944, Dahl was happy that "Marty Hemingway [had come] back last week from Italy and . . . was full of stories."[20] But she did not call on Dahl just to tell stories. She wanted to know if he could get Hemingway across the Atlantic. Space was scarce, reserved for war business. The air attaché controlled travel to Britain on Royal Air Force (RAF) planes. Dahl saw an opportunity. He could get a seat for Hemingway if he would agree to become an accredited war correspondent and report the war from an RAF viewpoint.[21] When Gellhorn conveyed Dahl's offer, Hemingway yielded to the inevitable and accepted. A grateful Gellhorn saluted Dahl for being "angelically helpful."[22]

Hemingway soon traveled from Cuba to New York, still sporting the full beard that he had grown during Operation Friendless. In Manhattan he touched base with *Collier's*, which was taking him on as a correspondent for the campaign in Europe, and met Dahl at the Hotel Gladstone. The two spent a memorable evening drinking champagne and eating caviar out of a seemingly bottomless, 2.2-pound jar with a man Dahl remembered as "some crazy boxing instructor."[23] Before he left for London, Hemingway told Gellhorn that women were not allowed on British aircraft (which was not true) and left her to cross the Atlantic by herself on a Norwegian freighter loaded with dynamite.

Gellhorn's success in getting Hemingway to Britain did nothing to save their marriage. Once in London, Hemingway moved into the Dorchester on Park Lane in Mayfair, which happened to be her favorite hotel. Relatively new—it opened in 1931—and built with reinforced concrete, Londoners considered it to be both luxurious and bombproof. It still attracted regulars like the British novelist Somerset Maugham. But now it also attracted many with new money who came to be safe. (One wag commented that, during the war, it was like being in expensive squalor on a transatlantic luxury liner, perhaps one that was now being used as a troopship; the Dorchester was a fortress where money bought you safety but could not always compensate for wartime shortages or guarantee that the right kind of people were sitting at the table next to you.[24])

Though he had never been to the British capital before, Hemingway found himself among an amazing variety of friends, family, and associates who kept him busy. In the spring of 1944, London was the epicenter of the Allied universe. Everything and everyone, it seemed, was focused on the upcoming invasion of northern Europe. Passing by in the street, in vehicles or on foot, singly and in groups, were throngs of soldiers, sailors, and airmen from all over the free world. The better restaurants and clubs were filled with their officers. Journalists came to cover the great event that everyone sensed was about to happen. Hemingway's brother Leicester, to whom he bragged about Operation Friendless, was there as part of a military film unit. When Gellhorn finally arrived in London,

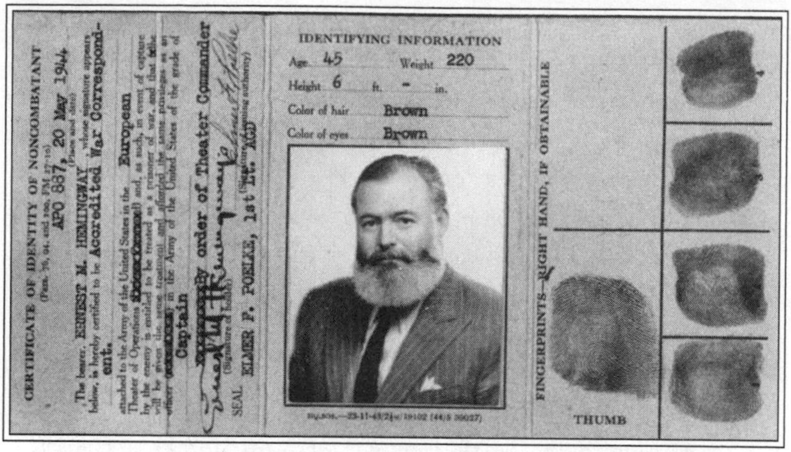

The officially accredited war correspondent: the ID card that the Army issued in 1944. *Ernest Hemingway Photo Collection, JFK Library.*

Hemingway had little time for her. Matters between them were worse than ever. They continued to fight, and he mocked her brutally in public. It did not help that he had developed an eye for Mary Welsh, the war correspondent from Minnesota who had worked with Leicester and talked to him about his big brother. She was a petite brunette, 5'2", with short curly hair and a friendly smile. The other correspondents thought she looked equally good in her uniform and the sweater she wore without a bra. Though still married to an Australian journalist, Mary soon became Ernest's mistress. After his divorce from Gellhorn, she would become his fourth wife.

There were even a few spies in the mix. One of them was from the NKVD, and he was looking for Hemingway. The record of the meeting is short. It declares simply that an unnamed operative met Hemingway in London in June. How did the Soviets know when and where to find him? It could have been by chance, or the result of a diligent search. Or perhaps, at the last meeting in Havana, Hemingway gave the Soviet "worker" there an idea of where to find him.

(According to hotel lore, the Dorchester had long been favored by Fifth Columnists and spies of all sorts.[25]) The Soviet contact and Hemingway might even have agreed on some kind of communications plan, perhaps that he would appear at a certain place at a certain time on a given day of the week.

The NKVD file suggests that this meeting was like the one that had occurred before Hemingway left Havana. It was, again, cordial and inconclusive, the Soviet probing for access and commitment, Hemingway sounding agreeable but stopping short of specific commitments:[26]

> *Our meetings with "Argo" [Hemingway's code name] in London and Havana were conducted with the aim of studying him and determining his potential for our work. . . . "Argo" did not give us any polit. Information [sic], though he repeatedly expressed his desire and willingness to help us.*

Over the past four years, the character of the war against fascism had changed significantly. The writer remained sympathetic to the Soviet Union and the Russian people, who continued to make enormous sacrifices in the war against the Nazis. But now more than ever, his own country was mobilized and engaged in what Eisenhower would call the Crusade in Europe. America had made good on her promise to be the arsenal of democracy, turning out untold quantities of ships, planes, and tanks, and putting millions of men under arms. Hemingway himself had already served proudly on land and at sea. In the spring of 1944, the U.S. Army was getting ready to challenge the Germans on the plains of northern Europe. There were new and worthy American stories to record, and opportunities to contribute to the war effort that did not involve the NKVD.

Hemingway did not need another lecture from Gellhorn to know that D-Day would be, for America, the turning point in the war in Europe. He called in favors to get himself as close to the invasion beaches as possible. From a thirty-eight-foot landing craft, he watched history unfolding in the waters off Normandy on June 6, 1944. Around and behind him was one of the greatest armadas in history: the "derrick-forested" transport ships, the smaller boats "over all the sea" like so many water bugs, "crawling forward toward France."[27] The battleship *Texas* was not far away; her main batteries spouted flame and sent shells the size of small passenger cars into the cliffs overlooking the beach code-named "Omaha." Amazingly, enough Germans survived the bombardment to shoot back at the invaders and create a killing zone at water's edge. Just inland, Hemingway could see two American tanks burning brightly after being hit by German fire.

Omaha turned out to be one of the Allies' greatest challenges on D-Day. The sector plan did not survive contact with the enemy. Confusion reigned. Most of the tanks designated for the beach sank offshore, infantry units could not find their objectives, and the German defenses in bunkers and pillboxes on the high ground held well into day. Some two thousand American soldiers died there in the surf and on the rocky beaches. But within the first twenty-four hours, the many survivors managed to rally and push a kilometer or two inland. They helped to establish the foothold on the Continent that would enable the American, Canadian, and British armies to battle their way through the difficult terrain of the coastal provinces in June and July before advancing east toward the River Seine and Paris in August.

After D-Day, Hemingway returned to London, and was finally able to fly with the RAF. Though now overweight, with a paunch above the beltline, he somehow fit into a British uniform with a shoulder tab labeling him as a correspondent. He even managed to buckle a life jacket and an oxygen mask over the uniform. In late June, he flew on sorties against V-1 "buzzbombs," the unmanned missiles that the Germans called revenge weapons and aimed at English cities. One afternoon, aloft in an RAF "Tempest," he watched a squadron of American B-25 bombers attack launch sites at a place called Droncourt in France. A few days later, on June 29, he flew over the south coast of England in a Mosquito, the RAF's fast, plywood fighter, engaged in the dangerous work of shooting down the missiles in flight. In between raids, he studied navigation, because he did not want to be just a "sand-bagging passenger." Here too he wanted to be useful. He began to enjoy learning about the war in the air and wanted to extend his "wonderful" time with the RAF.[28] At least for now, he was willing to forget his prior detest for His Majesty's Government, dating to its policy on the Spanish Civil War.

No matter what Hemingway's wishes, the land war was soon much more important, and it was time to give up his base in London. The editors at *Collier's* wanted him on the ground in France, where American soldiers were still fighting hard to push the Germans out of Normandy and Brittany. By mid-July, he had gotten himself accredited as a member of the press corps attached to the U.S. Army. Once on the Continent, he would remain true to the wartime criteria that he had established for himself. He had three goals: be useful to the fighting forces, find the best stories that he could, and operate on his own terms. They would lead to the high point of his career as a wartime spy.

After arriving in France, Hemingway befriended the commander of the 4th Infantry Division, Major General Raymond O. Barton, a tough, no-nonsense professional soldier, though one who was not humorless or close-minded. (For one thing, he tolerated the West Point nickname, "Tubby," that followed him throughout his career.) Barton was willing to give Hemingway a jeep and a driver, who was usually the private from upstate New York with bright red hair named Archie Pelkey, and let him explore Normandy on his own. Outfitted with maps and binoculars, armed with rifles and hand grenades, they covered a great deal of ground: from ancient small towns like Villedieu-les-Poêles, literally "God's City of Frying Pans," where Hemingway calmly watched street fights between German and American soldiers; to the maze of country lanes and back roads near St.-Pois where an ambush by deadly accurate German 88 mm antitank guns could have cost him his life; to the magical tidal island Mont-St.-Michel, whose twelfth-century abbey still soars some five hundred feet from the surrounding salt flats where he went to recover from the ambush for a few days.[29]

From the start, Hemingway shared what he learned and observed with the U.S. Army. There were small bits of information that Barton and others found useful—perhaps something that Heming-

Hemingway and his driver, Pvt. Archie Pelkey, on the road to adventure, France, 1944. *Ernest Hemingway Photo Collection, JFK Library.*

way gleaned from a Frenchman, perhaps something that he himself noticed. Hemingway knew the French countryside well, especially the parts that he had explored on a bicycle in the 1920s when he was living in Paris with his first wife and their son. He also had an eye for terrain features that made a difference in combat.

Barton had an ulcer, exacerbated by the stress of combat. Once when he was exhausted at the end of the day and needed to lie down, Hemingway lay with him on a blanket and spoke softly about where the Germans were "and whether they have left or not and how it is ahead."[30] When the Allied armies started to close in on Paris in mid-August, Barton knew there was a good chance that the 4th Division would help to liberate the city that was still so close to Hemingway's heart, and he gave the writer an unofficial reconnaissance mission: take your jeep and driver, and see what you can see on the road to Paris.[31]

Hemingway happily complied, heading east from the coast, leaving the cramped hedgerows of Normandy for the more open landscape of farms interspersed with the occasional copse of trees around Chartres. On August 19, 1944, he came across the two cars of bare-chested French guerrilla fighters armed with a haphazard assortment of weapons.[32] These were the young men from the communist Franc-Tireurs et Partisans Français (FTPF), the most radical, hard-left fringe of the French Resistance which was "frequently charged with lack of discipline or excessive zeal."[33]

Rapport was instant. The French irregulars were attracted to the large, energetic American who spoke their language, and they quickly attached themselves to him. He was equally happy to take them under his wing. It was not a formal relationship, but something that sprouted spontaneously on the battlefield. The Frenchmen were so taken with Hemingway that they soon began to copy his "sailor bear walk . . . [and, like him, spit] short sentences from the corners of their mouths . . . in different languages."[34] The American proceeded to scrounge captured weapons from nearby friendly units, and to outfit his men with odd bits of clothing and equipment from a U.S. Army truck that had been abandoned after an ambush. Soon the fighters were dressed and armed well enough, happily festooning strings of hand grenades about their waists and shoulders.[35]

Hemingway led his band to Rambouillet, now important because it sat astride one of the roads to Paris from the southwest. The German garrison had just evacuated; there was nothing between the small city and the enemy. This left a vacuum that Hemingway and his men could try to fill. He knew instinctively that he also needed to seek out the nearest American unit, to report where he was and what he had seen. So, on the morning of August 20, 1944, Hemingway drove a few miles back to the west to check in with the intelligence officer at the command post of the 5th Division outside the newly liberated Chartres, centered around the third-largest Gothic cathedral in Europe, its square towers and flying buttresses dominating the old town and the surrounding wheat fields. It was perhaps the bloated German and American corpses along the road that no one had yet had time to bury that impressed the senses more on that day, however.

At the command post the writer ran into David K. E. Bruce, the senior OSS officer in Western Europe. Even in plain GI battle dress, Bruce looked like the leader that he was: helmet squarely placed on his head, field jacket clean and buttoned, insignia of rank—a colonel's eagles—plain to see. His gaze was direct, his expression open and engaged, a sign that he had good people sense. In Chartres Bruce was (to use his words) "enchanted" by the "patriarchal" Hemingway, carried away by "his gray beard [and] imposing physique, much like God, as painted by Michelangelo."[36] Bruce's enchantment made it easy for Hemingway to persuade him that Rambouillet might hold the keys to the gates of Paris. Together they could accomplish one of Bruce's missions, that of finding out about the Germans' strength and intentions, especially by infiltrating spies through the lines into the territory the Germans still controlled.

About to step into "a bath of excitement": Hemingway and Colonel David K. E. Bruce of the OSS, with a member of the French Resistance, August 1944. Hemingway wears a captured German belt, and holds a glass, likely filled by the man on his left holding a bottle at the ready. *Ernest Hemingway Photo Collection, JFK Library.*

In the afternoon Bruce traveled the same road to Rambouillet that Hemingway had taken to and from Chartres. The colonel drove along the edge of a dense, old-growth forest that had been the king's hunting preserve in the days of the monarchy, then by a small, fairy-tale chateau, gray stucco with a rounded tower on each corner—the country house for French rulers when they wanted to get away from the capital. In the heart of town Bruce found an "ancient hotel, delightfully shaded."[37] With its own garden, the Grand Veneur looked more like another large country house than a small hotel. The four-story building had wooden shutters on its many double doors and windows, which, along with the dormers breaking up the pitch of the roof, gave the place an inviting air. Though named for the king's master huntsman (*veneur*), the Grand Veneur had been open to anyone who could pay to relax in style in the country.

Once inside the hotel, Bruce did not hesitate to plunge into the "bath of excitement" that Hemingway and his partisans had drawn for him.[38] By setting up an operations center in his room, Hemingway had already done some of Bruce's work for him, and they joined forces for the next few days. The patrols they sent out into the countryside between Rambouillet and Paris came back with reports that it was only lightly defended, key information for the Allied armies advancing on the French capital. Hemingway impressed Bruce as an expert interrogator and report writer, spending hours sifting the information he collected.[39] At one point, a French irregular asked Hemingway and Bruce for permission to leave their headquarters for "fifteen minutes to kill a civilian traitor"—something that was not unusual during the chaotic days between the occupation and the liberation, when members of the Resistance could settle old scores. Bruce wrote in his memoirs that they approved the request, and lent the man a pistol.[40]

Bruce charged Hemingway with keeping order at the Grand Veneur, and he did it in his own way. He is said to have come up with the novel idea of making his German prisoners take their pants off (on the theory that a man without pants was less likely to escape), and then put them to work peeling potatoes, onions, and carrots in the hotel kitchen. At dinnertime, the hotelier added insult to injury by making the prisoners put on frilly jackets and wait on their captors.[41]

When the word got out that troops were staging in Rambouillet for the liberation of Paris, the town was soon "jammed like a New Year's Eve party with . . . fairly trashy celebrants," including a number of fellow war correspondents who wondered why Hemingway seemed to be running the place.[42] He used his fists to keep order; as he put it later, he wound up hitting one newspaperman "squarely in the puss" and putting a hammerlock on a paratrooper who was "threatening everybody with his Sten gun to make them give him champagne."[43] The future diplomat Bruce would share a toned-down recap of that day with the writer Malcolm Cowley: "Ernest . . . was obliged, quite gently for such a Hercules of a man, to push a couple of them around with the back of his hand."[44] But even Bruce had to admit that the writer-spy could fly into rages at Rambouillet when he had had too much to drink.[45]

Bruce funneled the intelligence they produced to the advancing Allied forces. Some reports went directly to the field commanders, others onto the OSS wire—Bruce had his own encrypted radio and communicator. With a senior member of the Resistance, Bruce and Hemingway tried to brief the man who would lead the first Allied troops into Paris. The French division commander was a long-serving officer named Philippe François Marie Leclerc de Hautecloque, who had been fighting the Germans continuously since 1939. Bruce admired the fellow aristocrat: "tall, spare, handsome, stern-visaged . . . a striking figure."[46] Hemingway was less generous in one of his wartime dispatches: he told how, far from being grateful for their work, Leclerc called his three briefers unspeakable names in French and told them "to buzz off."[47] But the general's own intelligence officer sat down with them later at dinner, and Bruce gave him "a detailed summary, with sketches of the German strength between Rambouillet and Paris, along all routes, of the obstacles to be expected." Bruce believed that the information had "a determining effect upon the . . . march to Paris."[48]

Bruce valued Hemingway's contribution enough to arrange for their collaboration to continue after they left Rambouillet. The night before Leclerc advanced on Paris, the OSS officer wrote in pencil on a small scrap of lined paper to "Dear Mr. Hemingway." He, Bruce, would be leaving for Paris in the morning. Could Hemingway "arrange the transportation . . . of the twelve Resistance men who have done such excellent service here?" For Bruce it was "important to keep them together to be used for certain future purposes that I have in view." He closed with a formal "Very Sincerely Yours, D K E Bruce, Colonel, G.S.C., C.O. OSS, ETO."[49] Hemingway carefully saved this note, as he had done with the letter from Ambassador Braden about his work in Cuba.

On August 24, Bruce and Hemingway joined one of the long lines of Allied trucks, jeeps, and tanks as they started to make their way slowly through the forest in the direction of Paris. The weather did not cooperate—it rained for much of the day, soaking everyone to the skin within an hour of leaving Rambouillet—and neither did the few remaining Germans. More than once Hemingway and his private army stopped to take cover (and maybe to fight back) when the enemy opened fire from half a dozen or so carefully chosen positions, perhaps a tank hidden in the woods or one of the still dangerous 88 mm antitank guns on a piece of high ground.

The future CBS newscaster Andy Rooney, then a reporter for *Stars and Stripes,* was nearby when he heard cannon fire ahead. He knew instantly that it was not friendly fire and jumped out of his jeep, looking for—and finding—a roadside wall that was just high enough for him to hide behind if he crouched down low. Behind the same wall, some fifty feet away, he saw another figure who shouted, "We're going to be here a while!" The large man in a Canadian battle smock and officer's cap with a leather brim who then crawled over to him turned out to be Hemingway. Pulling bits of paper from his pockets, the writer proceeded to tell Rooney where the Germans were on the road ahead. Though he had reservations about Hemingway the rogue war correspondent, Rooney was impressed by the accuracy of the information and grateful for the warnings about trouble spots.[50]

By late afternoon on the twenty-fourth, Hemingway and Bruce were inside city limits, coming up on the River Seine that flows through the heart of Paris. Pockets of German resistance and jubilant crowds slowed progress to a crawl. Even where the two sides were still firing, the streets were lined with Parisians happily forcing fruit, flowers, and, above all, drinks on the liberators. "It was," Bruce wrote in his diary, "impossible to refuse [the gifts thrust upon us]. . . . In the course of the afternoon, we had beer, cider, white and red Bordeaux, white and red Burgundy, champagne, rum, whiskey, cognac, armagnac, and Calvados."[51] The combination was enough to wreck even Bruce's sturdy constitution and once night fell, he and Hemingway decided to put up for the night in a nearby house.

On August 25, the Americans woke to "a wonderful sunny day."[52] After taking the morning to collect themselves, the small group set out at twelve thirty on a grand tour of some of the most iconic sights in the City of Light, driving down the magnificent boulevard known as the Champs-Élysées, which sweeps from the Arc de Triomphe to the elegant Place de la Concorde. Though sniper fire continued to ring out through the area, six French veterans stood guard over the Tomb of the Unknown Soldier under the arch. Their captain allowed the Americans to go up on the roof to take in the breathtaking view—the sea of domes and roofs and spires above, tanks moving and firing in the streets below.

Later in the afternoon Bruce and Hemingway raced back up a now-deserted Champs-Élysées to No. 25, the home of the elite Travelers Club in the La Païva Mansion (named for a nineteenth-century courtesan also known as "la grande horizontale"). The club was mostly deserted, but they managed to find its president and joined him in a round of champagne. Then, after braving the crowds of cheering, drinking, and kissing Frenchmen in the Place de l'Opéra, they escaped to the relative calm of the Ritz, the venerable establishment in the heart of Paris, more like a chateau than a hotel, which was Hemingway's idea of heaven. ("When I dream of [the] afterlife . . . , the action always takes place in the Paris Ritz," Hemingway once wrote.[53]) There they settled in the bar with Hemingway's irregulars, a few correspondents, and Bruce's subordinates, ordering some fifty martinis, which the discerning Bruce dismissed as "not very good."[54] But dinner at the hotel that night, with Hemingway and a smaller entourage, was superb: the chef made the best of the few ingredients at his disposal, probably a cut of meat saved for a special occasion, along with some of the Ritz's wartime staples like vegetable broth, rice and creamed spinach with a special sauce, then a handful of raspberries in liqueur, all washed down with wines from one of the best cellars in the world (which had survived the occupation and the liberation intact). After dinner, the diners wrote the date on menu cards, which each of them then signed. The card that the military historian S. L. A. Marshall took home bore the caption: "We think we took Paris."[55]

They, of course, had not "taken" Paris in any sense of the word. But by most accounts they were in the vanguard, and their reports had proven useful, with solid facts about the enemy and the routes that were open.[56] It was a real contribution to the liberation of the French capital that probably saved lives. This was Hemingway at his lifetime best in the spy business. Ground combat with irregulars suited him well, better even than the war at sea and certainly better than the war in the air. Other forms of spying, like running the Crook Factory or working for the NKVD, paled in comparison. Marshall, who had seen Hemingway in action a number of times between August 23 and 25, and was a good judge of military prowess, concluded that he had "the courage of a saladang, and . . . was uncommonly good at managing guerrillas."[57] For his part, David Bruce concluded that Hemingway had displayed that rare combination of advised recklessness and caution that knows how properly to seize . . . a favorable opportunity which, once lost, is gone forever. He is a born leader of men, and, in spite of his strong independence of character . . . a highly disciplined individual."[58]

Marshall and Bruce were right. Hemingway could pick up a loosely organized team, become its leader, and lead it through the fog of war. But he was not just an independent guerrilla leader. He was careful to liaise with the regulars, and to make common cause with intelligence officers like Bruce. What Hemingway's driver said about the radical French partisans applied equally to the man who led them in August 1944. For Private "Red" Pelkey, they were "a good outfit. Best outfit I have ever been with. No [Army] discipline. Got to admit that. Drinking all the time. Got to admit that. But plenty fighting outfit," one that, with the right leader, got the job done.[59]

CHAPTER 10

AT THE FRONT

The Last Months of the Great War Against Fascism

In early September 1944, Hemingway and U.S. Army officer Charles T. Lanham stood on a hill overlooking the Belgian town of Houffalize, its gray and white stucco buildings clustered neatly around the town square on the far side of the River Ourthe. What Hemingway called "the rat race . . . through rolling, forested country" was coming to an end.[1] *The Allies had mostly driven the Germans out of France, then north and east through Belgium toward the Belgian–German frontier. The Americans could take pride in their achievements since D-Day in June, but the war was not yet over.*

On this day Hemingway and Lanham could see the Germans retreating over the bridge that spanned the small river, barely wider than a millrace, that now separated the two sides. To make sure that the Americans kept their distance, German artillery fired on the roads leading into town. Hemingway and Lanham each bet that he could reach the town square before the other. While Lanham took the back roads through the woods, Hemingway set off down the main road, "his" forces in two jeeps—one with his band of French irregulars, another with Private Pelkey at the wheel. Booby traps and downed trees made for slow going, and by the time Hemingway arrived at the water's edge, Lanham was already there—but neither could cross because the Germans had blown the bridge.

About ten days later, the two men were still testing each other. They were at dinner in an old farmhouse, eating a steak dinner in Hemingway's honor, when a German shell came through one wall and went out the other without exploding. While most of the other diners scurried for shelter, Hemingway calmly continued to cut his meat. Lanham told his guest to move, or at least to put on his helmet, but he refused and they argued while more shells tore through the walls, again and again, miraculously without exploding. Not to be outdone, Lanham took off his helmet, and resumed eating. The other diners—Lanham's officers—returned to the table after the shelling had tapered off. Some of them called Hemingway and Lanham brave, others hinted at bravado. Lanham settled the matter: it was a foolhardy test of fate.[2]

After the fall of Paris, Hemingway divided his time between the French capital and the front lines. In town he set up housekeeping at the Ritz with Mary Welsh, the American war correspondent whom he had courted in London in the spring even before his marriage to Gellhorn had completely disintegrated. Welsh used the word "horizontal" to describe how they rediscovered the pleasures they had first discovered in London.[3] Hemingway said that they now "loved each other very much with no clothes at all, no lies, no secrets, no pretenses . . . and only one shirt apiece."[4] Along the way, they helped other guests drink their way through the hotel's stock of Perrier-Jouët Brut, eventually forcing the sommeliers to fall back on lesser houses. When he was not with Mary, Hemingway attached himself to the Allied armies while they pushed the German army back to its homeland.

Most of the time, he was with what had become his favorite unit, the 22d U.S. Infantry Regiment of General Barton's 4th Infantry Division. Its commanding officer was Colonel Charles T. Lanham, the West Point graduate known to his friends simply as "Buck." Hemingway was drawn to this warrior-writer as he had been to Gustavo Durán in the Spanish war. Lanham liked to fight and write about it;

Mary Welsh, fellow war correspondent and future wife, dressed for war, ca. 1944. *Ernest Hemingway Photo Collection, JFK Library.*

he had even published a few poems and short stories about soldiering. In wartime pictures he is a little shorter than Hemingway, and nowhere near as heavy: Mary Welsh described him as "sprightly, prickly, sharp-witted."[5] His eyeglasses gave him a thoughtful air. But that did not keep him from being effective in combat. "It was," Hemingway remembered after the war, "always so much fun to be with a man who was literate, articulate, [and] completely brave. . . . [During a fight he was] absolutely intact, intelligent, humorous, and the best company in the world."[6]

The adventures at Houffalize and over dinner at the farmhouse were bonding rituals. Hemingway and Lanham never settled who was faster or braver, but they did lay the foundation for a friendship that grew on the battlefield and lasted for the rest of their lives. When they could relax after a day of combat, they stayed up late drinking and talking. Seizing the opportunity to pick the brain of a living legend of American letters, Lanham wanted to discuss literature and talk about his own writing. Hemingway was far more interested in courage on the battlefield—what Lanham would later call "this grace-under-pressure crap."[7] Courage, Lanham told Hemingway, was not "what a sober person discusses in public."[8] Even so, the writer who wanted to fight and the fighter who wanted to write complemented each other, and formed a bond as strong as any Hemingway ever had with another man. In 1948, looking back at the war, Hemingway mused that he had never "been closer to anyone, as a friend, than to Buck . . . nor admired anyone more."[9]

October brought an official investigation into his conduct at Rambouillet, an unwanted diversion from service with the 22d and from his love affair with Mary. Hemingway (and commanders with impeccable judgment like David Bruce) still felt that he had performed well on the road to Paris. Hemingway would later say, more than once, that he deserved a medal for finding the best route into the French capital, the one that the Germans were not defending in force. He noted how an OSS officer "got a DSC [Distinguished Service Cross] for the work I did about Rambouillet laying out everything so [the French general Phillipe] Leclerc . . . went in on a dime where it would have cost him at least $8.95."[10] Instead, he was now being called to account for conduct unbecoming a war correspondent. Probably levied by one or more of the other journalists whom he had literally pushed around at the Grand Veneur in August, the allegations were that he had stockpiled weapons, commanded troops, and joined the fight to liberate Paris. These allegations—all true—were violations of the U.S. Army regulations that war correspondents "will not exercise command, be placed in a position of authority over military personnel, nor will they be armed."[11] The penalties for "an intentional violation of these . . . regulations . . . may be . . . arrest to await deportation or trial by a court martial." Most of this was common knowledge among American war correspondents, whether experienced or not, but the Army still required them all to sign an agreement that spelled out the details.

Within a matter of weeks the allegations against Hemingway had spread widely enough to demand official attention. They were, after all, about a celebrity, and the newspapermen levying the charges knew how to make themselves heard. Eventually the inspector general (IG) of the Third Army felt compelled to investigate and summoned Hemingway to his headquarters, then in the French city of Nancy. The IG took written and oral testimony. Hemingway himself answered a series of questions under oath. Neither telling outright lies nor the whole truth, he talked around the issues. As he would put it years later, "I denied and kidded [my way] out of all of it and swore away everything I felt any pride in."[12]

This hurt. It was one thing not to get the recognition he thought he deserved; it was quite another to be the subject of an investigation that might lead to a court-martial in a war zone, ignominy for a man who cherished his reputation for courage under fire. Along the way, the investigation showcased Hemingway's ambivalent feelings for authority and the law. His last biographer, Michael S. Reynolds, put the Army investigation into a broader context and came to the conclusion that the writer had for most of his life "a profound, almost irrational fear of the law, its enforcers, and the courtroom. . . . He might joke about his sworn testimony . . . but at the same time there was nothing humorous about it" until the IG decided to drop the investigation.[13]

In November Hemingway was back with the 22d. By this time the regiment was facing the enemy's main line of resistance along the German–Belgian border, a set of fortifications that the Germans called the Westwall. The regiment's sector was in the Hürtgen Forest, where the network of bunkers and pillboxes was integrated into a landscape of dense woods, steep valleys, and waterways. Though only a few miles southeast of the German border city of Aachen, the forest was hard to get to, let alone to move through; there were few roads or even tracks, and many of the ones that existed in 1944 were narrow and unimproved. On his way in, Hemingway noted the succession of thickly wooded hills, some with clearings from which a soldier could see his enemy below.[14] In the late fall of 1944, cold and rain made it even harder for the 22d to move and fight.

During the heavy fighting from November 15 to December 4 that would cost the regiment over 2,700 casualties, Hemingway shadowed Lanham at his command post and on the battlefield, taking everything in and offering occasional bits of advice. One day they visited a frontline battalion commander in his solid bunker of earth and logs. The major had little energy, and Lanham commented to Hemingway that he was on the point of relieving him. Hemingway answered that Lanham did not need to relieve the man; he had the stink of death about him and would soon be dead. Within less than ten minutes, the report came through that the major had been killed when a piece of shrapnel passed through the walls of his bunker.[15]

Though not as active as he had been at Rambouillet, Hemingway did not hesitate to lend a hand in the many crises that occurred. When German infantry attacked the regimental command post on November 22, Hemingway grabbed a Thompson submachine gun and joined in the fray, helping to repel the attackers. During another counterattack a few days later around 4 A.M., German tanks and infantry swarmed around and through the regiment's defenses. The battalion commander who sounded the alarm was shooting Germans with one hand and holding a field telephone with the other. For once Hemingway and Lanham were not side by side, but

Lanham called for him while issuing stopgap orders. "I'll be right there, wait for me," was Hemingway's instant response. To get to Lanham, he dashed through a firebreak where many others had died, staying with the colonel until the Americans had fought the Germans to a standstill and left them no choice but to surrender by the dozen. It was for Lanham another pivotal moment in their relationship, one that he would never forget. Years later he would write that of all the things that he had carried in his heart from those days, none was more alive than the memory of that night.[16]

In the eyes of Lanham and his soldiers, Hemingway's performance in the Hürtgen Forest was exemplary. First, he was good company, sharing his whiskey and talking about subjects that mattered to him and were entertaining: how his son Jack had joined the OSS and parachuted into occupied France, how his undeserving wife Martha wanted a divorce, what the mating habits of African lions were. Hemingway even demonstrated how a lion got what he wanted from a lioness. And, though his job was to report on the fighting, he took the same risks as the men whose job was to fight. He went outside the wire with the attacking infantry, much farther forward than he had to go. Cool under pressure, willing to fight when he had to, he again displayed that sixth sense, what the Germans call the feeling in the tips of your fingers, that mark the best practitioners of the art of war.

On December 4, his last day in the forest, just as the members of the regiment who had survived the battle were being pulled back for a desperately needed rest, Hemingway's sixth sense saved his life and that of his friends. A thick ground fog made it impossible to see more than a few feet ahead as he rode slowly down a muddy road with a fellow correspondent named William Walton. Suddenly they heard a ripping sound that only Hemingway recognized, and he shouted "Oh, God, jump!" to Walton and their driver, Pelkey, pushing Walton into the roadside ditch and shielding his body seconds before a German fighter fired a stream of bullets into their jeep. The plane came back for a second pass, again firing down the middle of the road and missing the men in the ditch by a few feet—a very thin margin for a strafing. Hemingway calmly unhooked a canteen from his belt and offered Walton a premixed martini. The taste was metallic, but Walton had never enjoyed a drink more. The three picked themselves up, brushed the dirt off their clothes, and walked on past the smoldering wreck of their ride.[17]

Hemingway's last hurrah with the troops coincided with the Battle of the Bulge in the second half of December 1944. Hitler hurled German tanks and infantry—some thirty divisions in all—against a thinly defended part of the Allied line, a few miles to the north of where Lanham and his regiment were digging in. When the last great battle in the west started, Hemingway was in Paris with Mary. Once again, duty called; Barton, the division commander, told Hemingway over the phone that it was "a pretty hot show," one not to be missed.[18] Hemingway felt an obligation to go to the front and record the story.

By the time Hemingway arrived at the front, the German tide was beginning to ebb, and his appetite for battle was also winding down. Combat was exhilarating but it was also exhausting, especially in the winter of 1944–45, one of the coldest on record, when daily temperatures started out around 15 degrees Fahrenheit. Even the great writer-soldier could only push himself so far, and he accepted an invitation from Lanham to move in to his command post, then in a comfortable home near the town of Rodenbourg in the tiny country of Luxembourg. Hemingway shared a double bed with a fellow journalist (each man had his own bedroll) and he let the regimental doctor care for him. For some time he had been feverish, with a temperature that spiked at 104 degrees. Never quite warm enough even when wrapped in two sheepskin jackets, he was suffering from a chest cold and needed the quiet and the antibiotic sulfa drugs that the doctor gave him.[19]

By January 1945 the end of the war in Europe was predictable, a

A deceptively happy-looking Hemingway in the spring of 1945, on his way home to Cuba. *Copyright PAA, Ernest Hemingway Photo Collection, JFK Library.*

little like January 1939, when it had seemed just a matter of time before Franco's troops marched into Madrid. Hemingway did not need to wait to see the credits rolling down the screen to know how the movie would end. Instead he needed to leave the theater, and withdraw in order to recharge and to write. He was all too aware that he had not penned—or been paid for—much apart from news dispatches since publishing *For Whom the Bell Tolls* in 1940. The lack of new income made him feel "stony cold broke."[20]

Hemingway started looking for a way home, no easy task in early 1945. It took until early March for him to book a seat on a plane to take him back across the Atlantic. When he made it to Cuba, he focused again on what the war years had meant to him and how best to write about them in a novel.

At the Finca, Hemingway settled back into his routine of getting up before dawn and, alone except for a dog or a cat, either sitting at a desk or standing at a chest-high table, writing seriously for a few hours, usually in longhand, sometimes on a typewriter. He might be working on a book, or maybe writing letters, for him another way to practice his art. Later in the day, perhaps after lunch or after dinner, Hemingway might return to his desk to write long letters, often letting his guard down and expressing himself freely. On April 14, 1945, for example, he wrote seven letters in the morning, and was at it again in the late afternoon.[21]

Hemingway wrote love letters to his wives and mistresses, even to his first ex-wife, Hadley, and playful, affectionate letters to his sons. To publishers and lawyers, he dispatched sharp-tongued instructions, and more than once excoriated critics. It was hard for him to write short letters: one note to the journalist and critic Malcolm Cowley about his wartime exploits started with a promise to be short and tapered to a close more than once, but then there was just one more thing, and another. In the end the letter ran to four typewritten pages, with three more handwritten pages of postscripts.[22] It was as if he did not want to let go. Taken together, Hemingway's letters from this time reveal a man who wanted very badly to connect, and to stay connected, especially with those who were close to him.

Almost as soon as they were separated, Hemingway started writing to Lanham, telling him how much he missed him. On April 2, 1945, "absolutely homesick for the regiment," he wrote Lanham that he had "the Black Ass," his word for depression.[23] He added that he had not been depressed during the fighting, when there was a war to win and he had Lanham's companionship. Twelve days later, Hemingway told Lanham again that he was "lonesome for you and for [the] outfit."[24] In letters to others he praised Lanham the commander, the author, and above all the friend: "my pal and partner"[25] and "my best friend," feelings that Lanham reciprocated.[26] Together they had experienced life and death: Hemingway told Max Perkins that he had learned more while he and Buck were together than he had learned "altogether up until then."[27] This was a supreme compliment from a man who put such store by living life fully, and learning from it.

Hemingway's relationship with Lanham had nothing to do with spying. For the writer-soldier, war, especially ground combat, was the ultimate life experience. "It is wicked to say but that is the thing I love . . . best."[28] He felt most alive when risking his life, all of his senses fully engaged, putting his well-developed field and military skills to good use and not incidentally killing fascists. Hemingway relished being useful in this way. He also relished the comradeship that jelled in combat. Many of the friends whom he stayed in touch with for life were those he had been with on a battlefield, in Spain in the 1930s and France in 1944—men like the communist film maker Ivens, the patrician spy David Bruce, and the thoughtful soldier Lanham. The shared secret and risk of a meeting with the NKVD could make the pulse race; for many, spying was a substitute for battle. But for Hemingway it paled in comparison to actual combat, to being under fire, when a snap decision, moving to the left or the right, or a well-aimed shot, made reflexively, determined whether you lived or died.

No one in the NKVD had connected with Hemingway in the way that Ivens, Bruce, and Lanham did. The short Russian in the shabby clothes with the Boris-and-Natasha accent, the NKVD recruiter Jacob Golos was the kind of man Hemingway might have grown attached to: he was a true believer with heart and character, at a time when Hemingway was also a true believer (albeit in the allied cause of antifascism, not hard-line Marxism-Leninism). But Hemingway was only in touch with Golos for a short time, in peacetime New York in 1940 and 1941, and the NKVD operatives who reached out to Hemingway after Golos were unknowns, "workers" who had to conjure up introductions, met with the author once or twice without making much headway, and hoped for better results at the next meeting. When the Soviets dispatched another NKVD "worker" to meet with Hemingway in Cuba not long after he returned from Europe in 1945, the results were again inconclusive. But the Soviet record suggests that, until he received an "urgent summons out of the country," this "worker" nourished hopes of building a relationship with "Argo."[29]

Even if the Soviet operative and Hemingway had been granted the time to establish rapport, Hemingway's agenda was even more different now from the time when he had signed on with the NKVD in the winter of 1940–41, when his home country was sitting on the sidelines as the world burned. In 1945 there was no longer a compelling need to find the best way to fight fascism. World War II was over. Japan and Germany were literally in ruins. The armies of the East and the West faced each other warily on the plains of central Europe along a dividing line that ran through Germany and Austria.

CHAPTER 11

"THE CREEPS"

Not War, Not Peace

In September 1945, the war now finally over both in Europe and Asia, Buck Lanham was able to accept Hemingway's standing invitation to come to Cuba at "any hour of any day of any week of any month of any year."[1] *He shed his uniform for the first time in years and, with his wife, Mary, spent two weeks with the temporarily single writer drinking and talking among the palm trees around the pool at the Finca, shooting at the nearby Club de Cazadores, where the pigeons were clay and live, and fishing from* Pilar *in the Gulf Stream.*[2]

In the tropical sunlight, Lanham looked pale and stiff next to the tan and robust Hemingway, who drew his belly in and puffed his chest out for the photographer. Probably for Lanham's sake, the writer cinched up his shorts with the captured German belt with the "Gott mit uns" *buckle that he had worn in France in 1944. They enjoyed each other's company now as much as they had then. As they reminisced about the war and speculated about the future, their relationship easily made the transition from war to peace. But the writer was not sure about Mary Lanham. Ranging over subjects as diverse as bullfighting, world politics, and gender, they sized each other up in long conversations. Mary could not help noticing Hemingway's hostility to women, especially to his former wife Martha Gellhorn.*

A day or two before the Lanhams went home, Hemingway spent the evening with them at the plain wooden table in his small, light-

filled dining room. As the heads of deer and gazelle—his hunting trophies—looked down from the whitewashed walls, Hemingway started to talk about the need to coexist with the Soviet Union now that the war was over. Sitting a few feet away from the host, Mary Lanham interjected that his views sounded like "straight appeasement" to her.[3] *She was calling to mind British policy in 1938, a red flag for Hemingway, who detested the way that the British prime minister Neville Chamberlain had given in to Hitler at Munich, especially after failing to support the Spanish Republic.*

Face red, eyes blazing, Hemingway leapt to his feet and advanced on Mary, cocking his arm to throw a glass of wine in her face. At the last second, he restrained himself and returned to his place at the head of the table.

Right away he told her how sorry he was. But the damage was done. Mary Lanham and Hemingway would never be friends. The picture that Ernest gave Buck when the Lanhams went home showed the two men without Mary at the Floridita, and was inscribed only to "Buck from his best friend, always and whenever."[4]

With the end of the threat that had brought them together, the Soviet Union and the West began to redefine their relationship. Hemingway participated in the process, writing an introduction to *The Treasury of the Free World*. This was an anthology of essays by a number of prominent men, mostly left of center, who espoused a new world order. In that spirit, Hemingway called for Americans to rethink their place in the world. He noted that the United States was now "the strongest power" in both hemispheres, so strong that "[i]t would be easy for us, if we do not learn to understand the world and appreciate the rights, privileges and duties of all other countries and people, to represent in our power the same danger to the world that Fascism did"—words that would have angered some patriotic Americans when they were written in September 1945, probably before the Lanhams' visit.[5]

A friend for all seasons: Hemingway with Buck and Mary Lanham at the Finca in September 1945. Hemingway's belt is identical to the one that he wore in combat in 1944. *Ernest Hemingway Photo Collection, JFK Library.*

At roughly the same time, a thin, intense young man named Igor Gouzenko was getting ready to walk away from his job at the Soviet Embassy in Ottawa, Canada. Determined to find a better life for his family in the West, the code clerk would establish his bona fides with official telegrams. For a few weeks he had been stuffing a few pages of secrets into his shirt every night and hiding them at his apartment on Somerset Street, well away from the other Soviets in the Canadian capital. When he took the plunge on September 5, he went first to the *Ottawa Journal* and tried to explain what the telegrams showed. The night editor did not know what to make of the agitated Russian who stood in front of him and cried out again and again: "It's war, it's war, it's Russia!"[6]

Gouzenko returned to the newspaper the next day, to little effect, and then tried his luck with the Royal Canadian Mounted Police

(RCMP), the Mounties, who had an intelligence bureau—also to no avail. In the afternoon a driver from the embassy came to Somerset Street and banged on the door for a few minutes, shouting at Gouzenko to open up. Sympathetic neighbors called the local police, who did not know what to do. One of those neighbors, a Mrs. Elliott, offered the terrified Gouzenko family refuge in her apartment. Around midnight, the local NKVD *rezident* himself appeared with three or four young officers. Through a keyhole Gouzenko watched from across the hall as they broke down the door to his apartment and ransacked the place, looking for him and the secret documents. Someone called the local police again, who confronted the belligerent Soviets.

It was finally clear that the Gouzenkos needed protection from their own government. The next morning, two days after he had left his workplace, a policeman escorted Gouzenko to RCMP headquarters, where he began his life as a defector. When they started to read the telegrams, the Canadians learned how the Soviets had run an extensive spy ring in their country during World War II, and how that operation was connected to an even more extensive spy ring in the United States very much like the one that had touched Hemingway's life.

By early February 1946 bits of the sensational story had started to leak out. Canadian prime minister Mackenzie King tried to preempt further leaks by issuing a bland official statement. Others would come to consider the Gouzenko affair as the beginning of the Cold War. But King still thought of the Soviets as wartime allies and was reluctant to do anything to antagonize them. Nonetheless, by mid-February, the *New York Times* knew enough to run a front-page story on the defection of the "Soviet Embassy Ex-Aide" that implicated a surprising number of scientists and civil servants, one of them a ranking cabinet minister.[7] The *Times* story was just one of many articles on the Gouzenko affair that would continue to run well into March.[8]

When the news broke, Hemingway was at the Finca, hard at work on his novel about the war. He stopped what he was doing to focus on Gouzenko and came up with a unique interpretation of the affair. His choice of words implied that the Canadians had set a trap for the Soviets. He wrote to Lanham that, while he was "no professional Russki lover . . . , [t]his Canadian set-up" gave him "the creeps."[9] He placed the operations that Gouzenko unmasked on a par with the work of a typical military attaché, charged with collecting all manner of military information. This was a Panglossian interpretation of what the Soviets had been up to, which was aggressively spying on their allies—recruiting spies and stealing secrets from a friendly country. (By March the Canadians would arrest thirty-nine suspects on charges of spying. They ranged from atomic scientists to members of Parliament.) Hemingway went on to argue that the Soviets were simply behaving like all governments, including the U.S. government. That made it hypocritical for Americans to pretend to be "horrified" by the Soviet behavior.

Hemingway played a riff on that theme in the second half of the letter. American governments had routinely intervened in the internal affairs of Latin American countries since time immemorial. For that reason, the United States was in no position to complain when another great power intervened in the internal affairs of a small country. Besides, he continued, it was not right to lay the actions of every foreign communist at the Soviets' door. And if Britain and the United States persisted in maligning the Soviets, perhaps they would be forced to defend themselves by starting the Comintern up again.

A few weeks later, on March 5, 1946, Winston Churchill stood Hemingway's view on its head. Sharing a stage with President Harry Truman in the small college town of Fulton, Missouri, he delivered the first iconic Cold War speech, one that marked the shift from making common cause with the Soviets to countering Stalinist aggression:[10]

From Stettin in the Baltic to Trieste in the Adriatic, an iron curtain has descended across the Continent. Behind that line lie

> *all the capitals of the ancient states of Central and Eastern Europe . . . all . . . subject . . . to Soviet influence . . . and . . . control from Moscow. . . . The Communist parties, which were very small in all these . . . states . . . , are [now] seeking everywhere to obtain totalitarian control. . . .*

Churchill was careful to remember the "deep sympathy and goodwill" for Russia that had built up during the war, and to declare his resolve to work through any differences to establish lasting friendships. But, since the Soviets admired "nothing . . . so much as strength," the Western Allies needed to stand strong and vigilant in order to protect themselves, just as they had failed to do in the 1930s when Hitler and Mussolini threatened the established order.

Hemingway's comment on this speech, in a letter to a Soviet admirer, was that it was Churchill, not Stalin, who was a threat to world peace. The people of the United States and the Soviet Union would get along, he wrote, "if we could have understanding of each other instead of the repeat performance of a Churchill." Otherwise nothing stood between the friendship of their two countries, he concluded.[11]

Ten days later he was again writing about the Soviets. On June 30, he felt compelled to explain to Lanham that he had a "big prejudice in their favour on acct of knowing them in old days when [the] chips were down." He believed that every "lousy Russki . . . has as much right to his cut in the world" as any member of the British elite.[12] He reminded Lanham that there were still fascist regimes in the world—like that of Franco, not to mention Chiang Kai-shek, who presided over "the worst kind of slavery."

Once again, Hemingway was openly harking back to the Spanish Civil War, when the Soviets were supporting the Spanish Republic, the cause that he had believed in above all others. The British, on the other hand, had stayed on the sidelines, protecting their own interests. Then in World War II the United States and the Soviet Union had taken the lead in defeating the Germans and the Japanese. For Hemingway this meant that the fruits of victory were now "ours and theirs," not that of the old colonial powers, let alone the fascists who were still around.[13] After the war, he would tell Lanham in 1948, he had looked forward to seeing the world divided up between the United States and the Soviet Union "in a sound, hard-headed way;" he would grant the Soviets "all of Europe they could take and hold."[14] That was preferable to fighting to preserve the British Empire or the rights of oil companies.

Just as he had during and after the Spanish Civil War, Hemingway was willing to give the Soviets the benefit of the doubt. There was still not a word of criticism for the Soviet leadership, and he continued to downplay or excuse Stalin's purges. In his February 1947 handwritten draft of the letter to "Miss Craipeau" about Spain and communism, he would write that he had known "the Russians quite well in Spain and other places" and that "no one [he had] . . . admired there was ever executed." The key phrase was "no one [he had] admired." He went on to write that "many people" he knew "and thought deserved shooting were shot." After claiming that he knew nothing about the purges in the Soviet Union in the 1930s, he commented that he had read Koestler—"but knowing Koestler could not believe him altho [his] book was excellent."[15]

This was almost certainly a reference to the former communist Arthur Koestler's classic novel *Darkness at Noon* (published in 1940), which grew out his experiences in Spain when he had worked for Münzenberg. It became a bestseller and opened many eyes about Stalinism and the purges. Set in Moscow in 1938, it was the story of a member of the old guard, one Rubashov, who had dedicated his life to the revolution only to be accused of betraying it. Both Rubashov and his interrogators understand that it does not matter whether the charges are true; they are a matter of political convenience. The senior interrogator, an old friend, reasons with Rubashov, telling him that a confession will save his life. The junior interrogator is not so gentle. When he finally gives in to the inevitable and confesses, Rubashov finds it strangely liberating to do so. The experience has changed him. He is no longer a true believer, subject to party discipline, willing to accept every twist and turn of the party line. Instead he is "once more a human being, a man of feeling, of subjective sensibilities."[16]

The book hit so close to home that the party placed it on its index of works that members anywhere were forbidden to read, own, or discuss, even outside the Soviet Union.[17]

The obedient communist and gifted screenwriter Dalton Trumbo would later brag about his role in keeping *Darkness at Noon* from making it to the screen.[18] It was all right to film any number of tales about the Gestapo and its victims, but stories about the NKVD and its victims were off-limits.

The show trials, the most visible part of the purges in the 1930s, were far from secret. Though the full extent of Stalin's crimes, of the Gulag and its millions of victims, would not emerge for many years, the trials were fact, well known on both sides of the Atlantic. Hemingway would have been hard-pressed *not* to know about them. For long stretches in 1937, his communist friends in Spain talked of little else: "every day [they] . . . heard of new arrests, accompanied by incredible and frightening accusations. . . . The Terror was roaring across Russia, like a tidal wave drowning everything on its way."[19] The communist press he sometimes wrote for described the trials in hysterical detail, and the great American dailies that were on his bedside table reported the same stories in more muted tones. The *Daily Worker,* for example, described one of the trials as "the smashing of a fascist spy nest," and reported that Marshal Mikhail Tukhachevsky, the commander of the Red Army, had been a spy for the Gestapo.[20] On the same subject a few days later, the front page of the *New York Times* featured a sober analysis questioning the incredible charges against the Soviet military leader (all of which turned out to be false).[21]

A year after he wrote to Miss Craipeau, Hemingway would appear better informed in a letter to Lanham. He now seemed to acknowledge the existence and true purpose of the purges—while still expressing support for Stalin. He asked if, facing the same challenges, "Truman would have [been any] better than Stalin." He himself would have been "a damned sight worse." He hoped he would have been as ruthless "if it were for the good of my country."[22] This was Hemingway's way of saying that Stalin had to be ruthless in order to protect the Soviet Union from enemies like Hitler.

Hemingway was not alone in his attitude. Wartime sympathy for the Soviets—the victims of Nazi aggression who had fought back and won, at enormous cost—had ebbed. But there was still a reservoir of fellow feeling for our onetime allies. In 1946 many American public figures were not yet ready to heed Churchill's warning about the iron curtain. Even after Truman grudgingly admitted the British leader was probably right, there were others who continued to resist his conclusions. Among them were Eleanor Roosevelt and Henry Wallace, who from 1941 to 1945 had preceded Truman as Franklin Roosevelt's vice president, and who in 1948 would run for president as a third-party candidate against Truman. Wallace made some of the same arguments as Hemingway: the American government needed to make an effort to get along with the Soviets; they were, after all, just people like us. The Soviet Union had legitimate needs and aspirations like any other country. If we were hostile to them, they would be hostile to us. Hemingway acknowledged his kinship with Wallace in his unique way a year later when he wrote that Wallace seemed "unsound, unstable, possibly slightly nuts; yet right on many things."[23]

The problem was that neither Hemingway's nor Wallace's views were anywhere near the mainstream. As Cold War tensions deepened, the political center in America moved dramatically to the right.

Since 1932, the Democrats had controlled both the White House and Congress. Their New Deal had changed the country in hitherto unimaginable ways, laying the foundation for something like a welfare state. In November 1946, the pendulum started to swing the other way. The Republicans took control of both houses of Congress and wanted to reset the balance. Their platform was straightforward enough: it was time to take a stand against Roosevelt's creeping socialism, to say nothing of the communists and the liberals who tolerated them.

President Truman now found himself pushed to the right by circumstances abroad as well as by Republicans at home. The Soviets continued to make inroads into central and even Western Europe. When Britain announced that she could no longer afford to support traditional allies like Greece, then fighting communist insurgents, the president decided that the United States would shoulder that burden. In March 1947, he told Congress that it would be "the policy of the United States to support free peoples who are resisting subjugation" by Moscow or its surrogates.[24] The iron curtain that the Soviets had drawn across Europe and their expanding web of satellite states clearly sparked the president's declaration: "a number of countries . . . have recently had totalitarian regimes forced upon them against their will [by a system that] relies on terror and oppression, a controlled press and radio, fixed elections, and suppression of personal freedoms."

This policy became known as the Truman Doctrine. It was followed a few days later by the debut of a loyalty program to root out any communists or communist sympathizers in the federal government.[25]

The House Un-American Activities Committee (HUAC) flourished in this environment. Set up in 1938, HUAC featured a mix of southern Democrats, some of them toxic racists, and conservative Republicans, among them a smart, aggressive young representative from California named Richard Nixon. The committee's charter was to investigate "subversive and un-American propaganda," sponsored by foreign governments to undermine the republic.[26] Congressional committees were usually set up to gather the information that Congress needed to draft legislation. HUAC departed from the norm by also serving as political theater. It was a place where witnesses had few legal rights.

By now, the federal government had assembled a detailed picture of Soviet espionage in the United States through the end of World War II. Its information came from defectors and decrypted messages, which made it difficult to take cases to court. Much of the evidence was hearsay—what one old communist said about another—or still considered too secret to present to a jury. The government was a long way from declassifying a top secret program, code-named Venona, that broke thousands of messages between the NKVD station in New York and Moscow.[27] Many of the messages unmasked NKVD spies in the Roosevelt administration. As a result, it fell to HUAC to furnish the Congress and the American people with information about communist subversion, including what it called "Soviet espionage activities."[28]

The committee began by targeting communists in Hollywood because they seemed well placed to spread Soviet propaganda through their work. In the fall of 1947, HUAC investigated the composer Hanns Eisler, who happened to be Jewish, had fled Germany to escape from Hitler, and spent most of his time in the United States in Hollywood, writing "music for the movies."[29] Pudgy and bald, speaking in heavily accented English, Eisler did not look or sound like a threat to national security. His problem was a combination of guilt by association—his brother was a German communist who had antagonized the committee—and his own past. He *had* actually *been* a communist, and even though he had not done anything subversive in Hollywood, in the 1920s and 1930s he *had* worked with Hemingway's communist friend Joris Ivens, and he *had* written the music for communist songs that sounded far better in Berlin or Moscow than in Washington:[30]

We lunge to the fight . . .
We're coming with Lenin
For Bolshevik work.

While Eisler took the stand in September, Martha Gellhorn happened to be in the audience on Capitol Hill. She recorded how the large and ornate Caucus Room was almost empty that day but for a handful of newsmen and photographers, their lights focused relentlessly on the bewildered witness.[31] With his bad memory and limited English, Eisler was easy prey for HUAC counsel Robert E. Stripling, who was able to tangle the composer up in inconsistencies and make the far-fetched case that he was the Karl Marx of music.[32] In the end, Democratic congressman John E. Rankin of Mississippi rendered the judgment that changed Eisler's life, denouncing him for coming to the United States "to foment revolution" while "our boys were dying by the thousands . . . to get Hitler's heel off their necks."[33]

A few days later, federal authorities started proceedings to deport Eisler but then permitted him to leave of his own accord so long as he agreed not to return. At New York's LaGuardia Airport, before stepping onto a plane for Eastern Europe, he expressed his regret in a prepared statement: "I could well understand it when in 1933 the Hitler bandits put a price on my head and drove me out. They were the evil of the period; I was proud at being driven out. But I feel heart-broken over being driven out of this beautiful country in this ridiculous way."[34]

The next set of hearings, a few weeks later in October 1947, attracted far more attention than the Eisler hearings. The curtain was about to go up on "the hottest show in town," one that would feature studio directors, movie stars, and scriptwriters instead of the hapless composer.[35] The proceedings against them would displace world events on the front pages of every major American newspaper.

By the time the chairman called the Caucus Room to order on the first day of the hearings, every seat was taken, and many onlookers had to stand in the aisles. The lights were again turned up bright for the eight or nine news cameras—so bright that some of the cameramen, and even a witness or two, wore dark glasses. The fireworks began when the screenwriters took the stand to explain why they had allowed the communists to influence the content of movies in America.[36] The core of the group became famous as the Hollywood Ten, every one of them a communist or former communist, including Hemingway acquaintances Alvah Bessie and Ring Lardner, Jr. Hemingway and Bessie had met on the battlefields of Spain, where the writer had also known Lardner's son, Jim, who would be killed in action and movingly eulogized by Hemingway.

The Ten's performance on the stand grabbed more headlines than the actual charges of subversion. After receiving direction from the CPUSA, they produced their own political theater.[37] Their narrative was as compelling as the committee's, but no less misleading. John Howard Lawson—another Hemingway acquaintance—was the most disruptive. With bright brown eyes and "a great beak of a nose," he was short and energetic, with "drastic ideas on every subject under the sun."[38] Some remember him for his passion and talent, but for most party members he was a dogmatic Stalinist and humorless enforcer of communist discipline.[39]

Lawson fought back from the witness chair by invoking the Constitution:[40]

> Mr. Stripling: Are you a member of the Screen Writers Guild?
>
> Mr. Lawson: The raising of any question here in regard to membership, political beliefs, or affiliation . . .
>
> The Chairman: . . . [H]ave you ever been a member of the Communist Party?
>
> Mr. Lawson: I am framing my answer in the only way in which any American citizen can frame his answer to a question which absolutely invades his rights.
>
> The Chairman: Then you refuse to answer that question; is that correct? . . .
>
> Mr. Lawson: . . . I shall continue to fight for the Bill of Rights, which you are trying to destroy.

When the chairman ordered them "take this man away," the capitol guards escorted Lawson from the stand. Some members of the audience booed and others applauded.

In the end, one producer, one director, and eight screenwriters refused to answer questions about their membership in the Communist Party. For this, they were found to be in contempt of Congress by an overwhelming vote of the House of Representatives, 346 to 17. While many representatives on both sides of the aisle did not approve of the way the committee bullied its witnesses, only a handful were willing to tolerate the kind of spectacle that Lawson and his comrades had put on. The result was that the Ten faced fines and jail for up to a year. When they emerged from prison, they found themselves on the so-called Blacklist, started in November 1947 as a declaration by studio heads that they would not employ members of the Ten unless they renounced communism.

Hemingway was an attentive student of postwar politics because he sensed what was at stake for him. At the Finca, he covered tables and desks with the newspapers and magazines that he devoured every day. His library was filled with books about foreign countries and military affairs. The selection points to a special interest in Soviet espionage and the FBI.[41] This year he was reading and thinking about the events that occurred between Truman's speech to Congress in March and the HUAC hearings in the fall. There wasn't much that he liked about any of it. In a letter to Lanham—the correspondent to whom he continued to reveal himself more than any other about war and politics—Hemingway criticized the Truman Doctrine, particularly the idea that the United States should step in for his old nemesis, the British Empire, now without the means to maintain its traditional spheres of influence.[42]

Hemingway liked the president's loyalty program even less than his foreign policy. Tongue only partly in cheek, the writer told Lanham that the program put him, Hemingway, at risk because he had been a "pre-mature anti-fascist."[43] Now, Hemingway predicted, "in the course of the present witch hunt," all premature antifascists would probably end up in "concentration camps."[44] Continuing in the same vein, he told Lanham that if their friendship should ever become an embarrassment, the general should feel "absolutely free to denounce" the writer. (Lanham was, after all, still a serving officer. His politics were generally unremarkable; he was perhaps more open-minded than some of his brother officers but overall much closer to the center than his best friend. In 1948 he told Hemingway that he usually preferred Democrats to Republicans, and had nothing good to say about Wallace.[45]) Hemingway quipped that perhaps it would emerge that he had cultivated Lanham and his regiment "in order to learn . . . secrets . . . [and] transmit them to Moscu [*sic*]." He knew that he had been regarded as "a dangerous red" before the war. Then, during the war, when he had worked for American intelligence, he was regarded as a "fairly trustworthy character." But, he concluded, since he had never received any formal acknowledgment of his service, he would probably be persecuted anyway.

Strands of reality and fantasy mixed in Hemingway's thoughts. There were no concentration camps for American leftists. The Hollywood Ten did go to jail, but only after provoking the committee. Before America entered the war, the FBI had made note of Hemingway's sympathies for the left. His endorsement of Spanish Republican causes—like the Abraham Lincoln Battalion and a "Communist committee . . . to Aid Spanish Democracy"—had long since become a matter of record in the Bureau's internal security files.[46] After Pearl Harbor, Embassy Havana officers approached the FBI about their plans to use him to run the Crook Factory. That sparked the FBI's interest in Hemingway, who kept it alive by goading FBI agents and complaining about them to Joyce and Braden, in one case composing a fourteen-page screed against a Special Agent Knoblaugh alleging fascist sympathies. It was only after Hemingway tried to get Knoblaugh ejected from Cuba that Hoover directed his staff to summarize what the Bureau knew about the writer.[47]

The result was an exhaustive review, dated April 1943, of all open and confidential information on the writer, leading to the conclusion that the Bureau had "no information which would definitely tie him with the Communist Party or . . . indicate that he is or has been a Party member."[48]

By this time the Bureau had an official file on Hemingway—number 64-23312—that grew over the years as he made the news or when a Bureau representative happened to send in a report.[49] The classification "64" was for "Foreign Miscellaneous," a catch-all category that included Cuba. Much of the information in the file was about the turf battle between the Crook Factory and the FBI in Cuba, as well as Hemingway's qualifications for intelligence work. Other documents reflect the Bureau's concern that Hemingway might criticize the FBI in a forthcoming book, something Hoover was always at pains to avoid. A few documents in the file are fallout from other files, like that on the Abraham Lincoln veterans, or the in-depth look at Gustavo Durán for alleged communist sympathies, deemed far more serious than Hemingway's "liberalism."

File Number 64-23312 was not a counterintelligence or internal security file, and its content shows that the Bureau was not monitoring Hemingway in any systematic way, or investigating him with a view to indicting him for a crime like espionage.[50] Years later, in July 1955, an FBI employee would check a range of files back to 1938 and conclude that "[n]o investigation . . . has been conducted by the FBI concerning the captioned individual [Hemingway]."[51] The Bureau never particularly liked or trusted Hemingway, but he was simply wrong when he claimed, as early as 1942, that the U.S. government was keeping an eye on him because it had questions about his trustworthiness.[52] Like everyone else, his mail and his calls were subject to wartime censorship, but no one had singled him out for special attention, and no one was following him around New York or Havana to see what he was up to.

In June 1947 Hemingway went to the Embassy in Havana to receive a bit of official recognition for his wartime service: a Bronze Star Medal from the U.S. Army. A picture of the ceremony shows him in a long-sleeved white guayabera—an embroidered Cuban dress shirt, suitable for a formal occasion. A cheerful colonel in a Class A uniform—khaki jacket and tie, with campaign ribbons—leans in to pin the medal on the guayabera, probably just after an assistant has read the citation praising the war correspondent for his work in France after D-Day from July 20 to September 1, and then again from September 6 to December 6, covering the time at Rambouillet with David Bruce and at the front with the 22d Infantry after the fall

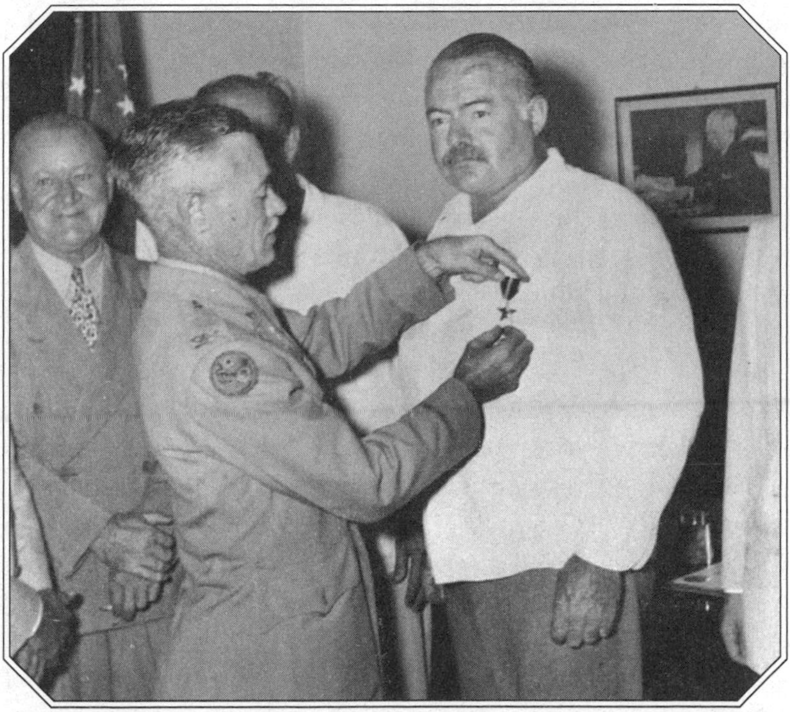

Not the medal that he wanted: Hemingway receiving the Bronze Star at the Embassy in Havana, June 1947. *Copyright Bettmann, Corbis Images.*

of Paris.[53] There was praise for his "familiarity with modern military science" and the way he circulated "freely under fire in combat areas," all in order to enable "readers to obtain a vivid picture of the difficulties and triumphs of the frontline soldier."

But the fine words did not make Hemingway happy. The expression on his face is that of a man who is ill at ease, who feels that something is not quite right. He accepts the medal and the citation, suitable for framing, and keeps them among his personal papers at the Finca, then reaches out almost immediately to Lanham to tell him that "the Bronze Star thing was very curious." He did not know the backstory, who had pushed it through the system or drafted the citation—but he found that it was "a very slippery piece of writing."[54] Part of the problem was that Hemingway wanted a more senior award, one that reflected his accomplishments on the battlefield, like the Distinguished Service Cross (DSC), which, as he liked to say, one of the OSS officers who had been at Rambouillet would wear in his stead.[55] Perhaps he thought that a DSC would protect him from the stigma of being a premature antifascist—one who had not only signed proclamations and given speeches but also gone to the extraordinary length of signing up with the NKVD.

In the absence of a DSC, life went on as before. In September he wrote Lanham that he once again had "every form of black ass [depression] and in spades" and that the political news from Washington was "very gloomy."[56] His comment that he had had enough war was another way to say that he still did not approve of the ever-hardening line that the Truman administration was taking toward the Soviets.[57]

Less than a month later, he praised Gellhorn's denunciation of HUAC's treatment of the German composer Eisler, published in the October 6 edition of the *New Republic*. Hemingway read her article and pronounced it "good. . . . She is at her best when she is fighting for something she believes in. . . ."[58]

In November 1947 he analyzed the Hollywood Ten hearings for Lanham. He came to the commonsense conclusion that "the whole thing was undignified . . . both the communists and the committee came out very chicken."[59] He speculated that they probably had bad consciences, not because they were communists, but because they were "whoreing [*sic*] instead of writing as well as they could"—that is, writing for the movies instead of crafting novels—and then becoming communists in order "to save their souls." This was a familiar refrain—Hemingway had often denounced writers who went to Hollywood to sell themselves to the studios instead of preserving their independence and artistic integrity.

In the next breath Hemingway went on to say what *he* would have done if he had been called by the committee. After denying that he had ever been a communist, he would have declared that the members of HUAC "appear[ed] to me to be c____ers [*sic*], saying it slowly and carefully for the microphone."[60] He would have concluded that he was in "complete contempt of them," and that his father, grandfather, and great-grandfather would also have been in contempt of them, and that he had known only four honest congressmen in the last thirty years.

The committee never gave Hemingway a chance to come to Washington for a confrontation. Although HUAC kept a file on the writer, it was like the FBI file about him (parts of which may have found their way to HUAC, as the two organizations cooperated on a regular basis). There were tidbits about his support for the Spanish Republic, and for the communists who had fought alongside him. But, like the FBI, the HUAC investigators were never able to show that Hemingway himself was a communist, let alone a Soviet spy. That, and his fame, were probably what kept him from receiving a subpoena. It was one thing to bully someone like Eisler, or clash with an out-and-out communist like Lawson, but quite another to put an American icon on the stand.[61]

For their part, the Hollywood Ten did not quietly exit stage left. Their behavior on the witness stand cost them the support of many Hollywood moderates. But others were still willing to protest on their behalf.[62] The playwright Arthur Miller proposed taking out full-page newspaper ads, and famous writers like Thomas Mann lent their names to the campaign.[63] Hemingway's old friend Archibald MacLeish spoke out against the committee, objecting that it was rendering quasi-legal judgments without offering their victims the protection of the law, and concluding that it had done more to undermine the defense of freedom "than all the Communists on earth."[64]

Several other old friends did their best to persuade Hemingway to speak out. Milton Wolff was the most persistent. When the two men met in Spain, Wolff was already a seasoned combat veteran who would go on to command the Abraham Lincoln Battalion of the International Brigades. Hemingway liked what he saw, writing that Wolff was as "tall as Lincoln, gaunt as Lincoln, as brave and as good a soldier as any that commanded battalions at Gettysburg."[65] During World War II, Wolff joined the U.S. Army and served with the OSS, earning a reputation as a "tempestuous, radical officer, a product of the depression and the Brooklyn liberalists . . . [and] a dissenting, trouble-making individual."[66] After the war, he continued the fight against the remaining fascist power, that of Franco's Spain.[67] He was a tireless organizer, writer, and speaker, more than once occupying the podium at Madison Square Garden in New York. He was not a member of the Communist Party, though he might as well have been one; he was on the same side of many issues as the party and consulted regularly with its leaders. His activism guaranteed him a prominent place on the lists of subversives maintained by the FBI and HUAC.[68]

Wolff and Hemingway had an on-again, off-again friendship. They had gotten off to a good start in Spain, but two years later, Wolff was one of the leftists who had attacked Hemingway for writing about Republican atrocities in *For Whom the Bell Tolls.*

Hemingway hit back hard, telling Wolff that he was the kind of "prick" who stabbed his friends in the back.[69] A few days later, Hemingway apologized for writing "such a tough letter" to the much younger man. He wanted to take his words back and wish him luck in all his ventures.[70] One story has Hemingway following up with a generous loan to Wolff, who immediately cabled his thanks, but added that he *still* thought the new novel was "a lousy book."[71]

In the summer of 1946, Wolff had first approached Hemingway to ask him to support the upcoming tenth anniversary of the Abraham Lincoln Battalion, offering Ernest "the Chairmanship job."[72] Wolff followed up with an international telephone call—an expensive proposition in 1946—and was disappointed

Never give up: Spanish Civil War veteran and activist Milton Wolff addressing a rally in New York, 1946. *Abraham Lincoln Collection, Tamiment Library.*

that Hemingway kept changing the subject, preferring to talk about his prowess on the battlefield in France in 1944.[73] To make sure Wolff got the message, Hemingway wrote out his answer on July 26 and put it in the mail: he was too busy with his novel to take on the chairmanship of "a political meeting," and he would not sign letters that he himself had not drafted.[74]

Hemingway's compromise was to agree to make a recording of his eulogy of Jim Lardner for Wolff. This he did in early 1947, adding a few words about how proud he was to be in the company of other "pre-mature anti-fascists," the classification that he and others had received because they had come early to the fight against fascism by going to Spain.[75]

But he did not now want to get any more deeply involved. In May 1947 a telegram from Wolff to Hemingway asked him to attend one or two commemorative events at Madison Square Garden in September: "We want persons most intimately connected with [the] struggle of [the] Spanish people. Wont you say yes."[76] There is no answer on file. Hemingway did not attend either of the events, and would keep his distance from politics on the mainland for years to come.[77]

CHAPTER 12

THE COLD WAR

No More Brave Words

"Red Ring Bared by Blond Queen": on July 21, 1948, the New York tabloids were adorned with banner headlines announcing a mystery women who would reveal what she knew about Soviet espionage in the United States.[1] *A few days later, HUAC—the House Un-American Activities Committee—called the "Blond Queen" to Washington to testify.*

The informant turned out to be a Vassar graduate named Elizabeth Bentley. Contrary to headline writers' fantasies, she had brown hair and, though only forty, something of a matronly look, with wide-set eyes and a high forehead. Her chin was undefined. For the hearings she dressed in dark suits with frilly blouses, and liked to wear strands of pearls wound tight around her neck. But this former communist made a strong impression. She seemed impervious to the standing-room-only audience, not to mention the hostility of the many prominent men and women she accused of being Soviet spies. Surrounded by newsmen crouching and standing in every available free space, "[b]lazed at by cameras . . . amid signals for the opening of radio and television circuits, Miss Bentley strode calmly to the witness chair and, after taking the oath and mopping her brow because of the heat of the klieg lights, told her story."[2]

The number of American spies she proceeded to name was breathtaking, and so were their positions—from the White House to the Treasury to the Department of State to the Department of

Justice, even the OSS, the wartime spy agency. She told the committee that an OSS officer named Duncan Lee, one of General Donovan's aides, had given her some of the same information that he had put in the general's in-box, knowing that its destination was another in-box in Moscow.

The only time she was not calm during her testimony was when asked about the Soviet spymaster she had worked for—and loved with a desperate intensity. That man was Jacob Golos, the old Bolshevik who had recruited Hemingway in the winter of 1940–41.[3]

Elizabeth Bentley had been a cutout, even a surrogate case officer, for the Soviets. This meant that she held face-to-face meetings with American spies on behalf of the NKVD. Based in New York, she traveled to Washington by train every two to three weeks, and met with her contacts in restaurants and parks across the city. Hardly anyone was likely to notice, let alone remember, the middle-aged American woman, with her plain looks, sitting in a booth at Martin's Tavern at Wisconsin and N in Georgetown with, say, a socially prominent OSS officer or a senior member of the administration. After the meetings, she gathered up their secrets in an oversize handbag or sometimes a shopping bag if there were many documents, and carried everything back to New York, where she passed it to her NKVD contact. From 1941 until his death in 1943, everything she collected flowed to Jacob Golos, that mainstay of Soviet espionage on the east coast.

Bentley not only worked for Golos, but also invited him into her modest but comfortable apartment at 58 Barrow Street in the West Village, a far less desirable address in 1941 than it would become fifty years later. One of the benefits of the brick townhouse was that it had a fireplace—useful for burning the papers that were the byproduct of their work. Golos was a good enough spy but kept cryptic notes in his pockets on bits of paper, and stored secret documents in a safe at the World Tourists Inc., the travel agency on Fifth Avenue where he and Bentley worked. He shared some, but not all, of his secrets with her. Although they lived and worked together in what one wag called "bourgeois sin and Leninist bliss," she testified he could be "very close-mouthed" and told her only what he thought she needed to know.[4]

Since she played no part in the Hemingway operation, she did not need to know about him, and likely never heard his name from Golos. For his part, Hemingway may not have recognized Golos from Bentley's testimony. Indeed he may not have known him by that name. (When he first met Bentley, Golos had introduced himself as "Timmy.") Photos of the Russian were (and are) scarce, and it would be three years before Bentley shared all of her loving impressions of this short, unusual-looking man with "the startlingly blue eyes" and "bright red hair."[5] But Hemingway understood what her testimony revealed about the larger political climate, and how it showed the committee's eagerness to uncover Soviet spies, even those who had never betrayed any official secrets.

On July 28, after the stories about Bentley had started to appear in the press, Hemingway wrote Lanham to say he knew that the times had changed. "In the old days" he felt free to go to "a top Russki" when he, Hemingway, wanted information, which the Russian would share with him "in confidence."[6] But, perhaps thinking of the Soviet spy who had contacted him in Cuba after his return from Europe in 1945, he went on to write that he had "not seen a Russki now for over two years." The reason was that Americans no longer trusted any communists. Since the U.S. government had started the Cold War with them, he had avoided "even social contact." Defensive in tone, Hemingway returned to the familiar themes of trust and loyalty. He claimed he had been like Jim Bridger, the nineteenth-century mountain man who had mediated between Indian tribes and encroaching settlers. There had never been any question of Bridger's loyalty; everyone trusted him because he embodied trustworthiness. He, Hemingway, had tried to be "trustworthy" all of his life, something he "would rather be . . . than anything in the world."

Hemingway would repeat himself in the coming months, telling

Lanham in one letter that he still did not believe in anything except fighting for his country whenever she sounded the call to arms.[7] He would later sum it all up for Lanham in a few words: he, Ernest Hemingway, was "no fucking traitor."[8]

In the meantime, the spectacle in Washington went on. Bentley and another former communist spy, *Time* editor Whittaker Chambers, continued to finger Americans who had spied for the Soviets, and the accused fought back, bitterly denying the allegations that would cost them their careers and even their lives. Assistant Secretary Harry Dexter White, Hemingway's onetime acquaintance at Treasury who had played a role in his travel to China in 1941, appeared before HUAC on August 13, 1948, to testify that he had "never been a communist, nor even close to becoming one" and that the principles by which he lived "made it impossible [for him] ever to do a disloyal act. . . ."[9] Like Lawson, he invoked the Constitution and the Bill of Rights. His creed was "the American creed":

> *. . . freedom of religion, freedom of speech, freedom of thought, freedom of the press. . . . I consider these principles sacred. I regard them as the basic fabric of our American way of life, and I believe in them as living realities, and not as mere words on paper. . . .*

Three days later White died of a heart attack. Documents that emerged after his death show beyond reasonable doubt not only that White passed official American secrets to the NKVD, but that he tried to promote Soviet as well as American interests when he was laying the groundwork for the postwar financial system. He was both an active spy *and* an agent of influence. His defense would have been to downplay Stalin's crimes and to say that the way of the future was for the Soviet Union and the United States to join hands. He might also have argued that he had not taken direction from the

The Red Spy Queen who told all, to the FBI, to Congress, and to the press, here testifying before HUAC in 1948. *Thomas D. McAvoy Photo, Getty Images.*

Soviets (at least not very much), and that he had worked with them on his own terms.[10]

In the fall of 1948, Hemingway had still more to tell Lanham about his own relationship with the Soviets. On November 24, he implied he was now at risk because of some of the "odd jobs" he had done for the Republican cause during the Spanish Civil War, "for any one of which you could be hanged now but in no one of which I was ever disloyal to my country. . . ."[11] He hinted that some of the "odd jobs" had been for the Soviets, not just the Republic, writing: "Have always told you straight all contacts I have had with Russkis, etc." He repeated that he had never been disloyal, adding that he knew "what is disloyal and what is not." The recent past showed that the "inquisitors," as he called them—presumably the FBI, whose ranks included Roman Catholics sympathetic to Franco, and HUAC, which followed leads from the FBI—were not likely to grasp why he had chosen to fight fascism in his own way. They would not be able to penetrate beneath the surface and appreciate that, at the end of the day, he had been a loyal American with "a clean and pure heart." For that reason he needed to be careful.

Two days later he wrote Lanham again, this time about the loyalty investigation of a good friend, to state his opinion that, in those days, "no one can be too careful who knows things."[12] A few weeks later, Hemingway reinforced the point, telling Lanham that he did not want to write about certain things because he did not have "any confidence in *any* mail, nor telephones, nor radios."[13]

Was Hemingway telling the truth to Lanham in his letters? Could the general take the writer at his word? The answer—yes, up to a point—is complicated. In Spain, as in France in 1944, he may have circumvented a few regulations, and played a more active role than a foreign correspondent should play, but everything he did was for a good cause—that is, antifascism, and getting what he called the "true gen" (the RAF slang for the "true genuine" story, or ground truth). Along the way he was never disloyal to his own country. This was true even though his political views put him on the fringe. There were some things a writer may not have wanted to tell his readers, but there was not anything to be ashamed of, either.

Hemingway omitted a vitally important fact—that he did not meet with the Soviets only to glean useful information. It was not just, or even mostly, about Spain. In the winter of 1940–41, after the end of the Spanish Civil War, he agreed to work hand in hand with the NKVD in the fight against fascism, and he met secretly with Soviet spies during World War II. It did not matter that he did not intend to be disloyal to his own country. His relationship with the NKVD was something he would never be able to explain away, especially not to HUAC, or to the FBI, the organization that would remember him not only for his political views but also for the insults to its agents in Havana in 1942 and 1943.

It came down to carrying an inner and outer burden. Hemingway could tell Lanham and one or two others about the outer burden of premature antifascism. But the inner burden of his relationship with the NKVD was something only he and the Soviets knew about. He could not share it with anyone else. To make matters worse, Hemingway would have to worry that there might one day be a defector, another Gouzenko or Bentley who happened to know his secret and would share it with the FBI or HUAC. It was not far-fetched for him to imagine that the Bureau was listening in on his telephone and intercepting his mail, or that he would one day find himself on the stand in the Caucus Room, being hounded by members of the committee. He pictured himself fighting back like John Lawson and the Hollywood Ten, and being in contempt of Congress, all of which could have made it difficult to work in his own country.

By the end of the decade, it was clear that victory in World War II would never pay a peace dividend. In August 1949, the Soviet Union tested its first atomic bomb and overturned America's monopoly on superweapons. A few months later, mainland China fell to the communists. Mao and Chou were now in charge, and Chiang had to make do with ruling the offshore island of Taiwan. In 1950 Stalinist North Korea invaded noncommunist South Korea, starting a war that would last into 1953. At home, the Red Scare intensified when Senator Joseph R. McCarthy of Wisconsin launched a witch hunt for communists that made HUAC's work seem careful and professional.

McCarthy seemed to point an accusing finger wherever he pleased and did not care whether there was any solid evidence to back up his charges so long as he stayed in the headlines. The senator began making his ever-more-sensational charges in 1950 and proceeded to conduct investigations and hearings through 1954. In March 1950 he charged that "official intelligence reports" showed that Hemingway's onetime close friend Gustavo Durán was "a rabid communist."[14] This forced Durán to hire lawyers and spend months defending his record before, during, and after the Spanish Civil War. Mutual friends like Ambassador Spruille Braden defended Durán under oath, and the story made the *Times*. Though his reaction is lost to history, the old newshound Hemingway must surely have followed Durán's misadventure.[15]

In March 1951, two American communists, Julius and Ethel Rosenberg, went on trial in New York for their role in stealing American atomic secrets and passing them to the NKVD. At their trial, Elizabeth Bentley testified that Jacob Golos—her lover and Hemingway's recruiter—had met secretly with Julius. It was not a key fact, but it was one that bolstered the case, especially after she declared that the Communist Party of the USA "only served the interests of Moscow, whether it be propaganda or espionage or sabotage."[16] During the trial, Bentley sold her story to *McCall's* magazine. In the summer, the magazine began publishing lengthy excerpts from her memoirs with sensational details about her life with Golos: how she "joined the underground" with the man she loved, how he recruited her for "special work," how she was "used by the Red spy ring," how he died in her arms on Thanksgiving Day in 1943.[17] If Hemingway was still reading *McCall's*, it would have been hard for him not to recognize the red-haired, blue-eyed Soviet spy who was the star of the June issue.

The irony is that the threat from Soviet espionage had receded by the time the Red Scare reached fever pitch. There were now fewer Americans spying for the NKVD than at any time in the past two decades, thanks to defectors like Bentley and to the U.S. government's ability to break Soviet codes.[18] The Soviet bench was so depleted that Moscow Center considered reanimating older cases, including Hemingway's.

In 1948 and then again in 1950, there was a flurry of message traffic between the Center and the Washington *rezidentura* about Hemingway, code name "Argo." On June 8, 1948, Moscow first asked about him, and then, apparently because Washington had not answered, sent another message on July 3, 1950: "Please determine the present location of 'Argo'—of whom we informed you previously. . . ."[19] The Center offered ploys for recontact, and went on to "remind [Washington] . . . that 'Argo' was recruited for our work on ideological grounds . . . by 'Sound' [Golos], that he has been studied little and has not been verified in practical work." Moscow offered to send Hemingway's material recognition signal to Washington "in case the need should arise."[20] Knowing its value, the NKVD had carefully kept the stamp that Hemingway had given to Golos in 1940; by presenting this token, an unknown Soviet could prove he was a genuine NKVD operative.

Hemingway had no idea that the NKVD was thinking about him. Recontact with the Soviet spy agency was close to the last thing he wanted. He continued to hold the same political ground he had occupied in 1947 and 1948. He remained critical of American foreign policy but refrained from criticizing that of the Soviets. He had mixed feelings about the Korean War: a twinge of regret that it was the first American war since 1918 that he did not go to—and then a lot of questions about strategy and the fitness of the generals fighting the war. Did it make sense to send troops to a land war in Asia when the main threat was on the plains of Europe? But he assured Lanham that if war broke out in Europe he would still be willing to fight for his country, perhaps as a partisan behind the lines, not unlike his fictional hero Robert Jordan.[21]

The hunt for communists at home kept him on edge. Hemingway continued to tell Lanham that, for him, trust and loyalty came first; they were fundamental, qualities that a man could sense. The writer claimed to be very sensitive to any talk of "treason, cowardice, conniving, and to the *good* qualities" that offset them.[22] He went on to divide the world into people you could and could not trust. On the one hand, he and Lanham were above suspicion, having "put it on the line for our government too many times." On the other hand, there were various untrustworthy groups: communists, Jesuits, and many (but not all) FBI agents. He concluded that it was a pity Washington did not recognize his trustworthiness. Even though he had worked selflessly "in a highly confidential capacity" for the U.S. government during the war, he had learned from an inside source that the censors in Miami had orders to hold all of his mail for two weeks, and commented bitterly that it was a poor reward for his service.

Putting it on the line for a cause like antifascism was now out of the question. His friend from the battlefields of Spain, Milton Wolff, continued to push Hemingway hard for endorsements and appearances. In the spring of 1950, Wolff asked Hemingway to come to New York to deliver "a handful of brave words" at a rally (probably against U.S. policy on Spain, where Franco was still in power).[23] Once again Hemingway did not attend, and he seems to have waited to reply until after the event. He wrote Wolff that he had been too busy to help. On the day of the rally he had corrected hundreds of pages of proofs, working all day and into the night to meet a deadline.[24] Then after finishing the proofs he slipped and fell on *Pilar*'s flying bridge, hitting a gaff—a murderous hook for large fish—and landing on a "big clamp." The result was yet another concussion, "complete with fireworks," a spout of bright red arterial blood, and an injury to his spine that immediately started to swell up. He told Wolff he was better now and wanted him to know that he was still willing to help anyone from Spain who had fallen on hard times. He mentioned the Lincoln Battalion's doctor, Eddie Barsky, who went to jail for refusing to answer questions for HUAC. But he, Hemingway, drew the line at supporting any more "Causas." *Causas* tended to have their own resources and did not need his help. Anyway, he added, Wolff and his comrades had made their own luck: "you guys sort of bought this." They had "hired out to be tough," and then complained when their enemies on the right hit back.[25]

Wolff would never forget how angry the line about buying trouble made him.[26] He had to keep his anger in check when he wrote back. The rally had been a success but the movement could be much stronger if it had Hemingway's support. He had "the kind of weight that would stir a great many of the confused, the timid, and the 'what is the use' crowd."[27] But "you didn't come and you haven't spoken and it's just too goddamned bad." There was one more thing Wolff wanted Hemingway to know: the young radical had always understood the risks of being an activist. He was *not* complaining about the consequences of his actions. "Please don't ever get the idea that we are hollering because we are getting what we 'bought.'" They were raising their voices because what was happening to them was only the beginning of a further slide to the right in America.

When Wolff reread the letters a decade later, they called to mind the difference between the Hemingway who was "wholly in the fight" during the Spanish war and the man who kept his distance in 1950, measuring what he would and would not do to help. The difference had made Wolff "weep deep inside."[28] What Wolff did not know was that Hemingway still agreed with many of the things that Wolff stood for. The writer had not changed his mind about Franco, and he regretted that politicians like red-baiting McCarthy were making life difficult for good men like Wolff. McCarthy was not the American Franco, but he was bad enough.

The day after he wrote his letter to Wolff, Hemingway considered buying some trouble himself. He typed and signed a letter to Senator McCarthy, then added a postscript, and signed his name a second time.[29] The letter itself is disjointed and obscene; parts of it make little sense. But the gist is clear. Hemingway begins by questioning McCarthy's courage and war record. "Some of us have seen the deads [*sic*] and counted them and counted the numbers of McCarthys. There were quite a lot [of deads] but you were not one [of them]. . . ." He tells McCarthy that he is "a shit" and invites him to come to Cuba for a private boxing match to settle their differences.

McCarthy should fight him instead of resorting to "sopoeanas" [*sic*] but he, McCarthy, did not "have the guts to fight a rabbit."

In the end, Hemingway probably did not send the letter; a signed copy is still among his papers.[30] What may have stayed his hand was a conviction that it was more important for him to keep writing books than to be an activist, someone who might wind up on a blacklist, unable to publish. In 1948 he had told his publisher, Charles Scribner, not to worry that his writing "might be regarded as subversive." He could take an oath "at any time" that he was not, and never had been, a communist.[31] Three years later, in 1951, he explained to A. E. Hotchner, the thin, eager-looking young writer and editor who first appeared in Hemingway's life in 1948, that these things were complicated. Not only did he need to be free of the communist taint; he also must avoid writing anything that might appear subversive. Of the antifascist work he had created in Madrid in 1937, he wrote that *The Fifth Column* was now "a subversive play."[32] It had not been subversive when written. But, he continued, he did not want to be "a TV personality" who had to explain to "some committee" that wouldn't believe him that he loved his country and was still willing to fight for her "against all enemies anytime anywhere." His time would be better spent writing novels than appearing before committees.

On at least two occasions during the 1950s, Hemingway refused requests to allow theater companies to stage *The Fifth Column*.[33] His tribute to the work of a communist counterspy working to save the Spanish Republic from fascist spies was obviously the work of a premature antifascist, written in the Hotel Florida under fire, with the added disadvantage that it was about spying. If he needed to stay clear of communists, it was doubly important for Hemingway to avoid communist spies. He knew better than anyone that, in 1950, it would not be easy to explain everything he had done in Spain—let alone his contacts with the NKVD in the 1940s. And if he did try to explain himself before a committee, he would be asked to name names of communists and fellow travelers, people like Milton Wolff and Joris Ivens. As he later told his friend Peter Viertel, he had no time for "stool pigeons" like the Hollywood personalities who had turned on their onetime friends.[34] Perhaps for the same reason, he did not respond to a plea from Arthur Koestler to speak out against the Stalinist oppression of artists in Eastern Europe.[35]

The book that Hemingway did publish in 1950 was decidedly not subversive. Set mostly in Venice, *Across the River and into the Trees* was the story of the last hours of a veteran U.S. Army officer. Richard Cantwell is exhausted and ready to die. He is not like the energetic Robert Jordan, the hero of *For Whom the Bell Tolls,* who is fighting to rid the world of fascism. Instead he seems to be an amalgam of Buck Lanham and Hemingway himself after they emerged from the Battle of the Bulge in 1945. But he is still willing to do his duty. Cantwell is a professional soldier, committed to fighting his country's enemies to the best of his abilities—no matter who they might be and what his personal feelings might be. At one point the fictional colonel sounds very much like Hemingway talking to Mary Lanham in 1945. Cantwell says the Russians "are our potential enemy. So, as a soldier, I am prepared to fight them. But I like them very much and I have never known finer people nor people more as we are."[36]

Hemingway hoped that *Across the River and into the Trees* would receive the same welcome as his last book. But the reviews were mixed. Typical was the review in the *Saturday Review of Literature,* which pronounced that the book was "a synthesis of everything bad in his [Hemingway's] previous work . . . [and] throws a doubtful light on the future."[37] Alfred Kazin of the *New Yorker* was sad that "so fine and honest a writer" had made "such a travesty of himself." *Time* magazine said the book showed that Hemingway, the previously acclaimed champ, was now over fifty and "on the ropes."[38]

The enraged Hemingway reacted by drafting a letter on the pages of the 1939 Warner's Calendar of Medical History—like the one that he had used in 1941 and 1942 as a log for Operation Friendless. He asked the editor of the *New Yorker* to tell "Mr. Alfred KAZIM (or

KAZIN) . . . that he can stick (STICK) his review up his ASS," and offered to supply the grease. The draft included an incomplete sentence that started, "It is not dishonorable to fight for your country," as if fighting for your country cleared the slate and offset a variety of transgressions, from poor writing to radical beliefs.[39]

Noting the publication of *Across the River and into the Trees,* Soviet spies in Washington clipped many of the reviews that were making Hemingway so angry and sent them to Moscow at the beginning of October 1950—presumably in order to keep the "Argo"/Hemingway file up to date. If they read the book, they missed the passage about how much Cantwell/Hemingway liked the Russians. Instead, they reported to Moscow that "he is said to adhere to [the] Trotskyite [camp]" and to have "attacked . . . the Soviet Union in his articles and pamphlets."[40]

None of this was even remotely true. Since the NKVD assassin had killed Stalin's rival Trotsky in Mexico in 1940, Trotskyites existed mostly in the collective imagination of the NKVD, and the word itself was still a catch-all label for the regime's enemies. (The same was true of the word "communist" for many Americans at the time.) Labeling Hemingway a Trotskyite was one way to dampen interest in the writer forever. If anyone in the NKVD thought about Hemingway after 1950, no one wrote it down. There is no evidence that the NKVD contemplated getting back in touch with him ever again or that he ever met another Soviet spy in the flesh.[41] But the writer-spy's memories of Spain and the NKVD and the FBI would never go away.

CHAPTER 13

NO ROOM TO MANEUVER

The Mature Antifascist in Cuba and Ketchum

In the spring of 1958, Hemingway took Mary fishing in bad weather off the north coast of Cuba. That was unusual in itself; he usually kept Pilar *at her berth when the sea was rough. Mary was even more surprised when she saw Gregorio Fuentes, the boat keeper, set "not quite fresh bait on the hooks"—bait that was past its prime, at the point where these two serious fishermen would normally have thrown it away. Nevertheless, once the outriggers were set, making her look like she was ready to fish, Hemingway steered* Pilar *out to sea, well out of sight of land about ten miles from shore.*[1] *He asked Mary to take the helm while he and Gregorio took care "of a little business."*

She watched them go below to open drawers and "tear bunks apart," unearthing an assortment of heavy guns, rifles, sawed-off shotguns, hand grenades, mysterious canisters, and belts of ammunition—the deadly cargo that she had slept on top of, blissfully unaware, on so many outings. Now it all went into the sea. There was so much that it took some thirty minutes to toss everything overboard.

Hemingway did not tell Mary where the supplies had come from, or why they were hidden on Pilar. *Gregorio later claimed Hemingway had let him hide "arms for the revolutionary movement" on* Pilar.[2] *So were the two men disposing of evidence of their support for Castro? All Hemingway said to Mary at the time was that the cache was "stuff left over from the old days," which could have been any time after 1942, and that no one could use it now.*[3] *When she mused that such a large store of weapons must be worth at least "a couple of grand," he replied opaquely, "My contribution to the revolution," adding, "Maybe we've saved a few lives."*[4]

Did he mean that he had helped to finance Castro's movement, or procured arms for him? Or that he just wanted to keep the weapons out of the hands of looters if law and order collapsed? But instead of explaining, the man who loved secrets and intrigue, and would one day write that his relationship to the revolution was "very complicated," swore Mary to secrecy and never revisited the subject.[5]

If *Across the River and into the Trees* was not very subversive, the next book Hemingway published had even less to do with subversion, let alone politics or war. It was also a triumphant popular success. *The Old Man and the Sea* is a novella about a poor Cuban fisherman named Santiago who is engaged in a personal struggle for survival. After going eighty-four days in his one-man skiff without a catch, he hooks a marlin that he battles for three days. He finally gets the enormous fish alongside and starts for home, only to have his catch devoured by sharks along the way. When he reaches port, he has only a skeleton to show for his triumph. But that is not the most important thing. As Santiago/Hemingway famously tells the reader, "A man can be destroyed but not defeated." Santiago fought the good fight and endured with style and grace. He triumphed in spirit.

A few critics were unhappy with this parable—judging it "hollow" and "soft and sentimental"[6]—but this time the book was literally a prize-winner, taking the Pulitzer for fiction in 1953. A year later, Hemingway was awarded the Nobel Prize for Literature, an award for lifetime achievement that nonetheless specifically mentioned *The Old Man and the Sea* in the official citation. Hemingway had for years coveted these two awards as much as the

Distinguished Service Cross. More than ten years earlier he had been on the verge of receiving the Pulitzer when the chairman of the board, the conservative Nicholas Murray Butler, had vetoed the award because he found *For Whom the Bell Tolls* to be offensive. In the years that followed, the writer had unhappily watched competitors, some of them barely known in North America, receive the Nobel. In 1953 it had gone to Winston Churchill for his books and speeches; Hemingway must have gritted his teeth when the old British imperialist got the prize—for *literature*! But now the Nobel committee was choosing a professional writer for "his mastery of the art of narrative, most recently demonstrated in *The Old Man and the Sea*, and for the influence that he has exerted on contemporary style."[7]

Easily the most prestigious literary award, the Nobel trumped all the critics, the nonbelievers, the competitors, both living and dead. Friends all over the world congratulated him. Hemingway saved many of the messages that poured into the Finca. The Swedish actress Ingrid Bergman wrote that the Swedes must "not [be] so dumb after all" if they were smart enough to give the prize to Hemingway, closing with "Love, Maria and Ingrid." (Ingrid had played Robert Jordan's lover Maria in the film version of *For Whom the Bell Tolls*.) A friend named Bill Allen praised Hemingway for showing everyone "the importance of truth." The great film director John Huston, himself a colorful and creative original, sent a three-word message: "Great, Papa, Great!"[8]

But Hemingway did not feel great. He did not travel to Stockholm to receive the award, and instead sent an acceptance speech that was a dark reflection on his life's work. "Writing at its best is a lonely life," he began.[9] The writer "grows in public stature as he sheds his loneliness and often his work deteriorates." But he should always strive to create "something that has never been done or that others have tried and failed."

Hemingway was not exaggerating when he told the committee he could not travel on account of his health. He had always been

Time starts to take its toll. Hemingway just before *The Old Man and the Sea* appeared in bookstores. *Lee Samuels Photo, NY Public Library.*

accident prone. In recent years he had sustained more than one head injury. The accident on *Pilar* in 1950 that he told Wolff about was more serious than he let on, coming after at least two serious concussions in World War II. In January 1954 he survived two plane crashes in Africa during a twenty-four-hour period. First the sightseeing flight that he chartered crash-landed in dense brush near Murchison Falls in Uganda. Hemingway suffered a mild concussion. Then the rescue plane that came for him and Mary inexplicably crashed and burned on takeoff. To escape, Hemingway literally butted the door open with his head, seriously compounding the earlier injury. In March a checkup showed that he was still far from well. He told Hotchner, who was by now a family friend, that "there was a rupture of kidneys—collapse of intestine—severe injuries [to the] liver—major concussion—severe burns [to] legs, belly, right forearm, left hand, head, lips . . . [and] dislocated right arms and shoulder."[10]

Hemingway would never fully recover from these injuries. Friends and biographers would look back on 1954 and say that it marked the start of an irreversible downward spiral, one that was accelerated by the accidents, and aggravated by various other illnesses and deep depression.[11] The thought that his work was deteriorating kept him up on more than one night. So, too, did the other fear that he had hinted at in the late 1940s and early 1950s: that his past as an antifascist would catch up with him, that, even though he was now a Nobel laureate, the FBI would one day come for him.

At least until 1957, Cuba was Hemingway's safe haven. After a difficult trip, the increasingly famous novelist could settle back into the familiar routine at the Finca that had nourished the body and the spirit in the past. He could still write in the morning, standing by the window in the bedroom and looking out over the lush green hills, swim a half mile in the pool after lunch, or take *Pilar* out into the Stream to troll for marlin. If the weather was rough and the fish weren't biting, there was still the shooting club or the occasional cockfight in the village. In the evening, he could linger over dinner with longtime Cuban friends who dropped by almost every day, or entertain visiting Americans downtown at La Florida. It was now air-conditioned and featured a bust of its most famous patron in a niche along one of the walls. Events in Washington and New York were just far enough away, across the water. But he could not always shut out Cuban politics, which, as the decade wore on, began to demand more and more of his attention.

The decade—and the couple—had good as well as bad moments. In one of the good moments, Hemingway and Mary pose outside the Finca. *Ernest Hemingway Photo Collection, JFK Library.*

The former Cuban army sergeant Fulgencio Batista had seized power in March 1952. He proclaimed the establishment of a "disciplined democracy." The phrase was window dressing for a kleptocracy whose main policy was to enrich Batista and his cronies while placating foreign investors. The United States was a reasonably good ally, and a major trading partner. Not a few American companies were in business on the island. So was the Mafia, involved in the casinos and hotels that made Havana an exotic destination for American tourists. All in all, Batista was a natural target for those on the left with any kind of democratic or anti-imperialist agenda. Opposition groups soon took aim at his regime.

By the time Batista seized power, the twenty-five-year-old Fidel Castro was already becoming a leader with whom to reckon. The radical lawyer had tried his hand at many kinds of activism. In 1947 Castro had signed up for an ill-fated expedition to overthrow Rafael Trujillo, the right-wing dictator of the nearby Dominican Republic. Though he and Castro would not meet until 1960, Hemingway had also supported the expedition, offering advice and perhaps money to its organizers. He wrote Lanham that he would have liked to do more but was too busy taking care of his grievously ill son, Patrick.[12]

Castro proceeded to run for office in Cuba on a populist platform and even mounted legal challenges to the regime before deciding the only way to overthrow Batista was through armed struggle. In 1953, this decision led to the famous assault on the Moncada Barracks in the city of Santiago, a tactical failure that would nevertheless add to Castro's mystique. During the trial that followed, Castro declared that, one day, history would absolve him of his alleged crimes, words that soon became a rallying cry.

Batista jailed Castro until 1955, when the dictator made the enormous mistake of believing that Castro was no longer a risk and set him loose. Castro fled to Mexico to plot his next move. Late in 1956, he and a small band of fighters landed on the Cuban coast from a secondhand American cabin cruiser called the *Granma* (short for "Grandma"), and eventually made for the rugged, remote Sierra Maestra mountains in Oriente Province, hundreds of miles southeast of Havana. There Castro established his headquarters and organized the 26th of July Movement, named for the day he and his men had stormed the Moncada Barracks.

After an initial setback that almost cost him his life, Castro built up his forces by fits and starts, stealing weapons and ammunition whenever he could, ambushing an enemy column here, briefly seizing and holding a town there. The idea was not to fight pitched battles, but to undermine confidence in the government. Batista played into Castro's hand by responding with conventional forces and generally overreacting. He used his air force to bomb suspected guerrilla camps in the jungle, and tried to contain the rebels in the hills with truckloads of foot soldiers in the valleys. For much of the time, he censored the press. This made it possible for every kind of rumor to flourish, including the story that Castro was dead, as the *New York Times* reported on December 3, 1956. Herbert L. Matthews, the onetime foreign correspondent now based in the paper's home office on Times Square, sensed that neither Castro nor his

"The man who invented Fidel": *New York Times* reporter Herbert L. Matthews. *Robert Capa Photo, ICP.*

movement was dead, and pressured his editor into letting him fly to Cuba and see for himself.[13]

The friendship between Matthews and Hemingway that started in Spain had never faltered. From the Hotel Florida, they had gone out onto the battlefield together. Joe North of *New Masses* had found the tall, thin man with the high forehead to be too detached, too much of a conventional reporter, not *involved* the way Hemingway was. At the wreck on the mountain road in southern Spain in May 1938, North had seen two very different personalities: Hemingway, the man who had leapt out of their car, grabbed a first-aid kit, and started to save lives—and Matthews, who had reached for his notepad, then stepped among and over the wounded, looking for someone to interview.[14]

North turned out to be wrong about Matthews. He did everything he could for the Republic, just in a slightly different way. The reporter made his entire contribution in writing, but he was no less committed than his more famous friend. "So long as there was hope I played it up strong," he reflected at the end of the war. "I guess I was fighting harder than the soldiers—at least on paper."[15] Like Hemingway, Matthews felt the Republican defeat deeply. It left wounds that never fully healed and influenced his work for decades to come.

Soon after the war Matthews wrote a series of books about Spain that met with Hemingway's approval. For the jacket of *Two Wars and More to Come,* Hemingway contributed high praise: for him, Matthews was "the straightest, the ablest, and the bravest war correspondent writing today."[16] He was not just a colleague. Their shared experiences in Spain had forged what Matthews called "a bond stronger than tempered steel." On his first visit to the Finca in 1952, Matthews found that "the best information" about local politics came from Hemingway; in the years to come he would feel comfortable turning to his old friend to help him understand what was going on in Cuba.[17]

When Matthews landed in Havana again in February 1957, the

fifty-seven-year-old was looking for one more great story, perhaps a sequel to Spain, ideally one with a better ending.[18] He started by making the rounds of the capital, meeting with prominent expatriates and a few well-placed Cubans before being smuggled out to the Sierra Maestra. It was a risky proposition. Since government troops surrounded the area, Matthews had to talk his way through a number of roadblocks. But his daring paid off when the tall, charismatic Castro, with his "flashing eyes" and "straggling beard," strode into the forest clearing where Matthews was waiting.

The reporter was carried away by Castro and his vision. While the two men puffed outsize cigars, Castro outlined his political goals, playing up his love for democracy and downplaying his communist ties without hiding his anti-imperialism. Matthews knew he had a great scoop. "I'm first," he exulted in his notes of the meeting. When he emerged from the hills, his wife, Nancie, found him "exhausted and unwashed," but also "triumphant and excited."[19]

On one of their last nights in Cuba, probably that of February 18, Matthews and Nancie went to the Finca for dinner with his old friend.[20] Joining them was another old friend, the Hemingway family doctor José Luis Herrera, a neurosurgeon once described as "a delicate[-looking] little guy . . . with fine hands like a musician," who had a lot in common with the two Americans.[21] This slight, balding man with thick black glasses was actually far from delicate. A veteran of the Spanish Civil War, he had repeatedly risked his life and livelihood for the Republic. After the war, he returned home to Cuba, where he continued to practice medicine and pay his dues to the Cuban Communist Party. During their student days, he and his neighbor, Fidel Castro, had started a friendship that would last a lifetime. Throughout the 1950s, Herrera kept Hemingway informed about Castro and his movement.[22]

At dinner that night Matthews could barely control himself. He did not hold back about his incredible adventure in the mountains. Once again he had a chance to make a difference with his writing—just as he and Hemingway had tried to do in Spain. Only this time the right side might win. A few years later Herrera told a Soviet researcher what he heard Matthews tell Hemingway that night.[23] First the reporter had confirmed that Castro was alive and continuing the struggle from his mountain hideout. Matthews then praised Castro as a man of great determination, one who was firmly in control of the movement. Well informed and well-read, he was mounting a serious challenge to Batista's regime. Castro's political views were "very liberal" and "leftist," Matthews reported.[24]

Matthews later wrote that he received "precious encouragement" from Hemingway, "who stood by me at all times." The novelist's support was appreciated all the more by Matthews because his reporting on Castro would often leave him "standing virtually alone among United States editors and newspapermen."[25] In this way, Hemingway helped to shape the reporter's ideas about the 26th of July Movement even before he first put pen to paper to write anything about Castro.

Hemingway himself had still to meet Castro, having only heard about him from mutual friends like Herrera.[26] Now the writer was presented the ground truth from a seasoned—and trusted—reporter for a great newspaper. What Matthews said about Castro was likely to capture the heart of a man who had committed himself to the struggle against fascism during the Spanish Civil War: a charismatic revolutionary was fighting a right-wing dictator, someone both Matthews and Hemingway detested. Castro was a leftist and an anti-imperialist, but not a communist. He was saying many of the same things about politics that Hemingway himself had said over the past few years. *And* he was conducting the kind of guerrilla warfare that had so fascinated Hemingway in the 1930s and 1940s.

Hemingway had no way of knowing that the respect was mutual. Castro had not only read but studied *For Whom the Bell Tolls;* he would later say that "we took . . . [the book] to the hills with us, and it taught us about guerrilla warfare."[27]

As soon as he could, Matthews flew home to New York with Nancie, who hid his notes in her girdle to get through security at the Havana airport, and drafted a series of articles that first appeared above the fold on the front page of the *Times*' Sunday edition. The subhead declared, "Castro Is Still Alive and Still Fighting in the Mountains."[28] The second article downplayed the role communists were playing in the opposition to Batista while the third, in contrast, predicted that

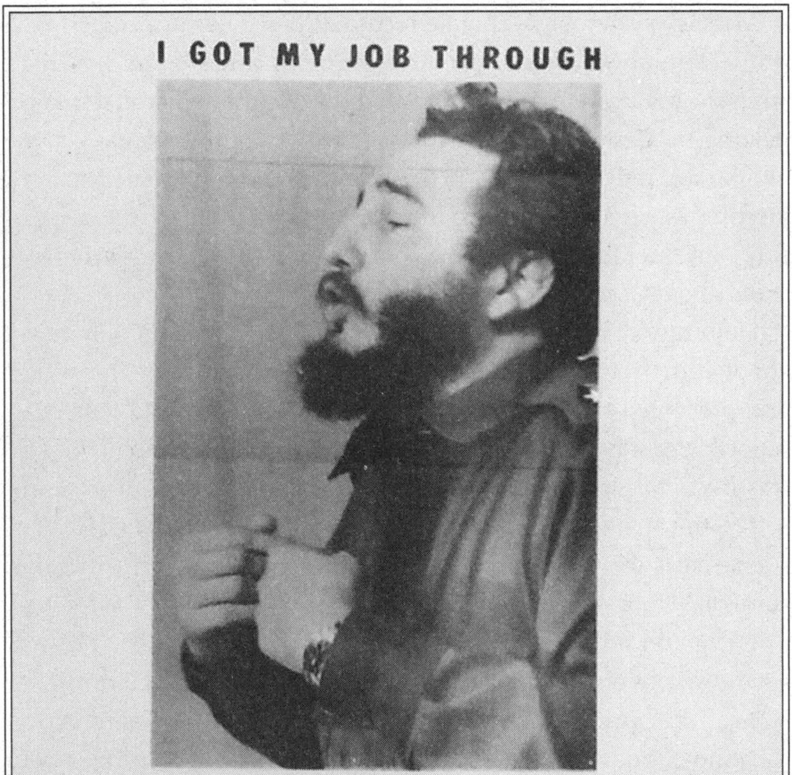

What one *New York Times* reader thought of Matthews's reporting after Castro started to show his true colors. *Herbert L. Matthews Papers, Columbia University.*

Castro's goal was not simply to replace Batista but to bring about thoroughgoing social change.

The immediate impact was enormous, and the aftereffects would reverberate "for months and years to come," leaving their mark on history.[29] Matthews's articles changed Castro's image "from hot-headed loser to noble rogue with broad ideals" and made him "the leading figure in the opposition."[30] Overnight the reporter became a hero to Cubans who were fighting Batista, and to many Americans on the left. The antifascist soldier turned political activist Milton Wolff, who had stayed in touch with Matthews as well as Hemingway, was not alone when he wrote Matthews to tell him that his articles had "stirred up long-suppressed desires for another go at something worthwhile."[31] Wolff, too, had instinctively grasped the parallels between Spain in the 1930s and Cuba in the 1950s.

In 1957 Castro leveraged the advantage that Matthews had given him. A natural expert at propaganda, he mixed his growing mystique with just enough on-the-ground reality to make his movement seem stronger than it was. Pinprick attacks, often small bombs, did not do much damage but kept the government and its supporters on edge. The number of defections from Batista's camp rose. The government continued to react with a heavy, arbitrary hand, engaging in wholesale torture and murder. Frequently it was the innocents who paid the price: Batista's soldiers began killing those who happened to live near the scene of a rebel attack, and then they displayed the victims' mutilated bodies to teach everyone else a lesson.

Hemingway felt Batista's heavy hand in mid-August. Early one morning, his dogs became agitated.[32] Hemingway's majordomo, René Villarreal, could tell by the way they were barking that the dogs were not welcoming a friend to the Finca.[33] The intruders turned out to be a detachment of eight or nine Rural Guards, dressed in khaki and carrying rifles. They reeked of alcohol. Hemingway cracked open his front door and demanded to know their business. The sergeant in charge said he was looking for "a certain oppositionist." Hemingway said there were no revolutionaries on his property and ordered the men to leave. After a moment of hesitation, the soldiers left without carrying out a search. The next morning, Machakos, one of the writer's dogs, was found dead near the kitchen steps, with a head wound, probably from a rifle butt. Hemingway immediately went to the local guard post to demand an explanation. Not surprisingly, the sergeant denied that his men had killed the animal. By the following week, Hemingway had told the story to the *New York*

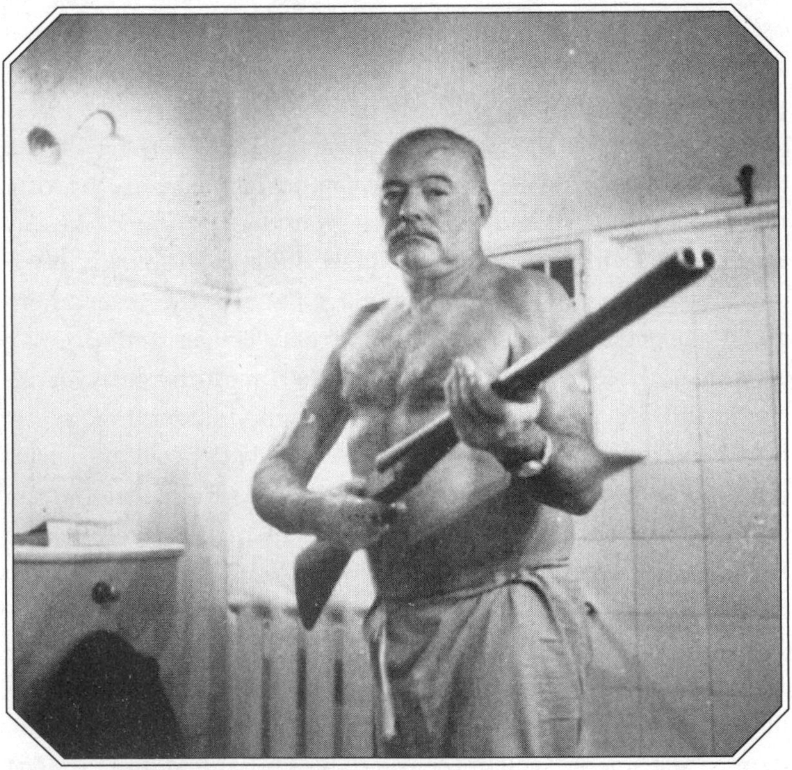

One of the bad, nighttime moments: Hemingway on guard at the Finca. *Ernest Hemingway Photo Collection, JFK Library.*

Times, which shared this bitter taste of life in Cuba in 1957 with its readers on August 22.[34]

Why was Hemingway a target? Dr. Herrera thought the local authorities were uneasy about the many gatherings Ernest hosted, with carloads of Cubans passing through the otherwise quiet town of San Francisco de Paula on their way to the Finca. Many of the American's guests were leftists. (As a communist, Herrera was not typical of Hemingway's friends; the writer's favorite revolutionaries were, like him, more independent.) Herrera said the gatherings were political only in the sense that everyone "always commented on the [political] situation, . . . the topic of the day everywhere."[35] But mostly, the doctor claimed, Hemingway ran films that he borrowed from the American Embassy, and then he and his guests sat around and chatted. On at least one occasion when Herrera was present even that was too much for the Rural Guards, and they came onto the property to confront Hemingway, who calmly explained they had nothing to worry about—the only conspiracy was one to drink whiskey.[36]

These were unpleasant reminders that the writer's position in Cuba was precarious. The balancing act was to keep Batista at arm's length without offending the regime and risking deportation. At the same time Hemingway sympathized with the rebels and offered discreet support to men he trusted—giving money to Herrera to support the movement or perhaps helping a local revolutionary buy and store weapons. He did not want to raise his political profile too high. He had not forgotten the lessons of being a premature antifascist.

There was a robust discussion of those lessons in 1958 when *Esquire* magazine moved to republish three of the short stories that Hemingway had written about the Spanish Civil War: "The Denunciation," "Night before Battle," and "The Butterfly and the Tank." The themes—and language—of the stories reflected the antifascist mood of the 1930s and clashed with the anticommunist mood of the 1950s. ("The Denunciation" is about turning an acquaintance in to the secret police, while "Night before Battle" lays out the political thinking of an American fighting for the Spanish Republic.) From Cuba Hemingway telephoned Alfred Rice, his lawyer in New York, and ordered him to object to republication on the grounds that *Esquire* (the original publisher) had only purchased the right to publish once.[37] The writer stressed that he did not want Rice to object "on any political basis."[38]

A lawyer who never shied away from a fight—one Hemingway biographer would call him "extremely rude and aggressive"—Rice proceeded in early August to file suit in New York State court to restrain *Esquire*.[39] He argued in court papers that the magazine's action would cause "great injury and irreparable damage to the plaintiff."[40] Rice reasoned: "passage of time can affect the writings of authors either favorably or unfavorably. . . . Illustrative is the change in attitude of people . . . to Russia," our wartime ally, now "perhaps our greatest enemy." Intentionally or not, Rice was echoing what Hemingway had said to Hotchner in 1951 when he observed *The Fifth Column* had become a "subversive" play after the Cold War started.[41]

Hemingway angrily claimed that Rice had blindsided him: when a *Times* reporter called for a comment, he erupted, saying that the man he later called a "goldefining [*sic*] conniver" had put "words in my mouth."[42] The writer distanced himself from Rice, saying he would drop the lawsuit. "Those statements were made by my lawyer . . . , and I have just called him up and given him hell for it."[43] He was particularly upset by the suggestion that political fear had spurred him to bar *Esquire* from republishing: "if anyone thinks I am worried about anyone reading political implications in[to] my stories, he is wrong." Two weeks later Hemingway wrote to thank the *Times* reporter for getting the story of the "frame-up" right and putting it on the wire.[44] Otherwise the only thing on record would have been Rice's version, which had been retransmitted "all over the world" by the Associated Press wire service, leaving readers with the impression that he, Hemingway, was "a turn-coat, or publicity seeker, or both."

Not everyone took Hemingway at his word. The day after the *Times* story appeared, the *Wall Street Journal* was not as kind to Hemingway. On August 8, it published a wicked parody called "The Old Man and the Fee":[45]

> *The writer has served with honor in many wars and does not care what people think about his politics. . . . It is not true that writer is worried about a change in public sentiment toward Russia in our time. The writer does not worry about such things.*

The *Journal* may have hit closest to the truth. Letters to his intimate friends in the 1950s had already shown a man who was very much attuned to U.S. public opinion. For more practical reasons, he still cared very much what the authorities in Cuba thought about his politics.

That spring and summer the struggle between Batista and Castro on the island made it difficult for anyone to let down his guard. When Castro called for a general strike, Batista authorized citizens to shoot strikers. The word on the street was that Castro, in turn, reacted by ordering the assassination of rebel leaders who did not strike. The upshot was that the citizenry stayed away from public places; even in large stores like Woolworth's, Mary found only a handful of customers.[46] Hemingway worried about recent kidnappings of Americans—"the latest . . . sport" that Castro's men were indulging in. The famous expatriate joked unhappily that Castro would be entertaining more Americans on the Fourth of July than the American ambassador and that he, Hemingway, had called the embassy to find out when Castro would start kidnapping FBI agents.[47] To Mary he observed that it was quite possible that looters would come to the Finca "when there was no law."[48] And if anyone or anything raised his political profile, would the Rural Guards return for a thorough search?[49] It was probably for both reasons that he took the precaution of ditching munitions he had concealed on *Pilar* and kept only a few weapons at home.[50]

Since life in Cuba was wearing them down, Mary and Hemingway decided to spend the fall and winter in Idaho. They missed the open spaces in the American West and felt a temporary change of scenery would do them good.[51] In August they arranged to rent a house in Ketchum; by October they had moved in. But Cuba was never far from Hemingway's mind. He kept an eye on developments on the island: the violence was not letting up, and there was no happy ending in sight. In November he was uncharacteristically fed up with everyone. "No one is right—both sides atrocious—. . . things aren't good and the overhead is murder," he wrote to his son Patrick. "Might pull out of there. Future looks very bad. . . ."[52]

A few weeks later, the incredible happened. A string of rebel victories in the late summer and fall of 1958 had further demoralized the Cuban army and police. Batista came to the conclusion that a Castro victory was inevitable, and decided to save himself before it was too late. In the early morning hours of January 1, 1959, he and his cronies loaded a few DC-4 airliners with their loot and fled to the Dominican Republic. By dawn Cuba had no government and Havana was quite literally lawless. Sometimes joyful, sometimes angry crowds took to the streets. As shots rang out here and there, looters entered the tourist hotels downtown and vandalized the gaming tables. Hundreds of miles away at the other end of the island, Castro broadcast an appeal for calm and started to make his way to the capital, riding on top of a tank with a dozen or so of his men hanging on to the sides. Jubilant crowds slowed his progress down the highway that ran along the island's spine. When he arrived in the capital, the celebration reminded the American reporter John H. Thompson of the liberation of Paris in 1944.[53] But Castro was not going to return to the status quo ante; he planned to change Cuban society forever. "Now the Revolution begins," he proclaimed.[54]

Castro Seizes Power: This photo captures the excitement and the confusion, and hints at his charisma. *Rolls Press, Popperfoto, Getty Images.*

The struggle, and the uncertainty that came with it, seemed to be over. Those who, like Hemingway, had opposed Batista and supported Castro, could now look forward to the future.

The news services tracked Hemingway down in Idaho and hounded him for a statement. Mary saw what he wrote on the back of a postcard before he spoke to anyone: "I believe in the historical necessity for the Cuban revolution and I believe in its long range aims."[55] When the *Times* called during the Rose Bowl game, Mary heard Hemingway say that he was "delighted" with the news from Cuba. She immediately took him to task; it was too early to predict the course of events. Castro might already be lining up firing squads. Hemingway resisted, but the man who had been more cautious than not throughout the 1950s eventually gave in, and called the *Times* newsroom to change "delighted" to "hopeful."[56]

Privately, Hemingway was more upbeat about the revolution. On

January 7, 1959, in a typical letter to his Italian friend Gianfranco Ivancich, he celebrated Batista's departure, wishing they could have seen him go: "Sic transit hijo de puta."[57] Two weeks later he was happy to report to a friend at Scribner's that "things are [still] OK with us in Cuba"—nothing had happened to the Finca—and that some of his friends now held government positions.[58] In early February, he was even more optimistic in a second letter to Gianfranco, proclaiming that "all the news from Cuba [was] good."[59] The new government would have a hard time because of the eight hundred American companies that had invested in the island nation; the United States would do "everything" to overthrow Castro. But since his people had "a decent chance for the first time ever," he wished Castro all the luck.

Hemingway's attitude did not change once he learned Mary had been right about the firing squads. Almost from the first, the revolutionaries started to execute their enemies. In the words of one insider, "In those January days, the topic on everyone's lips was the execution . . . of war criminals," who were mostly veterans of Batista's police force or army.[60] Days after the dictator's flight, Castro's brother Raúl had a group of some seventy prisoners shot in Santiago. Within two weeks the government staged somewhat more formal proceedings in Havana itself. On January 23, Ruby Phillips, the *Times* correspondent who had lived in Cuba for years (and styled herself R. Hart Phillips so that readers would take her seriously), reported on the first show trial of Batista's officers before a crowd of eighteen thousand enthusiastic spectators at the National Stadium.[61]

For those who did not subscribe to the *Times*, various news services filmed the trial. In neighborhood movie theaters in the United States or Great Britain, anyone could watch a minute-and-a-half story showing the crowded stadium. The first accused, a Major Jesus Sosa Blanco, was composed and smiling as he faced the three young bearded judges in fatigue uniforms. A barefoot twelve-year-old boy, with obvious coaching, pointed to Sosa Blanco, identifying him as the man who had killed his father. While the boy was speaking, the crowd chanted, "Kill him, kill him."[62]

Hemingway defended the trials during an interview in early March with a columnist from Seattle named Emmett Watson.[63] Hemingway and Watson first met on a Saturday night in the Duchin Room, a comfortable Sun Valley lounge whose dark paneling and deep red décor had attracted Hemingway since he first started coming to Idaho in the 1930s. Watson, on vacation, was at a table with other writers when Hemingway approached and sat down. Watson turned out to be the kind of journalist Hemingway liked: an original, brimming with grit, who had been a professional baseball player and worked in a shipyard during the war. It did not hurt that they had mutual acquaintances, or that the three-pack-a-day man knew something about whiskey. The thirty-minute chat was relaxed and friendly but hardly newsworthy.

Two days later, in the early afternoon, Watson ran into Hemingway again on a sidewalk in Sun Valley.[64] Hemingway was through working for the day, and ready to relax. Would Watson join him for a drink at the Ram, another Sun Valley institution? Once again in familiar surroundings—this time the décor was European and alpine—Hemingway was willing to talk, on the record, about Castro and Cuba, and gave the elated Watson the full scoop he had denied everyone else. For over an hour, while he sipped a glass of scotch and lime, the expatriate writer spoke "intently of the country he loves."[65]

Hemingway opened with his view that this was a real revolution, not just a changing of the guard. The trials were a necessary part of the revolution. Reacting to the outcry over the initial wave of executions, the new government had ordered the public trials but still faced criticism:[66]

People abroad began to yell, "Circus!" But the government had to do this to show it was in control, to give people a respect for law and order. . . . If the government doesn't shoot these criminals they would be killed anyway . . . for vengeance. . . . It would be bad, very bad.

Echoing Castro, Hemingway went on to say that he hoped capital punishment would be banned once the current wave of trials and executions had come to an end. Overall the future was bright. The revolution had the support of the Cuban people. (His only concern, which he asked Watson not to print, was that Castro might not prove strong enough to reorder Cuban society.[67]) Cuba was a "wonderful place to live," and he looked forward to returning.

When Mary and Hemingway landed at Havana's international airport on March 29, 1959, they found a busload of friends from San Francisco de Paula, the town outside the Finca's gates, waiting to greet them. When they reached the Finca itself, they were relieved to find their "marvelous home in perfect shape."[68] The next day an ecstatic Hemingway dictated a letter to his son Jack, repeating what he had said to Watson: "this is a *real* revolution. Something like what we [had] hoped for in Spain."[69]

This second chance energized Hemingway from the day he returned home. Everywhere he looked, people seemed to be reveling in their newfound freedom. Cuba was "bursting with libertarian fervor; you felt in the midst of a genuine, do-it-yourself revolution" that was *for* Cuba, not yet anti-American or pro-Soviet.[70] Hemingway took it all in, listening to the radio three times a day, reading every newspaper that he could lay his hands on, listening to (and perhaps even enjoying) Castro's seemingly endless speeches—they ran on and on for hours and while mostly about politics included digressions about almost anything.[71]

Days later, in early April, Hemingway spent a few hours drinking Papa Doble daiquiris at La Florida with the American playwright Tennessee Williams and the British film and drama critic Kenneth Tynan, who happened to be in town on assignment for *Holiday* magazine. Tynan remembered that, on that day, the fan in the air conditioner blew so hard that he had trouble lighting his cigarettes. Williams (in his yachting jacket with silver buttons) and Hemingway (in his white T-shirt and baseball hat) did not find much common ground, but Tynan found his host to be "in terrific form."[72] At some point a friendly journalist stepped in to invite Tynan to a nighttime open-air execution at Morro Castle, the sprawling old Spanish fort that still guarded the harbor. Tynan declined—he was against capital punishment—but Williams wanted to accept. It was, he said, the writer's duty to bear witness. Later Tynan asked Hemingway what he thought, and received the cryptic reply, "There are some refusals that are still permitted us." Nevertheless, he went on to declare that Castro's was "a good revolution, an *honest* revolution."[73]

Tynan and Williams soon realized they were late for an interview with Castro, and hurried over to the Presidential Palace, the ornate iron gates now guarded by boys in olive-green fatigues.[74] Castro suspended a cabinet meeting to greet the two foreign writers. They left duly impressed. Castro went back to the agenda for the day: his first, semiofficial visit to the United States. He had accepted an invitation to address the American Society of Newspaper Editors in Washington. Castro was still ambivalent about the United States, not sure which way to turn. The visit would be an opportunity to defend his record of revolutionary justice and perhaps set the stage for good Cuban-American relations.

When he heard about Castro's invitation to the United States, Hemingway offered to meet with the Cuban leader and prepare him for the questions that American reporters and politicians would ask. He passed the message through his good friend Dr. Herrera, who still was coming to dinner at the Finca a few times a month.[75] Castro himself did not accept the invitation, but he did send one of his subordinates to hear what Hemingway had to say.[76]

Late one night, Herrera drove a journalist named Euclides Vázquez Candela from Havana out to the Finca, where Hemingway received them at the door with a pistol in his pocket, testimony to the still unsettled times. An ardent anti-imperialist, Vázquez Candela was not sure what to expect from the famous *Yanqui*, but Hemingway quickly set his visitor at ease—and even charmed him.[77]

Hemingway sat with his guests in the Finca's fifty-foot-long living room, in the overstuffed chairs amid the writer's many books, hunting trophies, and world-class art collection. Classical music played softly in the background. They drank a chilled Italian white wine and snacked on nuts. Hemingway pulled out the notes he had prepared and started to explain how the American press worked, whom to watch out for, what the issues of the day were. He implied that, if Castro handled himself well, he could have whatever he wanted from the United States. Hemingway specifically mentioned the need to explain the "judicial decrees against obvious traitors," meaning the public trials and executions, and the question of communist influence. The last thing he did as he walked his guests back to their car was to ask Vázquez Candela to convey his wholehearted support for their revolution to the bearded ones in Havana.[78]

The Cuban leader's trip was a resounding public relations success.[79] In his rumpled fatigues and untrimmed beard, the thirty-three-year-old revolutionary seemed so authentic. Castro already knew how to charm a crowd, and spoke a "clumsy but clear" language some called "fidelenglish."[80] While in the United States, he literally reached out to anyone who came near him and calmly answered most questions put to him. Staying away from anti-imperialist rhetoric, he adeptly sidestepped questions about communists in his movement. During a speech from the bandstand in Central Park, Castro was eloquent but vague about his core political values: humanism and democracy. The only discordant notes came when he met with officials like Vice President Richard Nixon, who lectured him about the dangers of communism.[81]

For Hemingway another high point of 1959 was his summer trip to Spain.[82] The writer and his not inconsiderable entourage attended bullfights that he planned to write about for *Life* magazine. In July he celebrated his sixtieth birthday at La Consula, the palatial villa in Málaga on the Costa del Sol owned by the wealthy American expatriate Nathan "Bill" Davis, who was an aficionado of bullfighting.[83] The gardens reminded the Hemingways of the

Finca, but the large white house, built in the 1830s for a diplomat, was much more elaborate, with high ceilings and elegant, wrap-around balconies on two levels.

In response to Mary's invitations, old friends and family came from far away to attend the days-long extravaganza; they included the famous and near-famous, like Buck Lanham and David K. E. Bruce, now an ambassador, to say nothing of the great bullfighter Antonio Ordóñez and his followers. There were even two Indian maharajahs, one from Cooch Behar and one from Jaipur. The novelist's personal physician and good friend, Dr. George Saviers, and his wife, Pat, came from Ketchum. It turned out to be a bittersweet occasion, marked by dancing and music, fireworks, gifts, and toasts, including a tribute from David Bruce to the writer's "warmth, manliness, and generosity."[84] But everyone had to tolerate (or try to ignore) Hemingway's outbursts when he lashed out at the guests, even his best friend Lanham. Mary found it hard to put up with the cruel, senseless things he said to her in public, and the attention he paid to the much younger women he had insisted on inviting to the party.

Some three months after the melodrama in Málaga, Hemingway traveled to New York, and then back to Cuba, where revolutionary justice still held sway. He was, once again, met by a large crowd at the airport. This time it was not just friends and neighbors, but also reporters who wanted a statement. Hemingway told them that he did not believe the bad things in "the foreign press" about the revolution, and still supported the new Cuban government.[85] According to the Cuban news agency Prensa Latina, "he hoped Cubans would regard him not as a *Yanqui* . . . but [as] another Cuban," then grabbed and kissed a nearby Cuban flag.[86] He did it so quickly that the news photographers missed the gesture and asked him to repeat it. With a smile he said that he was a writer, not an actor, and went on his way. Something like twenty carloads of well-wishers escorted him home. The American Embassy in Havana reported the incident to Washington in a dispatch, commenting for "official use only" that it was "unfortunate" that, with his reputation, Hemingway would "publicly take a position which displays either (1) strong criticism of his government and compatriots, or (2) a remarkable ignorance concerning developments in Cuba since the first of the year."[87]

After an interlude in Idaho, Hemingway and Mary were back at the Finca in January 1960.[88] His old friend the *Times* reporter Herbert Matthews interpreted this as "a deliberate gesture" of support for the revolution by the artist who was the hero of the Cuban people.[89] On January 12, Hemingway wrote Lanham to say he still believed "completely in the historical necessity of the . . . revolution."[90] He was taking "the long view," looking forward to the day when Castro would be able to change Cuban society for the better. For that reason, he was less interested in the short-term, "day by day" drama, which was impossible for anyone to ignore: the huge "Cuba Si, Yanquis No!" banners throughout the capital and the radio that, day and night, condemned the United States, the cynical, murderous "Public Enemy No. 1."[91] It was as if Castro had read George Orwell's dystopian novel *1984* and liked the bits about totalitarian "newspeak."

With his sympathetic outlook, Matthews was all the more welcome when he came to lunch at the Finca in early or mid-March. Hemingway "was so pleased to see him . . . that their animated conversation continued well into the afternoon."[92] The increasingly isolated reporter, now out of step with the mainline press in America, was still upbeat about Castro, noting that he was moving ahead with plans for health, education, and welfare and that 75 percent of the people supported him. The problems he foresaw that day did not so much concern what Castro was doing at home, but rather how he was perceived and treated by the United States. Hemingway, the man who had coached Castro's aide on how to work with the American press, could not help but agree.[93]

In May 1960 Hemingway and Castro met for the first and perhaps only time.[94] The occasion was the annual Hemingway fishing competition. Apparently following all of the rules, Castro caught the biggest fish and won first prize. When Hemingway presented the

Winner take all: Castro and Hemingway at the fishing competition in May 1960. *Copyright Bettmann, Corbis Images.*

trophy, a large silver cup, the two men chatted for a few minutes. Castro told him how much he had admired—and learned—from *For Whom the Bell Tolls*.[95] An official photographer captured the occasion in a series of photos that shows them standing close together and sharing a few private words. A few inches taller than Hemingway in his plain green uniform and matching cap, Castro almost dominates the pictures. Hemingway alternates between appearing happy and engaged, and looking like an old man, somewhat frail with his wispy white hair and scraggly beard. There is a Band-Aid on his left hand.

The next morning a messenger delivered a set of prints to the Finca. Hemingway dedicated one of the pictures "To Dr. Fidel Castro . . . in friendship." Castro kept the picture on the wall of his office for years, next to a picture of his father.[96] For his part, Hemingway selected the print that he liked the best and, once framed, kept it on a table at the Finca with other souvenirs of memorable occasions.[97]

The fishing competition may have been the high point of Cuban-American relations in 1960. Like Matthews, Hemingway hoped the United States would give the benefit of the doubt to Cuba. They tended to look to Washington more than to Havana for compromise. But as Castro raised the ante, President Dwight D. Eisenhower doubled down. In May the United States cut the remaining aid programs. The largely apolitical René Villarreal, Hemingway's helpmate at the Finca, heard the resulting explosion: Hemingway used "his entire repertoire" of insults to denounce Eisenhower and said that his decision showed "the dictatorial face of the United States."[98] Mary disagreed, and after an angry exchange, the two retreated to sleep in separate bedrooms that night.

Even worse was the matter of the sugar quota, which had guaranteed sales of Cuba's main export to the United States at a good price. Hemingway hoped "to Christ" the United States would not cut the sugar quota. "That would really tear it. It will make Cuba a gift to the Russians."[99] But on the Fourth of July—the date was no coincidence—Castro staged a massive anti-American rally in downtown Havana, and two days later Eisenhower cut the quota. That day, the writer listened to the radio every half hour starting at six in the morning, almost as if he hoped that the news would improve over time.[100]

Hemingway knew this was a turning point. So did the American Embassy in Havana, which started advising American citizens in Cuba to leave the country.

The ambassador delivered the message to Hemingway in person. The tall, patrician Bonsal, yet another Yale graduate, so old-fashioned he referred to his wife as "Mrs. Philip W. Bonsal" in his memoirs, was actually a longtime, approachable friend. He had worked for the International Telephone & Telegraph Company in Havana before joining the State Department. Hemingway had fond memories of going on holiday with Bonsal in Salamanca, Spain, in the 1930s.[101] Bonsal had renewed their friendship when he became ambassador shortly after Castro took power in 1959. In the spring and summer of 1960 he was a regular dinner guest at the Finca.

Valerie Danby-Smith, Hemingway's young Irish secretary, joined the writer and the diplomat at one of those dinners, and listened as Bonsal conveyed "an important though informal" message from Washington.[102] He replayed the theme that the embassy had aired with Washington in its November 1959 dispatch about the famous expatriate who was speaking out in favor of the revolution.[103] Relations between the two countries had continued to deteriorate. Castro seemed to be going out of his way to antagonize the U.S. government, and American officials were uncomfortable that Hemingway was still living there. Perhaps he could live somewhere else and speak out against the Cuban regime? Hemingway protested: the Finca was home, the Cubans were friends and family. He told Bonsal that writing, not politics, was his business. Besides, he had proven his allegiance again and again; no one had ever questioned his loyalty to the United States.[104]

Bonsal did not let up. Diplomatic yet firm, he repeated that while he understood Hemingway's point of view, other members of the U.S. government did not. "If the writer was not prepared to take a stand as a public figure, there could be consequences."[105] Danby-Smith heard Bonsal use the word "traitor." She also remembered that Bonsal returned for dinner the following week and again told Hemingway that he "would have to make an open choice between his country and his home."[106] The rest of the conversation was strained that night; the old friends had to force themselves to make small talk. Valerie thought she saw tears in Hemingway's eyes when they parted.

Bonsal had touched a sensitive nerve in pressing Hemingway to choose between his home and his country and in lobbing the word "traitor" before the American icon. Hemingway had wrestled with questions of loyalty for decades now, from the Spanish Civil War, to the day in New York when he agreed to become a Soviet spy, through the Red Scares in the late 1940s and the early 1950s, to the day in 1951 when he insisted in the letter to Buck Lanham that he, Hemingway, was "no fucking traitor." The writer even employed many of the same words with Bonsal that he had used first with Lanham and later with Hotchner when discussing this troubling subject.

It was not just that he had intimate friends in Cuba, or that he had lived at the Finca longer than anywhere else in his life. There was something more. He had transferred his unrealized hopes for the Spanish Republic to the Cuban Revolution. What had happened from 1936 to 1939 still shaped the way he thought from 1952 to 1960; the Republic was the defining cause of his lifetime. Supporting Castro was equivalent to fighting Franco and Hitler in Spain. He did not fight as hard in Cuba as he had in Spain, but he had also been far from idle, no matter what he said to his friends or the press about staying out of Cuban politics. There was a reasonable chance that his hopes would be realized, but now his country's ambassador was asking him to turn his back on them for good. No wonder Valerie thought she saw tears.

Bonsal's message was all the more compelling because he was a friend and a moderate who had tried but failed to find common ground with the increasingly dictatorial Castro.[107] Hemingway had to admit that the ambassador's argument was not unreasonable. Castro's anti-American rhetoric was now over-the-top, and he was threatening Americans and American property on the island. It did not help that his speeches occasionally included a kind word about "Americans . . . like Hemingway," outliers who were friends of the revolution.[108] The revolution would never seize *their* property.[109] According to a Soviet scholar who lived and worked in Cuba, Castro even quoted the writer's defense of revolutionary justice.[110]

Castro's accolades put Hemingway in an awkward position. He confided in Hotchner, who was now both a regular companion and something like an unpaid assistant, that, personally, Castro did not bother him. Castro was likely to let the Hemingways live in peace at the Finca. The famous writer knew he was good publicity for the regime. But no matter how much he sympathized with Castro, or how much he hoped that the Cuban Revolution would make good the shortcomings of the Spanish Republic, he did not want to be the kind of exception that Castro praised. When Hotchner asked what bothered him most, he said he could not rest easy when other Americans were "being kicked out" and "his country [was] . . . being vilified."[111]

The events of the summer of 1960 likely sped up the decline begun a few years earlier. Hotchner could see the loss of physical strength in Hemingway—the man who loved to box looked thin, his once-powerful arms "as if they had been pared down by an unskilled whittler."[112] He had trouble with his kidneys and his eyesight. Perhaps worst of all, writing was much harder than it had ever been. The manuscript about bullfighting that he was working on for *Life* was spiraling out of control.[113] The magazine had asked for roughly forty pages. Working frenetically, Hemingway had produced 688 pages but could not bear to cut any of them. He had to ask Hotchner to fly down to Cuba from New York to help—and then resisted his edits for reasons that made no sense to the younger writer.

On July 25, Hemingway, Mary, and Valerie took the ferry from Havana to Key West. They had not made any final decisions about leaving Cuba. On the contrary, they intended to return in a few months, leaving many valued possessions at the Finca and keeping it fully staffed.[114] Hemingway made sure there was no fanfare when they departed. He did not want to draw attention to himself as he had in November. Most of all, he did not want anyone to think that his exit was meant to be a statement against Castro, whom he continued to support.[115]

At both ends of the journey, Hemingway was ill at ease, worrying about customs and immigrations formalities. Mary heard him muttering about "the dire consequences of lawbreaking."[116]

Continuing on by himself, Hemingway flew from Key West to New York, and then to Europe for the months of August and September. His friends in Spain were taken aback by how much he had deteriorated over the past year. Relying on firsthand testimony, the first Hemingway biographer, Carlos Baker, would sum up what he learned from them a few years later: they had all seen the writer "in most of his moods but none like this, . . . [showing] symptoms of extreme nervous depression: fear, loneliness, ennui, suspicion of the motives of others, insomnia, guilt, remorse, and failure of memory."[117]

On August 15, Hemingway wrote Mary that he feared a "complete physical and nervous crack up from deadly overwork."[118] This was only one of many pleas for help that he sent to her that month.

Mary and the loyal Hotchner did what they could to support Hemingway during the breakdown that played out in slow motion over the next year. Alarmed by what he was hearing from Spain, Hotchner flew to Europe to be with Hemingway, and, on October 8, escorted him back to New York. There Mary took charge of him, and the two traveled to Ketchum by train. By now both Hotchner and Mary knew that they were out of their depths when it came to caring for the man they loved, and they sought expert help, first consulting a psychiatrist in New York, and then, on his recommendation, arranging for treatment by doctors at the Mayo Clinic in Rochester, Minnesota. To avoid publicity, the clinic suggested he

A pensive Hemingway reading a letter at La Consula. *Mary Hemingway Photo, Ernest Hemingway Photo Collection, JFK Library.*

register under an alias, and so it was under the name of "George Saviers" (his doctor in Ketchum) that he went into a locked ward at St. Mary's Hospital, a Mayo affiliate, where he would stay from November 30, 1960, to January 22, 1961.

The main diagnosis was depression, complicated by paranoia. Hemingway's psychiatrist, Dr. Howard Rome, opted for electroconvulsive therapy, a treatment that at the time was not uncommon in severe cases.[119] Whether Hemingway himself, or Mary, signed the inevitable consent form, Hemingway was not a man with many choices, especially after consulting Dr. Rome and his colleagues. During the treatments, the doctors sedated Hemingway, strapped him to an operating table, and attached electrodes to his temples in order to run an electric current through his brain. The eleven to fifteen treatments seemed to lighten his depression, but he was convinced they were erasing his memory. (Indeed, memory loss was a common side effect.) This worried the writer who had never needed to take notes. As he told Hotchner, his memory was where he stored his capital; when he had depleted his capital, he would be out of business.[120]

The obsessions still would not go away.[121] Some were matters of demonstrable fact—like his notes on the cross-country drive from Key West to Idaho in November 1959, when he recorded the gallons of gas purchased, the number of miles driven, the times and distances. Some were out-and-out delusions. For example, Hemingway worried obsessively about Valerie Danby-Smith's U.S. visa (to allow her to reenter the United States and study in New York), which then led to the delusion that the U.S. Immigration and Naturalization Service was investigating him because he had sponsored Valerie.

Other delusions were about the FBI. He thought the FBI had been tailing him since his return from Europe in October 1960; for him any man who did not wear jeans and cowboy boots was suspect. (He imagined that FBI agents always dressed like they were going to work at their headquarters: in dark suits and white shirts.) In November, when he and Hotchner drove past a bank in Ketchum where the lights were still on after closing time, he was convinced federal agents were poring over his bank reports, looking for evidence of a crime that he would never specify. He also imagined they were bugging his hospital room and the cars he rode in; when Hotchner visited him in Rochester, Minnesota, he would not talk freely until they were walking through open fields. When Hotchner asked Hemingway why the FBI might be interested in him, he explained it was because of the "suspicious books" he had written, who his friends were, and where he lived—

"among Cuban communists."[122] At Christmas, Mary noted that, while he no longer insisted that there was a special agent in the bathroom with a tape recorder, Hemingway was still waiting for the FBI to pick him up and take him in for questioning.[123]

He even worried the FBI would investigate why he had registered at Mayo under an alias. Early in the new year, this prompted Hemingway's doctor to take the unusual step of asking the FBI field office in Minneapolis for "authorization" to tell Hemingway that the FBI didn't care about his use of an alias.[124] Dated January 13, 1961, the field agents' message to Washington suggests that the doctor's request came as a complete surprise to them. Their message went out over the wires in plain text, without any kind of priority—unlike messages about internal security investigations. In the original, the field for the file number was left blank; a date stamp suggests that it was added by hand eleven days later by a clerk in Washington. The Minneapolis office would have had the file number if it had been working on "the Hemingway case."

Since there was nothing at stake for them, the agents from Minneapolis felt free to advise Dr. Rome that they had "no objection" to his plan.[125] He presumably passed the message on to Hemingway. But the writer's paranoia about the government still did not lift. In mid-January he wrote Lanham ominously that "the true gen" (here his take on U.S. politics, loyalty, and the Soviets) he had shared with the general over the years was enough to send him to "the gallows."[126]

Still very much in the news in early 1961, Cuba was never far from Hemingway's mind in spite of his condition. On January 2, Matthews wrote Hemingway to lament the situation on the island. He deplored "the excesses, the links to communism, and the extravagant anti-Yankeeism of the Revolution."[127] Even so he felt "there is something precious . . . [in] this revolution that must not be lost." The Eisenhower administration clearly disagreed, severing diplomatic relations the next day. The resulting uncertainty gnawed at Hemingway. On the sixteenth he wrote Lanham that he and Mary might "lose everything in Cuba," or they might not.[128] He hinted that, perhaps, the Soviets would intervene on his behalf. But even this was "too much to write in a letter so keep it under your hat along with the other things we remember but don't write."[129]

While the new year was still young, rumors started to circulate among Cuban exiles and American journalists that Presidents Eisenhower and Kennedy (who took office on January 20, 1961) were planning some kind of action against Castro. Worried that Hemingway had not been able to absorb his earlier letter—the carbon copy in his files bears the handwritten note "Too ill then to read it. HLM"—Matthews wrote again to Hemingway on February 20. He was "of course unhappy about the way things have developed in Cuba," and imagined that Hemingway and Mary must be even more upset than he was. Still, he hoped the CIA would not destroy the revolution—he used the word "precious" again. Even if a CIA operation succeeded, "It would be a case of curing the patient by killing him."[130]

By now it was almost impossible to stop Operation Zapata, the plan to overthrow Castro that was conceived during the last year of the Eisenhower administration. In the early morning hours of April 17, 1961, a CIA-equipped and -trained force of Cuban exiles landed on the south coast of Cuba. By 11 A.M. on the same day, the Cuban representative to the United Nations declared that "Cuba was invaded this morning by a mercenary force . . . [outfitted] by . . . the United States."[131] The invaders, about 1,400 strong, fought bravely but were overwhelmed by the forces that Castro quickly mobilized to defeat the attack that he had feared for some time. On April 20, Castro declared victory over Cuban radio.[132] The *Times* printed his declaration the next day.

During the week of the so-called Bay of Pigs Invasion, American newspapers all over the country covered the story "with the kind of page-spanning, ink-drenched headlines usually reserved for presidential elections and national disasters."[133] Hemingway and Mary also heard it from radio and television broadcasts. Mary remembered that they were both "appalled" by the choice of landing site, a marshy swath of land much better suited for hunting ducks than maneuvering troops. Otherwise she wrote only that "our private preoccupations blurred our concerns with the distant fiasco."[134]

What were those concerns? Simply that the United States had chosen a bad landing site? Or that Castro had too much support (estimated at 75 percent by Mary and Matthews) among the Cuban people for the operation to succeed? Lanham thought he knew one answer. Three weeks later, he would write to Hemingway that he, Buck, imagined how painful it must have been for "an old beat-up military type" like Ernest to read about "such a monumental stupidity," adding that Castro was, sadly, turning out to be worse than Batista.[135]

Lanham seemed to sense that the prospects were slim for any outcome that would suit Hemingway. A victory for the U.S.-backed invasion would have made him uncomfortable; he had criticized the United States for acting like a nineteenth-century "great power" and being a bad neighbor in Latin America. It would also risk turning the clock back to the Batista era. A victory for Castro was little better for him. Castro would now be more anti-American than ever, and, though Hemingway loved Cuba, he would not go against his own country, ultimately. It was the kind of choice he had faced before, first in Spain, then during World War II and in the bitter peace that followed it. Perhaps he replayed Bonsal's warning about treason in his head and felt, one more time, all the pain it had evoked.

Mary implied that his private struggles had crowded out Hemingway's feelings about the invasion. But timing suggests the two may well have gone hand in hand.[136] On Tuesday, the second day of the invasion, he drafted a letter to his publisher saying that he had tried and failed to edit his memoirs about his life in Paris in the 1920s (work that would become *A Moveable Feast*); since his return from Minnesota, everything he tried simply made things worse.[137] This was not a passing complaint, but an acknowledgment of defeat. He simply could no longer do the work that had sustained him. The "distant fiasco" at the Bay of Pigs was another defeat, one that was almost as painful. He understood he would never be able to go home, to walk under the ceiba tree to the front door of the Finca, or steer *Pilar* out of the harbor past the old Spanish castle, or spend an afternoon drinking Papa Dobles at the Floridita with his friends. Nor would he be able to support a revolution that, for all its failings, was for him still a precious victory over the right. It was the end of an old and cherished dream, the one that had begun in Spain.

There was no easy way to soften any of this. When she went downstairs on the morning of Friday, April 21, Mary found Hemingway in the sitting room with his favorite shotgun in his hand and two shells on the windowsill within easy reach.[138] For a harrowing hour and a half, she gently talked to him about the things they could still do—go to Mexico, revisit Paris, maybe even Africa for another safari. When their good friend the family doctor Saviers arrived to take Hemingway's blood pressure, they were able to talk him into putting the weapon down. They took him to the local hospital and, as soon as possible, arranged to fly him back to the Mayo Clinic for another grim round of electroshock therapy in a locked ward. On the way, he tried at least twice to kill himself. At the airport in Casper, Wyoming, he attempted to walk into a whirling airplane propeller.

At the end of June, Hemingway's doctor at Mayo decided that his patient was ready to go home.[139] Mary suspected the truth, that her husband had manipulated the psychiatrist into signing the discharge papers. He was still leaving broad hints that he planned to commit suicide, like the letter that he wrote earlier in the month to René Villarreal, his Cuban "son" who was keeping the Finca up. Hemingway wrote that he was almost "out of gas." He was a shadow of his former self, down to a welterweight. He didn't "even have the will to read," a touchstone in his life that he had "loved above everything." "Writing," he remarked, was "even more difficult."[140] Hemingway asked René to look after his cats and dogs and his "beloved Finca," and assured him that, whatever happened, Papa would always remember him.

Despite her misgivings, Mary and George Brown, the boxer from New York who had been his friend for decades, picked Hemingway up at the clinic and drove him back to Ketchum, arriving on Friday, June 30.

On the warm and sunny morning of Saturday, July 1, Hemingway cajoled Brown into joining him for a long walk through the gentle hills north of the house, a small challenge for the New Yorker in his city shoes. The two men later drove around town, calling on old friends. They found Dr. Saviers in his office at the hospital, but the hunter Don Anderson was not at his workplace in Sun Valley. Another outdoorsman, Chuck Atkinson, came by the house before the sun went down, and chatted with Hemingway for an hour on the front porch.[141] At some point in the afternoon, Mary would tell Lanham, Hemingway reread the last letter he had received from the retired general.[142] Buck wrote to share news of mutual friends, but mostly to tell Ernest how concerned he, Buck, was about his old comrade in arms and how much he wanted for Ernest to get and feel better.[143]

In the evening Hemingway treated Brown and Mary to dinner at the familiar Christiania Restaurant downtown, where they sat at a corner table and could see who else was there. While they ate, Hemingway looked over at the next table and asked the waitress about the two men seated there. She thought they were salesmen from nearby Twin Falls.

Hemingway countered, "Not on Saturday." When the waitress shrugged, Hemingway explained in a low voice, "They're FBI."[144]

Early the next morning, Mary woke to what sounded like two drawers slamming shut, one after another, and went to investigate. She found Hemingway dead in the vestibule of the sitting room where she had disarmed him in April. He had gotten up before anyone else, padded quietly downstairs, and, with one of his double-barreled shotguns, killed what was left of the great American writer who had fought so hard for what he believed in.

EPILOGUE

Calculating the Hidden Costs

After the news spread, there was every kind of speculation about Hemingway's death.[1] It just did not make sense to anyone apart from a handful of insiders, especially after Mary put out the story that something had gone wrong while he was cleaning one of his guns. He had handled firearms all his life. How could the man who had taken so many risks—who had been on the front lines in three wars—die by accident in his own home? Emmett Watson, the journalist from Seattle who had scooped his rivals on Hemingway and Castro, made it his job to find out.

When Watson got to Ketchum, he felt like "every writer on earth was already there" to cover the funeral. Teaming up with another reporter, he worked Ketchum the way he would the backstreets of his hometown, avoiding the prominent citizens but interviewing everyone else "from bartenders, to . . . hunting pals, to maids, to waitresses, to his typist" to uncover the truth.[2] "Hemingway's Death Is Suicide" ran in the *Seattle Post-Intelligencer* on July 7 with the kind of details that would settle arguments.[3]

But Watson could not explain *why* the man who admonished us first to endure—one of his favorite sayings was "il faut d'abord durer"—would take his own life.

His many friends and readers began to search for the facts that would help them to understand Hemingway's death. Could it have been an incurable illness, perhaps something rare like hemochromatosis? Was there an old war wound that would not heal? Perhaps there had been trouble with Mary, or a financial crisis? And how much did the loss of the Finca contribute?

Over the years, a kind of consensus emerged: no one thing had driven this supremely talented man to suicide.[4] It was more complicated, and less satisfying, than that. Depression—what he called the "black ass"—had stalked him for much of his life, and gotten worse as time went on. Originally a simple pleasure, drinking became a complication, a multiplier of demons. Old age came early—and forcefully—for him, ushered in by the many accidents that had befallen him since the 1920s. The Cuban Revolution was at first an uplifting tonic and then another depressing complication; by 1961 there was little hope of resuming his life in Cuba or even seeing his beloved Finca again.

He could not even keep hold of his memories. Up to now, they had filled his mind and found new life in his short stories and novels. But the electroshock treatments at Mayo made him foggy, and took away the clarity for which he was famous. Without his memories he doubted he would ever be able to write again.

In 2011, on the fiftieth anniversary, A. E. Hotchner reopened the bidding about Hemingway's death. This considerably younger but still intimate friend, witness to events in the last months of Hemingway's life, advanced yet another theory that he called "Hemingway, Hounded by the Feds."[5] After reviewing the well-known explanations, Hotchner focused on the depression and paranoia that were part of the writer's life for most days in the 1950s. Hotchner wrote about the biographers who had portrayed Hemingway's obsessive worries about the FBI as delusions, and then about the file that the FBI had released in the 1980s in response to a claim under the Freedom of Information Act.

According to Hotchner, the file showed that Hemingway had not been wrong about the Bureau. Granted, the first entries date back to 1942, and are about the Crook Factory and the wartime hunt for fascists in Cuba. But, per Hotchner, the Bureau did not forget Hemingway when the war was over: "Over the following years agents filed reports on him and tapped his phones. The surveillance continued all through his confinement at St. Mary's hospital."[6] The FBI may have tapped the phone outside his room after all. Hotchner concluded that Hemingway had sensed the surveillance, and that it "substantially contributed to his anguish and his suicide."[7]

It is now clear that Hotchner understood Hemingway's state of mind better than he understood the Bureau's intent. A close reading of his FBI file shows that Hemingway was never under surveillance.[8] The FBI did not take the first step: the file opens with the ambassador's decision to use Hemingway to run an amateur counterintelligence bureau. The embassy announces the plan, and the Bureau reacts. First Hoover wants to know about the writer's background, and then he wants, above all, to avoid any unpleasant surprises that could embarrass the organization he had created in his own image.

At odd intervals in the years that followed, the Bureau continued to collect information on Hemingway that happened to come its way, sometimes from the writer himself, sometimes from other branches of the government, like the Department of State. A few entries were from newspapers. One or two reports came from confidential informants who met Hemingway socially and reported their impressions secretly to Hoover's men. Some of what they reported made the director worry that Hemingway might be writing a book that would cast him and his agents in a bad light. But he did not suspect Hemingway of any crimes, and the Bureau did not launch a formal investigation into his activities. Its agents did not tap his phones, open his mail, or follow him. In 1961, Hemingway's doctor brought the FBI in on his patient's case, not the other way around.[9]

The Bureau's hypothesis about Hemingway was always that he was not a communist, but simply a hard-core antifascist. Even after his death, Mary wanted to make sure that did not change. In 1964, after the Cuban post office issued a commemorative Hemingway stamp, Mary took the trouble to ask the journalist Quentin Reynolds to pass a message to Hoover. She wanted him to know that no one in the family had authorized the stamp, or supported the Cuban Revolution. Hemingway had welcomed Castro for ousting the right-wing dictator Batista. But "[h]e didn't know Castro well. Mary [said] he met Castro at a fishing party and talked to him for five minutes—period."[10] Hoover accepted the information at face value, writing and signing a memo for the file, his last known word on the case: "Knowing Hemingway as I did, I doubt he had any communist leanings. He was a rough, tough guy & always for the underdog."[11]

No matter how the Bureau viewed Hemingway, Hotchner is right that Hemingway was anxious about the Bureau. Hoover and his agents knew only a little about the various "subversive" activities in the writer's past, and nothing about his meetings with the NKVD. They did not hound Hemingway to death. But he was never able to forget what he did for the causes he cared about—especially his own brand of antifascism and his support for Castro—and fretted that his actions had put him on the Bureau's radar. His obsessive worry about government surveillance deepened his depression and made his final illness worse. He could not rest, "knowing" that federal agents were coming to arrest him for crimes that were not entirely imaginary.

This lifelong rebel resented the authority they represented. Just as he was *for* the underdog, Hemingway was *against* anyone who (he thought) was an instrument of oppression. From 1937 until the end of his life, he did everything he could to fight fascism, especially the virulent European strains. Theirs was the worst kind of authority, not only oppressing the underdog but also stifling the arts. The militant writer attacked American and British politicians who did not share his agenda, and he saw traces of fascism in American institutions, like the FBI and HUAC. In Cuba he passionately supported the revolutionaries against the established order and once again found that his own government's agenda was different from his.

He especially resented government intrusion into his private life. From 1942 on, this naturally conspiratorial man worried he was under some kind of surveillance. He pushed back when he thought the FBI was undermining his work at the Crook Factory and was angry when he learned that wartime censors in Miami were reading his mail. In 1944, he could barely bring himself to answer the Army inspector general who questioned him about being a fighter instead of a reporter at Rambouillet. He hated having to lie about the record that showed he had been a part of the action, not just an observer.

During the early years of the Cold War, he worried even more about what the government might have in store for him, to the point where it made him think twice about what he was writing and publishing. The man who had "honestly and undauntedly" reproduced "the hard countenance of the age" in the 1930s took to censoring himself in the 1950s.[12]

Hemingway said the government was watching him because it viewed him as untrustworthy because he had been a "pre-mature anti-fascist." He never mentioned the best reason the government might have had to watch him: this premature antifascist had signed up with the NKVD. That he had never actually spied for the Soviets was immaterial; good people were hauled up in front of committees for far less during the McCarthy years. It was far from unreasonable for him to worry that his secret could derail his career.

Writing, Hemingway told the Nobel committee, was a lonely life. He might have added that secrets can make a writer even lonelier. He could have lightened his burden by sharing it, but he almost certainly did not. In his letters he stopped short of telling the whole truth to Lanham, the man he trusted most, and likely said even less to Gellhorn, Mary, or Hotchner. He certainly revealed nothing to the federal government or to the public. The cost of isolating himself—of locking up his explosive secret—was dire; worry descended into obsession and delusion.

Could this chapter of the Hemingway biography have ended differently? Many former communists, like his acquaintance Koestler, openly turned their backs on "the God that failed."[13] More than one American who spied for the NKVD walked into the nearest FBI office and told the agents everything he (or she) knew, and then spoke out against Comrade Stalin. For some it was cathartic, a good way to come in out of the cold. But Hemingway could not renounce communism, because he had not been a communist, and he could not imagine how to tell the complicated story of his relationship with the NKVD in a way that would make sense to anyone willing to listen. Besides, his makeup made it difficult for him to turn on his former allies; he detested "stool pigeons" and "turncoats."

Ambassador Bonsal suggested one way out in the summer of 1960: go back to the United States and speak out against Castro's excesses. This would put him right with America. But that too was a near-impossible choice. Hemingway had not given up on the Cuban Revolution. Longer than other Americans, he nurtured hopes for its future and he could not bring himself to denounce a guerrilla chieftain who had carried a copy of *For Whom the Bell Tolls* in his rucksack *and* overthrown a right-wing dictator.

Hemingway did not share much with Bonsal during their last meeting at the Finca. He said a few words about his love for America and his attachment to Cuba. While he understood what the ambassador was telling him, he did not go on to say that he still planned to continue living by his own rules—as he had for most of his life. Living by his own rules had enabled him to create a wonderful, pioneering body of work. He had, almost single-handedly, changed the way Americans looked at the world and wrote about what they saw and felt.

Living by his own rules allowed him to take risks that were not just restricted to writing. Between 1937 and 1960, he was deeply engaged in politics and intrigue, first for the Spanish Republic, then with the Soviets, and next for his own country during World War II. After the Cold War started, he lowered his political profile in America, but he was hardly a passive observer of events in Cuba during the 1950s.

From the day he saw the bodies of the veterans strewn on a Florida beach in 1935, the political Hemingway was almost as active and independent as the literary Hemingway. For the most part, he worked on his own and did what he thought needed to be done, seizing opportunities as they came along, as he did when he met the

NKVD recruiter Golos in 1940. He thought he could make his own foreign policy. Like other powerful men who have become spies, he believed that he could control his relationships with the Soviet—and American—intelligence bureaus. He was only partly right. Surprisingly good at this, his second career, he was not the expert he thought he was. The ultimate professional when it came to writing, in politics and intrigue he was a gifted but overconfident amateur. Until it was too late, he did not pause to consider the costs he would one day have to pay for his secret adventures.

SOURCES

PRIMARY SOURCES

FBI website

File Number 64-23312 (Ernest Hemingway), in vault.fbi.gov

Franklin D. Roosevelt Presidential Library

Henry Morgenthau, Jr., Diaries

John F. Kennedy Presidential Library

Ernest Hemingway Collection

Hoover Institution Library and Archives, Stanford University

J. Arthur Duff Papers
Joseph Freeman Papers
Myers G. Lowman Papers

Library of Congress

A. E. Hotchner Papers
Alexander Vassiliev Papers
Archibald MacLeish Papers
Communist International Archives
Philip W. Bonsal Papers

Marine Corps History Division, Quantico, VA

John W. Thomason, Jr., Personnel File

National Archives I, Washington, DC

HUAC Files, Records of the House of Representatives (RG 233)

National Archives II, College Park, MD

Alexander Orlov Papers
Department of the Treasury Records (RG 56)
FBI Records (RG 65)
OSS Records (RG 226)

U.S. Navy Records (RG 38)
Department of State Records (RG 59)

National Archives, Kew, England
Gustav Regler Personal File, Records of the Security Service

New York Public Library
Hemingway Legal Files

Princeton University
Firestone Library, Rare Books and Special Collections
Carlos Baker Papers (C0365)
Charles T. Lanham Papers (C0305)
Lanham-Hemingway Papers (C0067)
Scribner's Sons Archive (C0101)
Mudd Library, Rare Books and Special Collections
Charles T. Lanham Papers (MC081)

Rare Books and Manuscripts Library, Columbia University, New York
Herbert L. Matthews Papers
Spruille Braden Papers

Roald Dahl Museum and Story Centre, Buckinghamshire, England
Roald Dahl Correspondence

Special Collections, Georgetown University Library, Washington, DC
Edward P. Gazur Papers

Tamiment Library, New York University
Milton Wolff Papers

Library of the University of California, San Diego
Southworth Spanish Civil War Collection

Virginia Historical Society, Richmond
David K. E. Bruce Papers

Beinecke Rare Book and Manuscript Library, Yale University
Robert Joyce Papers

BOOKS AND ARTICLES

Aaron, Daniel. *Writers on the Left*. New York: Avon, 1961.

Aldrich, Nelson W., ed. *George, Being George*. New York: Random House, 2008.

Andrew, Christopher, and Vasili Mitrokhin. *The Sword and the Shield*. New York: Basic Books, 2001.

Baker, Carlos. *Ernest Hemingway: A Life Story*. New York: Scribner, 1969.

———, ed. *Ernest Hemingway: Selected Letters*. New York: Macmillan, 1989.

Bentley, Elizabeth. *Out of Bondage*. New York: Ivy, 1988.

Bentley, Eric, ed. *Thirty Years of Treason: Excerpts from Hearings Before the House Committee on Un-American Activities 1938–1968*. New York: Thunder's Mouth Press, 1971.

Bessie, Alvah. *Men in Battle*. New York: Chandler & Sharp, 1975.

Bessie, Dan, ed. *Alvah Bessie's Spanish Civil War Notebooks*. Lexington: University Press of Kentucky, 2002.

Billingsley, Kenneth Lloyd. "Hollywood's Missing Movies: Why American Films Have Ignored Life Under Communism." *Reason*, June 2000.

———. *Hollywood Party: How Communism Seduced the American Film Industry in the 1930s and 1940s*. Roseville, CA: Forum, 2000.

Brack, Fred. "Emmett Watson Reminisces." *Seattle Post-Intelligencer*, October 21, 1981.

Braden, Spruille. *Diplomats and Demagogues: The Memoirs of Spruille Braden*. New Rochelle, NY: Arlington House, 1971.

Bradley, Mark A. *A Very Principled Boy: The Life of Duncan Lee, Red Spy and Cold Warrior*. New York: Basic Books, 2014.

Brasch, James D. "Hemingway's Doctor: José Luis Herrera Sotolongo Remembers Ernest Hemingway." *Journal of Modern Literature* 13, no. 2 (July 1986).

Brasch, James D., and Joseph Sigman. *Hemingway's Library: A Composite Record*. Boston: JFK Library Electronic Edition, 2000.

Brian, Denis. *The True Gen*. New York: Grove, 1988.

Briggs, Ellis O. *Proud Servant: Memoirs of a Career Ambassador*. Kent, OH: Kent State University Press, 1998.

———. *Shots Heard Around the World*. New York: Viking, 1957.

Bruccoli, Matthew J., ed. *Conversations with Ernest Hemingway*. Jackson, MS, and London: University Press of Mississippi, 1986.

———, ed. *Hemingway and the Mechanism of Fame*. Columbia: University of South Carolina Press, 2006.

———, ed. *The Only Thing That Counts: The Ernest Hemingway–Maxwell Perkins Correspondence*. New York: Scribner's, 1996.

Capa, Robert. *Slightly Out of Focus*. New York: Random House, 1999.

Carpenter, Iris. *No Woman's World*. Boston: Houghton Mifflin, 1946.

Carr, Virginia S. *Dos Passos: A Life*. New York: Doubleday, 1984.

Carroll, Peter N., and James D. Fernandez, eds. *Facing Fascism: New York & the Spanish Civil War*. New York: NYU Press, 2007.

Carroll, Peter N. *The Odyssey of the Abraham Lincoln Brigade: Americans in the Spanish Civil War*. Stanford, CA: Stanford University Press, 1994.

Castro, Fidel, and Ignacio Ramonet. *Fidel Castro: My Life: A Spoken Autobiography*. New York: Scribner, 2008.

Chamberlin, Brewster. *The Hemingway Log*. Lawrence: University Press of Kansas, 2015.

Charney, David L. "True Psychology of the Insider Spy." *Intelligencer* 18, no. 1 (Fall/Winter 2010).

Churchill, Winston S. *The Second World War*. New York: Houghton Mifflin, 1959.

Cockburn, Claud. *I, Claud*. London: Penguin, 1967.

Conant, Jennet. *The Irregulars: Roald Dahl and the British Spy Ring in Wartime Washington*. New York: Simon & Schuster, 2008.

Conquest, Robert. *The Great Terror: A Reassessment*. New York: Oxford University Press, 2008.

Copeland, Miles. *The Game Player*. London: Aurum Press, 1989.

Costello, John, and Oleg Tsarev. *Deadly Illusions: The KGB Orlov Dossier*. New York: Crown Books, 1993.

Cowley, Malcolm. *The Dream of the Golden Mountains: Remembering the 1930s*. New York: Penguin, 1981.

Craig, R. Bruce. *Treasonable Doubt: The Harry Dexter White Spy Case*. Lawrence: University Press of Kansas, 2004.

DeFazio III, Albert J., ed. *"Dear Papa, Dear Hotch": The Correspondence of Ernest Hemingway and A. E. Hotchner*. Columbia: University of Missouri Press, 2005.

de la Mora, Constancia. *In Place of Splendor*. New York: Harcourt, Brace, 1939.

del Vayo, Julio Alvarez. *Give Me Combat: The Memoirs of Julio Alvarez del Vayo*. Boston: Little, Brown, 1973.

DePalma, Anthony. *The Man Who Invented Fidel: Castro, Cuba, and Herbert L. Matthews of the New York Times*. New York: PublicAffairs, 2006.

Donaldson, Scott. *Archibald MacLeish: An American Life*. Boston and New York: Houghton Mifflin, 1992.

Donovan, Robert J. *Conflict and Crisis: The Presidency of Harry S Truman, 1945–1948*. New York: Norton, 1971.

Dmytryk, Edward. *Odd Man Out: A Memoir of the Hollywood Ten*. Carbondale: Southern Illinois University Press, 1996.

Dubois, Jules. *Fidel Castro: Rebel, Liberator, or Dictator?* New York: Bobbs-Merrill, 1959.

Eakin, Hugh. "Stalin's Reading List." *New York Times*, April 17, 2005.

Eby, Cecil B. *Comrades and Commissars: The Lincoln Battalion in the Spanish Civil War*. University Park: Pennsylvania State University Press, 2007.

Ehrenburg, Ilya. *Memoirs: 1921–1941*. Cleveland and New York: World, 1964.

Fensch, Thomas. *Behind Islands in the Stream: Hemingway, Cuba, the FBI, and the Crook Factory*. New York: iUniverse, 2009.

Franqui, Carlos. *Family Portrait with Fidel*. New York: Vintage, 1985.

Fuentes, Norberto. *Hemingway in Cuba*. Secaucus, NJ: Lyle Stuart, 1984.

Fuller, Robert. "Hemingway at Rambouillet." *Hemingway Review* 33, no. 2 (Spring 2014).

Gazur, Edward P. *Alexander Orlov: The FBI's KGB General*. New York: Carroll & Graf, 2001.

Gellhorn, Martha. "Cry Shame." *New Republic*, October 6, 1947.

———. *Travels with Myself and Another*. New York: Penguin, 2001.

Gerogiannis, Nicholas, ed. *Ernest Hemingway: 88 Poems*. New York and London: Harcourt, Brace, Jovanovich, 1979.

Gingrich, Arnold. *Nothing But People: The Early Days at Esquire*. New York: Crown, 1978.

Glantz, David M., and Jonathan House. *When Titans Clashed: How the Red Army Stopped Hitler*. Lawrence: University Press of Kansas, 1995.

Goodman, Walter. *The Committee: The Extraordinary Career of the House Committee on Un-American Activities*. New York: Farrar, Straus, 1968.

Grimes, Larry, and Bickford Sylvester, eds. *Hemingway, Cuba, and the Cuban Works*. Kent, OH: Kent State University Press, 2014.

Groth, John. *Studio: Europe*. New York: Vanguard, 1945.

Gurney, Jason. *Crusade in Spain*. London: Faber & Faber, 1974.

Haberkern, E., and Arthur Lipow, eds. *Neither Capitalism nor Socialism: Theories of Bureaucratic Collectivism*. Alameda, CA: Center for Socialist History, 2008.

Hailey, Jean R. "Maj. Gen. Charles Lanham Dies." *Washington Post*, July 22, 1978.

Haines, Gerald K., and David A. Langbart. *Unlocking the Files of the FBI: A Guide to Its Records and Classification System*. Wilmington, DE: Scholarly Resources, 1993.

Haynes, John Earl, Harvey Klehr, and Alexander Vassiliev. *Spies: The Rise and Fall of the KGB in America*. New Haven, CT: Yale University Press, 2009.

Hemingway, Ernest. *The Fifth Column*. New York: Simon & Schuster, 1969.

———. *The Green Hills of Africa*. New York: Scribner, 1935.

———. "'I Saw Murder Done in Spain'—Hemingway's Lost Report." *Chicago Tribune*, November 29, 1982.

———, ed. *Men at War: The Best War Stories of All Time*. New York: Crown, 1942.

———. "Who Killed the Vets?" *New Masses*, September 17, 1935.

Hemingway, Ernest, et al. *Somebody Had to Do Something: A Memorial to James Phillips Lardner*. Los Angeles: James Lardner Memorial Fund, 1939.

Hemingway, Gregory H. *Papa: A Personal Memoir*. Boston: Houghton Mifflin, 1976.

Hemingway, Leicester. *My Brother, Ernest Hemingway*. Sarasota, FL: Pineapple Press, 1996.

Hemingway, Leicester, and Anthony Jenkinson. "A Caribbean Snoop Cruise." *Reader's Digest* 37 (1940).

Hemingway, Mary Welsh. *How It Was*. New York: Ballantine, 1977.

Hemingway, Valerie. *Running with the Bulls: My Years with the Hemingways*. New York: Ballantine, 2005.

Hendrickson, Paul. *Hemingway's Boat: Everything He Loved in Life, and Lost*. New York: Knopf, 2011.

Herbst, Josephine. *The Starched Blue Sky of Spain*. New York: HarperCollins, 1991.

Hickam, Homer H., Jr. *Torpedo Junction: U-Boat War off America's East Coast, 1942*. Annapolis, MD: Naval Institute Press, 1996.

Hicks, Granville. *Where We Came Out*. New York: Viking, 1954.

Hochschild, Adam. *Spain in Our Hearts: Americans in the Spanish Civil War, 1936–1939*. Houghton Mifflin, 2016.

Horne, Gerald. *The Final Victim of the Blacklist: John Howard Lawson, Dean of the Hollywood Ten*. Berkeley: University of California Press, 2006.

Hotchner, A. E. *Hemingway and His World*. New York and Paris: Vendome Press, 1989.

———. "Hemingway, Hounded by the Feds." *New York Times Magazine*, July 11, 2011.

———. *Hemingway in Love: His Own Story*. New York: St. Martin's Press, 2015.

———. *Papa Hemingway*. New York: Random House, 1966.

Isaacson, Walter, and Evan Thomas. *The Wise Men*. New York: Touchstone, 1986.

Jenkinson, Sir Anthony. *America Came My Way*. London: Arthur Barker, 1936.

———. *Where Seldom a Gun Is Heard*. London: Arthur Barker, 1937.

Kale, Verna. *Ernest Hemingway*. London: Reaktion Books, 2016.

Kert, Bernice. *The Hemingway Women: Those Who Loved Him—The Wives and Others*. New York: Norton, 1983.

Kessler, Lauren. *Clever Girl: Elizabeth Bentley, the Spy Who Ushered in the McCarthy Era*. New York: Perennial, 2003.

Knight, Amy. *How the Cold War Began: The Igor Gouzenko Affair and the Hunt for Soviet Spies*. New York: Carroll & Graf, 2006.

Knightley, Philip. *The Master Spy: The Story of Kim Philby*. New York: Knopf, 1989.

Koch, Stephen. *The Breaking Point: Hemingway, Dos Passos, and the Murder of José Robles*. New York: Counterpoint, 2005.

———. *Double Lives: Spies and Writers in the Secret Soviet War of Ideas against the West*. New York: Free Press, 1994.

Koestler, Arthur. *Invisible Writing: The Second Volume of an Autobiography, 1932–1940*. New York: Stein & Day, 1984.

———. *Spanish Testament*. London: Gollancz, 1937.

Kowalski, Daniel. *Stalin and the Spanish Civil War*. New York: Columbia University Press, 2004.

Langer, Eleanor. *Josephine Herbst*. Boston: Northeastern University Press, 1994.

Lankford, Nelson. *The Last American Aristocrat: The Biography of Ambassador David K. E. Bruce*. Boston: Little, Brown, 1996.

———, ed. *OSS Against the Reich: The World War II Diaries of Colonel David K. E. Bruce*. Kent, OH: Kent State University Press, 1991.

Lash, Joseph P. *Eleanor: The Years Alone*. New York: Norton, 1972.

Leighton, Frances S. "Letters from Hemingway; Unadulterated, Uninhibited—and Unpublishable." *American Weekly*, May 12, 1963.

Levin, Elizabetha. "In Their Time: The Riddle behind the Epistolary Friendship between Ernest Hemingway and Ivan Kashkin." *Hemingway Review* 32, no. 2 (2013).

Luddington, Townsend, ed. *The 14th Chronicle: Letters and Diaries of John Dos Passos*. New York: Gambit, 1973.

Lynn, Kenneth S. *Hemingway*. Cambridge, MA: Harvard University Press, 1995.

Marshall, S. L. A. *Bringing Up the Rear*. San Francisco: Presidio Press, 1979.

Matthews, Herbert L. *Castro: A Political Biography*. London: Penguin, 1969.

———. "Castro Is Still Alive and Still Fighting in the Mountains." *New York Times*, February 24, 1957.

———. *The Cuban Story*. New York: George Braziller, 1961.

———. *Education of a Correspondent*. New York: Harcourt, Brace, 1946.

———. *Two Wars and More to Come*. New York: Carrick & Evans, 1938.

———. *A World in Revolution: A Newspaperman's Memoir*. New York: Scribner, 1971.

Matthews, Nancie. "Journey to Sierra Maestra: Wife's Version." *Times Talk* 10, no. 7 (March 1957).

McGilligan, Patrick, and Paul Buhle. *Tender Comrades: A Backstory of the Hollywood Blacklist*. New York: St. Martin's, 1971.

Mellow, James R. *Hemingway: A Life Without Consequences*. Boston: Houghton Mifflin, 1992.

Merriman, Marion, and Warren Lerude. *American Commander in Spain: Robert Hale Merriman and the Abraham Lincoln Brigade*. Reno: University of Nevada Press, 1986.

Meyers, Jeffrey. *Hemingway: A Biography*. New York: DaCapo, 1999.

———. *Hemingway: Life into Art*. New York: Cooper Square, 2000.

———. "The Hemingways: An American Tragedy." *Virginia Quarterly Review*, Spring 1999.

Mickelson, Erik D. "Seattle By and By: The Life and Times of Emmett Watson." M.A. Dissertation, University of Montana, 2002.

Moorehead, Caroline. *Gellhorn: A Twentieth-Century Life*. New York: Henry Holt, 2004.

———, ed. *Selected Letters of Martha Gellhorn*. New York: Henry Holt, 2006.

Moreira, Peter. *Hemingway on the China Front: His WWII Spy Mission with Martha Gellhorn*. Washington, DC: Potomac Books, 2007.

Mort, Terry. *The Hemingway Patrols*. New York: Scribner, 2009.

National Security Agency and Central Intelligence Agency. *Venona: Soviet Espionage and the American Response, 1939–1957*. Washington, DC: NSA and CIA, 1996.

North, Joseph. *No Men Are Strangers*. New York: International, 1968.

Olmstead, Kathryn S. *Red Spy Queen: A Biography of Elizabeth Bentley*. Chapel Hill: University of North Carolina Press, 2002.

O'Rourke, Sean. *Grace Under Pressure: The Life of Evan Shipman*. Boston: Harvardwood, 2010.

Paporov, Yuri. *Hemingway en Cuba*. Mexico City and Madrid: Siglo Veintiuno Editores, 1993.

Phillips, R. Hart. *The Cuban Dilemma*. New York: Ivan Obolensky, 1962.

Pleshakov, Constantine. *Stalin's Folly*. Boston: Houghton Mifflin, 2005.

Preston, Paul. *We Saw Spain Die*. London: Constable, 2009.

Price, Ruth. *The Lives of Agnes Smedley*. Oxford: Oxford University Press, 2005.

Radosh, Ronald, Mary R. Habeck, and Grigory Sevostianov, eds. *Spain Betrayed: The Soviet Union in the Spanish Civil War*. New Haven, CT, and London: Yale University Press, 2001.

Radosh, Ronald, and Allis Radosh. *Red Star over Hollywood*. San Francisco: Encounter Books, 2005.

Rasenberger, Jim. *The Brilliant Disaster: JFK, Castro, and America's Doomed Invasion of Cuba's Bay of Pigs*. New York: Scribner, 2011.

Regler, Gustav. *Das grosse Beispiel*. 1940; reprint, Cologne, Germany: Kiepenhauer & Witsch, n.d.

———. *Dokumente und Analysen*. Saarbrücken, Germany: Saarbrücker Druckerei und Verlag, 1985.

———. *The Great Crusade*. New York: Longman, Green, 1940.

———. *The Owl of Minerva*. New York: Farrar, Straus, 1960.

Reynolds, Michael S. *Hemingway: The Final Years*. New York: Norton, 1999.

Reynolds, Nicholas. "A Spy Who Made His Own Way: Ernest Hemingway, Wartime Spy." *Studies in Intelligence* 56, no. 2 Extracts (June 2012).

Robinson, Daniel. "'My True Occupation Is That of a Writer': Hemingway's Passport Correspondence." *Hemingway Review* 24, no. 2 (Fall 2005).

Romerstein, Herbert, and Eric Breindel. *The Venona Secrets: Exposing Soviet Espionage and America's Traitors*. Washington, DC: Regnery, 2000.

Rooney, Andy. *My War*. New York: PublicAffairs, 2000.

Sanders, David. "Ernest Hemingway's Spanish Civil War Experience." *American Quarterly* 12, no. 2 (1960).

Sbardellati, John. *J. Edgar Hoover Goes to the Movies: The FBI and the Origins of Hollywood's Cold War*. Ithaca, NY: Cornell University Press, 2012.

Scammell, Michael. *Koestler*. New York: Random House, 2009.

Schoonover, Thomas D. *Hitler's Man in Havana*. Lexington: University Press of Kentucky, 2008.

Schoots, Hans. *Living Dangerously: A Biography of Joris Ivens*. Amsterdam: Amsterdam University Press, 2000.

Scott, Phil. *Hemingway's Hurricane*. New York: McGraw-Hill, 2006.

Setlowe, Rick. "Hemingway and Hollywood: For Whom the Camera Rolled." *Los Angeles Times*, October 14, 1979.

Sigal, Clancy. *Hemingway Lives! Why Reading Ernest Hemingway Matters Today*. New York and London: OR Books, 2013.

Smedley, Agnes. *China Correspondent*. London and Boston: Pandora, 1984.

Smith, Richard Harris. *OSS: The Secret History of America's First Intelligence Agency*. Berkeley: University of California Press, 1981.

Stein, Jacob A. "General Buck Lanham, Ernest Hemingway, and That Woman in Venice." *Washington Lawyer*, January 2003.

Stoneback, H. R. "Hemingway's Happiest Summer—'The Wildest, Most Beautiful, Wonderful Time Ever Ever' or, The Liberation of France and Hemingway." *North Dakota Quarterly* 64, no. 3 (Summer 1997).

Straight, Michael. *After Long Silence*. New York: Norton, 1983.

Sweet, Matthew. *The West End Front*. London: Faber & Faber, 2011.

Szurek, Alexander. *The Shattered Dream*. Boulder, CO: East European Monographs, 1989.

Tannenhaus, Sam. *Whittaker Chambers: A Biography*. New York: Random House, 1997.

Thomas, Hugh. *The Spanish Civil War*. Revised by the author. New York: Modern Library, 2001.

Thompson, Hunter S. "What Lured Hemingway to Ketchum?" *National Observer*, May 25, 1964.

Tierney, Dominic. *FDR and the Spanish Civil War*. Durham, NC: Duke University Press, 2007.

Tuchman, Barbara W. *Practicing History*. New York: Knopf, 1981.

Turner, Martha Anne. *The World of John W. Thomason, USMC*. Austin, TX: Eakin Press, 1984.

Tynan, Kathleen, ed. *Kenneth Tynan Letters*. New York: Random House, 1994.

Tynan, Kenneth. "A Visit to Havana." *Holiday* 27, no. 2 (February 1960): 50–58.

———. *Right & Left*. London: Longmans, 1967.

U.S. House of Representatives. *This Is Your House Committee on Un-American Activities*. Washington, DC: U.S. Government Printing Office, 1954.

Vernon, Alex. *Hemingway's Second War: Bearing Witness to the Spanish Civil War.* Ames: University of Iowa Press, 2011.

Viertel, Peter. *Dangerous Friends: At Large with Huston and Hemingway in the 1950s.* New York: Doubleday, 1992.

Villarreal, René, and Raúl Villarreal. *Hemingway's Cuban Son: Reflections on the Writer by His Longtime Majordomo.* Kent, OH: Kent State University Press, 2009.

Watson, Emmett. *My Life in Print.* Seattle: Lesser Seattle, 1993.

Watson, William B. "Investigating Hemingway: The Novel." *North Dakota Quarterly* 60, no. 1 (Winter 1991).

———. "Investigating Hemingway: The Story." *North Dakota Quarterly* 59, no. 1 (Winter 1991).

———. "Investigating Hemingway: The Trip." *North Dakota Quarterly* 59, no. 3 (Summer 1991).

———. "Joris Ivens and the Communists: Bringing Hemingway Into the Spanish Civil War." *Hemingway Review* 18, no. 2 (Fall 1990).

Weinstein, Allen, and Alexander Vassiliev. *The Haunted Wood.* New York: Modern Library, 1999.

Wheelock, John H., ed. *Editor to Author: The Letters of Maxwell E. Perkins.* New York: Scribner's, 1950.

White, Theodore H. *In Search of History.* New York: Harper & Row, 1978.

White, William, ed. *By-Line: Ernest Hemingway.* New York: Touchstone, 1967.

Wilmers, Mary-Kay. *The Eitingons: A Twentieth-Century Story.* London: Faber & Faber, 2010.

Wyden, Peter. *The Passionate War: The Narrative History of the Spanish Civil War.* New York: Simon & Schuster, 1983.

Zheng, Kaimei. "Hemingway in China." *North Dakota Quarterly* 70, no. 4 (2003).

ACKNOWLEDGMENTS

When he received the Nobel Prize in 1954, Hemingway reminded us that writing was a lonely life occasionally "palliated" by organizations for writers. For a genius who was writing fiction, that was especially true. He was drawing on his imagination and his skill with words; so much of his professional life was literally in his head. For someone who is not a genius, and is writing nonfiction, it is still a lonely business, with long periods in the chair by yourself. But there are facts to find, and places to go to find them, and a supporting cast of scholars, archivists, librarians, editors, and other researchers, not to mention agents and friends. There are many people who have been with me on this journey, and it is my pleasure to thank them.

In the beginning there was Mark Bradley, longtime friend and fellow historian. I was lucky enough to be a member of his team of readers when he was writing about Duncan Lee, the descendant of Robert E. Lee who spied for the Soviets. I learned a great deal from the process, both about the subject matter and about writing a book. Mark more than repaid the favor when I embarked on this project, and I will not ever be able to thank him enough. Toni Hiley, the director of the CIA Museum, tolerated and encouraged my research when I was starting out. I am convinced that there is not, on this planet, a better museum director to work for. Jill R. Hughes, at the Editor's Mark, played a vital role in helping me to shape the first five chapters that I used to market the book.

At my first meeting of the Hemingway Society, in Petoskey, Michigan, in 2012, Jean Jespersen Bartholomew and I were on a panel where I presented my first, very tentative findings. We struck up a conversation, then an email correspondence, then a literary partnership. I found out soon that she is the real deal. A longtime Hemingway scholar and aficionado, she became the irreplaceable friend, reader, and editor, someone I came to call "JMax" to evoke Hemingway's relationship with Max Perkins.

Other scholars have been willing to correspond and share sources: Daniel Robinson was kind enough to send me copies of FOIA releases that no one in the government could find anymore; Hans Schoots corresponded with me about Joris Ivens; Jeffrey Meyers shared the results of his work on Hemingway's lawyer; Joel Christenson told me about the history of the American Embassy in Havana. Kenneth W. Rendell, the founder of the Museum of World War II in Boston, sent me copies of useful letters in his collection. At the Library of Congress, John Haynes discussed the sources for *Spies,* his groundbreaking book on Soviet espionage in America, and pointed me in the direction of collections with Hemingway potential. At the National Archives, William Davis was an excellent guide to the HUAC files. Throughout my good friend Hayden Peake was an invaluable resource on the study of intelligence.

The Tabardiers, writers who meet at a round table at the Tabard Inn in downtown Washington, have palliated this writer's loneliness for the last two years. We read and critique each other's work, trade tips and references, and offer support. My heartfelt thanks go to Carol Meyers, Danielle Polen, and Kimberly Wilson. They were there during my somewhat depressing quest for a literary agent—when I couldn't even get enough traction to be rejected. Danielle suggested I approach RossYoon, the DC firm that became the home team. Andrew Simon spotted the manuscript, Anna Sproul-Latimer developed the relationship, and Howard Yoon took me on for the long haul. Howard does it all for his writers: therapist, coach, salesman, editor, teacher. Two other friends, Richard Bangs and Anthony Vinci, listened patiently to all of my breathless updates on the book, and were kind enough to share contacts from their Rolodexes.

I have also been blessed with wonderful friends who have read and critiqued all or part of the manuscript, and pointed out a lot of things that I missed or could have done better: Tommy Sancton, Paul Nevin, Samuel Cooper-Wall, Bill Foster, Ann Todd, and my sister Mary Jane Miltner. Sam and I shared an office for over a year, and he was always willing to serve as a sounding board and provide his wise counsel. Ann brainstormed the title with me. The exceptional expatriate/writer/editor Abby Rasminsky worked with me on the last, hardest part of the book—how to write the introduction.

The results landed on the desk of Executive Editor Peter Hubbard at William Morrow, to whom I will be forever indebted for patiently and professionally shepherding author and manuscript through the publishing process. Thanks to his sure touch, and the careful work of assistant editor Nick Amphlett, production editor David Palmer, and copy editor Tom Pitoniak, this is a far, far better book than it would otherwise have been. Along with Gena Lanzi, Senior Director of Media Relations Sharyn Rosenblum has enthusiastically promoted the project from the day we met.

Late in 2015, my friend Kristie Miller invited me along to a meeting of the Washington Biography Group, a remarkably talented and supportive group that I have already learned a lot from. The same is true of Professor Sandra Aistars and her students at George Mason University Law School, who ran a clinic for writers. Another supportive group was at the CoworkCafé, in Arlington, Virginia, where I spent many hours finishing up the manuscript in comfortable surroundings.

The staff at the JFK Presidential Library, which houses the Ernest Hemingway Collection, has been uniformly helpful. On my first day there, Hannah German offered me a tour of the Hemingway Research Room (the place is set up like his living room in Cuba) and an associated display of memorabilia—starting off my research on just the right note. On subsequent visits staff members were good enough to listen to me expound on my ideas at a noontime talk, and to bring particular sources to my attention. Stephen Plotkin, Michael Desmond, Laurie Austin, Jessica Green, and Connor Anderson all made my work easier.

When it comes to research, no one can beat Mary Ellen Cortellini, who roamed the Net searching for useful tidbits that I otherwise would never have found. Similarly, Annette Amerman at the Marine Corps History Division is unbeatable when it comes to ferreting out and delivering odd bits of information about the Marine Corps at the cyclic rate. My good friend Nick Welch was kind enough to check out a lead at the National Archives in London, as did Katie and Peggy Lindsey at the Virginia Historical Society in Richmond. Another old friend, Dr. Samuel Yelin Zabicky, helped with facts about Mexico City in 1942.

I would be remiss if I failed to mention the many Hemingway scholars on whose shoulders I stand. The first biographer, Professor Carlos Baker of Princeton, laid the foundations for the rest of us with his painstakingly thorough research, conducted while memories were still fresh. Of the biographers who followed Baker, I have found the works of Jeffrey Meyer and Michael Reynolds (no relation, alas) to be especially useful. Brewster Chamberlin's very thorough chronology of Hemingway's life was always within reach while I worked. Almost every day I checked a source in the *Hemingway Review,* whose authors I salute.

The Hemingway Society offers a great deal of scholar support, on line and in person, for which I am grateful. The staff of the International Center of Photography, especially Susan Carlson, made it easy and fun to source wonderful old photographs. Doug Miller, the administrator for the Pan Am Foundation, was equally helpful; I enjoyed corresponding with him about the glory days of America's flagship airline.

As a former employee writing about intelligence, I had to submit my manuscript to the CIA for review of any possibly classified material. I would like to extend my thanks to the Publications Review Board for staying in touch during the process. The Board requested that I include the following standard disclaimer:

"This [book] does not constitute an official release of CIA information. All statements of fact, opinion, or analysis are those of the author and do not reflect the official positions or views of the CIA or any other US Government agency. Nothing in the contents should be construed as asserting or implying US Government authentication of information or CIA endorsement of the author's views. This material has been reviewed solely for classification."

And finally the home front. No book about Hemingway would be complete without a few words about what writing does to writers while they are working, and the temporary insanity that occurs along the way. My hat's off, my head humbly bowed, to my wife, Becky, for cheerfully enduring the process.

One last word. Any mistakes of fact or interpretation are mine, and mine alone.

PERMISSIONS

For permitting the use of photos and text, thanks are due to the following:

Random House for a quotation from the work of W. H. Auden; the Pan Am Foundation for a photo of Hemingway on Pan Am; Getty Images for McAvoy and Popper photos; Corbis Images for Bettmann photos; the International Center of Photography for Robert Capa photos; the Tamiment Library for photos from the Abraham Lincoln Collection; the Nederlands Fotomuseum for a Fernhout photo; Annemay Regler-Repplinger for the photo of Gustav Regler in 1944, used under the terms of the GNU Free Documentation License.

ENDNOTES

INTRODUCTION

1. The story of the OSS files as they moved around Washington from OSS to CIA to NARA is admirably told in "Records of the Office of Strategic Services (Record Group 226), About the Records," archives .gov (accessed July 2016).
2. John Earl Haynes, Harvey Klehr, and Alexander Vassiliev, *Spies: The Rise and Fall of the KGB in America* (New Haven, CT: Yale University Press, 2009).

CHAPTER I: AWAKENING: WHEN THE SEA TURNED THE LAND INSIDE OUT

1. Anders Österling, Award Ceremony Speech for Literature, http://www.nobelprize.org/nobel_prizes/literature/laureates/1954/press.html (accessed October 2015).
2. Carlos Baker, ed., *Ernest Hemingway: Selected Letters: 1917–1961* (New York: Scribner's, 1979), 420–21n.
3. Elizabetha Levin, "In Their Time: The Riddle behind the Epistolary Friendship between Ernest Hemingway and Ivan Kashkin," *Hemingway Review* 32, no. 2 (2013): 95–108.
4. Ivan Kashkin to Ernest Hemingway (EH), July 25, 1935, in Incoming Correspondence, Ernest Hemingway Collection, JFK Presidential Library, Boston.
5. EH to Ivan Kashkin, August 19, 1935, in Baker, ed., *Selected Letters*, 417.
6. In a letter to Max Perkins on April 19, 1936, Hemingway expressed his pleasure in his popularity in Russia. Matthew J. Bruccoli, ed., *The Only Thing That Counts: The Ernest Hemingway–Maxwell Perkins Correspondence* (New York: Scribner's, 1996), 242. EH to Konstantin Simonov, June 20, 1946, in Baker, ed., *Selected Letters*, 607–9, contains Hemingway's praise for Kashkin.
7. EH to Ivan Kashkin, August 19, 1935, in Baker, ed., *Selected Letters*, 418–19.
8. David Sanders, "Ernest Hemingway's Spanish Civil War Experience," *American Quarterly* 12, no. 2 (1960): 136, discusses these passages. Bernice Kert, *The Hemingway Women* (New York: Norton, 1983), 273,

includes a good discussion of the critical response to *The Green Hills of Africa.* "One Trip Across" was first published in *Cosmopolitan* in 1934.

9. *Time,* April 26, 1926.
10. Quoted in James R. Mellow, *Hemingway: A Life without Consequences* (Boston: Houghton Mifflin, 1992), 473–74.
11. Joseph North, *No Men Are Strangers* (New York: International, 1968), 110.
12. Daniel Aaron, *Writers on the Left* (New York: Avon, 1961), esp. 172–73, offers a good description of these times.
13. Anon., "History of Sloppy Joe's," www.sloppyjoes.com (accessed October 2015).
14. Phil Scott, *Hemingway's Hurricane* (New York: McGraw-Hill, 2006), 2–3.
15. John Dos Passos to Stewart Mitchell, March 27, 1935, in Townsend Luddington, ed., *The 14th Chronicle: Letters and Diaries of John Dos Passos* (New York: Gambit, 1973), 469.
16. EH, *The Green Hills of Africa* (New York: Scribner's, 1935), 191.
17. EH to Maxwell Perkins, September 7, 1935, in Baker, ed., *Selected Letters,* 421–22.
18. Ibid. See also Bruccoli, ed., *The Only Thing That Counts,* 226–27.
19. EH to Maxwell Perkins, September 7, 1935.
20. Discussed in Kenneth S. Lynn, *Hemingway* (Cambridge, MA: Harvard University Press, 1995), 454.
21. Aaron, *Writers on the Left,* 325.
22. Ibid.; Carlos Baker, *Ernest Hemingway: A Life Story* (New York: Scribner's, 1969), 615n.
23. Malcolm Cowley, *The Dream of the Golden Mountains: Remembering the 1930s* (1964; reprint, New York: Penguin, 1981), 292.
24. Baker, *Hemingway,* 279.
25. *New Masses,* September 17, 1935, 3 and 9–10. Hemingway later claimed that the editors changed his slightly less inflammatory title, "Who Killed the Vets?" Baker, *Hemingway,* 615n. But since he himself had used the word "murdered" in his letter to Perkins, and since the article itself was inflammatory, it is hard to accuse the editors of exceeding their brief. He was still happy enough with the article in 1937 to consider putting it in an anthology of his works and would write to Perkins that he wanted to get it into a book. Bruccoli, ed., *The Only Thing That Counts,* 250–51.
26. *New Masses,* September 17, 1935, 10.
27. "Catastrophe: After the Storm," *Time,* September 23, 1935, 23.

28. Ernest Hemingway, "Who Killed Vets in Florida? Asks Hemingway," *Daily Worker*, September 13, 1935.
29. Mellow, *Hemingway*, 482.
30. Edward P. Gazur, *Alexander Orlov: The FBI's KGB General* (New York: Carroll & Graf, 2001): "Hemingway was no stranger to the KGB [NKVD] and the Information Section as they were already aware of his background. . . . Hemingway had written an article for the ultra-left periodical *New Masses*. . . ."
31. Their cases, and others like them, are outlined in Haynes et al., *Spies*, 196–245.
32. For a discussion of this topic see for example Daniel Kowalski, *Stalin and the Spanish Civil War* (New York: Columbia University Press, 2004), 2.
33. Gazur, *Alexander Orlov*, 124. Standing alone, relying on memory and unsupported by original documents, Orlov and Gazur are not the most compelling witnesses to the past. Gazur reports that he took copious notes of his conversations with Orlov (which occurred years after the events they addressed) and used them to write this book. However, once this testimony is placed in context and matched with other memoirs, events, and documents, Gazur gains in credibility. On this particular point, whether the NKVD or the Comintern or both paid any attention to a writer like Hemingway in 1935, consider Stephen Koch's conclusion that the Comintern was "aware of them [Hemingway and Dos Passos] both" as early as the mid-1920s. Koch does not have documentary proof, but the circumstantial evidence he discusses, especially the company that the two writers kept in Paris, and that company's connections to the Soviets, bolsters Gazur's case. Stephen Koch, *Double Lives: Spies and Writers in the Secret Soviet War of Ideas against the West* (New York: Free Press, 1994), 213–14. For more on these points, consult the notes to Chapter 2 that discuss Gazur's and Orlov's papers.
34. Gazur, *Alexander Orlov*, 124. Orlov's claim that the NKVD was reading the foreign press is consistent with other reports. "The Cadre Department, a sinister branch of the Comintern . . . kept files on leading communists" and coordinated with the NKVD. In the fall of 1940, that department noted that an anti-Stalinist book by Gustav Regler was "particularly significant" because it contained a preface by Hemingway. Hugh Eakin, "Stalin's Reading List," *New York Times*, April 17, 2005, F19. The NKVD would later obtain a copy of *For Whom the Bell Tolls* for its file on Hemingway, who by then was joining forces with the Soviets. See Chapter 5.

CHAPTER 2: THE WRITER AND THE COMMISSAR: GOING TO WAR IN SPAIN

1. Hans Schoots, *Living Dangerously, A Biography of Joris Ivens* (Amsterdam: Amsterdam University Press, 2000), 127. Hemingway left a vivid description of being strafed, perhaps of this strafing, in a July 1938 article: When the enemy plane fires on your car, "you swerve to the side of the road and jump out of the car. You lie flat . . . with your mouth dry." Ernest Hemingway, "'I Saw Murder Done in Spain'—Hemingway's Lost Report," *Chicago Tribune*, November 29, 1982.
2. For a discussion of the Soviet role in Spain, see Ronald Radosh, Mary R. Habeck, and Grigory Sevostianov, eds., *Spain Betrayed: The Soviet Union in the Spanish Civil War* (New Haven, CT, and London: Yale, 2001) and Kowalski, *Stalin and the Spanish Civil War*. The best general biography of Orlov is John Costello and Oleg Tsarev, *Deadly Illusions: The KGB Orlov Dossier* (New York: Crown Books, 1993).
3. For a very readable portrait of the Cambridge Five, see Philip Knightley, *The Master Spy: The Story of Kim Philby* (New York: Knopf, 1989).
4. Jason Gurney, *Crusade in Spain* (London: Faber & Faber, 1974), 183.
5. One of the NKVD's leading assassins in Spain was responsible for "the construction . . . of a secret crematorium which enabled the NKVD to dispose of its victims without leaving any trace of their remains." Christopher Andrew and Vasili Mitrokhin, *The Sword and the Shield* (New York: Basic Books, 2001), 74. The authors cite more than one source for this amazing story.
6. Radosh et al., *Spain Betrayed*, xxiii and xxiii.
7. Gazur, *Alexander Orlov*, 123–24.
8. Marginal note by J. Bell dated February 24, 1937, on EH passport application bearing same date. Department of State FOIA release to author. Also quoted in Daniel Robinson, "'My True Occupation Is That of a Writer': Hemingway's Passport Correspondence," *Hemingway Review* 24, no. 2 (2005): 87–94. See also Hemingway to Perkins, October 28, 1938, in Baker, ed., *Selected Letters*, 473–75. Here Hemingway describes how he was offered "a staff captaincy" with an unnamed French unit but had to turn it down on account of his contract with Jack Wheeler of NANA and his promise to Pauline not to fight in another war.
9. Josephine Herbst, *The Starched Blue Sky of Spain* (New York: HarperCollins, 1991), 150.
10. Ibid.
11. In A. E. Hotchner, *Papa Hemingway* (New York: Random House, 1966), 197, the transcript of a Hemingway interview puts the em-

phasis on the Republic: ". . . I watched the people write their constitution. This was the last republic that had started in Europe, and I believed in it."

12. EH to Maxwell Perkins, December 15, 1937, in Baker, ed., *Selected Letters*, 455.
13. Ibid., 456.
14. EH to Pfeiffer Family, February 9, 1937, in Baker, ed., *Selected Letters*, 457.
15. EH to Archibald MacLeish, June 28 [year not specified, from context ca. 1933] in Box 10, MacLeish Papers, Library of Congress (LoC), Washington, DC.
16. Archibald MacLeish to Whittaker Chambers, March 18, 1941, in Box 10, MacLeish Papers, LoC.
17. http://library.sc.edu/spcoll/amlit/hemingway/images/spainflames.jpg (accessed December 2013).
18. Schoots, *Living Dangerously*, esp. 71. Ivens was a member of the Communist Party of Holland from at least 1931 to 1936. There were other times in his life when his membership may have lapsed, but his politics did not change.
19. Cowley, *The Dream of the Golden Mountain*, 233.
20. Ronald Radosh and Allis Radosh, *Red Star over Hollywood* (San Francisco: Encounter Books, 2005), 1–2; Arthur Koestler, *Invisible Writing: The Second Volume of an Autobiography, 1932–1940* (New York: Stein & Day, 1984), 251, 381. Koch, *Double Lives*, also offers an overview of Münzenberg's life and work.
21. Koestler, *Invisible Writing*, 251, 381.
22. Schoots, *Living Dangerously*, 47–48.
23. Scott Donaldson, *Archibald MacLeish: An American Life* (Boston and New York: Houghton Mifflin, 1992), 264.
24. Hemingway biographer Baker coined the term. Baker, *Hemingway*, 307. The MIT historian William B. Watson went further, writing that Ivens functioned more or less as Hemingway's "case officer," that is, like an intelligence professional running a spy case. Although I am indebted to Watson's analysis, on which I rely up to a point, I think that he overstates the case somewhat. Hemingway was certainly influenced by Ivens and other communists, but he was never under the kind of control that a case officer would have liked to exert. Moreover, Ivens was a propagandist, not a spy. William B. Watson, "Joris Ivens and the Communists: Bringing Hemingway Into the Spanish Civil War," *Hemingway Review* 18, no. 2 (Fall 1990).

25. These files are available as part of the INCOMKA, Communist International Archives, project at a terminal in the European Reading Room, LoC, accessed October 2013.
26. Described in Koestler, *Invisible Writing*, 387 et seq.
27. Wertheim's story can be found in Peter Wyden, *The Passionate War: The Narrative History of the Spanish Civil War* (New York: Simon & Schuster, 1983), 405. Wyden's source is an interview with Tuchman. It is intriguing to note that Hemingway knew, or knew of, Katz, and said that he did not like him. Gustav Regler, *The Owl of Minerva* (New York: Farrar, Straus, 1960), 357.
28. Barbara W. Tuchman, *Practicing History* (New York: Knopf, 1981), 6.
29. James D. Brasch and Joseph Sigman, *Hemingway's Library: A Composite Record* (Boston: JFK Library Electronic Edition, 2000), 372.
30. Watson, "Joris Ivens," 13.
31. Ibid., 12.
32. Ibid. More generally, see Schoots, *Living Dangerously*, 123–24.
33. Ilya Ehrenburg, *Memoirs: 1921–1941* (Cleveland and New York: World, 1963), 383.
34. Watson, "Joris Ivens," 13.
35. Joris Ivens to EH, April 26, 1937, in Incoming Correspondence, Ernest Hemingway Collection, JFK Library.
36. Undated fragment, circa June 1937, of note from Ivens to Hemingway, beginning "Hannah at the typewriter for Joris" in Incoming Correspondence, Ernest Hemingway Collection, JFK Library. See also Baker, *Hemingway*, 313.
37. Denis Brian, *The True Gen* (New York: Grove, 1988), 111. Watson makes the related point that, thanks to Ivens, most of the people Hemingway met on his first trip to Spain appear to have been communists. This is an educated guess. For most of his life, Hemingway was in touch with people from many walks of life. Ivens kept a film log that shows that Hemingway spent a great deal of time with the crew on his first visit to Spain. But that log did not account for all of his time, even on that visit. There is no surviving daily diary or calendar that shows what else Hemingway may have been up to. Similarly, the lack of detailed evidence makes it hard to subscribe to the theories in Stephen Koch, *The Breaking Point: Hemingway, Dos Passos, and the Murder of José Robles* (New York: Counterpoint, 2005), which posits even more communist control and manipulation of Hemingway in Spain. For Koch, Hemingway is "a useful idiot," that is, a semi-witting or unwitting collaborator who did the

Comintern's bidding. In this book, Koch explores the complicated controversy about Hemingway's and Herbst's roles in telling Dos Passos about Robles's death.

38. Luddington, ed., *14th Chronicle*, 527.
39. Koch, *Two Lives*, 254–55.
40. Luddington, ed., *14th Chronicle*, 528.
41. Ibid.
42. Herbst, *Starched Blue Sky*, 150–51.
43. Schoots, *Living Dangerously*, 127.
44. Joris Ivens to EH, April 26, 1937.
45. Quoted in Virginia S. Carr, *Dos Passos: A Life* (New York: Doubleday, 1984), 368. See also Herbst, *Starched Blue Sky*, 154.
46. Carr, *Dos Passos*, 372, describes the scene at the train station, and cites multiple sources for the event. Brewster Chamberlin, *The Hemingway Log* (Lawrence: University Press of Kansas, 2015), 185, places the final confrontation on May 11. I also relied on the shipping and weather news from the Paris editions of the *New York Herald Tribune* for May 10, 11, 12, and 13, 1937, which contain references to Hemingway's activities in Paris on this visit and report that he himself was scheduled to sail for the United States on the liner *Normandie* on May 13.
47. Luddington, ed., *14th Chronicle*, 496. I take Hemingway's comment about the critics to mean that they would crucify Dos Passos because, by criticizing the Republic, he was shifting to the right, away from the left-wing orthodoxy they espoused.
48. Ibid., 496.
49. Schoots, *Living Dangerously*, 138.
50. The text of the cable appears in Paul Preston, *We Saw Spain Die* (London: Constable, 2009), 106.
51. EH to John Dos Passos, circa March 26, 1938, published in Baker, ed,. *Selected Letters*, 463–64.
52. The article is quoted in Alex Vernon, *Hemingway's Second War: Bearing Witness to the Spanish Civil War* (Ames: University of Iowa Press, 2011), 165; the comment to MacLeish is in EH to Archibald MacLeish, December 25, 1943, in Box 10, MacLeish Papers, LoC.
53. Hotchner, *Papa Hemingway*, 132–33.
54. EH to Archibald MacLeish, October 5, 1952, in Box 10, MacLeish Papers, LoC.
55. Adam Hochschild, *Spain in Our Hearts: Americans in the Spanish Civil War, 1936–1939* (New York: Houghton Mifflin, 2016), esp. ch.

4, is an excellent description of the political and social climate in Barcelona.

56. Hugh Thomas, *The Spanish Civil War,* revised by the author (New York: Modern Library, 2001), 639 and 680–86. Constancia de la Mora, *In Place of Splendor* (New York: Harcourt, Brace, 1939), 327, represents the Republican party line. Radosh et al., *Spain Betrayed,* esp. 171–78, is an excellent discussion of the Soviets' role in the crisis.
57. Thomas, *Spanish Civil War,* 631.
58. Orlov's personal participation in the Nin affair is covered in ibid., 684, and thoroughly aired in Costello and Tsarev, *Deadly Illusions,* esp. 287–91. Years later, after accusations about his role had surfaced, Orlov would tell the FBI a version of the far-fetched cover story. He insisted that he himself had had nothing to do with Nin's death. Gazur, *Alexander Orlov,* 340–46.
59. Hemingway mentions Nin in his March 26, 1938, letter to Dos Passos. Baker, ed., *Selected Letters,* 463–64.
60. Chamberlin, *The Hemingway Log,* 187; Schoots, *Living Dangerously,* 129.
61. "Writers Hear Browder at Congress," *Daily Worker,* June 5, 1935; "The Writers' Congress an Outstanding Event," *Daily Worker,* June 4, 1935.
62. Ibid., 130.
63. Joseph Freeman, "Death in the Morning," July 11, 1961, 65, in Freeman Papers, Hoover Institution, Stanford University. This is a draft of a long article by Freeman, who remembered how he went looking for Hemingway that evening, going from bar to bar until he turned up.
64. Alvah Bessie, *Men in Battle* (New York: Chandler & Sharp, 1975), 113. This book was originally published in 1939.
65. The entire text was printed in *New Masses,* June 22, 1937, and included Hemingway's attack on fascist forces for murdering civilians in indiscriminate bombardments.
66. Baker, *Hemingway,* 314. See also Amanda Vail, *Hotel Florida* (New York: Farrar, Strauss, 2014), 202–3.
67. Max Perkins to EH, June 17, 1937, in Bruccoli, ed., *The Only Thing That Matters,* 251.
68. *New Masses,* June 22, 1937.
69. EH to Ralph M. Ingersoll, July 18, 1938, in Box 10, MacLeish Papers, LoC.
70. Undated fragment, circa June 1937, of note from Ivens to Hemingway, beginning "Hannah at the typewriter for Joris," Incoming

Correspondence, Ernest Hemingway Collection, JFK Library. See also Baker, *Hemingway*, 313.

71. Martha Gellhorn to Eleanor Roosevelt, July 8, 1937, in Caroline Moorehead, ed., *Selected Letters of Martha Gellhorn* (New York: Henry Holt, 2006), 55.
72. EH to Mrs. Paul Pfeiffer, August 2, 1937, in Baker, ed., *Selected Letters*, 459–61.
73. Ibid.
74. Quoted in Schoots, *Living Dangerously*, 130, from original sources. Dominic Tierney, *FDR and the Spanish Civil War* (Durham, NC: Duke University Press, 2007), 34. Tierney puts the visit in the broader context of FDR's policies. Initially neutral, FDR eventually came to sympathize with those who saw the need to oppose German and Italian intervention in Spain.
75. Eleanor Roosevelt, "My Day," *Atlanta Constitution*, July 12, 1937. Roosevelt's dateline is Friday, July 9; the article did not appear in the *Constitution* until the following week.
76. Gellhorn to Roosevelt, July 8, 1937.
77. In a July 27, 1938, letter to Ralph Ingersoll, Hemingway mentions that he paid Pauline's fare for the trip to the coast to show the picture. Box 10, MacLeish Papers, LoC.
78. Rick Setlowe, "Hemingway and Hollywood: For Whom the Camera Rolled," *Los Angeles Times*, October 14, 1979.
79. Schoots, *Living Dangerously*, 131.
80. Quoted in Marion Merriman and Warren Lerude, *American Commander in Spain: Robert Hale Merriman and the Abraham Lincoln Brigade* (Reno: University of Nevada Press, 1986), 201–2.
81. Baker, *Hemingway*, 316.
82. Vernon, *Hemingway's Second War*, esp. 117 and 130.
83. Schoots, *Living Dangerously*, 136. His source was an interview with Gellhorn.
84. Ibid, 136.

CHAPTER 3: RETURNING TO SPAIN: TO STAY THE COURSE

1. This story has been admirably researched and told by Professor Watson of MIT. William B. Watson, "Investigating Hemingway: The Story," *North Dakota Quarterly* 59, no. 1 (Winter 1991): 36–68; "Investigating Hemingway: The Trip," *North Dakota Quarterly* 59, no. 3 (Summer 1991): 79–95; and "Investigating Hemingway: The Novel," *North Dakota Quarterly* 60, no. 1 (Winter 1991): 1–39. See

also Vernon, *Hemingway's Second War*, 169–70. The original source is Alexander Szurek, *The Shattered Dream* (Boulder, CO: East European Monographs, 1989), esp. 143–51. Citing Gellhorn's diary, Hochschild, *Spain in Our Hearts*, 254–55, puts the first visit to Alfambra in September.

2. Joris Ivens to EH, January 28, 1938, in Incoming Correspondence, Ernest Hemingway Collection, JFK Library.
3. See, for instance, Hans Kohn, "Yesterday's Landmarks," *New York Times*, March 20, 1960. This favorable review of Regler's memoirs by a distinguished historian is a good introduction to Regler's life and work.
4. Regler, *Owl of Minerva*, 203 and 291.
5. Ibid., 263.
6. "First-Hand Picture of Conflict in Spain Given by Volunteer Here," *Washington Post*, March 18, 1938.
7. Regler, *Owl of Minerva*, 295.
8. Gurney, *Crusade in Spain*, 54, 183–84, is a firsthand description of Marty by an English soldier.
9. Regler, *Owl of Minerva*, 292.
10. Ibid.
11. Ibid.
12. Gazur, *Alexander Orlov*, 126–28, tells the story of the first Hemingway-Orlov meeting.
13. Ibid., 129. It would have been difficult for the Soviets to miss: *New Masses* published a version of his speech in its June 22, 1937, issue.
14. Gazur, *Alexander Orlov*, 129.
15. Mary-Kay Wilmers, *The Eitingons: A Twentieth-Century Story* (London: Faber & Faber, 2010), 275. Wilmers offers a full portrait of Eitingon, who would go on to orchestrate the murder of Trotsky in 1940. Trotsky's killer was a Spaniard, originally spotted by the NKVD during the Spanish Civil War.
16. Gazur, *Alexander Orlov*, 130–31.
17. Ibid., 131 and 140.
18. Dan Bessie, ed., *Alvah Bessie's Spanish Civil War Notebooks* (Lexington: University Press of Kentucky, 2002), 133.
19. This is a quote from page 1 of Chapter 23 of the original manuscript of Gazur, *Alexander Orlov*, among the Edward P. Gazur Papers, Georgetown University Library Special Collections, which differs somewhat from the printed version. Regarding Hemingway the True Believer, the famous writer Marjorie K. Rawlings commented

to similar effect in a letter to their mutual editor, Max Perkins, on April 23, 1938, that she could not help but "mistrust" Hemingway's current work, given his "present violently partisan mood." Rawlings Folder, Box 11, Carlos Baker Papers, Princeton University Library (PUL). Orlov meant to put the stress on Hemingway's antifascist mindset, not on any pro-communist feelings. But what exactly did Orlov mean by "true believer"? He spoke and read English with ease, especially after spending the more than three decades between 1938 and 1971 in the United States. He knew what he was saying when he called Hemingway a "true believer." Introduced by the "longshoreman philosopher" Eric Hofer, the term came into vogue in the United States in the 1950s among the politically literate, a category that certainly included Orlov. He devoured books on politics, especially those that had anything to do with communism, and was a careful reader of the *New York Times,* whose columnists were familiar with the term. (Orlov's reading habits are evident from his extensive clipping collection among his papers. See Alexander Orlov Papers, NARA II, College Park, MD.) He is likely to have read about Hofer, and perhaps even to have read Hofer's book by the same name, before talking to Gazur about Hemingway. As coined by Hofer, the term denotes the kind of person who subsumes his identity in a political movement like communism or fascism, or anticommunism and antifascism, and does so to the point where passion begins to displace reason.

20. Gazur, *Alexander Orlov,* 138. To focus on Hemingway's role was disingenuous. Orlov omits the problematic Soviet role: first giving material support to Republic, then conducting the divisive secret internal war against the far left, finally limiting material support.
21. Brian, *True Gen,* 121; Baker, *Hemingway,* 335.
22. Brian, *True Gen,* 121.
23. Preston, *We Saw Spain Die,* 371.
24. North, *No Men are Strangers,* 169.
25. Vernon, *Hemingway's Second War,* 39.
26. Bowers to SecState, April 2, 1938, in U.S. Department of State, *Foreign Relations of the United States,* vol. 1 (Washington, DC: U.S. Government Printing Office, 1938), 279.
27. Bessie, *Men in Battle,* 113–16. See also Dan Bessie, ed., *Civil War Notebooks,* 25, and Vernon, *Hemingway's Second War,* 44, which shows that Bessie's memoirs are consistent with Hemingway's reporting.
28. Reprinted as Ernest Hemingway, "'I Saw Murder Done in Spain'—

Hemingway's Lost Report," *Chicago Tribune*, November 29, 1982. The story of the article is in William B. Watson, "A Surprise from the Archives," *Chicago Tribune*, November 29, 1982. The language is similar to that Hemingway used in his June 1937 speech at Carnegie Hall.

29. I am indebted to the analysis in David Sanders, "Ernest Hemingway's Spanish Civil War Experience," *American Quarterly* 12, no. 2 (1960), esp. 139–40. Compendia of his articles were published in Ernest Hemingway, "Hemingway Reports Spain," *New Republic*, 94, no. 1221 (April 27, 1938), and 95, no. 1227 (June 8, 1938); and Ernest Hemingway, *By-Line: Ernest Hemingway* (New York: Simon & Schuster, 1967).
30. Vernon, *Hemingway's Second War*, p. 39. Vernon analyzes Hemingway's reporting during the war.
31. Lynn, *Hemingway*, 453.
32. Ernest Hemingway, *The Fifth Column* (New York: Simon & Schuster, 1969). The play opened on Broadway in 1940.
33. EH to Ada MacLeish, October 5, 1952, in Hemingway Correspondence, 1938–1958, Box 10, MacLeish Papers, LoC.
34. W. H. Auden, "Spain 1937," quoted in and discussed by Thomas, *The Spanish Civil War*, 333.
35. Ernest Hemingway, "On the American Dead in Spain," in Ernest Hemingway et al., *Somebody Had to Do Something: A Memorial to James Phillips Lardner* (Los Angeles: James Lardner Memorial Fund, 1939). This was a commemorative pamphlet. Most of Hemingway's article was reprinted in *New Masses*, February 14, 1939.
36. De la Mora, *In Place of Splendor*, 373. Thomas, *Spanish Civil War*, 830–31, describes the withdrawal itself.
37. Martha Gellhorn to David Gurewitsch [?1950], in Moorehead, ed., *Selected Letters*, 222.
38. Ibid., 222.
39. Ibid. See also Chamberlin, *The Hemingway Log*, 205, and Moorehead, *Gellhorn*, 153.
40. Quoted in Regler, *Owl of Minerva*, 298.
41. Ehrenburg, *Memoirs*, 387.

CHAPTER 4: THE BELL TOLLS FOR THE REPUBLIC: HEMINGWAY BEARS WITNESS

1. De la Mora, *In Place of Splendor*, 387.
2. Szurek, *The Shattered Dream*, 276–77.

3. EH to Mrs. Paul Pfeiffer, February 6, 1939, in Baker, ed., *Selected Letters,* 475–78.
4. Ibid.
5. EH to Max Perkins, February 7, 1939, in Baker, ed., *Selected Letters,* 478–79.
6. EH to Mrs. Paul Pfeiffer, February 6, 1939.
7. EH to Max Perkins, February 7, 1939.
8. Thomas, *Spanish Civil War,* 893–901, includes a discussion of the last chapter and the aftermath of the war.
9. Martha Gellhorn to Charles Colebaugh, October 22, 1938, in Moorehead, ed., *Selected Letters,* 67–70.
10. EH to Ivan Kashkin, March 23, 1939, in Baker, ed., *Selected Letters,* 480–81.
11. EH to Max Perkins, February 7, 1939.
12. Available in various editions, including Ernest Hemingway, *The Fifth Column and Four Stories of the Spanish Civil War* (New York: Simon & Schuster, 1969).
13. This agreement was also known as the Hitler-Stalin Pact, and the Molotov-Ribbentrop Pact.
14. Aaron, *Writers on the Left,* 376. To the same effect, see Granville Hicks, *Where We Came Out* (New York: Viking, 1954), 49, 70–71, 80.
15. Regler, *Owl of Minerva,* 353–54.
16. Jay Allen to Archibald MacLeish, March 24, 1940: "Ernest has deposited a sum of money for him in Paris to keep him and to pay his fare." Box 1, Archibald MacLeish Papers, LoC. It did not matter that Regler had a long track record as an anti-Nazi, and it did not help that he had been a communist, which landed him on various watch lists, including that of the British Security Service, which noted Hemingway's financial support for a potential subversive. Dr. Gustav Regler, Personal File, KV 2/3506, Records of the Security Service, National Archives, Kew, England.
17. Regler, *Owl of Minerva,* 316.
18. Gustav Regler, *The Great Crusade* (New York: Longman, Green, 1940), 187. Ironically, the book was translated from the German by Whittaker Chambers, himself a disillusioned former communist, who would figure prominently in the investigation of Soviet spying in America. Chambers and Regler do not appear to have met.
19. Ibid., vii–xi. See also Regler, *Owl of Minerva,* 310–11.
20. See, for example, Robert Conquest, *The Great Terror: A Reassessment* (New York: Oxford University Press, 2008), 209 and 409–12, where Conquest discusses the fate of the Internationals. To the same effect,

see Thomas, *Spanish Civil War,* 926: "To have been a member of the International Brigades was as bad as having intervened in Russia against the bolsheviks in 1919."

21. Ernest Hemingway, preface to Regler, *Great Crusade,* ix. The wording in the original German version of the book is clearer: the pact was "after the Soviet Union lost any trust in the democracies" ("*als die Sowjetunion jedes Vertrauen in die Demokratien verloren hatte*"). Gustav Regler, *Das grosse Beispiel* (1940; reprint, Cologne, Germany: Kiepenhauer & Witsch, n.d.), 13–14.
22. Hemingway was not alone in this interpretation. The thoughtful communist professor Granville Hicks wrote that Munich was for many as great a betrayal as the pact, which had showed Stalin that he could not depend on England and France and "that he must take care of Hitler in his own way." Hicks, *Where We Came Out,* 81.
23. Regler, *Owl of Minerva,* 357.
24. Ibid.
25. Ibid., 296.
26. Martha Gellhorn to Clara Spiegel, May 17, 1940, in Spiegel Folder, Box 12, Carlos Baker Papers, PUL.
27. Martha Gellhorn to Hortense Flexner and Wyncie King, May 17, 1940, in Moorehead, ed., *Selected Letters,* 90.
28. EH to Max Perkins, December 8, 1939, in Baker, ed., *Selected Letters,* 498.
29. EH to Max Perkins, circa May 1, 1940, in Baker, ed., *Selected Letters,* 505.
30. "Writer's Influence," *Time,* June 24, 1940, 92. See also Donaldson, *MacLeish: An American Life,* 334–35.
31. EH to Max Perkins, July 13, 1940, in Baker, ed., *Selected Letters,* 506.
32. Discussed in EH to Charles Scribner, August 15, 1940, in Baker, ed., *Selected Letters,* 507–10.
33. Hotchner, *Papa Hemingway,* 131. Hotchner is reporting what Hemingway told him.
34. EH to Ivan Kashkin, March 23, 1939, in Baker, ed., *Selected Letters,* 480–81.
35. Edmund Wilson, "Return of Ernest Hemingway," reprinted in *Literary Essays and Reviews of the 1930s & 40s* (New York: Literary Classics, 2007), 885.
36. Julio Alvarez del Vayo, *Give Me Combat: The Memoirs of Julio Alvarez del Vayo* (Boston: Little, Brown, 1973), 188.
37. Alvah Bessie, Review of *For Whom the Bell Tolls,* in *New Masses,* November 5, 1940, 25–29.
38. Ibid. See also Cecil B. Eby, *Comrades and Commissars: The Lincoln*

Battalion in the Spanish Civil War (University Park: Pennsylvania State University Press, 2007), 434–35.

39. Bessie, Review, 28–29.
40. Brian, *True Gen,* 122–25.
41. Schoots, *Living Dangerously,* 140.
42. Regler, *Dokumente und Analysen,* 51. Regler and the multitalented Republican division commander Gustavo Durán discussed whether to talk about the Republic's shortcomings. Durán said, "We can only get the authority to be . . . leader[s] in the future by telling . . . the truth about us too."
43. Regler, *Owl of Minerva,* 293.
44. EH to Max Perkins, December 8, 1939, in Baker, ed., *Selected Letters,* 498–99.
45. Regler, *Owl of Minerva,* 293.

CHAPTER 5: THE SECRET FILE: THE NKVD PLAYS ITS HAND

1. Robert van Gelder, "Ernest Hemingway Talks of Work and War," *New York Times,* August 11, 1940. Hemingway intimate Arnold Gingrich likewise commented on his upbeat, almost manic frame of mind when he finished the novel. Arnold Gingrich, *Nothing but People: The Early Days at Esquire* (New York: Crown, 1971), 247.
2. EH to Max Perkins, July 13, 1940, in Baker, ed., *Selected Letters,* 506.
3. EH to John Hemingway, October 15, 1942, in Outgoing Correspondence, Ernest Hemingway Collection, JFK Library.
4. EH to Charles Scribner, October 21, 1940, in Baker, ed., *Selected Letters,* 519–20.
5. Martha Gellhorn to Hortense Flexner, October 30, 1940, in Moorehead, ed., *Selected Letters,* 103–6. She wrote that the "Burma Road is out. *Collier's* has sent someone else, some other girl." Ibid., 106–7, contains an editorial comment on what happened next.
6. Transcripts of Meeting "Re Debt Limit," January 27, 1941, Diaries of Henry Morgenthau, Jr., Series 1: Morgenthau Diaries, vol. 351, 239–60, Franklin D. Roosevelt Presidential Library, Hyde Park, NY.
7. Ibid. See also Peter Moreira, *Hemingway on the China Front: His WWII Spy Mission with Martha Gellhorn* (Washington, DC: Potomac Books, 2007), 14–20. Moreira has unearthed interesting facts about the trip and about White. He does not, however, make a convincing case for his thesis—namely, that Hemingway was on a spy mission in China and that the mission kindled his wartime fascination with intelligence. I explore this issue in more detail in Chapter 6.

8. EH to Henry Morgenthau, Jr., July 30, 1941, in Outgoing Correspondence, Ernest Hemingway Collection, JFK Library. It is also reprinted in Moreira, *Hemingway on the China Front*, 201-8.
9. See, for example, Michael Warner, *The Office of Strategic Services: America's First Intelligence Agency* (Washington, DC: CIA, 2000), 3.
10. Hemingway's attitude can be inferred from EH to Henry Morgenthau, Jr., July 30, 1941.
11. EH to Hadley Mowrer, December 26, 1940, in Baker, ed., *Selected Letters*, 520–21. Hemingway's next letter to Hadley was dated from New York on January 26, 1941. Ibid., 521. He was almost certainly in New York when he spoke to Harry Dexter White on January 26 or 27. Moreira, *Hemingway on the China Front*, 16 and 214n.
12. Golos has been described in many works, including Haynes et al., *Spies*, esp. 496–500; Lauren Kessler, *Clever Girl: Elizabeth Bentley, the Spy Who Ushered in the McCarthy Era* (New York: Perennial, 2003); Elizabeth Bentley, *Out of Bondage* (New York: Ivy, 1988), esp. 65–73; and Herbert Romerstein and Eric Breindel, *The Venona Secrets: Exposing Soviet Espionage and America's Traitors* (Washington, DC: Regnery, 2000), 145–50.
13. Words on a slip of paper dated November 20, 1928, recorded in an FBI inventory titled "The Personal Papers of Jacob Golos," October 13, 1948, in File 65-14603, vol. 146, Silvermaster Files, http://education-research.org/PDFs/Silvermaster146.pdf (accessed February 2014). Golos's personal papers reflected his interests and lifestyle.
14. Alexander Vassiliev, "White Notebook," 123 and 129, in Vassiliev Papers, LoC. There are various versions of these papers: handwritten Russian, typewritten Russian, and English translation. The handwritten Russian papers are Vassiliev's transcriptions of secret NKVD/KGB files made between 1993 and 1995. My citations refer to the English translations, and to the page numbers of the translations (visible on the upper right hand corner of each page), not to page numbers cited in Vassiliev's text. These papers have also been intermittently available online. See, for example, "Vassiliev Notebooks," digitalarchive.wilsoncenter.org (accessed October 2015), which contains an explanation of their provenance. Haynes et al., *Spies*, explores their provenance and content in great detail.
15. See, for example, Kessler, *Clever Girl*, 55–89, for a description of the process.
16. Gazur, *Alexander Orlov*, 124–29.
17. Alexander Vassiliev, "Operations in the U.S. in 1941–45," undated and without pagination, in "Summary Narratives," Alexander Vas-

siliev Papers, LoC. These narratives were prepared by Vassiliev to enable Russian intelligence officers to vet the information that could be released to a Western historian who would then write the history and share some of the proceeds with his Russian counterparts (as discussed below in this chapter). Kathryn S. Olmstead, *Red Spy Queen: A Biography of Elizabeth Bentley* (Chapel Hill: University of North Carolina Press, 2002), 23–26, contains a good description of how Golos went about recruiting another spy.

18. Hugh Eakin, "Stalin's Reading List," *New York Times*, April 17, 2005, F19. The summary of Hemingway's KGB file, prepared in June 1948, sets out what the KGB knew about him. It is printed nearly verbatim in Haynes et al., *Spies,* 154. As transcribed by Vassiliev, the original is "Report on 'Argo,'" June 8, 1948, in Vassiliev, *Black Notebook*, 89.
19. Bentley, *Out of Bondage*, 107–8.
20. Reprinted in Matthew J. Bruccoli, ed., *Hemingway and the Mechanism of Fame* (Columbia: University of South Carolina Press, 2006), 72.
21. Douglas M. Jacobs to Carlos Baker, March 5, 1964, in folder for 1940, Box 19, Baker Papers, PUL. Jacobs witnessed their reunion.
22. Haynes et al., *Spies,* 153.
23. Eleanor Langer, *Josephine Herbst* (Boston: Northeastern University Press, 1994), 269.
24. Joris Ivens to EH, January 10 [1939], in Incoming Correspondence, Museo Ernest Hemingway, Ernest Hemingway Collection, JFK Library.
25. "Report on 'Argo,'" June 8, 1948, in Vassiliev, *Black Notebook*, 89.
26. Haynes et al., *Spies,* 145–46. The chapter in *Spies* on "Journalist Spies" explores the subject in some detail and gives examples of how the NKVD used some American journalist spies, such as to collect information from their sources and serve as cutouts between NKVD officers and spies. Journalists could also write articles that were favorable to Soviet policies. However, this does not seem to have been the NKVD's prime motivation in seeking out American journalists around this time.
27. Ibid., 153 and 574n. The original is in Vassiliev, *White Notebook #1*, 29. At least on January 23, 1941, Hemingway was apparently in New City at the Lombardy Hotel. See EH to Milton Wolff, January 23, 1941, in Box 1, Milton Wolff Papers, Tamiment Library, New York University.
28. The difficulties that Hemingway and Gellhorn encountered when they were making travel arrangements is usually explained by a shortage of seats or berths on the carrier they wanted. But perhaps

there was a search for a way to China via the Soviet Union that further complicated matters. Moreira, *Hemingway on the China Front*, 13–14, discusses their travel plans.

29. Vassiliev, "Operations in the U.S." The original note to Moscow from New York is in Vassiliev, *Black Notebook*, 90.
30. Vassiliev, "Operations in the U.S."
31. Hemingway's FBI file is available at vault.fbi.gov/ernest-miller-hemingway (accessed February 2014).
32. The story is told in two parts in Haynes et al., *Spies*, ix–xx and xxvii–liii. The first part is the preface by Haynes and Klehr; the second is the introduction by Vassiliev, "How I Came to Write My Notebooks, Discover Alger Hiss, and Lose to His Lawyer."
33. The summaries that Vassiliev prepared were used, more or less according to the SVR plan, to write Allen Weinstein and Alexander Vassiliev, *The Haunted Wood* (New York: Modern Library, 1999). This book contains fewer details and names than Haynes et al., *Spies*, the book based on Vassiliev's raw notes. *The Haunted Wood* mentions Hemingway in passing but does not refer to him as an NKVD spy.
34. Costello and Tsarev, *Deadly Illusions*.
35. Haynes et al., *Spies*, xlii.
36. My analysis generally follows the argument in ibid., ix–xx.
37. See Chapter 12.
38. In print Gellhorn was silent on the subject, which proves little. I have not been able to check the Martha Gellhorn Papers at the Gottlieb Archival Research Center, Boston University, for any hints on the subject. The archivists' answers to me have been that the papers are to remain sealed until 2023, twenty-five years after her death (although some writers have been granted access).
39. EH to Ada MacLeish, n.d., in Hemingway Correspondence 1938–1958, MacLeish Papers, LoC. The context suggests that Hemingway wrote the letter in December 1940 or January 1941.
40. In 1948 he would imply that he had had a secret relationship with the Soviets that *he* controlled, saying that he would go to "a top Russki," ask him what he wanted to know, and the Russian would reply in confidence. EH to Charles T. Lanham, July 28, 1948, in Box 1, Lanham-Hemingway Papers, PUL. See also discussion in Chapter 12.
41. Draft of telegram to "Walter," bearing the annotation "1940," in Outgoing Correspondence, Ernest Hemingway Collection, JFK Library. In 1948, he would compare his dealings with the Soviets to those of

the mountain man Jim Bridger with the Indians on the frontier. EH to Charles T. Lanham, July 28, 1948, in Box 1, Lanham-Hemingway Papers, PUL. See also the discussion in Chapter 12.

42. This act is still on the books. See www.fara.gov (accessed February 21, 2014). A more remote possibility would have been a violation of the Smith Act of 1940, which made it a crime to advocate the violent overthrow of the U.S. government, part of the communist program until the United States entered World War II.

43. "Mr. Hemingway showed Mrs. Shipley a copy of the contract to do regular reporting in Spain" and assured her that was all he intended to do. J. Bell marginal note, dated February 24, 1937, on EH passport application signed on the same day. Department of State FOIA release to author. After the war, he would say that the government considered him untrustworthy for being a "pre-mature anti-fascist." See Chapters 11–12.

44. Ernest Hemingway, "Old Newsman Writes: A Letter from Cuba," December 1943, in White, ed., *By-Line*, 179–85.

CHAPTER 6: TO SPY OR NOT TO SPY: CHINA AND THE STRAIN OF WAR

1. This wonderful description of wartime Chungking is from Theodore H. White, *In Search of History: A Personal Adventure* (New York: Harper & Row, 1978), 67–70, esp. 69.
2. Martha Gellhorn, *Travels with Myself and Another* (New York: Penguin, 2001), 51–52.
3. Ibid., 52.
4. Ibid., 10.
5. Ibid., 11.
6. Ibid., 12.
7. EH to Martha Gellhorn, undated but with note "After 16 May 1941" in Outgoing Correspondence, Ernest Hemingway Collection, JFK Presidential Library.
8. Quoted in Bruccoli, ed., *Hemingway and the Mechanism of Fame*, 138.
9. Gellhorn, *Travels*, 30.
10. Ibid., 14.
11. White, ed., *By-Line*, 306. Even the gloomy American communist Agnes Smedley had to agree that Hong Kong in 1941 was still a good place for a foreigner to relax and drink—and to forget the danger of imminent attack. Agnes Smedley, *China Correspondent* (London and Boston: Pandora, 1984), 360.

12. EH to Bernard Peyton, April 5, 1947, in Peyton Folder, Box 11, Carlos Baker Papers, PUL, contains his drink mix and the claim that it did almost as much as the Japanese army to bring down the colony. Smedley, *China Correspondent*, 361, describes the tall tales.
13. Smedley, *China Correspondent*, 361.
14. White, ed., *By-Line*, 305.
15. Ibid., 319.
16. Baker, *Hemingway*, 364. What he wrote for public consumption was that Hong Kong was "excellently defended," if vulnerable to having its food cut off. White, ed., *By-Line*, 305.
17. Moreira, *Hemingway on the China Front*, 135.
18. White, ed., *By-Line*, 316.
19. Moreira, *Hemingway on the China Front*, 210–11. Gellhorn, *Travels*, 48, reports an unlikely stay of "several weeks." See also White, ed., *By-Line*, 308.
20. Gellhorn, *Travels*, 49. The other "generalissimo" known to Hemingway was of course Franco.
21. Ibid., 51.
22. Ibid.
23. Ibid., 52–53.
24. EH to Henry Morgenthau, Jr., July 30, 1941, in Outgoing Correspondence, Ernest Hemingway Collection, JFK Presidential Library. Reprinted in Moreira, *Hemingway on the China Front*, 201–8. One of Hemingway's Chinese interpreters said that the American had praised Chou as "intellectually versatile and sensitively diplomatic" even though he "over-emphasized the Communist role in the . . . war." Kaimei Zheng, "Hemingway in China," *North Dakota Quarterly* 70, no. 4 (2003): 184–85.
25. "Report on 'Argo,'" June 8, 1948, in Vassiliev, *Black Notebook*, 89.
26. Anna Wong, the European who arranged the meeting, wrote in her memoirs that the meeting lasted for about an hour and that it was dominated by Hemingway, not Chou, which seems unlikely. Moreira, *Hemingway on the China Front*, 130. Hemingway knew how to play the part of the good journalist who listens to what his source has to say.
27. White, ed., *By-Line*, 307.
28. Quoted in Moreira, *Hemingway on the China Front*, 207.
29. White, ed., *By-Line*, 317. Hemingway did not explain where or how he had first met the officer.
30. See, for example, David L. Charney, "True Psychology of the Insider

Spy," *Intelligencer* 18, no. 1 (Fall/Winter 2010): 47–54, which surveys the psychological stage of spying.

31. "The true gen" was British military slang for "true genuine," meaning "the inside story" or "the full scoop."
32. EH to Archibald MacLeish, October 5, 1952, Hemingway Correspondence 1938–1958, Box 10, MacLeish Papers, LoC. Hemingway was trying to explain the pressures he was under and how they made him difficult to deal with. Gellhorn made a similar comment on August 23, 1940, when she wrote that "[i]t is a big year when you have to get out a book, get a divorce, and decide about buying a house. . . . I am sure E is as exhausted as I am." Martha Gellhorn to Charles Scribner, Gellhorn Folder, Box 778, Scribner's Sons Archive, PUL.
33. EH to Ada MacLeish, October 5, 1952, in Hemingway Correspondence 1938–1958, Box 10, MacLeish Papers, LoC.
34. EH to Max Perkins, April 29, 1941, in Baker, ed., *Selected Letters*, 522–23.
35. Baker, *Hemingway*, 364.
36. William J. Lederer to Carlos Baker, May 11, 1966, in folder for Far East Trip, Box 19, Carlos Baker Papers, PUL.
37. EH to Martha Gellhorn, undated but with note "After 16 May 1941," in Outgoing Correspondence, Ernest Hemingway Collection, JFK Library. See also Baker, *Hemingway*, 364–65.
38. EH to Martha Gellhorn, undated but with note "After 16 May 1941."
39. EH to Henry Morgenthau, Jr., July 30, 1941.
40. White, ed., *By-Line*, 303–14.
41. EH to Henry Morgenthau, Jr., July 30, 1941. A reference to a previous meeting in Washington when "we talked" suggests that the meeting was relatively short. Earlier Hemingway had conveyed his regards and best wishes for Morgenthau's work "in these difficult times," which suggests his eagerness to please Morgenthau. Harry Dexter White to Henry Morgenthau, Jr., "Hemingway's and Bond's comments on Chinese transportation," May 29, 1941, Morgenthau Diaries, FDR Library. Treasury had asked Hemingway to take a look at transportation networks in China, a task for which Hemingway had only limited enthusiasm and delegated to a Pan Am official named H. L. Bond. H. L. Bond to Carlos Baker, April 15, 1966, in folder for Far East Trip, Box 19, Carlos Baker Papers, PUL.
42. H. L. Bond to Carlos Baker, April 15, 1966, suggesting another possible topic of conversation and Hemingway's willingness to make recommendations.

43. EH to Henry Morgenthau, Jr., July 30, 1941. Two weeks later White summarized the letter for Morgenthau. Harry Dexter White to Henry Morgenthau, Jr., "Digest of Mr. Hemingway's Letter on China," August 14, 1941, Morgenthau Diaries, FDR Library.
44. EH to Henry Morgenthau, Jr., July 30, 1941.
45. Haynes et al., *Spies*, 258. This source contains an excellent summary of the evidence about White's activities as a Soviet spy (258–62). R. Bruce Craig, *Treasonable Doubt: The Harry Dexter White Spy Case* (Lawrence: University Press of Kansas, 2004), gives White the benefit of the doubt.
46. John H. Wheelock, ed., *Editor to Author: The Letters of Maxwell E. Perkins* (New York: Scribner's, 1950), contains letters to Thomason going back to 1927. In January 1940 Perkins happened to meet Sweeny, "a man who looked exactly like he ought to" (153).
47. Baker, *Hemingway*, 365. Thomason worked for Naval Intelligence from the summer of 1940 through March 1943 and was mostly responsible for Latin America. "Record of Thomason, John W. Jr.," Officer Qualification Record, Marine Corps History Division, Quantico, VA; Martha Anne Turner, *The World of John W. Thomason, USMC* (Austin, TX: Eakin Press, 1984), 311.
48. Gellhorn, *Travels*, 53.
49. John W. Thomason to Maxwell Perkins, June 3 or 4, 1941, in folder for 1941, Box 19, Carlos Baker Papers.

CHAPTER 7: THE CROOK FACTORY: A SECRET WAR ON LAND

1. Leddy reported the American Gestapo remark to Washington. LegAtt to Director, October 8, 1942, reprinted in Thomas Fensch, *Behind Islands in the Stream: Hemingway, Cuba, the FBI, and the Crook Factory* (New York: iUniverse, 2009), 13–16. The same documents are available on the FBI website at vault.fbi.gov/ernest-miller-hemingway (accessed July 2014). Joyce described the midnight encounter in his unpublished memoirs. He did not name Guest or Leddy, but his description leaves little doubt as to their identities. Robert Joyce Memoirs in Robert Joyce Papers (MS 1901), Box 1, Folder 5, 50, Yale University Library (YUL).
2. Hemingway described the Gulf Stream and life in Cuba in some of his reporting, including "Marlin off the Morro: A Cuban Letter," *Esquire*, Autumn 1933; "Out in the Stream: A Cuban Letter," *Esquire*, August 1934; and "On the Blue Water: A Gulf Stream Letter," *Esquire*, April 1936. All three stories were reprinted in White, ed., *By-Line*.

3. Spruille Braden, *Diplomats and Demagogues: The Memoirs of Spruille Braden* (New Rochelle, NY: Arlington House, 1971), 285.
4. Braden to George Messersmith, February 20, 1945, Diplomatic Correspondence for 1945, Spruille Braden Papers, Rare Books and Manuscript Library (RBML), Columbia University, New York City.
5. Hemingway to Prudencio de Pereda, August 14, 1941, in Baker, ed., *Selected Letters*, 526.
6. See, for example, Constantine Pleshakov, *Stalin's Folly* (Boston: Houghton Mifflin, 2005), 86–87.
7. Winston S. Churchill, *The Second World War* (New York: Houghton Mifflin, 1959), vol. 1, 159. This is the condensed version of his memoirs.
8. See, for example, David M. Glantz and Jonathan House, *When Titans Clashed: How the Red Army Stopped Hitler* (Lawrence: University Press of Kansas, 1995), esp. 53 and 292.
9. See, for example, the discussion in Mark A. Bradley, *A Very Principled Boy* (New York: Basic Books, 2014), 124–25. By comparison, the number of American dead in World War II was around 407,000.
10. Joseph Freeman, untitled essay on the German invasion of the Soviet Union, August 1941, in Folder 4, Box 111, Joseph Freeman Papers, Hoover Institution, Stanford University.
11. Moscow Center to New York, November 27, 1941, quoted in Vassiliev, *White Notebook*, 30.
12. Joyce Papers, Box 1, Folder 5, 55, YUL. Joyce did not record when Hemingway showed him the telegram, but it would have been while they were both in Cuba from the summer of 1941 through mid-1943.
13. See, for example, his words of praise in ibid., 55–56, and EH to Konstantin Simonov, June 20, 1946, in Baker, ed., *Selected Letters*, 607.
14. Hemingway to Maxwell Perkins, December 11, 1941, in Baker, ed., *Selected Letters*, 531.
15. Ibid.
16. Hemingway to Charles Scribner, December 12, 1941, in Baker, ed., *Selected Letters*, 432–33. Martha wrote to Scribner the next time on motel stationery. Martha Gellhorn to Charles Scribner, December 13, 1941, in Gellhorn Folder, "Ernest Hemingway Related Correspondence," Box 778, Scribner's Sons Archive, PUL.
17. Martha Gellhorn and EH to "Bill" Davis, March 5, 1942, Gellhorn Personal Papers, Ernest Hemingway Collection, JFK Library. Bullfighting has been a fixture in Mexico since the sixteenth century. Mexico City still has an active bullring.
18. Regler, *Owl of Minerva*, 356–57.

19. Ibid., 357. Regler added that Hemingway mistrusted "only one of my slanderers, a man who . . . [would be] hanged by his party in Prague in 1953." This is an intriguing reference to Otto Katz, the Comintern agent who had worked for Willi Münzenberg during the Spanish Civil War and tried to recruit Barbara Wertheim (the future Barbara Tuchman). Where might Hemingway and Katz have crossed paths, and why did Hemingway distrust him?
20. Regler, *Owl of Minerva,* 357. As one Hemingway scholar has pointed out, this outburst was not unlike his 1937 attempt to get Dos Passos back on message. Chamberlin, *The Hemingway Log,* 185.
21. Regler, *Owl of Minerva,* 357.
22. EH to "Miss Craipeau," February 13, 1947, Outgoing Correspondence, Hemingway Collection, JFK Library. "Miss Craipeau" is not further identified. From Hemingway's letter, it appears that she sent Hemingway an article and a book about the Soviet Union, and that he was commenting on both. Craipeau may well have been related to Yvan Craipeau, a French Trotskyite who was the author of works about the Soviet Union. See, for example, a 1937 article by Yvan Craipeau, "The Fourth International and the Russian Counterrevolution," in E. Haberkern and Arthur Lipow, eds., *Neither Capitalism nor Socialism: Theories of Bureaucratic Collectivism* (Alameda, CA: Center for Socialist History, 2008), 25–39.
23. Martha Gellhorn to Charles Colebaugh, July 17, 1941, in Moorehead, ed., *Selected Letters,* 112–13.
24. Ibid.
25. Ross E. Rowell, "Attaché Report," September 25, 1939, in Box 27, Stack Area 370, Row 15, Compartment 29, Shelf 4, U.S. Navy Records (RG 38), NARA II, College Park, MD.
26. J. Edgar Hoover to Adolf Berle, July 29, 1942, in Box 239, Stack Area 370, Row 14, Compartment 19, Shelf 1, RG 38.
27. Hayne D. Boyden, Intelligence Report, August 6, 1940, in Box 27, Stack Area 370, Row 15, Compartment 29, Shelf 4, RG 38. Gellhorn reported the same incident in a letter: "He [the Nazi] sounded awfully big until E called him [out] and then he evaporated." Martha Gellhorn to Charles Scribner, Summer 1940, in Box 778, Scribner's Sons Archive, PUL.
28. Joyce Papers, Box 1, Folder 5, 45, YUL.
29. Ibid., 46.
30. Ibid. Joyce and his boss, Ambassador Braden, even believed that Hemingway was the right man to use to tamp down enthusiasm for Soviet propaganda in Latin America. There is a note to that effect

from Joyce to Hemingway. Joyce to Hemingway, n.d. (most likely summer 1942), in Incoming Correspondence, Ernest Hemingway Collection, JFK Library. See also Braden, *Diplomats and Demagogues,* 302–3.

31. Carlos Baker, "Information from Robert Joyce," November 17, 1963, in folder for 1942, Box 19, Carlos Baker Papers, PUL.
32. Ellis O. Briggs, *Proud Servant: Memoirs of a Career Ambassador* (Kent, OH: Kent State University Press, 1998), 174.
33. Braden, *Diplomats and Demagogues,* 283.
34. Ibid.
35. LegAtt to Director, October 8, 1942, reprinted in Fensch, *Behind Islands in the Stream,* 13–16.
36. Joyce Papers, Box 1, Folder 1, 50, YUL.
37. Braden, *Diplomats and Demagogues,* 283.
38. LegAtt to Director, October 8, 1942.
39. Joyce Papers, Box 1, Folder 5, 47–48, YUL. R-42 was probably Winston Guest, the loyal member of Hemingway's entourage in Cuba.
40. Ibid.
41. Joyce Papers, Box 1, Folder 5, 54, YUL.
42. D. M. Ladd, "Memorandum for the Director RE: Ernest Hemingway," April 27, 1943, reprinted in Fensch, *Behind Islands in the Stream,* 30.
43. Braden to L. Duggan, November 20, 1942, File Series 852.01, Department of State Records (RG 59), NARA II, College Park, MD. See also Braden to Hemingway, March 7, 1944, Spruille Braden Papers, RBML, Columbia University: "The highly confidential intelligence activities which you undertook . . . were of the utmost value . . . in assisting us to evaluate certain developments in the interpretation of which your background, experience, and abilities gave you a unique preparation."
44. LegAtt to Director, October 8, 1942, reprinted in Fensch, *Behind Islands in the Stream,* 13–16.
45. D. M. Ladd, "Memorandum for the Director RE: Ernest Hemingway, December 17, 1942, reprinted in Fensch, *Behind Islands in the Stream,* 21–23.
46. Ibid., and Leddy, "Memorandum," June 13, 1943, reprinted in Fensch, *Behind Islands in the Stream,* 50.
47. Joyce Papers, Box 1, Folder 5, 50, YUL.
48. Ibid., 50. Hemingway displayed a similar attitude in a letter to his brother at about the same time, lecturing the younger man about

the difference between intelligence and journalism. EH to Leicester Hemingway, June 28, 1941, in Leicester Hemingway, *My Brother, Ernest Hemingway* (Sarasota, FL: Pineapple Press, 1996), 300–1.

49. J. Edgar Hoover, "RE: Ernest Hemingway," December 17, 1942, reprinted in Fensch, *Behind Islands in the Stream,* 25.

50. C.H. Carson, "Memorandum for Mr. Ladd Re: Intelligence Activities of Ernest Hemingway in Cuba," June 13, 1943, and J. Edgar Hoover, "Memorandum for Mr. Tamm [and] Mr. Ladd," December 19, 1942, both reprinted in Fensch, *Behind Islands in the Stream,* 27 and 57.

51. J. Edgar Hoover, "Memorandum for Mr. Tamm [and] Mr. Ladd," December 19, 1942. A 1943 note by Hoover directing his subordinates to "let me have memo on Ernest Hemingway" attests to Hoover's personal interest in the author. Memo from the Office of the Director, n.d., probably written in February or March 1943, in vault.fbi.gov/ernest-miller-hemingway (accessed July 2014). Hoover was probably reacting to Hemingway's campaign against an FBI special agent named Edward Knoblaugh earlier in the year. Hemingway tried to persuade Ambassador Braden to send Knoblaugh home from Havana by writing a long, detailed memorandum about his alleged fascist sympathies during the Spanish Civil War. EH to Spruille Braden, February 10, 1943, in Outgoing Correspondence, Ernest Hemingway Collection, JFK Library. The ambassador initially agreed, then reversed himself, but apparently not before Hemingway was able to gloat over his interim victory. Baker, *Hemingway,* 380–81; Fensch, *Behind Islands in the Stream,* 60.

52. Joyce Papers, Box 1, Folder 5, 54–55, YUL.

53. LegAtt to Director, October 9, 1942, reprinted in Fensch, *Behind Islands in the Stream,* 17–18.

54. Quoted in C. H. Carson, "Memorandum for Mr. Ladd Re: Intelligence Activities of Ernest Hemingway in Cuba," June 13, 1943, reprinted in Fensch, *Behind Islands in the Stream,* 51.

55. Her brother-in-law Michael Straight would later be unmasked as the only American in the NKVD's Cambridge University spy ring, and is mentioned at the end of Chapter 8. The Soviet spymaster Orlov also played a role in that operation.

56. Joyce Papers, Box 1, Folder 5, 54, YUL. LegAtt to Director, October 9, 1942, reprinted in Fensch, *Behind Islands in the Stream,* 17–18, reported that the ambassador had interceded with Washington on Hemingway's behalf to secure Durán's services "for the special purpose of assisting Mr. Hemingway."

57. Joyce Papers, Box 1, Folder 5, 54–55, YUL.

58. Baker, "Information from Robert Joyce," November 17, 1963.
59. Joyce Papers, Box 1, Folder 5, 55, YUL. According to the FBI, "Hemingway's organization was disbanded and its work terminated as of April 1, 1943." LegAtt to Director, April 21, 1943, reprinted in Fensch, *Behind Islands in the Stream,* 28.

CHAPTER 8: *PILAR* AND THE WAR AT SEA: A SECRET AGENT OF MY GOVERNMENT

1. *Pilar* Logbook in "Other Material," Ernest Hemingway Collection, JFK Library. It is also reprinted in Terry Mort, *The Hemingway Patrols* (New York: Scribner, 2009), 185–88.
2. Gregory H. Hemingway, *Papa: A Personal Memoir* (Boston: Houghton Mifflin, 1976), 88. Gregory claims to have been on the boat on that particular day but this is likely hearsay. The diligent chronologist puts him in Key West on that day. Chamberlin, *The Hemingway Log,* 240.
3. EH to Lillian Ross, June 3, 1950, in folder for 1942, Box 19, Carlos Baker Papers, PUL.
4. See EH, "First Poem to Mary in London," Nicholas Gerogiannis, ed., *Ernest Hemingway, 88 Poems* (New York: Harcourt, Brace, Jovanovich, 1979), 104.
5. *Pilar* Logbook.
6. EH to Charles T. Lanham (CTL), January 5, 1949, in Box 1, Lanham-Hemingway Papers, PUL.
7. Paul Hendrickson, *Hemingway's Boat: Everything He Loved in Life, and Lost* (New York: Knopf, 2011), 9.
8. Ibid., 74.
9. See Chapter 1.
10. EH to Leicester Hemingway, June 28, 1941, reprinted in Leicester Hemingway, *My Brother, Ernest Hemingway,* 300–301.
11. Ernest Hemingway, ed., *Men at War: The Best War Stories of All Time* (New York: Crown, 1942). Baker, *Hemingway,* 371, describes how Crown asked Hemingway to work on the book, and how Hemingway planned to "lean heavily on the editorial and military experience" of his friends Perkins, Thomason, and Sweeny.
12. EH, ed., *Men at War,* xi.
13. Ibid., xxiii. Smedley wrote a few paragraphs in her memoirs about her meeting with Hemingway. See Chapter 6 and, more generally, Ruth Price, *The Lives of Agnes Smedley* (Oxford: Oxford University Press, 2005).

14. EH, ed., *Men at War*, xx.
15. Ibid., xxvii.
16. EH to Malcolm Cowley, April 9, 1948, in Outgoing Correspondence, Ernest Hemingway Collection, JFK Library.
17. Braden, *Diplomats and Demagogues*, 283–84.
18. EH to Alfred Rice, December 15, 1948, in Baker, ed., *Selected Letters*, 654–56.
19. Gregory Hemingway, *Papa*, 70.
20. EH to Malcolm Cowley, June 28, 1948, in Outgoing Correspondence, Ernest Hemingway Collection, JFK Library.
21. Leicester Hemingway, *My Brother, Ernest Hemingway*, 223. I have been unable to document Jenkinson's naval intelligence assignment. It was, presumably, with British naval intelligence. Ernest Hemingway's first contact with Jenkinson may have come when the Englishman visited Key West in 1937. Jenkinson also had a connection through Joris Ivens. While reporting for the London *Daily Sketch*, Jenkinson met Ivens in China in 1938 and started corresponding with Hemingway about the situation in the Far East. See Chamberlin, *The Hemingway Log*, 202.
22. Sir Anthony Jenkinson, *America Came My Way* (London: Arthur Barker, 1936), and *Where Seldom a Gun Is Heard* (London: Arthur Barker, 1937).
23. EH to Charles T. Lanham, November 15, 1948, in Box 1, Lanham-Hemingway Papers, PUL.
24. Leicester Hemingway, *My Brother, Ernest Hemingway*, 223.
25. Ibid.
26. Leicester Hemingway to EH, March 19, 1940, in Norberto Fuentes, *Hemingway in Cuba* (Secaucus, NJ: Lyle Stuart, 1984), 316–18.
27. Leicester Hemingway, *My Brother, Ernest Hemingway*, 223.
28. See, for example, EH to Anthony Jenkinson, May 1, 1940, in Fuentes, *Hemingway in Cuba*, 318–19.
29. Leicester Hemingway and Anthony Jenkinson, "A Caribbean Snoop Cruise," *Reader's Digest* 37 (1940): 128.
30. Ibid.
31. T. J. Wilkinson to William J. Donovan, March 24, 1942, in "Leicester Hemingway" Folder, COI/OSS Central Files, Entry 92, OSS Records (RG 226), NARA II.
32. EH to Grace Hemingway, July [n.d.], 1940, in Leicester Hemingway, *My Brother, Ernest Hemingway*, 297. Hemingway was not just being polite about Leicester because he was writing to his mother.

He also praised his work in a postwar letter to his best friend. See EH to Charles Lanham, November 25, 1948, in Lanham-Hemingway Papers, PUL.

33. See Chapter 7.
34. See, for example, Ross E. Rowell, "Attaché Report," January 27, 1940, in "Monograph Type Documents," Box 27, Stack Area 370, Row 15, Compartment 29, Row 4, Office of Naval Intelligence Files, RG 38, NARA II.
35. Homer H. Hickam, Jr., *Torpedo Junction: U-Boat War off America's East Coast, 1942* (Annapolis, MD: Naval Institute Press, 1996), 159, 291.
36. George S. Messersmith to Laurence Duggan, January 30, 1942, DoS Designator 837.24, Box 4649, Department of State Files (RG 59), NARA II. Messersmith was Braden's predecessor. A similar message two months later mentioned a sinking near Cuba. Ellis O. Briggs to Philip W. Bonsal, March 27, 1942, DoS Designator 800.20237, Box 3220, DoS Files, NARA II.
37. EH to Leicester Hemingway, June 28, 1941, in Leicester Hemingway, *My Brother, Ernest Hemingway*, 300
38. Ibid, 224.
39. EH to Leicester Hemingway, June 28, 1941.
40. Braden, *Diplomats and Demagogues*, 283. Braden gives the impression that this conversation occurred after the Crook Factory closed its doors; in fact there was considerable overlap between the two operations.
41. Ibid., 283–84.
42. Ibid.
43. EH, "Notes 1935–1944," n.d., in "Other Material," Ernest Hemingway Collection, JFK Library.
44. Ellis Briggs, *Shots Heard Round the World: An Ambassador's Hunting Adventures on Four Continents* (New York: Viking 1957), 55–60. Briggs was a ranking officer at the Embassy in 1942 and took part in the consultations. See also Anonymous to EH, November 9, 1942, a note in "Caribbean Submarine War," World War II, Ernest Hemingway Collection, JFK Library, referring to Thomason's "conversation with you in Havana." Hemingway himself corresponded about Operation Friendless with Malcolm Cowley after the war. See EH to Malcolm Cowley, April 9, 1948, and June 28, 1948, in Outgoing Correspondence, Ernest Hemingway Collection, JFK Library.
45. Briggs, *Shots Heard Round the World*, 58–59.
46. EH to Malcolm Cowley, April 9, 1948.

47. EH to Robert Joyce, November 9, 1942, in Outgoing Correspondence, Ernest Hemingway Collection, JFK Library. See also EH to Don Saxon, January 13, 1949, in Box 11, Carlos Baker Papers, PUL. "Cucu" or "Cuckoo"—both spellings appear in Hemingway letters—may have been Boyden's informal but permanent call sign as a Marine aviator.
48. Briggs, *Shots Heard Round the World*, 59–60. An email from the Historical Reference Branch of the Marine Corps History Division on August 18, 2014, provided basic information on Saxon's service.
49. Hayne D. Boyden to Whom It May Concern, May 18, 1943, in Incoming Correspondence, Museo EH Collection, Ernest Hemingway Collection, JFK Library.
50. EH to Hayne D. Boyden, November 2, 1942, in Outgoing Correspondence, Ernest Hemingway Collection, JFK Library.
51. EH to Malcolm Cowley, June 28, 1948.
52. Ibid.
53. Office of Legal Attaché to Director, FBI, September 21 1943, in Fensch, *Behind Islands in the Stream*, 87–89. The file refers only to "Confidential Informant . . . # 396," which suggests that the intent was to protect his identity from those outside the Bureau. For whatever reason, Hemingway appears to have been careful about what he told 396, and said nothing controversial to him.
54. Martha Gellhorn to EH, June 26, 1943, in Moorehead, ed., *Selected Letters*, 145.
55. Baker, *Hemingway*, 381.
56. EH to Malcolm Cowley, June 28, 1948.
57. Entry for December 10, 1942, WWII War Diaries, Caribbean Sea Frontier, April 1942 to December 1943, Records of the Office of the CNO, RG 38, NARA II. Michael Reynolds, *Hemingway: The Final Years* (New York: Norton, 1999), 72–81, cites similar messages and tells the story of Operation Friendless in good detail.
58. Spruille Braden to EH, March 7, 1944, in "Catalogued Correspondence," Spruille Braden Papers RBML, Columbia University. After the war, Hemingway mentioned that he had given the letter to his lawyer for safekeeping. EH to Alfred Rice, December 15, 1948, in Baker, ed., *Selected Letters*, 655.
59. EH to Spruille Braden, March 21, 1944, in "Catalogued Correspondence," Spruille Braden Papers, RBML, Columbia University.
60. EH to Archibald MacLeish, circa May 5, 1943, in Baker, ed., *Selected Letters*, 544–46. A few months later, he wrote Max Perkins that he

"wouldn't trade [his] present job for anybody's." EH to Maxwell Perkins, August 2, 1943, in ibid., 547–48.

61. Leicester Hemingway, *My Brother, Ernest Hemingway*, 229–30.
62. Ibid., 230.
63. The relevant sentence in the 1948 file summary in the Vassiliev Papers: "In Sept. 1943, when 'Argo' was in Havana, where he owned a villa, our worker contacted him and, prior to his departure for Europe, met with him only twice." Vassiliev, *Black Notebook*, 89.
64. See, for example, his wartime remarks about the Soviets recorded in Joyce Papers, Box 1, Folder 5, 55–56, YUL.
65. Michael Straight, *After Long Silence* (New York: Norton, 1983), 129–30.
66. Ibid.
67. Vassiliev, *Black Notebook*, 89.

CHAPTER 9: ON TO PARIS: BRAVE AS A SALADANG

1. Nelson Lankford, ed., *OSS Against the Reich: The World War II Diaries of Colonel David K. E. Bruce* (Kent, OH: Kent State University Press, 1991), 160; Attachment to David Bruce to EH, June 12, 1955, in Incoming Correspondence, Ernest Hemingway Collection, JFK Library. See also Robert Fuller, "Hemingway at Rambouillet," *Hemingway Review* 33, no. 2 (Spring 2014): 68–70.
2. Lankford, ed., *OSS Against the Reich*, 160.
3. EH to Mary Welsh (MW), August 27, 1944, in Baker, ed., *Selected Letters*, 564.
4. David Bruce to EH, June 12, 1955.
5. Martha Gellhorn to Clara Spiegel, March 4, 1942, in Spiegel Folder, Box 12, Carlos Baker Papers, PUL.
6. Moorehead, ed., *Selected Letters*, 149–60.
7. Joyce describes his disengagement from the Foreign Service in Joyce Papers, Box 1, Folder 6, 1, YUL. His OSS personnel record also contains material relating to his application to, and service in, OSS. Robert P. Joyce Personnel File, OSS Files, NARA II.
8. Joyce to Shepardson, March 16, 1944, CIA FOIA Release. This letter contains references to an earlier message from Joyce to Shepardson on February 9, 1944, that was not among the other messages. These records were subsequently moved to NARA in College Park, Maryland, where I have been unable to locate them. I obtained the material in this FOIA release, which apparently occurred in February 1983, courtesy of the scholar Daniel Robinson.

9. McBaine to Shepardson, February 14, 1944, CIA FOIA Release.
10. Joyce to Shepardson, March 16, 1944, CIA FOIA Release.
11. Magruder to Shepardson, April 6, 1944, CIA FOIA Release.
12. Ibid. Buxton's note is on the same page as Magruder's memorandum to Shepardson.
13. Bigelow to Shepardson, April 21, 1944, CIA FOIA Release.
14. Shepardson to Joyce, May 1, 1944, "METO Pouch Review" (February 1–May 27, 1944), Box 53, Entry 99, OSS Files, NARA II. This is a summary of miscellaneous communications received in the field and does not include other messages relating to Hemingway.
15. Baker, *Hemingway*, 385.
16. Moorehead, *Gellhorn*, 212.
17. Kert, *The Hemingway Women*, 391–92.
18. Jennet Conant, *The Irregulars: Roald Dahl and the British Spy Ring in Wartime Washington* (New York: Simon & Schuster, 2008), is a description of his work.
19. Roald Dahl to "Dear Mama," October 19, 1943, Roald Dahl Museum and Story Centre (RDMSC), Buckinghamshire, England.
20. Roald Dahl to "Dear Mama," March 21, 1944, RDMSC.
21. Draft of a letter from Roald Dahl to an unnamed recipient (probably Carlos Baker), July 28, 1965, RDMSC.
22. Martha Gellhorn to Eleanor Roosevelt, April 28, 1944, in Moorehead, ed., *Selected Letters*, 160–61.
23. Draft of Roald Dahl to unnamed recipient (probably Carlos Baker), July 28, 1965, RDMSC. The boxer was George Brown. Baker, *Hemingway*, 386.
24. Matthew Sweet, *The West End Front* (London: Faber & Faber, 2011), 91.
25. See, for example, ibid., esp. 82–92.
26. Vassiliev, *Black Notebook*, 89. Also quoted in Haynes et al., *Spies*, 154.
27. EH, "Voyage to Victory," in White, ed., *By-Line*, 340–41.
28. EH to Charles Poore, March 16, 1953, in Box 11, Carlos Baker Papers, PUL; EH to Konstantin Simonov, June 20, 1946, in Baker, ed., *Selected Letters*, 607–9.
29. H. R. Stoneback, "Hemingway's Happiest Summer—'The Wildest, Most Beautiful, Wonderful Time Ever' or, The Liberation of France and Hemingway," *North Dakota Quarterly* 64, no. 3 (Summer 1997): 184–220, is a peerless review of the literature on the subject, as well

as a wonderful piece in its own right. I have also relied on Reynolds, *Hemingway: The Final Years*, esp. 101–9.

30. Quoted in Baker, *Hemingway*, 404.
31. EH to Charles Poore, March 16, 1953, in Poore Folder, Carlos Baker Papers, PUL.
32. EH, "Battle for Paris," in White, ed., *By-Line*, 365. Another good source is EH to MW, August 27, 1944, in Outgoing Correspondence, Ernest Hemingway Collection, JFK Library.
33. Richard Harris Smith, *OSS: The Secret History of America's First Intelligence Agency* (Berkeley: University of California Press, 1981), 191.
34. Robert Capa, *Slightly Out of Focus* (New York: Random House, 1999), 179.
35. David Bruce to EH, June 12, 1955, in Incoming Correspondence, Ernest Hemingway Collection, JFK Library. Bruce attached the typescript of his recollections of Rambouillet that he had prepared for "a writer," possibly Denis Brian or Malcolm Cowley.
36. Quoted in Nelson Lankford, *The Last American Aristocrat: The Biography of Ambassador David K. E. Bruce* (Boston: Little, Brown, 1996), p. 155. See also Lankford, ed., *OSS Against the Reich*, 160.
37. S. L. A. Marshall, *Bringing Up the Rear* (San Francisco: Presidio Press, 1979), 101. This book contains a reprint of an article about 1944 first published in 1961.
38. Lankford, ed., *OSS Against the Reich*, 160.
39. David Bruce to Carlos Baker, December 13, 1965, in David Bruce Papers, Virginia Historical Society, Richmond.
40. Lankford, ed., *OSS Against the Reich*, 166.
41. Miles Copeland, *The Game Player* (London: Aurum Press, 1989), 55. Copeland was an OSS officer who reached the hotel by August 21. Hemingway's slightly different version is in EH, "Battle for Paris," in White, ed., *By-Line*, 369.
42. EH to CTL, November 8, 1948, in Lanham-Hemingway Papers, PUL.
43. Ibid.
44. David Bruce to EH, June 12, 1955.
45. David Bruce to Carlos Baker, November 23, 1965, in David Bruce Papers, Virginia Historical Society, Richmond. "I did . . . occasionally see him in rages, especially when he had too much to drink."
46. Lankford, ed., *OSS Against the Reich*, 168.
47. EH, "How We Came to Paris," in White, ed., *By-Line*, 374.

48. David Bruce to EH, June 12, 1955; Lankford, ed., *OSS Against the Reich*, 169. See also EH to Charles Poore, March 16, 1953, which includes the claim that he worked out two alternate routes to Paris "where you would only have to fight twice." Poore Folder, Box 11, Carlos Baker Papers, PUL.
49. David Bruce to EH, August 23, 1944, in Incoming Correspondence, Ernest Hemingway Collection, JFK Library.
50. Andy Rooney, *My War* (New York: PublicAffairs, 2000), 205.
51. Lankford, ed., *OSS Against the Reich*, 171. The source is Bruce's wartime diary.
52. Ibid., 172–73. Bruce does not specifically state whether Hemingway climbed the arch with him, but from his diary and other sources it is near certain that the writer was with Bruce before and after the climb.
53. Quoted in A. E. Hotchner, *Hemingway and His World* (New York and Paris: Vendome Press, 1989), 162.
54. Lankford, ed., *OSS Against the Reich*, 174.
55. Marshall, *Bringing Up the Rear*, 95. Iris Carpenter, *No Woman's World* (Boston: Houghton Mifflin, 1946), 113, describes the food at the Ritz after the liberation. Mary Welsh Hemingway (MWH) does the same in *How It Was* (New York: Ballantine, 1977), 144.
56. There is an excellent discussion of this topic in Fuller, "Hemingway at Rambouillet," 66–80.
57. Marshall, *Bringing Up the Rear*, 101. A saladang is a wild ox that was common in Asia.
58. David Bruce to EH, June 12, 1955.
59. EH, "Battle for Paris," 383.

CHAPTER 10: AT THE FRONT: THE LAST MONTHS OF THE GREAT WAR AGAINST FASCISM

1. EH, "War in the Siegfried Line," in White, ed., *By-Line*, 392.
2. Reynolds, *Hemingway: The Final Years*, 111–12, tells these stories well.
3. MWH, *How It Was*, 143.
4. EH to MW, September 11, 1944, in Baker, ed., *Selected Letters*, 506.
5. MWH, *How It Was*, 184.
6. EH to Helen Kirkpatrick, November 12, 1948, in Baker, ed., *Selected Letters*, 652.
7. Jacob A. Stein, "General Buck Lanham, Ernest Hemingway, and That Woman in Venice," *Washington Lawyer*, January 2003.

8. Ibid.
9. EH to Helen Kirkpatrick, November 12, 1948, in Baker, ed., *Selected Letters*, 652.
10. EH to Raymond O. Barton, June 9, 1948, in Baker, ed., *Selected Letters*, 640. See also Reynolds, *Hemingway: The Final Years*, 222, containing a reference to Hemingway's claims that he had been recommended for the Distinguished Service Cross three times.
11. War Department, FM 30-26: Regulations for Correspondents Accompanying U.S. Army Forces in the Field (Washington, DC: War Department, 1942), 2.
12. Quoted in Reynolds, *Hemingway: The Final Years*, 116.
13. Ibid.
14. EH to MW, September 13, 1944, in Baker, ed., *Selected Letters*, 568.
15. Baker, *Hemingway*, 434.
16. Ibid., 438. Lanham wrote about the event in letters to Hemingway after the war. CTL to EH, November 6, 1954, and March 9, 1960, in Incoming Correspondence, Ernest Hemingway Collection, JFK Library.
17. There are various versions of this incident: Reynolds, *Hemingway: The Final Years*, 123; Stoneback, "Hemingway's Happiest Summer," 204; and Baker, *Hemingway*, 438. Both Stoneback and Baker rely on firsthand testimony from Walton.
18. Baker, *Hemingway*, 439.
19. Ibid., 439–40.
20. EH to Alfred Rice, December 15, 1948, in Baker, ed., *Selected Letters*, 656.
21. EH to MW, April 14, 1945, in Baker, ed., *Selected Letters*, 584.
22. EH to Malcolm Cowley, April 9, 1948, and April 13, 1948, in Outgoing Correspondence, Hemingway Research Collection, JFK Library.
23. EH to CTL, April 2, 1945, in Baker, ed., *Selected Letters*, 578–81. Hemingway's depression may have been a form of PTSD after his intense experiences in combat in 1944. In another one of his letters to Lanham, he described an apparent symptom of PTSD: waking up at home, not knowing where he was, and kicking Mary awake to tell her that "this fucking house" was indefensible and they needed to leave. EH to CTL, January 5, 1949, in Box 1, Lanham-Hemingway Papers, PUL.
24. EH to CTL, April 14, 1945, in Box 1, Lanham-Hemingway Papers, PUL.
25. EH to Maxwell Perkins, July 23, 1945, in Baker, ed., *Selected Letters*, 593–95.

26. EH to Konstantin Simonov, in Baker, ed., *Selected Letters,* 608. In 1946, Lanham would write that Hemingway was one of two people in the world who understood him, and that the only way that he was able to relax, "apart from fornication," was to write a letter to Hemingway. CTL to EH, July 15, 1946, in Incoming Correspondence, Ernest Hemingway Collection, JFK Library.
27. EH to Maxwell Perkins, July 23, 1945, in Baker, ed., *Selected Letters,* 594.
28. EH to CTL, May 23, 1953, in Box 1, Lanham-Hemingway Papers, PUL. In this passage he wrote Lanham about loving "the science and practice of doing away with the Kraut."
29. Vassiliev, *Black Notebook,* 89; also quoted in Haynes et al., *Spies,* 154.

CHAPTER 11: "THE CREEPS": NOT WAR, NOT PEACE

1. Mary Lanham to EH, October 10, 1945, in Incoming Correspondence, Ernest Hemingway Collection, JFK Library.
2. The Lanham visit began on September 22. See EH to MW, September 28, 1945, in Baker, ed., *Selected Letters,* 601–3.
3. Mary Lanham to Carlos Baker, June 1, 1964, in folder for 1945, Box 20, Baker Papers, PUL. This is my principal source for this story.
4. The photo is in Box 1, Lanham-Hemingway Correspondence, PUL.
5. Quoted in Bruccoli, ed., *Hemingway and the Mechanism of Fame,* 90.
6. This account follows Amy Knight, *How the Cold War Began: The Igor Gouzenko Affair and the Hunt for Soviet Spies* (New York: Carroll & Graf, 2005), esp. 32–35.
7. P. J. Philip, "Soviet Embassy Ex-Aide Gave Tip On Leak of Canada's Science Data," *New York Times,* February 19, 1946.
8. See, for example, Walter Isaacson and Evan Thomas, *The Wise Men* (New York: Touchstone, 1986), 357.
9. EH to CTL, February 21, 1946, Box 1, Lanham-Hemingway Papers, PUL.
10. The full text of the speech can be found in Winston S. Churchill, "Mr. Churchill's Address Calling for United Effort for World Peace," *New York Times,* March 6, 1946.
11. EH to Konstantin Simonov, June 20, 1946, in Baker, ed., *Selected Letters,* 607–9.
12. EH to CTL, June 30, 1946, in Box 1, Lanham-Hemingway Papers, PUL.
13. Ibid.
14. EH to CTL, January 17, 1948, in Box 1, Lanham-Hemingway Papers, PUL.

15. Hemingway to "Miss Craipeau," February 13, 1947, Outgoing Correspondence, Ernest Hemingway Collection, JFK Library. Craipeau, first name unknown, had apparently sent Hemingway a book and article about the Soviet Union, and may have asked for his reaction. See also the discussion of the letter in Chapter 7.
16. Harold Strauss, "The Riddle of Moscow's Trials," *New York Times*, May 25, 1941. This is a review of *Darkness at Noon.*
17. Edward Dmytryk, *Odd Man Out: A Memoir of the Hollywood Ten* (Carbondale: Southern Illinois University Press, 1996), 14–15.
18. Kenneth L. Billingsley, "Hollywood's Missing Movies: Why American Films Have Ignored Life Under Communism," *Reason*, June 2000, and Billingsley, *Hollywood Party: How Communism Seduced the American Film Industry in the 1930s and 1940s* (Roseville, CA: Forum, 2000).
19. Koestler, *Invisible Writing*, 451. Koestler and Hemingway had many mutual friends.
20. "Smashing of Fascist Spy Nest," *Daily Worker*, June 16, 1937.
21. Harold Denny, "Many Doubts Rise in Russia on Guilt of Eight Generals," *New York Times*, June 25, 1937. Today there is virtually no doubt that Tukhachevsky was innocent of the charges against him and guilty only of being a brilliant military leader who might one day overshadow Stalin. In the 1930s and 1940s three interpretations of the purges were common in the United States. Especially during the war, some Americans—like the former ambassador to the Soviet Union, William Davis—liked to believe that the accused were guilty, and that Stalin was dealing with real enemies. Another approach was to suspect that the show trials were just that, but to acknowledge that there was little that the United States could or should do about them. That made sense during the war; the Soviet Union could treat its own citizens any way it liked. The third approach was to side with Churchill and to reserve the right to denounce the dictator whose bloodthirsty excesses easily rivaled those of Hitler. See, for instance, the discussion in Ronald Radosh and Allis Radosh, *Red Star over Hollywood* (San Francisco: Encounter Books, 2005), 94–95.
22. EH to CTL, January 17, 1948, in Box 1, Lanham-Hemingway Papers, PUL.
23. Ibid. For general background see for example the discussion in Joseph P. Lash, *Eleanor: The Years Alone* (New York: Norton, 1972), 82–89, of liberals who were somewhat sympathetic to the Soviets. When Wallace became blind to Soviet transgressions, even Eleanor reluctantly parted company with him.

24. Robert J. Donovan, *Conflict and Crisis: The Presidency of Harry S Truman, 1945–1948* (New York: Norton, 1971), 284.
25. There are many discussions of this period. Those that I have found particularly helpful are Bradley, *A Very Principled Boy*; Sam Tannenhaus, *Whittaker Chambers: A Biography* (New York: Random House, 1997); and Walter Goodman, *The Committee: The Extraordinary Career of the House Committee on Un-American Activities* (New York: Farrar, Straus, 1968).
26. Eric Bentley, ed., *Thirty Years of Treason: Excerpts from Hearings Before the House Committee on Un-American Activities 1938–1968* (New York: Thunder's Mouth Press, 1971), 57. Nazi sympathizers were the committee's primary prewar target.
27. This would happen in 1996. See National Security Agency and Central Intelligence Agency, *Venona: Soviet Espionage and the American Response, 1939–1957* (Washington, DC: NSA and CIA, 1996).
28. U.S. House of Representatives, *This Is Your House Committee on Un-American Activities* (Washington, DC: U.S. Government Printing Office, 1954), 17.
29. Goodman, *The Committee*, 204.
30. Bentley, ed., *Thirty Years of Treason*, 84, 91–92.
31. Martha Gellhorn, "Cry Shame," *New Republic*, October 6, 1947.
32. Bentley, ed., *Thirty Years of Treason*, 86.
33. Ibid, 106.
34. Hanns Eisler, "Statement on Leaving the USA," March 27, 1948, available at www.eislermusic.com (accessed June 9, 2015).
35. Dmytryk, *Odd Man Out*, 39.
36. John Sbardellati, *J. Edgar Hoover Goes to the Movies: The FBI and the Origins of Hollywood's Cold War* (Ithaca, NY: Cornell University Press, 2012), esp. 197–208, is an excellent discussion of fears of communist subversion, and the criteria that were applied to mostly unremarkable films. See also Billingsley, "Hollywood's Missing Movies" and *Hollywood Party*, esp. 282. The Communist Party had hoped to influence the content of movies in America through party members like the Hollywood Ten. They *had* succeeded to some extent, just not in the way that the committee imagined. With a few exceptions, Hollywood did not make movies that glorified communism or the Soviet Union. What the Ten had been able to do was their bit to keep Hollywood from making serious movies about Lenin or Stalin and their crimes against humanity. Between 1941 and 2015, Hollywood has turned out any number of movies about the Third Reich, keeping fresh the image of Hitler's terrible worldview. But, thanks in

part to the Ten, there are almost no movies that depict Stalin and his murderous paranoia: little or nothing about the famines that he caused, or the purges that he ordered, or the great archipelago of concentration camps that he established in Siberia.

37. See, for example, Gerald Horne, *The Final Victim of the Blacklist: John Howard Lawson, Dean of the Hollywood Ten* (Berkeley: University of California Press, 2006), 195.
38. Ibid., esp. 35–36.
39. Ibid., and Dmytryk, *Odd Man Out*, 21.
40. Bentley, ed., *Thirty Years of Treason*, 154 and 158–59.
41. James D. Brasch and Joseph Sigman, *Hemingway's Library: A Composite Record* (Boston: JFK Library Electronic Edition, 2000). The authors have indexed the books by subject, with books on espionage on page 403; the OSS on page 423; Russia and the Soviet Union on page 429; secret services on 430; and the FBI on 435. Included on the list are at least two books that focus on the case of Alger Hiss, the high-profile spy whom Bentley and Chambers unveiled. Bentley's book is not listed but Chambers's famous memoir, *Witness*, was on the shelves at the Finca.
42. EH to CTL, March 28, 1947, in Box 1, Lanham-Hemingway Papers, PUL. Along similar lines, he would comment on April 15, 1948, that he did not like many of Truman and Forrestal's policies. EH to CTL, April 15, 1948, in Baker, ed., *Selected Letters*, 634.
43. Edward Dmytryk, one of the Hollywood Ten, explained in his memoirs that the phrase was "used before, during and long after the war as one of the leading loyalty-check guides. . . . It meant that anyone who was . . . against . . . Mussolini's Italy, or Hitler's Germany [after Pearl Harbor] was OK. . . . But anyone who had been against the same regimes before December 7, 1941, was just as obviously an extreme and dangerous leftist, since only the communists officially resisted the spread of fascism at that time." Dymtryk, *Odd Man Out*, 3.
44. EH to CTL, March 28, 1947.
45. See, for instance, CTL to EH, (1) June 19, 1946, and (2) January 13, 1948, in Incoming Correspondence, Ernest Hemingway Collection, JFK Library, where (1) Lanham sets clear limits to his tolerance for the Soviets and (2) talks about his political preferences. Given the amount of time it took for letters to arrive at their destination, the EH–CTL correspondence often seems disjointed, as if their letters were figuratively as well as literally crossing in the mail.
46. See, for example, FBI, "North American Spanish Aid Committee,

An Internal Security Case," March 12, 1941, File 100-HQ-7058, Box 1176, FBI Records (RG 65), NARA II.

47. See "Memo from the Office of the Director," undated, in vault.fbi.gov/ernest-miller-hemingway (accessed July 2014). This memo comes after a December 1942 entry and before an April 1943 entry. The memo contains the additional note, "4/27/43 memo Dir," a reference to the memo prepared in response to Hoover's request.
48. D. M. Ladd, "Memorandum for the Director Re: Ernest Hemingway," April 27, 1943, vault.fbi.gov/ernest-miller-hemingway (accessed July 2014), reproduced in Fensch, *Behind Islands in the Stream*, 30–31.
49. The file is available in its entirety on the FBI website at vault.fbi.gov/ernest-miller-hemingway (accessed August 2015). As documents or parts of documents are declassified, the FBI occasionally still adds content to the holdings on its website, making it a slightly better source than Fensch's book, *Behind Islands in the Stream*, which reprints most of the file that was available in 2009. File Number 64-23312 appears to be devoted exclusively to Hemingway. See Gerald K. Haines and David A. Langbart, *Unlocking the Files of the FBI: A Guide to Its Records and Classification System* (Wilmington, DE: Scholarly Resources, 1993), esp. 63, explaining Classification 64 and stating that it includes "a file relating to Ernest Hemingway." There is no evidence that the Bureau opened any other files on Hemingway. Trust me, I looked and asked, many times!
50. For a different point of view, see Jeffrey Meyers, *Hemingway: Life into Art* (New York: Cooper Square, 2000), 109, and the discussion in the epilogue to this book.
51. Blind Memorandum on "Ernest Hemingway," July 20, 1955, vault.fbi.gov/ernest-miller-hemingway (accessed August 2015), reproduced in Fensch, *Behind Islands in the Stream*, 96–98. If the Bureau had investigated Hemingway, it would have tried to make a case that he had committed a crime, and there would have been a different file number. And the file would have been much longer. For example, Joris Ivens's FBI file ran to 650 pages. Schoots, *Living Dangerously*, 169. Years later, Hoover would tell his subordinates that he did not think Hemingway had any communist leanings. Marginal comment in Hoover's handwriting on Quentin Reynolds to J. Edgar Hoover, January 6, 1964, vault.fbi.gov/ernest-miller-hemingway (accessed August 2015). In other words, the Bureau regarded Hemingway as an occasional nuisance, especially in 1942 and 1943 in Cuba, but not as a communist, let alone a communist spy. See also discussion in epilogue.
52. EH to CTL, January 5, 1949, in Box 1, Lanham-Hemingway Papers,

PUL: Hemingway told Lanham that from 1942 to 1944, his source was "a kid in censorship."

53. "Citation for Bronze Star Medal," undated, in World War II folder, Other Material, Ernest Hemingway Collection, JFK Library.
54. EH to CTL, July 1, 1947, in Box 1, Lanham-Hemingway Papers, PUL.
55. Ibid. Hemingway later referred to his Bronze Star as "the highest piece of junk they could give a civilian." EH to Alfred Rice, December 15, 1948, in Baker, ed., *Selected Letters*, 656.
56. EH to CTL, September 3, 1947, Box 1, Lanham-Hemingway Papers, PUL. During the summer of 1947, George Kennan published his famous article on the need for "U.S. policy towards the Soviet Union [to] be that of a long-term, patient but firm and vigilant containment of Russian expansive tendencies" and Congress was discussing whether to provide economic aid to Western Europe under the Marshall Plan.
57. EH to CTL, April 15, 1948, in Baker, ed., *Selected Letters*, 634.
58. EH to Charles Scribner, October 29, 1947, in Baker, ed., *Selected Letters*, 630.
59. Hemingway shorthand for "chickenshit," a favorite noun or adjective. EH to CTL, November 27, 1947, in Box 1, Lanham-Hemingway Papers, PUL.
60. Ibid. He used similar language in EH to Charles Scribner, July 22, 1949, in Baker, ed., *Selected Letters*, 659.
61. See entries for Hemingway in Individual Name Files, Box 131 and Master Name Index, Box 291, Un-American Activities Committee, Records of the House of Representatives (RG 233), NARA, Washington, DC. HUAC started its work by following a lead of some sort—perhaps from a news article, or a concerned citizen, or another part of the government. If the lead seemed promising, the committee proceeded with a preliminary investigation by one or more of a dozen investigators. The investigators included a number of former Secret Service and FBI special agents, who could call on the contacts they had built up over their professional lives. Once they had assembled enough information, the investigators presented their findings to the chairman, who would confer with the members of the committee and then decide whether to proceed to formal hearings. The process is described in U.S. House of Representatives, *This Is Your House Committee on Un-American Activities*.
62. Radosh and Radosh, *Red Star over Hollywood*, 203, 205, 216.
63. Ibid., 216.
64. Quoted in Donaldson, *Archibald MacLeish*, 398. He would later speak out against McCarthy. Ibid., 426–29.

65. Quoted in Peter N. Carroll, *The Odyssey of the Abraham Lincoln Brigade: Americans in the Spanish Civil War* (Stanford, CA: Stanford University Press, 1994), 73.
66. John A. Kneip, "Evaluation of Milton Wolff" [on Form 2725, n.d., circa 1945], Wolff Personnel File, OSS Records, NARA II.
67. The United States and Spain would sign an agreement in 1953 that made them allies against the Soviets. Franco only released his grip on power when he died in 1975.
68. Carroll, *The Odyssey of the Abraham Lincoln Brigade*, 279–90, is an excellent description of Wolff's activism after the war.
69. EH to Milton Wolff, January 1941 [n.d.], reprinted in Baker, *Hemingway*, 357.
70. EH to Milton Wolff, January 23, 1941, in Box 1, Milton Wolff Papers, Tamiment Library, New York University.
71. Peter Viertel, *Dangerous Friends: At Large with Huston and Hemingway in the 1950s* (New York: Doubleday, 1992), 11. Viertel claimed to have heard the story from Hemingway.
72. EH to Milton Wolff, July 26, 1946. Copy of letter supplied by private collector. Especially after the war, the word "brigade" replaced the original word "battalion" in the unit designation.
73. Hemingway mentioned the call in his letter to Wolff. Ibid. Wolff also mentioned it in a letter to Carlos Baker. MW to Carlos Baker, March 9, 1964, in Box 13, Carlos Baker Papers, PUL.
74. EH to Milton Wolff, July 26, 1946.
75. Irving Fajans, Tape Recording of Hemingway, February 1947, in folder for 1947, Box 20, Carlos Baker Papers, PUL. See also Wolff's description of the transaction in Milton Wolff, "We Met in Spain," *American Dialogue* 1, no. 2 (October–November 1964): 8–9.
76. Milton Wolff to EH, May 27, 1947, in "Other Material," Museo Ernest Hemingway, Ernest Hemingway Collection, JFK Library.
77. Chamberlin, *The Hemingway Log*, 264–65, places Hemingway elsewhere in September 1947.

CHAPTER 12: THE COLD WAR: NO MORE BRAVE WORDS

1. Quoted in Kessler, *Clever Girl*, 159.
2. C. P. Trussell, "Woman Links Spies to U.S. War Offices and the White House," *New York Times*, July 31, 1948.
3. Golos and Bentley's relationship started in 1938. She remembered starting her work as an intermediary in July 1941.
4. U.S. House of Representatives, *Hearings before the Committee on*

Un-American Activities (Second Session, 1948) (Washington, DC: Superintendent of Documents, 1948), sec. 526. See also Kessler, *Clever Girl*, 63–64.

5. Elizabeth Bentley, *Out of Bondage* (New York: Devin-Adair, 1951), 65. The book was serialized in *McCall's* magazine in May, June, and July 1951.
6. EH to CTL, July 28, 1948, in Box 1, Lanham-Hemingway Papers, PUL. He later wrote that he spoke to a senior Soviet official in Spain who was willing to show him "how everything was run" in order to enable him to report accurately. EH to Bernard Berenson, October 14, 1952, in Baker, ed., *Selected Letters*, 789.
7. EH to CTL, November 27, 1948, in Box 1, Lanham-Hemingway Papers, PUL.
8. EH to CTL, January 8, 1951, in Box 1, Lanham-Hemingway Papers, PUL.
9. Craig, *Treasonable Doubt*, 276.
10. Ben Steil, "Red White: Why a Founding Father of Postwar Capitalism Spied for the Soviets," *Foreign Affairs*, March–April 2013, provides an excellent summary of the White case, more compelling to me in most ways than Craig's *Treasonable Doubt*. The book based on Vassiliev's NKVD files comes to the same conclusion as Steil. See Haynes et al., *Spies*, 258–62, concluding that the "evidence is overwhelming. . . . White assisted Soviet military intelligence in the 1930s and the KGB from 1943 to 1945 and perjured himself in his congressional testimony."
11. EH to CTL, November 24, 1948, in Box 1, Lanham-Hemingway Papers, PUL.
12. EH to CTL, November 26, 1948, in Box 1, Lanham-Hemingway Papers, PUL.
13. EH to CTL, December 22, 1948, in Box 1, Lanham-Hemingway Papers, PUL.
14. "M'Carthy's Charge Is Denied by Duran," *New York Times*, March 15, 1950. This time there was some truth in McCarthy's allegations. Durán was never rabid about anything, but he had been a fellow traveler and he had served, if only briefly, as head of Republican military intelligence, which was largely under the control of the NKVD. It probably did not help that his wife's brother-in-law was the Soviet spy Michael Straight.
15. Ibid. The same story included Braden's defense of Durán.
16. Quoted in Kessler, *Clever Girl*, 211.
17. Elizabeth Bentley, "I Joined the Underground with the Man I

Loved," *McCall's*, June 1951; Elizabeth Bentley, "How I Was Used by the Red Spy Ring," *McCall's*, July 1951; and Elizabeth Bentley, "I Met Tragedy and Disillusion," *McCall's*, August 1951. As noted above, her memoirs were published in book form in the same year. Bentley, *Out of Bondage*.

18. See, for instance, Haynes et al., *Spies*, 543.
19. "Operational Letter," July 3, 1950, in Vassiliev, *Black Notebook*, 95.
20. Ibid. Years later, in the NKVD's secret archive, the researcher Vassiliev saw a related "list of agents with whom the Wash. station was asked to renew contact in '48–'50 . . . [that] includes 'Argo,'" identified as a "well-known journalist, recruited in 1941" who had "not given valuable information." Vassiliev, *Black Notebook*, 81 and 83.
21. EH to CTL, January 8, 1951, in Box 1, Lanham-Hemingway Papers, PUL; Hotchner, *Papa Hemingway*, 69.
22. EH to CTL, January 5, 1949, in Box 1, Lanham-Hemingway Papers, PUL.
23. Milton Wolff to EH, August 8, 1950, in Incoming Correspondence, Ernest Hemingway Collection, JFK Library. U.S. policy was moving toward collaboration with Franco against the Soviets. For Wolff's reaction to that policy, see, for example, Carroll, *The Odyssey of the Abraham Lincoln Brigade*, 293; Peter N. Carroll and James D. Fernandez, *Facing Fascism: New York and the Spanish Civil War* (New York: NYU Press, 2007), 180–81.
24. EH to Milton Wolff, May 7, 1950, in Milton Wolff Papers, Tamiment Library, NYU. The accident was memorable enough for Hemingway to also describe it to Hotchner. Hotchner, *Papa Hemingway*, 68.
25. EH to Wolff, May 7, 1950. An interesting example of Hemingway's support for individual veterans was that of Evan Shipman, who wrote Hemingway in 1950 to describe his "very lonely" political position on account of his service in Spain. When he fell ill later in the year, Hemingway cared for him in Cuba. See Sean O'Rourke, *Grace Under Pressure: The Life of Evan Shipman* (Boston: Harvardwood, 2010), ch. 11.
26. Milton Wolff, "We Met in Spain," *American Dialog* 1, no. 2 (October–November 1964).
27. Milton Wolff to EH, August 8, 1950.
28. Wolff, "We Met in Spain."
29. EH to Joseph McCarthy, May 8, 1950, in Baker, ed., *Selected Letters*, 693. This would not have been the only angry letter that Hemingway drafted but probably did not send in 1950. See the discussion in Chamberlin, *The Hemingway Log*, 279.
30. Baker, ed., *Selected Letters*, 693.

31. EH to Charles Scribner, Jr., June 29, 1948, in Baker, ed., *Selected Letters*, 641.
32. EH to A. E. Hotchner, March 25, 1951, in Albert J. DeFazio III, ed., *"Dear Papa, Dear Hotch": The Correspondence of Ernest Hemingway and A. E. Hotchner* (Columbia: University of Missouri Press, 2005), 119. The scholar Richard K. Sanderson has made a similar argument about the introduction to *Men at War,* analyzing postwar revisions made by Hemingway to bring it in line with changes in the political climate. "Cold War Revisions of Hemingway's *Men at War,*" *Hemingway Review* 20, no. 1 (Fall 2000): 29–60.
33. See, for example, Alfred Rice to Vojtech Strnad, August 28, 1957, in Box 4, Hemingway Legal Files, New York Public Library.
34. Viertel, *Dangerous Friends*, 252.
35. Koestler's initiative occurred in 1950. Michael Scammell, *Koestler* (New York: Random House, 2009), 372, 639n.
36. EH, *Across the River and Into the Trees* (New York: Scribner, 1950), 70.
37. The *Saturday Review* and Kazin reviews are quoted in Hendrickson, *Hemingway's Boat*, 331–35.
38. "Books: On the Ropes," *Time*, September 11, 1950.
39. Quoted in Hendrickson, *Hemingway's Boat*, 334–35. Hendrickson was probably the first to publish the draft of Hemingway's letter. See also Chamberlin, *The Hemingway Log*, 279.
40. Washington to Center, October 1, 1950, in Vassiliev, *Black Notebook*, 96. The message contains the intriguing note that Hemingway still maintained "friendly relations" with Joe North, now of the *Daily Worker,* the journalist who had urged Hemingway to write about the hurricane of 1935 for *New Masses* and may have introduced Hemingway to Golos.
41. Vassiliev, *Black Notebook*, 81, refers to a list dated December 23, 1949, that describes Hemingway as the well-known agent recruited in 1941 who did not give valuable information. He was one of the agents with whom "ties" had not been "renewed" as of that date. A similar notation appears on page 83 of the same source.

CHAPTER 13: NO ROOM TO MANEUVER: THE MATURE ANTIFASCIST IN CUBA AND KETCHUM

1. MWH, *How It Was*, 569. Her memoirs are the primary source for this paragraph.
2. Fuentes, *Hemingway in Cuba*, 273. It is also possible that the weapons were left over from some other time, perhaps even World War II, and that he had kept them because he was a pack rat, or because he

wanted to keep his options open. However, he probably purged his wartime armory after the contretemps over his alleged support for the expedition against Trujillo in 1947.

3. MWH, *How It Was*, 569.
4. Ibid. Gregorio told Fuentes that he had been a longtime Castro supporter. Fuentes, *Hemingway in Cuba*, 273.
5. Quoted in Larry Grimes and Bickford Sylvester, eds., *Hemingway, Cuba, and the Cuban Works* (Kent, OH: The Kent State University Press, 2014), 29.
6. See, for example, Clancy Sigal, *Hemingway Lives! (Why Reading Ernest Hemingway Matters Today)* (New York and London: OR Books, 2013), ch. 13.
7. Anders Österling, Award Ceremony Speech for Literature.
8. "2013 Materials" from Museo Ernest Hemingway, Ernest Hemingway Collection, JFK Library. The Nobel Prize Committee is Swedish and Norwegian.
9. EH, "Nobel Prize Acceptance Speech," reprinted in Matthew J. Bruccoli, ed., *Conversations with Ernest Hemingway* (Jackson, MS, and London: University Press of Mississippi, 1986), 196.
10. Quoted in Chamberlin, *The Hemingway Log*, 293.
11. See, for example, Reynolds, *Hemingway: The Final Years*, esp. 280.
12. EH to CTL, October 24, 1947, in Box 1, Lanham-Hemingway Papers, PUL. Although he claimed that he had only given advice to the plotters, he worried enough about possible repercussions to flee to Miami for a few days until it was clear that the Cuban government did not want to question him about his role. Chamberlin, *The Hemingway Log*, 266. Interviews in Cuba with Hemingway intimates by Yuri Paporov for *Hemingway en Cuba* (Mexico City and Madrid: Siglo Veintiuno Editores, 1993), 87–105, suggest that Hemingway's role went further than simply giving advice and recommendations. Fuentes, *Hemingway in Cuba*, 253–54, quotes a statement by Herrera that Hemingway "gave some money for the . . . thing."
13. Anthony DePalma, *The Man Who Invented Fidel: Castro, Cuba, and Herbert L. Matthews of the New York Times* (New York: PublicAffairs, 2006); Herbert L. Matthews, *The Cuban Story* (New York: George Braziller, 1961).
14. See Chapter 3.
15. Quoted in DePalma, *The Man Who Invented Fidel*, 60.
16. Quoted in Bruccoli, ed., *Hemingway and the Mechanism of Fame*, 60.
17. HLM to Carlos Baker, November 15, 1961, in Box 22, Carlos Baker

Papers, PUL. See also DePalma, *The Man Who Invented Fidel*, 65; Chamberlin, *The Hemingway Log*, 287; Matthews, *The Cuban Story*, 299.

18. Matthews, *The Cuban Story*, 15–45, describes Matthews's adventure, as does DePalma, *The Man Who Invented Fidel*, 79–92. The quotations are at pages 80 and 81, and in one of the illustrations of Matthews's handwritten notes.
19. De Palma, *The Man Who Invented Fidel*, 80; Nancie Matthews, "Journey to Sierra Maestra: Wife's Version," *Times Talk* 10, no. 7 (March 1957).
20. Matthews, *The Cuban Story*, 44. See also DePalma, *The Man Who Invented Fidel*, 91.
21. Quoted in Hunter S. Thompson, "What Lured Hemingway to Ketchum?" *National Observer*, May 25, 1964.
22. Fuentes, *Hemingway in Cuba*, 272. James D. Brasch, "Hemingway's Doctor: José Luis Herrera Sotolongo Remembers Ernest Hemingway," *Journal of Modern Literature* 13, no. 2 (July 1986): 185–210, offers a portrait of Herrera.
23. Paporov, *Hemingway en Cuba*, 390–91; Fuentes, *Hemingway in Cuba,* 270. Both Paporov and the Cuban scholar Norberto Fuentes use direct quotations from Herrera. The books have very similar titles, and overlap somewhat, but are not identical in content.
24. Paporov, *Hemingway en Cuba*, 391.
25. Matthews, *The Cuban Story*, 299.
26. Fuentes, *Hemingway in Cuba*, 272, quotes Herrera's testimony.
27. Quoted in Kenneth Tynan, *Right & Left* (London: Longmans, 1967), 336. Tynan interviewed Castro in 1959. The Cuban leader claimed to have read *For Whom the Bell Tolls* at least four times. Fidel Castro and Ignacio Ramonet, *Fidel Castro: My Life: A Spoken Autobiography* (New York: Scribner, 2008), 209.
28. DePalma, *The Man Who Invented Fidel*, 99; Herbert L. Matthews, "Castro Is Still Alive and Still Fighting in the Mountains," *New York Times*, February 24, 1957.
29. DePalma, *The Man Who Invented Fidel,* 109.
30. Ibid., 109.
31. Milton Wolff to Herbert L. Mathews, April 4, 1957, in Box 1, Matthews Papers, RBML, Columbia University. Four days later, Matthews replied: "I understand how you feel about doing something before becoming completely senile because that was exactly the way I felt and still feel. . . ." Matthews to Wolff, April 10, 1957, Box 1, Matthews Papers.

32. Based on contemporary information from Hemingway himself, the best source for this story appears to be "Hemingway Dog Slain," *New York Times*, August 22, 1957.
33. René Villarreal and Raúl Villarreal, *Hemingway's Cuban Son: Reflections on the Writer by His Longtime Majordomo* (Kent, OH: Kent State University Press, 2009), 123.
34. "Hemingway Dog Slain." Yet another version of this story is MWH, *How It Was*, 566, which mentions "someone shooting our dog, Machakos, in the night." Machakos is a place-name in Kenya, the home of Hemingway's friend, the big-game hunter Philip Percival.
35. Fuentes, *Hemingway in Cuba*, 62.
36. Ibid., 62.
37. EH to CTL, September 18, 1958, in Box 1, Lanham-Hemingway Papers, PUL.
38. EH to Layhmond Robinson, August 23, 1958, in Outgoing Correspondence, Ernest Hemingway Collection, JFK Library. This is a typewritten draft edited in Hemingway's handwriting. He also wrote to Hotchner claiming that Rice had done "exactly what I told him not to do" and attributed "that shit" to his client. EH to A. E. Hotchner, August 26, 1958, in DeFazio, ed., *Dear Papa, Dear Hotch*, 232.
39. Jeffrey Meyers, "The Hemingways: An American Tragedy," *Virginia Quarterly Review*, Spring 1999, 273. Meyers discusses Hemingway's up-and-down relationship with Rice.
40. "Hemingway Would Bar Reprints," *Washington Post and Times Herald*, August 6, 1958.
41. EH to A. E. Hotchner, March 25, 1951, in DeFazio, ed., *Dear Papa, Dear Hotch*, 119.
42. The description of Rice is in EH to CTL, September 18, 1958, in Lanham-Hemingway Papers, PUL. The conversation with the reporter is in Layhmond Robinson, "Hemingway Says He Will Drop Suit, Asserts That Political Fear Did Not Spur Attempt to Bar Reprint of Stories," *New York Times*, August 7, 1958. Rice believed that *Esquire* did in fact have the right to reprint the stories. See Alfred Rice to EH, July 30, 1958, in Incoming Correspondence, Ernest Hemingway Collection, JFK Library. For that reason, he apparently decided to rely on the political argument, which he had heard from Hemingway over the phone. See Meyers, *Hemingway*, 516, for a slightly different version of this story. Hemingway's claim that Rice blindsided him is partly misleading because Rice sent him a terse cable after filing the court papers. Rice added that the hearing would take place

five days later. Alfred Rice to EH, August 1, 1958, in Incoming Correspondence, Ernest Hemingway Collection, JFK Library.

43. Robinson, "Hemingway Says He Will Drop Suit."
44. EH to Layhmond Robinson, August 23, 1958.
45. "The Old Man and the Fee," *Wall Street Journal*, August 8, 1958, and mentioned in Arnold Gingrich, "Scott, Ernest, and Whoever," *Esquire*, December 1966, 324. Gingrich and Hemingway had been friends for years, but Gingrich never heard from Hemingway again after this contretemps. See also "Hemingway's Suit," *Washington Star*, August 11, 1958: the stories reflected "his sentiments of that period [b]ut now, even though he still adheres to that sentiment, he apparently wishes he had written them in a different way," one "designed to make sure that they will never return to haunt him."
46. MWH, *How It Was*, 568.
47. EH to Mr. and Mrs. William D. Horne, July 1, 1958, in Baker, ed., *Selected Letters*, 884. Matthews condemned the practice in his reporting. See Herbert L. Matthews, "Castro's Kidnapping Shows War Is Still On; But Methods He Uses Have Cost Him Support of Friends in US," *New York Times*, July 6, 1958.
48. MWH, *How It Was*, 569, 571.
49. This is my interpretation based on the circumstances, and also that of scholars such as Michael Reynolds. See, for example, Reynolds, *Hemingway: The Final Years*, 312, and Chamberlin, *The Hemingway Log*, 307.
50. MWH, *How It Was*, 569.
51. Ibid., 572–73.
52. EH to Patrick Hemingway, November 24, 1958, in Baker, ed., *Selected Letters*, 888. The "both sides atrocious" remark probably reflected his feeling about the political kidnappings by Castro's men.
53. Jules Dubois, *Fidel Castro: Rebel, Liberator, or Dictator* (New York: Bobbs-Merrill, 1959), 363.
54. DePalma, *The Man Who Invented Fidel*, 141–43, is the vivid description of these events upon which I have relied.
55. MWH, *How It Was*, 579. He would use many of the same words in a letter in Lanham in 1960. See EH to CTL, January 12, 1960, in Baker, ed., *Selected Letters*, 899.
56. MWH, *How It Was*, 579. It is not clear whether the *Times* used the quote. A diligent search for the quote came up empty-handed.
57. EH to Gianfranco Ivancich, January 7, 1959, in Baker, ed., *Selected Letters*, 890. This was a play on the Latin "sic transit gloria mundi"—

"thus passes the glory of the world." One translation of "hijo de puta" is "son of a bitch."

58. EH to L. H. Brague, Jr., January 24, 1959, in Baker, ed., *Selected Letters*, 891–92. To similar effect, see John Crosby, "Peppery Radio Station Puts Zip into News," *Washington Post and Times Herald*, February 9, 1959. Crosby recounted that, in early February, he was "sitting home minding my own business and listening to New York's peppy independent [radio station], WNEW, when the announcer broke in with a recorded interview with Ernest Hemingway, the writer and occasional revolutionist. Hemingway was asked what he thought about the revolution in Cuba, . . . and he said he was very happy about it. . . ."

59. EH to Gianfranco Ivancich, February 2, 1959, in Outgoing Correspondence, Ernest Hemingway Collection, JFK Library.

60. Carlos Franqui, *Family Portrait with Fidel* (New York: Vintage, 1985), 17.

61. R. Hart Philips, "Cuban Show Trial of Batista Aides Opens in Stadium," *New York Times*, January 23, 1959.

62. See, for example, "Havana-Trials Make Roman Holiday," February 2, 1959 (Film ID 1567.21), from the archives of British Pathé (accessed on youtube.com, July, 2015 and September, 2016).

63. Fred Brack, "Emmett Watson Reminisces," *Seattle Post-Intelligencer*, October 21, 1981; Emmett Watson, *My Life in Print* (Seattle: Lesser Seattle, 1993), 66–68.

64. Watson, *My Life in Print*, 68–69. Watson describes the circumstances in some detail: how he did not take notes during the conversation but typed them out immediately as soon as it was over, how he offered to show the notes to Hemingway (who declined to review them), and how he heard from a mutual friend that Hemingway liked the column and "was relieved" that Watson had quoted him accurately.

65. Ibid., 70.

66. Emmett Watson, "Hemingway on Cuba and Castro," *Seattle Post-Intelligencer*, March 9, 1959, reproduced in Watson, *My Life in Print*, 69–74. The wire services picked up the story and it appeared in newspapers all over the world, sometimes in an abbreviated version. See, for example, Emmett Watson, "Hemingway Defends Cuban Trials," *Milwaukee Sentinel*, March 11, 1959. For an earlier reflection of Hemingway's views on revolutionary justice (which became only slightly more conservative over time), see EH to "Miss Craipeau," February 13, 1947, in Outgoing Correspondence, Ernest Hemingway Collection, JFK Library, discussed in Chapter 7.

67. Watson, *My Life in Print*, 69.
68. EH to William Seward, March 31, 1959, in Box 12, Carlos Baker Papers, PUL.
69. EH to Jack Hemingway, March 30, 1959, in Box 22, Carlos Baker Papers, PUL. The letter is in Mary's handwriting.
70. Tynan, *Right & Left*, 62.
71. This paragraph is based on the testimony of Robert Herrera, Dr. Herrera's son, who worked at the Finca in various capacities. He picked the Hemingways up at the airport upon their return, and discussed the revolution with Hemingway. Paporov, *Hemingway en Cuba*, 396–97.
72. Kenneth Tynan to Bill and Annie Davis, April 30, 1959, in Kathleen Tynan, ed., *Kenneth Tynan Letters* (New York: Random House, 1994), 232–33. He wrote this letter after his return from Cuba, and included a comment about Hemingway's praise for Castro. See also Kenneth Tynan, "A Visit to Havana," *Holiday* 27, no. 2 (February 1960): 50–58.
73. Tynan, *Right & Left*, 334. In the end, the execution was rained out and no one attended. A secondhand, somewhat garbled version of this story appears in Nelson W. Aldrich, ed., *George, Being George* (New York: Random House, 2008), 145–46.
74. Kenneth Tynan to Terence Kilmartin, April 11, 1959, in Tynan, *Letters*, 231–32. The circumstances are described in Tynan, *Right & Left*, 335–36.
75. Paporov, *Hemingway en Cuba*, 397.
76. Vázquez Candela was one of the editors of the newspaper *Revolución*. Both his and Herrera's testimony were recorded and printed by Paporov, *Hemingway en Cuba*, 398–99. See also Fuentes, *Hemingway in Cuba*, 275. He cites an article about the meeting: Euclides Vázquez-Candela, "Hemingway Worried About Cuba and Fidel," *Cuban Gazette* 2, no. 13 (February 13, 1963), which I have not been able to find.
77. Paporov, *Hemingway en Cuba*, 398.
78. Ibid., 399. Reynolds, *Hemingway: The Final Years*, 322–23, is an excellent description of the same meeting. Reynolds points out that the notes Hemingway prepared for this meeting are among his papers at the JFK archive.
79. Franqui, *Family Portrait with Fidel*, 31–32, is a description of these events by an insider who reports that Castro listened to the advice that he bought from an American public relations firm.

80. Franqui appears to have coined the word "fidelenglish." Ibid., 31. The "clumsy but clear" phrase is Tynan's. Tynan, *Right & Left*, 336. See also R. Hart Phillips, *The Cuban Dilemma* (New York: Ivan Obolensky, 1962), 72.
81. Franqui, *Family Portrait with Fidel*, 32.
82. My source for this paragraph is Baker, *Hemingway*, 547–48.
83. Davis had also been Hemingway's host in 1942 in Mexico, where he had gone to attend some bullfights and visit Gustav Regler.
84. MWH, *How It Was*, 598.
85. "Ernest Hemingway Again in Cuba Arrives," *Revolución*, November 5, 1959 (reproduced in Fuentes, *Hemingway in Cuba*, 274). See also "Hemingway Back in Cuba," *New York Times*, November 6, 1959: "Mr. Hemingway told newsmen he had every sympathy with Prime Minister Fidel Castro's regime." When asked to elaborate on his comments a few days later, Hemingway had nothing to say. "Hemingways Plan Sun Valley Visit," *Washington Evening Star*, November 10, 1959.
86. Quoted in Embassy Havana to Department of State Washington, November 6, 1959, which found its way into Hemingway's FBI file and is reproduced in Fensch, *Behind Islands in the Stream*, 100–101.
87. Ibid. In a letter to Buck Lanham he would claim that the "Yanqui thing" was taken out of context. "To say you are not a Yanqui Imperialist but an old San Francisco de Paula boy" was not the same as renouncing his American citizenship." EH to CTL, January 12, 1960, in Baker, ed., *Selected Letters*, 899. He also cared enough about his reputation in the United States to send a "corrective" message to the gossip columnist Leonard Lyons. Ibid.
88. Hemingway wrote Lanham that they would spend the hurricane months in Idaho, and the rest of the time in Cuba. Ibid.
89. Herbert L. Matthews, *Castro: A Political Biography* (London: Penguin 69), 156. Matthews noted that he recorded this impression in a memo that he wrote after his March 1960 trip. Earlier, Mary had written Matthews, and speaking for herself and Hemingway, praised his "sound analysis" and "defense of the revolution." MH to Herbert L. Matthews, January 27, 1960, in Matthews Papers, RBML, Columbia University.
90. EH to CTL, January 12, 1960, in Baker, ed., *Selected Letters*, 899. Matthews would develop a similar analysis about what he too called "the long view" in a letter to Hemingway in 1961. Herbert L. Matthews to EH, January 2, 1961, in Matthews Papers, RBML, Columbia University. Joseph Alsop, "Hemingway's Guest at a Cockfight,"

Washington Post and Times Herald, March 9, 1960, describes the atmosphere in Havana during his visit, as does Ruby Phillips, the *Times* correspondent who lived in Havana for decades. See Phillips, *The Cuban Dilemma*, ch. 14.

91. EH to CTL, January 12, 1960.
92. Valerie Hemingway, *Running with the Bulls: My Years with the Hemingways* (New York: Ballantine, 2005), 116, is the primary source for this meeting. See also Mary Hemingway to CTL, March 16, 1960, in Box 1, Lanham-Hemingway Papers, PUL. Mary described Matthews's visit and said that the local scene continued to be "fascinating" as the regime moved further and further out on a political and economic limb. Like Hemingway she stressed this was not just a change of the palace guard but a real revolution, one supported by 75 percent of the population. The meeting may have taken place on March 8, the date Matthews proposed. Herbert L. Matthews to MWH, February 1, 1960, in Box 2, Matthews Papers, RBML, Columbia University.
93. After their talk, Matthews made a note that he and Hemingway continued to agree about Cuban politics. Quoted in Fuentes, *Hemingway in Cuba*, 428. See also Herbert L. Matthews to Carlos Baker, November 15, 1961, in Box 22, Carlos Baker Papers, PUL.
94. Castro said that he was able to talk to Hemingway "twice, quite briefly" during "the first year of the Revolution." Castro and Ramonet, *Fidel Castro: My Life*, 592.
95. Valerie Hemingway, *Running with the Bulls*, 119.
96. Castro and Ramonet, *Fidel Castro: My Life*, 1.
97. Paporov, *Hemingway en Cuba*, 402.
98. Ibid., 402.
99. Hotchner, *Papa Hemingway*, 235.
100. EH to Charles Scribner, Jr., July 6, 1960, in Baker, ed., *Selected Letters*, 906. In his memoirs, Bonsal approvingly quoted Hemingway's argument against abolishing the quota. Philip W. Bonsal, *Cuba, Castro, and the United States* (Pittsburgh: University of Pittsburgh Press, 1971), 151.
101. EH to L. H. Brague, Jr., January 24, 1959, in Baker, ed., *Selected Letters*, 891–92. Matthews also found Bonsal approachable even when they did not agree. See Herbert L. Matthews to Nancie Matthews, July 9, 1959, in Box 2, Matthews Papers, RBML, Columbia University.
102. Valerie Hemingway, *Running with the Bulls*, 106–7, is the principal source for this meeting and the one that followed a week later. She

places these conversations with Bonsal in April, and writes that they occurred just before he was recalled. However, Bonsal's final recall was in October 1960, by which time Hemingway was out of the country. Bonsal's memoirs state that the embassy started advising American citizens to leave Cuba in July, which may be a more likely month for this meeting. Bonsal, *Cuba, Castro, and the United States*, 167. See also Villarreal and Villarreal, *Hemingway's Cuban Son*, 133, which states that U.S. diplomats were pressuring Hemingway to leave Cuba, and implies that the meetings occurred during the summer, as does Mary Hemingway, who discusses this issue after commenting on the weather in June. MWH, *How It Was*, 613.

103. Embassy Havana to Department of State Washington, November 6, 1959, which found its way into Hemingway's FBI file and is reproduced in Fensch, *Behind Islands in the Stream*, 100–101.
104. Valerie Hemingway, *Running with the Bulls*, 106.
105. Ibid., 107.
106. Ibid.
107. See, for example, Bonsal, *Cuba, Castro, and the United States*, 51: "During my first weeks in Havana I endeavored through as many channels as possible to convey goodwill and a readiness to enter into serious negotiations on any matters the regime might wish to raise." The messages in Box 1, Philip W. Bonsal Papers, LoC, also track his early attempts to reach out to Castro.
108. This favorable mention of Hemingway by Castro appeared in Fidel Castro, "Statements," *Revolución*, July 9, 1960 (reproduced in Fuentes, *Hemingway in Cuba*, 427). Hemingway kept the newspaper clipping among his papers at the Finca, and underlined that particular line.
109. The *New York Times* reported that Castro specifically mentioned Hemingway. R. Hart Phillips, "Havana Rejects Seizure Protest," *New York Times*, July 9, 1960.
110. Paporov, *Hemingway en Cuba*, 399, claims that Castro quoted from Hemingway's interview with Emmett Watson, apparently on this or another occasion in July. There are no footnotes in Paporov's book, and I have been unable to confirm his claim even after reading through the mind-numbing transcripts of Castro's speeches for that month.
111. Hotchner, *Papa Hemingway*, 243.
112. Ibid., 242.
113. It would be published both as a magazine article in 1960 and as

a book, Ernest Hemingway, *The Dangerous Summer* (New York: Scribner, 1984).

114. MWH, *How It Was,* 614.

115. Paporov, *Hemingway en Cuba,* 434, quotes his friend Mario Menocal, who accompanied Hemingway to the terminal. A search of the American press for July 1960 suggests that he succeeded in leaving Cuba without attracting attention. In September 1960, Hemingway wrote Matthews to assure him that "the reports saying he [Hemingway] had 'gone sour' on Fidel and the Cuban Revolution were false." Matthews, *The Cuban Story,* 299. The letter that Matthews referred to is probably EH to Herbert L. Matthews, September 13, 1960, in Box 2, Matthews Papers, RBML, Columbia University. In that letter Hemingway told Matthews that he should not listen to secondhand reports on his views, and that he, Hemingway, told the editor of the *Saturday Review* that Matthews was the man best qualified to write about Cuba.

116. MWH, *How It Was,* 614.

117. Baker, *Hemingway,* 554.

118. Ibid.

119. Meyers, *Hemingway,* 546–50, is a good discussion of Hemingway's time at Mayo. A. E. Hotchner, *Hemingway in Love: His Own Story* (New York: St. Martin's Press, 2015), 157–58, reflects Hemingway's attitude to his doctors. Jeffrey Meyers, "The Hemingways: An American Tragedy," *Virginia Quarterly Review,* Spring 1999, 267–79, reports his impression that Mary authorized the treatments and that Hemingway's doctor did not fully inform her about the procedure. This is consistent with Gregory Hemingway's report of his conversation with the Mayo doctor (probably Dr. Rome), who told him almost nothing. Gregory Hemingway, *Papa,* 115–16.

120. Hotchner, *Papa Hemingway,* 280.

121. For this paragraph I have relied on ibid., 264–99; Baker, *Hemingway,* 555–64; and Reynolds, *Hemingway: The Final Years,* 317–59.

122. Hotchner, *Hemingway in Love,* 162.

123. MWH, "Christmas 1960 Note to Self," as quoted in Reynolds, *Hemingway: The Final Years,* 351.

124. SAC, Minneapolis to Director, FBI, January 13, 1961, in vault.fbi.gov/ernest-miller-hemingway (accessed August 2015). Scholars have argued that the FBI tracked Hemingway to the Mayo Clinic, and that was one of the high points of their "unsuccessful attempts to control, mock, and vilify him." Meyers, *Hemingway,* 109. As I note elsewhere, my reading of the matter is different. If the FBI had been

tracking Hemingway, his file would have been much larger than 124 pages—filled with detailed surveillance reports from the field, and guidance from the Seat of Government, as Hoover liked to call Washington.

125. SAC, Minneapolis to Director, FBI, January 13, 1961.
126. EH to CTL, January 16, 1961, in Box 1, Lanham-Hemingway Papers, PUL.
127. Herbert L. Matthews to EH, January 2, 1961, in Box 2, Matthews Papers, RBML, Columbia University.
128. EH to CTL, January 16, 1961, in Box 1, Lanham-Hemingway Papers, PUL.
129. Ibid. I can only speculate that this is a reference to the courtesy call that Soviet foreign minister Anastas Mikoyan paid on Hemingway at the Finca in February 1960, when he offered to pay, over a period of ten years, the royalties that the Soviet Union owed to Hemingway. MWH to Clara Spiegel, February 29, 1960, in Box 12, Carlos Baker Papers, PUL; MWH to Alfred Rice, November 19, 1961, in Box 6, Hemingway Legal Files, New York Public Library. Other letters reflected his troubled mood about Cuba. On January 16, he commented to his son Patrick that events in Cuba were "much more complicated than what you read," and on the next day he wrote his fishing friend Thomas Shevlin that, while the Finca had not been touched, "nothing [was] too clear about Cuba." EH to Patrick Hemingway, January 16, 1961, in Baker, ed., *Selected Letters*, 911–12; EH to Thomas Shevlin, January 17, 1961, in Box 12, Carlos Baker Papers, PUL.
130. Herbert L. Matthews to EH, February 20, 1961, in Box 2, Matthews Papers, RBML, Columbia University.
131. Quoted in Jim Rasenberger, *The Brilliant Disaster* (New York: Scribner, 2011), 252, an up-to-date source on the invasion and the circumstances surrounding it.
132. "Communique by Castro," April 21, 1961, *New York Times*.
133. Rasenberger, *Brilliant Disaster*, 313.
134. MWH, *How It Was*, 631. She would later wonder where the planners could have gotten the information that persuaded them to believe the operation could ever succeed. Was it from "the bottom of the dozenth double rum?" MWH to CTL, October 20, 1961, in Box 1, Charles T. Lanham Papers, Firestone Library, PUL.
135. CTL to EH, May 9, 1961, in Incoming Correspondence, Ernest Hemingway Collection, JFK Library.
136. MWH, *How It Was*, 631. Reynolds, *Hemingway: The Final Years*, 354,

makes the connection between the Bay of Pigs and Hemingway's state of mind. Reynolds credits fellow Hemingway scholar Susan Beegel with first pointing this out. My chronology is slightly different from his. I focus on the dates of the ground combat, the part of the operation that generated the most publicity.

137. Described in Reynolds, *Hemingway: The Final Years,* 354. They would be published after his death as *A Moveable Feast.*
138. Described in MWH, *How It Was,* 630.
139. Ibid., 633.
140. Villarreal and Villarreal, *Hemingway's Cuban Son,* 134. Villarreal received the letter in late June 1961 and committed it to memory. The original is lost.
141. MWH, *How It Was,* 635, and Baker, *Hemingway,* 563, are the primary sources for the events of that day.
142. According to Lanham, Mary told him how Hemingway had reread the general's most recent letter on his last afternoon, information that somehow made it into a careful obituary writer's file. Jean R. Hailey, "Maj. Gen. Charles Lanham Dies," *Washington Post,* July 22, 1978. The same claim appears in Frances S. Leighton, "Letters from Hemingway; Unadulterated, Uninhibited—and Unpublishable," *American Weekly,* May 12, 1963. There are no footnotes in either source, but the claim is plausible. In the summer of 1961, Mary and Lanham talked and wrote extensively about Lanham's letters to Ernest. See, for example, CTL to MH, November 21, 1961, in Box 1, Charles T. Lanham Papers, Firestone Library, PUL.
143. Carbon copies of Lanham's last letters to Hemingway, dated June 5 and June 28, 1961, are similar in content. The first was mailed to Rochester, the second to Sun Valley. Box 3, Charles T. Lanham Papers, Firestone Library, PUL.
144. MWH, *How It Was,* 635–36.

EPILOGUE: CALCULATING THE HIDDEN COSTS

1. See, for example, Meyers, *Hemingway,* 565–66.
2. Watson, *My Life in Print,* 75.
3. Reprinted in ibid., 76–77.
4. For further insights on Hemingway's relationships with Mary and his treatment at Mayo, see Meyers, "The Hemingways: An American Tragedy," 267–79. Or, among other interesting discussions, Gregory Hemingway, *Papa,* esp. pp. 114–19, and Hotchner, *Papa Hemingway,* esp. 277–303.

5. A. E. Hotchner, "Hemingway, Hounded by the Feds," *New York Times Magazine*, July 11, 2011.
6. Ibid.
7. Ibid.
8. vault.fbi.gov/ernest-miller-hemingway (accessed August 2015). This paragraph recaps my discussion of the file in Chapter 11.
9. Since Hemingway had registered at the clinic under the name of George Saviers, he worried that the FBI might want to know what he was hiding. See discussion in Chapter 13.
10. Quentin Reynolds to J. Edgar Hoover, January 6, 1964, in vault.fbi.gov/ernest-miller-hemingway (accessed August 2015). The prominent journalist Reynolds was apparently on good terms with Hoover, and happy to write on Mary's behalf.
11. Ibid. Marginal comment in Hoover's handwriting on the Reynolds letter.
12. The phrase is from: Anders Österling, Award Ceremony Speech for Literature.
13. The title of a book by Koestler. Arthur Koestler et al., *The God That Failed: A Confession* (New York: Harper Brothers, 1949).

INDEX

P.S.

Insights, Interviews & More . . .

*

Meet Nicholas Reynolds

Becky Reynolds

NICHOLAS REYNOLDS has worked in the fields of modern military history and intelligence off and on for forty years, with some unusual detours. Freshly minted PhD from Oxford University in hand, he joined the United States Marine Corps in the 1970s, serving as an infantry officer and then as a historian. As a colonel in the reserves, he eventually became officer in charge of field history, deploying historians around the world to capture history as it was being made. When not on duty with the USMC, he served as a CIA officer at home and abroad, immersing himself in the very human business of espionage. Most recently, he was the historian for the CIA Museum, responsible for developing its strategic plan and helping to turn remarkable artifacts into compelling stories. He has taught as an adjunct professor for Johns Hopkins University and, with his wife, Becky, cares for rescue pugs.

A Message That Still Resonates: Hemingway in the Twenty-first Century

Even after I discovered his dalliance with the NKVD, it took me a while to figure out I wanted to write about Hemingway's political journey. I began by simply wanting to look into the breathtaking claim that Soviet spies had successfully recruited him for their work, and so went in search of sources to corroborate or explain this transaction. Anyone who has read this far will remember some of the milestones in my journey to find every bit of available evidence: how one archive visit led to the next, how I eventually had enough for a journal article, and ultimately how a book began to form, almost on its own. I revisit this journey to make the point that I was not responding to external events. I had no idea how timely the book would be.

"I had no idea how timely the book would be."

In March 2016, President Obama made a state visit to Havana, part of his initiative to normalize relations between Cuba and the United States. Mrs. Obama took the opportunity to make a side-trip to the Hemingway *finca*. Speechwriter and lifelong Hemingway fan Cody Keenan went along, and was thrilled to find the house more or less as he had imagined it, hunting trophies lining the walls, "photos and mementos of his escapades . . . scattered everywhere, and books—thousands and thousands of books" throughout.* The Obama visit contributed to a flurry of interest in the old farmstead, and its preservation by a Cuban-American consortium, one issue on which the two countries have been able to agree over the years. Reports from the *finca* showed how the Cubans have been preserving the Hemingway legacy ever since the day he left the island.

The living room at the *finca* as it looked when Hemingway left Cuba and at the time of the Obama visit more than half a century later. *Maurizio Giovanni Bersanelli Photo, Copyright 123RF.com.*

Roughly a year later, the spring of 2017 turned out to be the season for new books about Hemingway—not just the hardback version of my work, but also several others, including Mary Dearborn's *Ernest Hemingway*, a comprehensive biography, the first from a female ▶

* Cody Keenan, "Inside Finca Vigía, Hemingway's Home in Cuba," Medium, March 23, 2016 (accessed October 27, 2017).

perspective; Andrew Farah's *Hemingway's Brain*, a forensic psychiatrist's discourse on the many illnesses that dogged the writer, especially head trauma; and James McGrath Morris's *The Ambulance Drivers*, a close look at Hemingway's friendship with John Dos Passos. I have read, enjoyed, and admired them all, struck by the extent to which each of us has staked out his or her own ground, for the most part complementing rather than competing with one another. (Citing the book *Spies* and an early version of my work, only Dearborn treats Hemingway's relationship with the NKVD.)

This confluence is remarkable. Hemingway died in 1961. Thousands of books and articles about him are already on library shelves. So how can there still be so much fertile ground to till? More than once I've been asked why we are still transported by Hemingway and his work. My answer is that this is due not only to the richness of his writing, but also to the amazing variety and complexity of his life experiences. Just as there is a Hemingway creation that seems to speak to each of us so clearly that it might have been a private message, there is also something for almost everyone in his life story: the fisherman, the war-fighter, the cosmopolitan involved in the affairs of his day, the disciplined writer who began every day by writing for hours.

"There is also something for almost everyone in his life story."

The spring turned into a stormy summer. As it neared the Keys, Hurricane Irma seemed on track to damage, if not destroy, the nineteenth-century

Hemingway house at 907 Whitehead Street in Key West, like the unnamed hurricane of 1935. Both were Category 5, and both in the end spared Hemingway's house and grounds, along with the fifty or so six-toed cats now roaming the property, some of which are said to be descended from one of his cats. The earlier hurricane was more of a killing machine. The worst storm of the twentieth century to strike Florida, it killed hundreds of men and women in the Upper Keys, and changed Hemingway's life forever. He motored up in his cabin cruiser *Pilar* to witness the devastation and do what he could to help. ▶

Concerned staff member Lori Sumacki with one of her charges on the grounds of the Hemingway home, boarded up in anticipation of Hurricane Irma's approach to the Keys in 2017. *Hemingway Home & Museum.*

A Message That Still Resonates *(continued)*

Outraged by the number of deaths, including the many destitute veterans the Roosevelt administration had sent to the Keys to work on relief, Hemingway experienced a political awakening. Now he simply could not return to the status quo of fishing and writing after what he had seen. Before, he had been largely apolitical, as if what he wanted most from government was to be left alone. After, he began speaking up for the underdog and attacking oppressive leaders, especially if they were autocrats on the right. That put him on the road that would lead him to Spain, where in 1936 the left and the right became embroiled in a long and bloody civil war. There he saw the common man pitted against the forces of reaction led by Francisco Franco and became a true believer in the anti-fascist cause. Along the way, he got to know the Soviets who came to Spain to join the fight against Franco. Before long, he embraced them as allies in that cause. It was their secret service, the NKVD, that recruited Hemingway "for our work" at the end of the decade.

"Now he simply could not return to the status quo of fishing and writing after what he had seen."

By agreeing to work with the NKVD, Hemingway did not become a traitor to his own country; he did not take money from the Soviets, and he did not betray American secrets. He was never that kind of spy. But he did open himself up to potential prosecution under the Foreign Agents Registration Act, enacted in 1938 in the service of transparency. It applied to those who represented the interests of a foreign power in "a political or quasi-political capacity," which included everything from spying to lobbying. Hemingway's NKVD recruiter, the longtime Bolshevik *and* U.S. citizen Jacob Golos, quite rightly fell afoul of the law. The basic idea was to keep everyone honest; if you represented another country you needed to say so. You needed to avoid even the appearance of a conflict of interest. The law remains on the books in 2017; the news of the day tells us that it is far from a dead letter.

In his dealings with the Soviets, Hemingway entered the never-never land where the difference between American and Soviet interests started to blur. Even today it is hard, sometimes impossible, to know when he was speaking with his independent—and very American voice—and when he was doing some favor for the Soviets—writing for *Pravda*, the official newspaper of the Communist Party, or producing a propaganda film on Spain directed by Joris Ivens, an agent of the Communist International, or lobbying President Roosevelt about Spain alongside Ivens. Then came the topper: agreeing to a secret relationship with the NKVD in a series of meetings with Golos in 1940 and 1941 in New York City. Hemingway would later admit privately to doing a few "odd jobs" during and after the civil war for the anti-fascist cause—represented by the Spanish Republic and its Soviet ally. He would also insist that, in his dealings with the Soviets, he had been like the nineteenth-century mountain man ▸

"Hemingway would later admit privately to doing a few 'odd jobs' during and after the civil war for the anti-fascist cause."

Jim Bridger, who moved between two worlds on the frontier, that of the white settler and that of the Native American. But the parallel doesn't stand scrutiny. The American and Soviet governments would both have been surprised to learn that Hemingway was anyone's intermediary. Bridger may have been an intermediary, but he was not a secret agent. And none of the great chiefs was anything like the totalitarian dictator Stalin.

Like many of my readers, I am struck by a different parallel, that between Hemingway's situation in the 1940s and the consequences of Russian intervention in the 2016 presidential election. Where is the dividing line between legitimate American and legitimate Russian interests? When do they diverge? When do Americans, wittingly or unwittingly, do the Russians' bidding and by so doing undermine American democracy? As I wrote in an op-ed in the spring, Hemingway's experiences tell a cautionary tale.**

"Where is the dividing line between legitimate American and legitimate Russian interests?"

First are the continuities in Russian history. No matter whether it is called NKVD, KGB, or SVR, the Russian secret service has since 1934 worked hard to gather information on and exert influence in the United States. Its officials have never forgotten that it is in their interest to understand and

** Nicholas Reynolds, "How Russia Recruited Ernest Hemingway," Daily Beast, March 18, 2017.

manipulate the great power across the ocean, something they have always been most comfortable doing behind the scenes.

The Cuban government honored Hemingway in a series of postage stamps, including this 1963 issue. It depicts the author with his late-in-life comb-over along with a scene from *For Whom The Bell Tolls,* the book that Castro claimed to have carried in his backpack. *Gors4730 Photo, Copyright 123RF.com.*

Second, as in the Hemingway case, those initiatives are not always as clear cut as outright spying or influence peddling. No doubt the instances of classic espionage are easiest to understand and categorize: Soviet spies targeting American and British officials with access to state secrets who, after being recruited, stole those secrets and passed them to the Soviets. But there were also many other, less straightforward cases, where the Soviets wanted to acquire insider information that was not top secret, or exert influence in a subtler way. They were after leads to prominent men or women who might be willing to lend a sympathetic ear to Moscow, share a confidence, recast a policy, perhaps shade a headline. That is what the NKVD wanted from ▶

"The instances of classic espionage are easiest to understand and categorize. . . . But there were also many other, less straightforward cases."

A Message That Still Resonates ***(continued)***

"journalist spies," their category for Hemingway—newsmen both well-connected and wise in the ways of the world, as comfortable in the dining room of the White House as the waiting room of a house of ill repute in Havana.

So, some seventy-five years later, Hemingway's private foreign policy still resonates, and not in a reassuring way. Most of us who read and love his work do so because his writing—honest, direct, independent—evokes so many American values. We want Hemingway the author we read, and read about, to be transparent, not someone following a hidden agenda. Few of us want to learn that our literary icon was in a secret relationship with a foreign power, especially one whose values have always been so different from ours. The equivalency between America and Russia that Hemingway posited in the late 1940s is as troubling as President Trump's attitude to Russia today. I am old-fashioned enough to think that America is not just another great power but a unique experiment in self-government and democracy, a true republic unlike any Russian government to date, Soviet or post-Soviet. This, sadly, is something that one of America's greatest writers never fully grasped.

"Some seventy-five years later, Hemingway's private foreign policy still resonates, and not in a reassuring way."